SAMS
Teach Yourself

PHP, MySQL® and Apache

Julie C. Meloni

All in One

SAMS   *800 East 96th Street, Indianapolis, Indiana, 46240 USA*

Sams Teach Yourself PHP, MySQL and Apache All in One

International Standard Book Number: 0-672-32620-5

Library of Congress Catalog Card Number: 2003109401

Printed in the United States of America

First Printing: December 2003

06 05 04   7   6   5   4

Trademarks

All terms mentioned in this book that are known to be trademarks or service marks have been appropriately capitalized. Sams Publishing cannot attest to the accuracy of this information. Use of a term in this book should not be regarded as affecting the validity of any trademark or service mark.

Warning and Disclaimer

Every effort has been made to make this book as complete and as accurate as possible, but no warranty or fitness is implied. The information provided is on an "as is" basis. The author and the publisher shall have neither liability nor responsibility to any person or entity with respect to any loss or damages arising from the information contained in this book or from the use of the CD or programs accompanying it.

Bulk Sales

Sams Publishing offers excellent discounts on this book when ordered in quantity for bulk purchases or special sales. For more information, please contact

U.S. Corporate and Government Sales
1-800-382-3419
corpsales@pearsontechgroup.com

For sales outside of the U.S., please contact

International Sales
+1-317-428-3341
international@pearsontechgroup.com

Acquisitions Editor
Shelley Johnston

Development Editor
Chris Newman

Managing Editor
Charlotte Clapp

Project Editor
Dan Knott

Copy Editor
Krista Hansing

Indexer
Sharon Shock

Proofreader
Mike Henry

Technical Editor
Chris Newman

Publishing Coordinator
Vanessa Evans

Multimedia Developer
Dan Scherf

Designer
Gary Adair

Page Layout
Julie Parks

Contents at a Glance

Table of Contents

Part V: Basic Projects

About the Authors

Lead author

Julie C. Meloni is the technical director for i2i Interactive (http://www.i2ii.com), a multimedia company located in Los Altos, California. She's been developing Web-based applications since the Web first saw the light of day and remembers the excitement surrounding the first GUI Web browser. She has authored several books and articles on Web-based programming languages and database topics, and you can find translations of her work in several languages, including Chinese, Italian, Portuguese, Polish, and even Serbian.

Contributing authors

Matt Zandstra is a writer and consultant specializing in server programming. With his business partner, Max Guglielmino, he runs Corrosive (http://www.corrosive.co.uk), a technical agency that plans, designs and builds Internet applications. Matt is interested in all aspects of object-oriented programming, and is currently exploring enterprise design patterns for PHP 5. When he is not reading, writing, or thinking about coding in PHP and Java, Matt shoots alien invaders in the park with his four-year-old daughter, Holly. He lives by the sea in Brighton, Great Britain, with his partner Louise McDougall, and their children Holly and Jake.

Daniel López Ridruejo is the founder of BitRock, a technology company providing multiplatform installation and management tools for a variety of commercial and open source software products. Previously, he was part of the original engineering team at Covalent Technologies, Inc., which provides Apache software, support, and services for the enterprise. He is the author of several popular Apache and Linux guides, the mod_mono module for integrating Apache and .NET, and of Comanche, a GUI configuration tool for Apache. Daniel is a regular speaker at open source conferences such as Linux World, ApacheCon, and the O'Reilly Open Source Convention. He holds a Master of Science degree in Telecommunications from the Escuela Superior de Ingenieros de Sevilla and Danmarks Tekniske Universitet. Daniel is a member of the Apache Software Foundation.

Acknowledgments

The Apache Foundation, the PHP Group, and MySQL AB deserve much more recognition than they ever get for creating these super products that drive a great portion of the Web.

Daniel Lòpez (author of *Sams Teach Yourself Apache 2 in 24 Hours*) and Matt Zandstra (author of *Sams Teach Yourself PHP in 24 Hours*) wrote super books, which form a portion of this book. Obviously, this book would not exist without their work!

Great thanks especially to all the editors and layout folks at Sams who were involved with this book, for all their hard work in seeing this through! Thanks as always to everyone at i2i Interactive for their never-ending support and encouragement.

We Want to Hear from You!

As the reader of this book, *you* are our most important critic and commentator. We value your opinion and want to know what we're doing right, what we could do better, what areas you'd like to see us publish in, and any other words of wisdom you're willing to pass our way.

You can email or write me directly to let me know what you did or didn't like about this book—as well as what we can do to make our books stronger.

Please note that I cannot help you with technical problems related to the topic of this book, and that due to the high volume of mail I receive, I might not be able to reply to every message.

When you write, please be sure to include this book's title and author as well as your name and phone or email address. I will carefully review your comments and share them with the author and editors who worked on the book.

Email: opensource@samspublishing.com

Mail: Mark Taber
      Associate Publisher
      Sams Publishing
      800 East 96th Street
      Indianapolis, IN 46240 USA

Reader Services

For more information about this book or others from Sams Publishing, visit our Web site at www.samspublishing.com. Type the ISBN (excluding hyphens) or the title of the book in the Search box to find the book you're looking for.

Introduction

Welcome to *Sams Teach Yourself PHP, MySQL, and Apache All in One*! This book combines the lessons found in *Sams Teach Yourself Apache 2 in 24 Hours*, *Sams Teach Yourself PHP in 24 Hours*, and *Sams Teach Yourself MySQL in 24 Hours*, along with several additional chapters, to provide you with a solid and painless introduction to the world of developing Web-based applications using these three technologies.

Over the course of this book, you'll learn the concepts necessary for configuring and managing Apache, the basics of programming in PHP, and the methods for using and administering the MySQL relational database system. The overall goal of the book is to provide you with the foundation you need to understand how seamlessly these technologies integrate with one another, and to give you practical knowledge of how to integrate them.

Who Should Read This Book?

This book is geared toward individuals who possess a general understanding of the concepts of working in a Web-based development environment, be it Linux/Unix or Windows. Installation and configuration lessons assume that you have familiarity with your operating system and the basic methods of building (on Linux/Unix systems) or installing (on Windows systems) software.

The lessons that delve into programming with PHP assume no previous knowledge of the language, but if you have experience with other programming languages, such as C or Perl, you will find the going much easier. Similarly, if you have worked with other databases, such as Oracle or Microsoft SQL Server, you will have a good foundation for working through the MySQL-related lessons.

The only real requirement is that you understand static Web content creation with HTML. If you are just starting out in the world of Web development, you will still be able to use this book, although you should consider working through an HTML tutorial. If you are comfortable creating basic documents and can build a basic HTML table, you will be fine.

How This Book Is Organized

This book is divided into seven parts, corresponding to particular topic groups. The lessons within each part should be read one right after another, with each lesson building on the information found in those before it:

▶ Part I, "Laying the Groundwork," walks you through the installation and configuration of MySQL, Apache, and PHP. You'll need to complete the lessons in Part I before moving on, unless you already have access to a working installation of these technologies. Even if you don't need to install and configure MySQL, Apache, and PHP in your environment, you should still skim these lessons so that you understand the basics.

▶ Part II, "PHP Language Structure," is devoted to teaching you the basics of the PHP language, including structural elements such as arrays and objects. The examples will get you in the habit of writing code, uploading it to your server, and testing the results.

▶ Part III, "Getting Involved with the Code," consists of lessons that cover intermediate-level application-development topics, including working with forms and files, restricting access, and completing other small projects designed to introduce a specific concept.

▶ Part IV, "PHP and MySQL Integration," contains lessons devoted to working with databases in general, such as database normalization, as well as using PHP to connect to and work with MySQL. Included is a basic SQL primer, which also includes MySQL-specific functions and other information.

▶ Part V, "Basic Projects," consists of lessons devoted to performing a particular task using PHP and MySQL, integrating all the knowledge gained so far. Projects include an address book, a discussion forum, and a basic online storefront, among others.

▶ Part VI, "Administration and Fine Tuning," is devoted to administering and tuning Apache and MySQL. It also includes information on virtual hosting and setting up a secure Web server.

▶ Part VII, "Looking Toward the Future," contains information regarding the upcoming major releases of PHP 5.0 and MySQL 4.1.

If you find that you are already familiar with a topic, you can skip ahead to the next lesson. However, in some instances, lessons refer to specific concepts learned in previous chapters, so be aware that you might have to skim a skipped lesson so that your development environment remains consistent with the book.

At the end of each chapter, a few quiz questions test how well you've learned the material. Additional activities provide another way to apply the information learned in the lesson and guide you toward using this newfound knowledge in the next chapter.

Conventions Used in This Book

This book uses different typefaces to differentiate between code and plain English, and also to help you identify important concepts. Throughout the lessons, code, commands, and text you type or see onscreen appear in a `computer typeface`. New terms appear in *italics* at the point in the text where they are defined. Additionally, icons accompany special blocks of information:

A "By the Way" presents an interesting piece of information related to the current topic.

By the Way

A "Did You Know" offers advice or teaches an easier method for performing a task.

Did you Know?

A "Watch Out" warns you about potential pitfalls and explains how to avoid them.

Watch Out!

PART I

Laying the Groundwork

CHAPTER 1

Installing and Configuring MySQL

Welcome to the first chapter of *Sams Teach Yourself PHP, MySQL, and Apache*. This is the first of three installation-related chapters, in which you will learn how to set up a development environment. We'll tackle the MySQL installation first, primarily because the PHP installation is much simpler when MySQL is already installed.

In this chapter, you will learn

- ► How to install MySQL
- ► Basic security guidelines for running MySQL
- ► How to work with the MySQL user privilege system

Current and Future Versions of MySQL

The installation instructions in this chapter refer to MySQL 4.0.15, which is the current production version of the software. This version number can be read as minor release number 15 of the major version 4.0 software. MySQL AB, the company responsible for creating and distributing MySQL, uses minor release numbers for updates containing security enhancements or bug fixes. Minor releases do not follow a set release schedule; when enhancements or fixes are added to the code and thoroughly tested, MySQL AB releases a new version, with a new minor version number.

It is possible that by the time you purchase this book, the minor version number will have changed, to 4.0.16 or beyond. If that is the case, you should read the list of changes at http://www.mysql.com/doc/en/News-4.0.x.html for any changes regarding the installation or configuration process, which makes up the bulk of this chapter.

Although it is unlikely that any installation instructions will change between minor version updates, you should get in the habit of always checking the changelog of software that you install and maintain. If a minor version change does occur during the time you are reading this book, but no installation changes are noted in the

changelog, simply make a mental note and substitute the new version number wherever it appears in the installation instructions and accompanying figures.

How to Get MySQL

MySQL AB, the company that develops and maintains the MySQL database server, distributes MySQL on its Web site: `http://www.mysql.com/`. Binary distributions for all platforms, as well as RPMs and source code files for Linux/Unix platforms, can be found at the Web site. Additionally, you can purchase boxed versions of the software—that is, software in a box and with a printed version of the comprehensive MySQL manual—from the MySQL AB online store, for a very reasonable price.

The installation instructions in this chapter are based on the official MySQL 4.0.x distribution from MySQL AB. All files can be downloaded from `http://www.mysql.com/downloads/mysql-4.0.html`, and the current versions as of the time of writing are also found on the CD included with this book.

By the Way

> For instructions on installing MySQL from the CD, please refer to Appendix A, "Installing MySQL, Apache, and PHP from the CD-ROM."

Installing MySQL on Linux/Unix

The process of installing MySQL on Linux/Unix is straightforward, whether you use RPMs or install the binaries. For a minimal installation from RPMs, you will need two files:

- ▶ `MySQL-server-VERSION.i386.rpm`—The MySQL server
- ▶ `MySQL-client-VERSION.i386.rpm`—The standard MySQL client libraries

To perform a minimal installation from RPMs, type the following at your prompt:

```
#> rpm -i MySQL-server-VERSION.i386.rpm MySQL-client-VERSION.i386.rpm
```

By the Way

> Replace VERSION in the filename with the actual version you downloaded. For example, the current MySQL 4.0 server RPM is called `MySQL-server-4.0.15-0.i386.rpm`, and the client libraries RPM is called `MySQL-client-4.0.15-0.i386.rpm`.

Another painless installation method is to install MySQL from a binary distribution. This method requires `gunzip` and `tar` to uncompress and unpack the distribution, and also requires the ability to create groups and users on the system. The first series of commands in the binary distribution installation process has you adding a group and a user and unpacking the distribution, as follows:

> Replace VERSION-OS in the filename with the actual version you downloaded. For example, the current MySQL 4.0 Linux/i386 binary is called `mysql-max-4.0.15-pc-linux-i686.tar.gz`.

By the Way

```
#> groupadd mysql
#> useradd -g mysql mysql
#> cd /usr/local
#> gunzip < /path/to/mysql-VERSION-OS.tar.gz | tar xvf -
```

Next, the instructions tell you to create a link with a shorter name:

```
#> ln -s mysql-VERSION-OS mysql
#> cd mysql
```

Once unpacked, the README and INSTALL files will walk you through the remainder of the installation process for the version of MySQL you've chosen. In general, the following series of commands will be used:

```
#> scripts/mysql_install_db
#> chown -R root  /usr/local/mysql
#> chown -R mysql /usr/local/mysql/data
#> chgrp -R mysql /usr/local/mysql
#> chown -R root /usr/local/mysql/bin
```

You're now ready to start the MySQL server, so skip down to the section called "Basic Security Guidelines." If you had any issues with your installation, check the "Troubleshooting Your Installation" section.

Installing MySQL on Windows

The MySQL installation process on Windows is also quite simple—the developers from MySQL AB have packaged up everything you need in one zip file with a setup program! Download the zip file, extract its contents into a temporary directory, and run the `setup.exe` application. After the `setup.exe` application installs the MySQL server and client programs, you're ready to start the MySQL server.

The following steps detail the installation of MySQL 4.0.x on Windows, when the installer is downloaded from MySQL AB. The install sequence looks similar, regardless if you have a Windows 98, Windows NT, Windows 2000, or Windows XP environment for testing and development. Many users install MySQL on personal Windows machines just to get a feel for working with the database before deploying MySQL in a production environment.

> If you have the tools and skills to compile your own Windows binary files, the Cygwin source code is also available from MySQL AB. Follow the instructions contained in the source distribution, to build your own executable files.

Jumping right into the installation sequence, assuming you have download the Windows installer from the MySQL AB Web site, follow these steps:

1. Extract the contents of the zip file into a temporary directory and find the setup.exe file, and then double-click it to start the installation. You will see the first screen of the installation wizard, as shown in Figure 1.1. Click Next to continue.

FIGURE 1.1
The first step of the MySQL installation wizard.

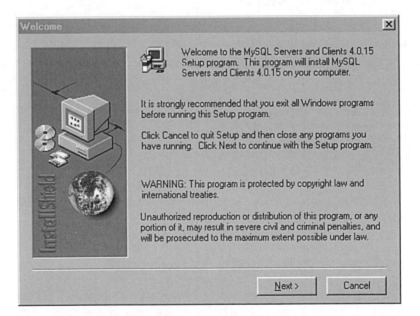

2. The second screen in the installation process contains valuable information regarding the installation location (see Figure 1.2). The default installation location is C:\mysql. If you plan to install MySQL in a different location, this screen shows you a few changes that you will have to make on your own. The information on this screen is also important for Windows NT users

who want to start MySQL as a service. Read the information and note anything relevant to your situation, and then click Next to continue.

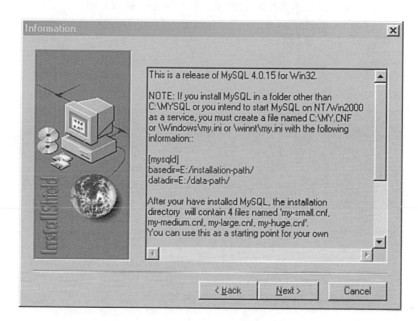

FIGURE 1.2
Step 2 of the MySQL installation wizard. Note any relevant information before continuing.

3. The third screen in the installation process has you select the installation location (see Figure 1.3). If you want to install MySQL in the default location, click Next to continue. Otherwise, click Browse and navigate to the location of your choice, and then click Next to continue.

4. The fourth screen asks you to select the installation method—Typical, Compact, or Custom (see Figure 1.4). The Custom option allows you to select elements of MySQL to install, such as documentation and help files. Select Typical as the installation method, and click Next to continue.

5. The installation process will now take over and install files in their proper locations. When the process is finished, you will see a confirmation of completion, as in Figure 1.5. Click Finish to complete the setup process.

There are no fancy shortcuts installed in your Windows Start menu after an installation of MySQL from MySQL AB, so now you must start the process yourself. If you navigate to the MySQL applications directory (usually C:\mysql\bin\ unless you changed your installation path), you will find numerous applications ready for action (see Figure 1.6).

FIGURE 1.3
Step 3 of the
MySQL installation
wizard. Select
an installation
location.

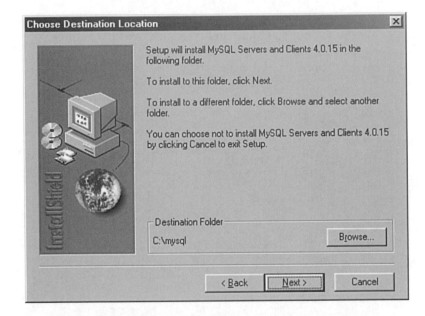

FIGURE 1.4
Step 4 of the
MySQL installation
wizard. Select an
installation type.

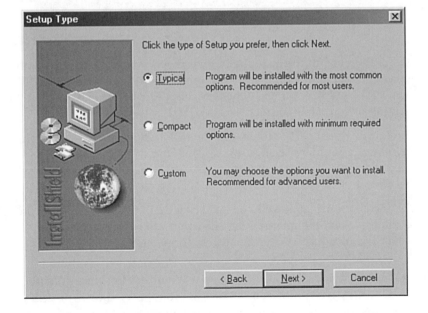

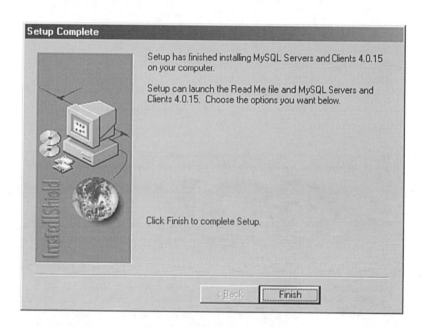

FIGURE 1.5
MySQL has been
installed.

FIGURE 1.6
A directory listing
of MySQL
applications.

The winmysqladmin.exe application is a great friend to Windows users who are just getting started with MySQL. If you double-click this file, it will start the MySQL server and place a stoplight icon in your taskbar.

When you start WinMySQLadmin for the first time, you will be prompted for a username and password (see Figure 1.7). The application will create the initial MySQL user account on a Windows system.

FIGURE 1.7
Creating the initial
MySQL account.

When you are finished creating the account, or whenever you right-click the stop-light icon in your taskbar, the graphical user interface will launch. This interface, shown in Figure 1.8, provides an easy way to maintain and monitor your new server.

WinMySQLadmin will automatically interpret environment information, such as IP address and machine name. The tabs across the top allow you to view system information and edit MySQL configuration options.

For example, if you select the Variables tab, as shown in Figure 1.9, you can also view server configuration information. This information is similar to the output of the MySQL SHOW VARIABLES command.

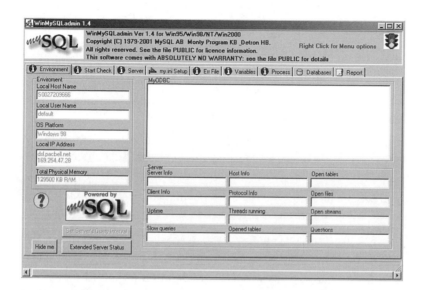

FIGURE 1.8
WinMySQLadmin started and ready for action.

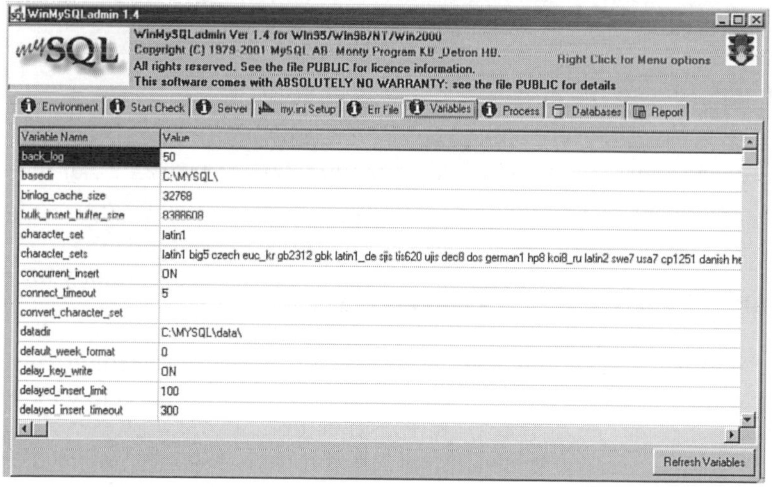

FIGURE 1.9
Server configuration information.

To shut down the MySQL server and/or the WinMySQLadmin tool, right-click again on the stoplight icon in your taskbar and select the appropriate option (stop or start). As long as the MySQL server is running, you can run additional applications through a console window, such as the MySQL monitor.

Troubleshooting Your Installation

If you have any problems during the installation of MySQL, the first place you should look is the "Problems and Common Errors" chapter of the MySQL manual, which is located at `http://www.mysql.com/doc/P/r/Problems.html`.

The following are some common problems:

- ▶ On Linux/Unix, incorrect permissions do not allow you to start the MySQL daemon. If this is the case, be sure you have changed owners and groups to match those indicated in the installation instructions.

- ▶ If you see the message `Access denied` when connecting to MySQL, be sure you are using the correct username and password.

- ▶ If you see the message `Can't connect to server`, make sure the MySQL daemon is running.

- ▶ When defining tables, if you specify a length for a field whose type does not require a length, the table will not be created. For example, you should not specify a length when defining a field as `TEXT` (as opposed to `CHAR` or `VARCHAR`).

If you still have trouble after reading the manual, sending email to the MySQL mailing list (see `http://lists.mysql.com/` for more information) will likely produce results. You can also purchase support contracts from MySQL AB for a very low fee.

Basic Security Guidelines

Regardless of whether you are running MySQL on Windows or Linux/Unix, and no matter whether you administer your own server or use a system provided to you by your Internet service provider, you must understand basic security guidelines. If you are accessing MySQL through your Internet service provider, there are several aspects of server security that you, as a non-root user, should not be able to modify or circumvent. Unfortunately, many Internet service providers pay no mind to security guidelines, leaving their clients exposed—and for the most part, unaware of the risk.

Starting MySQL

Securing MySQL begins with the server startup procedure. If you are not the administrator of the server, you won't be able to change this, but you can certainly check it out and report vulnerabilities to your Internet service provider.

If your MySQL installation is on Linux/Unix, your primary concern should be the owner of the MySQL daemon—it should not be root. Running the daemon as a non-root user such as mysql or database will limit the ability of malicious individuals to gain access to the server and overwrite files.

You can verify the owner of the process using the ps (process status) command on your Linux/Unix system. The following output shows MySQL running as a non-root user (see the first entry on the second line):

```
#> ps auxw | grep mysqld
mysql 153  0.0  0.6 12068 2624 ? S Nov16  0:00 /usr/local/bin/mysql/bin/mysqld
--defaults-extra-file=/usr/local/bin/mysql/data/my.cnf
--basedir=/usr/local/bin/mysql --datadir=/usr/local/bin/mysql/data
--user=mysql --pid-file=/usr/local/bin/mysql/data/mike.pid --skip-locking
```

The following output shows MySQL running as the root user (see the first entry on the second line):

```
#> ps auxw | grep mysqld
root 21107  0.0  1.1 11176  1444  ?  S  Nov 27 0:00 /usr/local/mysql/bin/mysqld
--basedir=/usr/local/mysql --datadir=/usr/local/mysql/data --skip-locking
```

If you see that MySQL is running as root on your system, immediately contact your Internet service provider and complain. If you are the server administrator, you should start the MySQL process as a non-root user or specify the username in the startup command line:

```
mysqld --user=non_root_user_name
```

For example, if you want to run MySQL as user mysql, use

```
mysqld --user=mysql
```

However, the recommended method for starting MySQL is through the safe_mysqld startup script in the bin directory of your MySQL installation:

```
#> /usr/local/bin/mysql/bin/safe_mysqld &
```

Securing Your MySQL Connection

You can connect to the MySQL monitor or other MySQL applications in several different ways, each of which has its own security risks. If your MySQL installation is on your own workstation, you have less to worry about than users who have to use a network connection to reach their server.

If MySQL is installed on your workstation, your biggest security concern is leaving your workstation unattended with your MySQL monitor or MySQL GUI administration tool up and running. In this type of situation, anyone can walk over and delete data, insert bogus data, or shut down the server. Utilize a screen saver or lock screen mechanism with a password if you must leave your workstation unattended in a public area.

If MySQL is installed on a server outside your network, the security of the connection should be of some concern. As with any transmission of data over the Internet, it can be intercepted. If the transmission is unencrypted, the person who intercepted it can piece it together and use the information. Suppose the unencrypted transmission is your MySQL login information—a rogue individual now has access to your database, masquerading as you.

One way to prevent this from happening is to connect to MySQL through a secure connection. Instead of using Telnet to reach the remote machine, use SSH. SSH looks and acts like Telnet, but all transmissions to and from the remote machine are encrypted. Similarly, if you use a Web-based administration interface, such as phpMyAdmin (see `http://phpmyadmin.sourceforge.net` for more information) or another tool used by your Internet service provider, access that tool over a secure HTTP connection.

In the next section, you'll learn about the MySQL privilege system, which helps secure your database even further.

Introducing the MySQL Privilege System

The MySQL privilege system is always on. The first time you try to connect, and for each subsequent action, MySQL checks the following three things:

- ▶ Where you are accessing from (your host)
- ▶ Who you say you are (your username and password)
- ▶ What you're allowed to do (your command privileges)

All this information is stored in the database called mysql, which is automatically created when MySQL is installed. There are several tables in the mysql database:

- ▶ columns_priv—Defines user privileges for specific fields within a table
- ▶ db—Defines the permissions for all databases on the server
- ▶ func—Defines user-created functions
- ▶ host—Defines the acceptable hosts that can connect to a specific database
- ▶ tables_priv—Defines user privileges for specific tables within a database
- ▶ user—Defines the command privileges for a specific user

These tables will become more important to you later in this chapter as you add a few sample users to MySQL. For now, just remember that these tables exist and must have relevant data in them in order for users to complete actions.

The Two-Step Authentication Process

As you've learned, MySQL checks three things during the authentication process. The actions associated with these three things are performed in two steps:

1. MySQL looks at the host you are connecting from and the username and password pair that you are using. If your host is allowed to connect, your password is correct for your username, and the username matches one assigned to the host, MySQL moves to the second step.

2. For whichever SQL command you are attempting to use, MySQL verifies that you have the ability to perform that action for that database, table, and field.

If step 1 fails, you'll see an error about it and you won't be able to continue on to step 2. For example, suppose you are connecting to MySQL with a username of joe and a password of abc123 and you want to access a database called myDB. You will receive an error message if any of those connection variables is incorrect for any of the following reasons:

- ▶ Your password is incorrect.
- ▶ Username joe doesn't exist.
- ▶ User joe can't connect from localhost.
- ▶ User joe can connect from localhost but cannot use the myDB database.

You may see an error like the following:

```
#> /usr/local/mysql/bin/mysql -h localhost -u joe -pabc123 test
Error 1045: Access denied for user: 'joe@localhost' (Using password: YES)
```

If user joe with a password of abc123 is allowed to connect from localhost to the myDB database, MySQL will check the actions that joe can perform in step 2 of the process. For our purposes, suppose that joe is allowed to select data but is not allowed to insert data. The sequence of events and errors would look like the following:

```
#> /usr/local/mysql/bin/mysql -h localhost -u joe -pabc123 test
Reading table information for completion of table and column names
You can turn off this feature to get a quicker startup with -A

Welcome to the MySQL monitor.  Commands end with ; or \g.
Your MySQL connection id is 61198 to server version: 4.0.15-log
Type 'help;' or '\h' for help. Type '\c' to clear the buffer.

mysql> select * from test_table;
+----+------------+
| id | test_field |
+----+------------+
+----+------------+
|  1 | blah       |
|  2 | blah blah  |
+----+------------+
2 rows in set (0.0 sec)

mysql> insert into test_table values ('', 'my text');
Error 1044: Access denied for user: 'joe@localhost' (Using password: YES)
```

Action-based permissions are common in applications with several levels of administration. For example, if you have created an application containing personal financial data, you might grant only SELECT privileges to entry-level staff members, but INSERT and DELETE privileges to executive-level staff with security clearances.

Working with User Privileges

In most cases when you are accessing MySQL through an Internet service provider, you will have only one user and one database available to you. By default, that one user will have access to all tables in that database and will be allowed to perform all commands. In this case, the responsibility is yours as the developer to create a secure application through your programming.

If you are the administrator of your own server or have the ability to add as many databases and users as you want, as well as modify the access privileges of your users, these next few sections will take you through the processes of doing so.

Adding Users

Administering your server through a third-party application might afford you a simple method for adding users, using a wizard-like process or a graphical interface. However, adding users through the MySQL monitor is not difficult, especially if you understand the security checkpoints used by MySQL, which you just learned.

The simplest method for adding new users is the GRANT command. By connecting to MySQL as the root user, you can issue one command to set up a new user. The other method is to issue INSERT statements into all the relevant tables in the mysql database, which requires you to know all the fields in the tables used to store permissions. This method works just as well but is more complicated than the simple GRANT command.

The simple syntax of the GRANT command is

```
GRANT privileges
ON databasename.tablename
TO username@host
IDENTIFIED BY "password";
```

The privileges you can grant are

- ▶ ALL—Gives the user all the following privileges
- ▶ ALTER—User can alter (modify) tables, columns, and indexes
- ▶ CREATE—User can create databases and tables
- ▶ DELETE—User can delete records from tables
- ▶ DROP—User can drop (delete) tables and databases
- ▶ FILE—User can read and write files; this is used to import or dump data
- ▶ INDEX—User can add or delete indexes
- ▶ INSERT—User can add records to tables
- ▶ PROCESS—User can view and stop system processes; only trusted users should be able to do this

- ▶ REFERENCES—Not currently used by MySQL, but a column for REFERENCES privileges exists in the user table

- ▶ RELOAD—User can issue FLUSH statements; only trusted users should be able to do this

- ▶ SELECT—User can select records from tables

- ▶ SHUTDOWN—User can shut down the MySQL server; only trusted users should be able to do this

- ▶ UPDATE—User can update (modify) records in tables

- ▶ USAGE—User can connect to MySQL but has no privileges

If, for instance, you want to create a user called john with a password of 99hjc, with SELECT and INSERT privileges on all tables in the database called myDB, and you want this user to be able to connect from any host, use

```
GRANT SELECT, INSERT
ON myDB.*
TO john@"%"
IDENTIFIED BY "99hjc";
```

Note the use of two wildcards: * and %. These wildcards are used to replace values. In this example, * replaces the entire list of tables, and % replaces a list of all hosts in the known world—a very long list indeed.

Here's another example of adding a user using the GRANT command, this time to add a user called jane with a password of 45sdg11, with ALL privileges on a table called employees in the database called myCompany. This new user can connect only from a specific host:

```
GRANT ALL
ON myCompany.employees
TO jane@janescomputer.company.com
IDENTIFIED BY "45sdg11";
```

If you know that janescomputer.company.com has an IP address of 63.124.45.2, you can substitute that address in the hostname portion of the command, as follows:

```
GRANT ALL
ON myCompany.employees
TO jane@'63.124.45.2'
IDENTIFIED BY "45sdg11";
```

One note about adding users: Always use a password and make sure that the password is a good one! MySQL allows you to create users without a password, but that leaves the door wide open should someone with bad intentions guess the name of one of your users with full privileges granted to them!

If you use the GRANT command to add users, the changes will immediately take effect. To make absolutely sure of this, you can issue the FLUSH PRIVILEGES command in the MySQL monitor to reload the privilege tables.

Removing Privileges

Removing privileges is as simple as adding them; instead of a GRANT command, you use REVOKE. The REVOKE command syntax is

```
REVOKE privileges
ON databasename.tablename
FROM username@hostname;
```

In the same way that you can grant permissions using INSERT commands, you can also revoke permissions by issuing DELETE commands to remove records from tables in the mysql database. However, this requires that you be familiar with the fields and tables, and it's just much easier and safer to use REVOKE.

To revoke the ability for user john to INSERT items in the myCompany database, you would issue this REVOKE statement:

```
REVOKE INSERT
ON myDB.*
FROM john@"%";
```

Changes made to the data in the privilege tables happen immediately, but in order for the server to be aware of your changes, issue the FLUSH PRIVILEGES command in the MySQL monitor.

Summary

Installing MySQL on Windows is a very simple process, thanks to a wizard-based installation method. MySQL AB provides a GUI-based administration tool for Windows users, called WinMySQLadmin. Linux/Unix users do not have a wizard-based installation process, but it's not difficult to follow a simple set of commands to unpack the MySQL client and server binaries. Linux/Unix users can also use RPMs for installation.

Security is always a priority, and there are several steps you can take to ensure a safe and secure installation of MySQL. Even if you are not the administrator of the server, you should be able to recognize breaches and raise a ruckus with the server administrator!

The MySQL server should not run as the root user. Additionally, named users within MySQL should always have a password, and their access privileges should be well defined.

MySQL uses the privilege tables in a two-step process for each request that is made. MySQL needs to know who you are and where you are connecting from, and each of these pieces of information must match an entry in its privilege tables. Also, the user whose identity you are using must have specific permission to perform the type of request you are making.

You can add user privileges using the GRANT command, which uses a simple syntax to add entries to the user table in the mysql database. The REVOKE command, which is equally simple, is used to remove those privileges.

Q&A

Q. *How do I completely remove a user? The* REVOKE *command just eliminates the privileges.*

A. To completely remove a user from the privilege table, you have to issue a specific DELETE command from the user table in the mysql database.

Q. *What if I tell my Internet service provider to stop running MySQL as* root, *and it won't?*

A. Switch providers. If your Internet service provider doesn't recognize the risks of running something as important as your database as the root user, and doesn't listen to your request, find another provider. There are providers, with plans as low as $9.95/month, that don't run important processes as the root user!

Workshop

The workshop is designed to help you anticipate possible questions, review what you've learned, and begin learning how to put your knowledge into practice.

Quiz

1. True or False: Telnet is a perfectly acceptable method to securely connect to MySQL from a remote host.

2. Which three pieces of information does MySQL check each time a request is made?

3. What command would you use to grant SELECT, INSERT, and UPDATE privileges to a user named bill on localhost to all tables on the BillDB database? Also, what piece of information is missing from this statement that is recommended for security purposes?

Answers

1. False. The key word is *secure*, and Telnet does not encrypt data between hosts. Instead, use SSH to connect to your server.

2. Who you are, where you are accessing from, and what actions you're allowed to perform.

3. The command is

```
GRANT SELECT, INSERT, UPDATE
ON BillDB.*
TO bill@localhost;
```

The important missing piece is a password for the user!

Activities

1. Think of situations in which you might want to restrict command access at the table level. For example, you wouldn't want the intern-level administrator to have shutdown privileges for the corporate database.

2. If you have administrative privileges in MySQL, issue several GRANT commands to create dummy users. It doesn't matter whether the tables and databases you name are actually present.

3. Use REVOKE to remove some of the privileges of the users you created in activity 2.

CHAPTER 2

Installing and Configuring Apache

In this second of three installation-related chapters, you will install the Apache Web server and familiarize yourself with its main components, including log and configuration files.

In this chapter, you will learn

- ▶ How to install the Apache server on Linux/Unix
- ▶ How to install the Apache server on Windows
- ▶ How to make configuration changes to Apache
- ▶ Where Apache log and configuration files are stored

Current and Future Versions of Apache

The installation instructions in this chapter refer to Apache HTTPD server version 2.0.47, which is the current production version of the software. The Apache Software Foundation uses minor release numbers for updates containing security enhancements or bug fixes. Minor releases do not follow a set release schedule; when enhancements or fixes are added to the code and thoroughly tested, the Apache Software Foundation will releases a new version, with a new minor version number.

It is possible that by the time you purchase this book, the minor version number will have changed, to 2.0.48 or beyond. If that is the case, you should read the list of changes, which is linked from the download area at http://httpd.apache.org/ download.cgi, for any changes regarding the installation or configuration process, which makes up the bulk of this chapter.

Although it is unlikely that any installation instructions will change between minor version updates, you should get in the habit of always checking the changelog of software that you install and maintain. If a minor version change does occur during the time you are reading this book, but no installation changes are noted in the

changelog, simply make a mental note and substitute the new version number wherever it appears in the installation instructions and accompanying figures.

Choosing an Installation Method

You have several options when it comes to getting a basic Apache installation in place. Apache is open source, meaning that you can have access to the full source code of the software, which in turn enables you to build your own custom server. Additionally, pre-built Apache binary distributions are available for most modern Unix platforms. The examples in this chapter will teach you how to build Apache from source if you are using Linux/Unix, and how to use the installer if you plan to run Apache on a Windows system.

By the
Way

> For instructions on installing Apache from the CD, please refer to Appendix A, "Installing MySQL, Apache, and PHP from the CD-ROM."

Building from Source

Building from source gives you the greatest flexibility because it enables you to build a custom server, remove modules you do not need, and extend the server with third-party modules. Building Apache from source code enables you to easily upgrade to the latest versions and quickly apply security patches, whereas updated versions from vendors can take days or weeks to appear.

The process of building Apache from the source code is not especially difficult for simple installations, but can grow in complexity when third-party modules and libraries are involved.

Installing a Binary

Linux/Unix binary installations are available from vendors and can also be downloaded from the Apache Software Foundation Web site. They provide a convenient way to install Apache for users with limited system administration knowledge, or with no special configuration needs. Third-party commercial vendors provide prepackaged Apache installations together with an application server, additional modules, support, and so on.

The Apache Software Foundation provides an installer for Windows systems—a platform where a compiler is not as commonly available as in Linux/Unix systems.

Installing Apache on Linux/Unix

This section explains how to install a fresh build of Apache 2.0.x on Linux/Unix. The steps necessary to successfully install Apache from source are

1. Downloading the software

2. Running the configuration script

3. Compiling the code and installing it

The following sections describe these steps in detail.

Downloading the Apache Source Code

The official Apache download site is located at http://httpd.apache.org/. You can find several Apache versions, packaged with different compression methods. The distribution files are first packed with the tar utility and then compressed either with the gzip tool or the compress utility. Download the .tar.gz version if you have the gunzip utility installed in your system. This utility comes installed by default in open source operating systems such as FreeBSD and Linux. Download the tar.Z file if gunzip is not present in your system. (It isn't included in the default installation of many commercial Unix operating systems.)

The file you want to download will be named something similar to httpd-2.0.*version*.tar.Z or httpd-2.0.*version*.tar.gz, where *version* is the most recent release version of Apache. For example, Apache version 2.0.47 is downloaded as a file named httpd-2.0.47.tar.gz. Keep the downloaded file in a directory reserved for source files, such as /usr/src/ or /usr/local/src/.

Uncompressing the Source Code

If you downloaded the tarball compressed with gzip (it will have a tar.gz suffix), you can uncompress it using the gunzip utility (part of the gzip distribution).

Tarball is a commonly used nickname for software packed using the tar utility.

By the Way

You can uncompress and unpack the software by typing the following command:

```
# gunzip < httpd-2.0*.tar.gz | tar xvf -
```

If you downloaded the tarball compressed with compress (tar.Z suffix), you can issue the following command:

```
# cat httpd-2.0*.tar.Z ¦ uncompress ¦ tar xvf -
```

Uncompressing the tarball creates a structure of directories, with the top-level directory named httpd-2.0_version. Change your current directory to this top-level directory to prepare for configuring the software.

Preparing to Build Apache

You can specify which features the resulting binary will have by using the configure script in the top-level distribution directory. By default, Apache will be compiled with a set of standard modules compiled statically and will be installed in the /usr/local/apache2 directory. If you are happy with these settings, you can issue the following command to configure Apache:

```
#./configure
```

However, in preparation for the PHP installation in Chapter 3, you will need to make sure that mod_so is compiled into Apache. This module, named for the Unix shared object (*.so) format, enables the use of dynamic modules such as PHP with Apache. To configure Apache to install itself in a specific location (in this case, /usr/local/apache2/) and to enable the use of mod_so, issue the following command:

```
#./configure --prefix=/usr/local/apache2 --enable-module=so
```

The purpose of the configure script is to figure out everything related to finding libraries, compile-time options, platform-specific differences, and so on, and to create a set of special files called *makefiles*. Makefiles contain instructions to perform different tasks, called *targets*, such as building Apache. These files will be read by the make utility, which will carry out those tasks. If everything goes well, after executing configure, you will see a set of messages related to the different checks just performed, and will be returned to the prompt:

```
...
creating test/Makefile
config.status: creating docs/conf/httpd-std.conf
config.status: creating include/ap_config_layout.h
config.status: creating support/apxs
config.status: creating support/apachectl
config.status: creating support/dbmmanage
config.status: creating support/envvars-std
config.status: creating support/log_server_status
config.status: creating support/logresolve.pl
```

```
config.status: creating support/phf_abuse_log.cgi
config.status: creating support/split-logfile
config.status: creating build/rules.mk
config.status: creating include/ap_config_auto.h
config.status: executing default commands
#
```

If the `configure` script fails, warnings will appear, alerting you to track down additional software that must be installed, such as compilers or libraries. After you install any missing software, you can try the `configure` command again, after deleting the `config.log` and `config.status` files from the top-level directory.

Building and Installing Apache

The `make` utility reads the information stored in the makefiles and builds the server and modules. Type `make` at the command line to build Apache. You will see several messages indicating the progress of the compilation, and you will end up back at the prompt. After compilation is finished, you can install Apache by typing `make install` at the prompt. The makefiles will install files and directories, and return you to the prompt:

```
...
Installing header files
Installing man pages and online manual
mkdir /usr/local/apache2/man
mkdir /usr/local/apache2/man/man1
mkdir /usr/local/apache2/man/man8
mkdir /usr/local/apache2/manual
Installing build system files
make[1]: Leaving directory `/usr/local/src/httpd-2.0.40'
#
```

The Apache distribution files should now be in the `/usr/local/apache2` directory, as specified by the `--prefix` switch in the `configure` command. To test that the `httpd` binary has been correctly built, type the following at the prompt:

```
# /usr/local/apache2/bin/httpd -v
```

You should see the following output (your version and build date will be different):

```
Server version: Apache/2.0.47
Server built:   Sep  28 2003 11:47:22
```

Unless you want to learn how to install Apache on Windows, skip ahead to the "Apache Configuration File Structure" section to learn about the Apache configuration file.

Installing Apache on Windows

Apache 2.0 runs on most Windows platforms and offers increased performance and stability over the 1.3 versions for Windows. You can build Apache from source, but because not many Windows users have compilers, this section deals with the binary installer.

Before installing Apache, you'll probably want to make sure that you are not currently running a Web server (for instance, a previous version of Apache, Microsoft Internet Information Server, or Microsoft Personal Web Server) in your machine. You might want to uninstall or otherwise disable existing servers. You can run several Web servers, but they will need to run in different address and port combinations.

Before downloading the installer, take a moment—a very important moment—and look for a statement on the downloads page (found at http://httpd. apache.org/download.cgi) that says If you are downloading the Win32 distribution, please read these important notes. The direct URL to these notes is http://www.apache.org/dist/httpd/binaries/win32/README.html.

The Apache Software Foundation maintains this page for the benefit of all Windows users who want to run a version of the Apache server. On this page, there are notes for nearly every flavor of Windows still in use, and as such it will be in your best interest to read the information that is presented. I guarantee that if you are running Apache either as a production or development server, you find relevant information on the notes page. Once you're ready to begin the installation, look for the link labeled Win32 Binary (MSI Installer). After you download the installer, double-click on the file to start the installation process. You will get a welcome screen, as shown in Figure 2.1. Select Next to continue the installation process, and you will be prompted to accept the Apache license. Basically the license says that you can do whatever you want with the software—including making proprietary modifications—except claim that you wrote it, but be sure to read the license so that you fully understand the terms.

After you accept the license, the installer presents you with a brief introduction to Apache. Following that, it asks you to provide basic information about your computer, as shown in Figure 2.2. This includes the full network address for the server (for instance, mycomputer.mydomain.com) and the administrator's email address. The server name will be the name that your clients will use to access your server, and the administrator email address will be added to error messages so that visitors know how to contact you when something goes wrong.

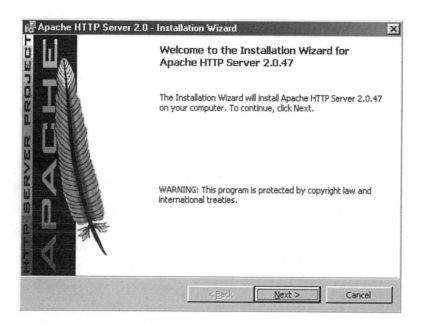

FIGURE 2.1
The Windows installer welcome screen.

If your machine does not have a full network address, use localhost or 127.0.0.1 as the server name.

By the Way

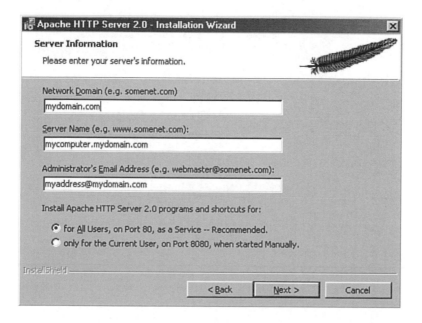

FIGURE 2.2
The basic informa-tion screen.

In the next step, you can install Apache as a service or require it to be started manually. Installing Apache as a service will cause it to run every time Windows is started, and you can control it through the usual Windows service administration tools. Choose this option if you plan to run Apache in a production environment or otherwise require Apache to run continuously. Installing Apache for the current user will require you to start Apache manually and set the default port on which Apache listens to requests to 8080. Choose this option if you use Apache for testing or if you already have a Web server running on port 80.

The next screen enables you to choose the type of installation, as shown in Figure 2.3. *Typical* installation means that Apache binaries and documentation will be installed, but headers and libraries will not. This is the best option to choose unless you plan to compile your own modules.

FIGURE 2.3
The installation
type selection
screen.

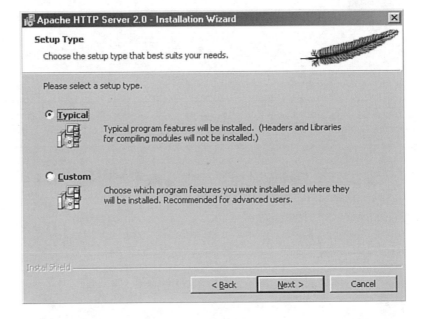

A *custom* installation enables you to choose whether to install header files or documentation. After selecting the target installation directory, which defaults to c:\Program Files\Apache Group, the program will proceed with the installation process. If everything goes well, it will present you with the final screen shown in Figure 2.4.

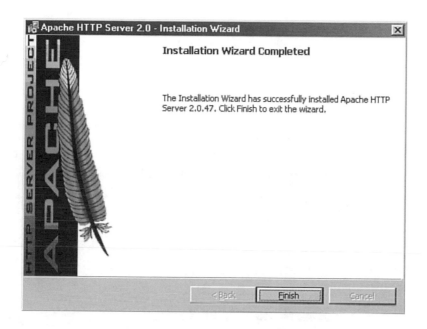

FIGURE 2.4
The successful installation screen.

In the next section, you'll learn about the Apache configuration file, and eventually start up your new server.

Apache Configuration File Structure

Apache keeps all of its configuration information in text files. The main file is called `httpd.conf`. This file contains directives and containers, which enable you to customize your Apache installation. *Directives* configure specific settings of Apache, such as authorization, performance, and network parameters. *Containers* specify the context to which those settings refer. For example, authorization configuration can refer to the server as a whole, a directory, or a single file.

Directives

The following rules apply for Apache directive syntax:

- ▶ The directive arguments follow the directive name.
- ▶ Directive arguments are separated by spaces.
- ▶ The number and type of arguments vary from directive to directive; some have no arguments.

▶ A directive occupies a single line, but you can continue it on a different line by ending the previous line with a backslash character (\).

▶ The pound sign (#) should precede the directive, and must appear on its own line.

In the Apache server documentation, found online at `http://httpd.apache.org/docs-2.0/`, you can browse the directives in alphabetical order or by the module to which they belong. You'll soon learn about some of the basic directives, but you should supplement your knowledge using the online documentation.

Figure 2.5 shows an entry from the documentation for the `ServerName` directive description. You can read this description in the online documentation at `http://httpd.apache.org/docs-2.0/mod/core.html#servername`.

FIGURE 2.5
Directive description example.

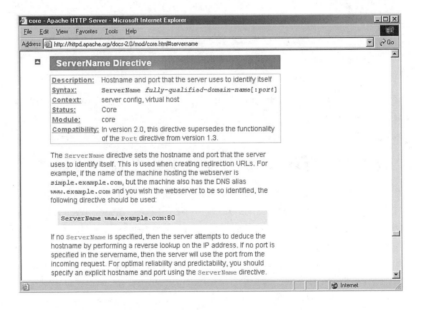

The schema, as detailed in the documentation at `http://httpd.apache.org/docs-2.0/mod/directive-dict.html`, is the same for all directives:

▶ **Syntax**—This entry explains the format of the directive options. Compulsory parameters appear in italics, optional parameters appear in italics and brackets.

▶ **Default**—If the directive has a default value, it will appear here.

▶ **Context**—This entry details the containers or sections in which the directive can appear. Containers are explained in the next section. The possible values are server config, virtual host, directory, and .htaccess.

▶ **Status**—This entry indicates whether the directive is built in Apache (core), belongs to one of the bundled modules (base or extension, depending on whether they are compiled by default), is part of a Multi-Processing Module (MPM), or is bundled with Apache but not ready for use in a production server (experimental).

▶ **Module**—This entry indicates the module to which the directive belongs.

▶ **Compatibility**—This entry contains information about which versions of Apache support the directive.

▶ **Override**—Apache directives belong to different categories. The override field is used to specify which directive categories can appear in .htaccess per-directory configuration files.

A brief explanation of the directive follows these entries in the documentation, and a reference to related directives or documentation might appear at the end.

Containers

Directive containers, also called *sections*, limit the scope for which directives apply. If directives are not inside a container, they belong to the default server scope (server config) and apply to the server as a whole.

These are the default Apache directive containers:

▶ <VirtualHost>—A VirtualHost directive specifies a virtual server. Apache enables you to host different Web sites with a single Apache installation. Directives inside this container apply to a particular Web site. This directive accepts a domain name or IP address and an optional port as arguments. You will learn more about virtual hosts in Chapter 26, "Apache Performance Tuning and Virtual Hosting."

▶ <Directory>, <DirectoryMatch>—These containers allow directives to apply to a certain directory or group of directories in the file system. Directory containers take a directory or directory pattern argument. Enclosed directives apply to the specified directories and their subdirectories. The DirectoryMatch container allows regular expression patterns to be specified as an argument. For example, the following allows a match of all second-level subdirectories of the www directory that are made up of four numbers, such as a directory named after a year and month (0902 for September 2002):

```
<DirectoryMatch "^/www/.*/[0-9]{4}">
```

▶ `<Location>`, `<LocationMatch>`—These containers allow directives to apply to certain requested URLs or URL patterns. They are similar to their `Directory` counterparts. `LocationMatch` takes a regular expression as an argument. For example, the following matches directories containing either "`/my/data`" or "`/your/data`":

```
<LocationMatch "/(my¦your)/data">
```

▶ `<Files>`, `<FilesMatch>`—Similar to `Directory` and `Location` containers, `Files` sections allow directives to apply to certain files or file patterns.

Containers surround directives, as shown in Listing 2.1.

LISTING 2.1   Sample Container Directives

```
 1: <Directory "/some/directory">
 2: SomeDirective1
 3: SomeDirective2
 4: </Directory>
 5: <Location "/downloads/*.html">
 6: SomeDirective3
 7: </Location>
 8: <Files "\.(gif¦jpg)">
 9: SomeDirective4
10: </Files>
```

Sample directives *SomeDirective1* and *SomeDirective2* will apply to the directory /www/docs and its subdirectories. *SomeDirective3* will apply to URLs referring to pages with the .html extension under the /download/ URL. *SomeDirective4* will apply to all files with .gif or .jpg extensions.

Conditional Evaluation

Apache provides support for conditional containers. Directives enclosed in these containers will be processed only if certain conditions are met.

▶ `<IfDefine>`—Directives in this container will be processed if a specific command-line switch is passed to the Apache executable. The directive in Listing 2.2 will be processed only if the -D*MyModule* switch was passed to the Apache binary being executed. You can pass this directly or by modifying the apachectl script, as described in the "Apache-Related Commands" section later in this chapter.

IfDefine containers allow the argument to be negated. That is, directives inside a <IfDefine !*MyModule*> section will be processed only if no -D*MyModule* parameter was passed as a command-line argument. For example, if -DSSL is not passed, listening on the SSL port (usually 443) will not occur.

▶ <IfModule>—Directives in an IfModule section will be processed only if the module passed as an argument is present in the Web server. For example, Apache ships with a default httpd.conf configuration file that provides support for different MPMs. Only the configuration belonging to the MPM compiled in will be processed, as you can see in Listing 2.3. The purpose of the example is to illustrate that only one of the directive groups will be evaluated.

LISTING 2.2 IfDefine **Example**

```
1: <IfDefine MyModule>
2: LoadModule my_module modules/libmymodule.so
3: </IfDefine>
```

LISTING 2.3 IfModule **Example**

```
 1: <IfModule prefork.c>
 2: StartServers          5
 3: MinSpareServers       5
 4: MaxSpareServers      10
 5: MaxClients           20
 6: MaxRequestsPerChild   0
 7: </IfModule>
 8:
 9: <IfModule worker.c>
10: StartServers          3
11: MaxClients            8
12: MinSpareThreads       5
13: MaxSpareThreads      10
14: ThreadsPerChild      25
15: MaxRequestsPerChild   0
16: </IfModule>
```

ServerRoot

The ServerRoot directive takes a single argument: a directory path pointing to the directory where the server lives. All relative path references in other directives are relative to the value of ServerRoot. If you compiled Apache from source on Linux/Unix, as described earlier in this chapter, the default value of ServerRoot is /usr/local/apache2. If you used the Windows installer, the ServerRoot is c:\Program Files\Apache Group.

Per-Directory Configuration Files

Apache uses per-directory configuration files to allow directives to exist outside the main configuration file, httpd.conf. These special files can be placed in the file system. Apache will process the content of these files if a document is requested in a directory containing one of these files or any subdirectories under it. The contents of all the applicable per-directory configuration files are merged and processed. For example, if Apache receives a request for the /usr/local/apache2/htdocs/index.html file, it will look for per-directory configuration files in the /, /usr, /usr/local, /usr/local/apache2, and /usr/local/apache2/htdocs directories, in that order.

Enabling per-directory configuration files has a performance penalty. Apache must perform expensive disk operations looking for these files in every request, even if the files do not exist.

Per-directory configuration files are called .htaccess by default. This is for historical reasons; they were originally used to protect access to directories containing HTML files.

The directive AccessFileName enables you to change the name of the per-directory configuration files from .htaccess to something else. It accepts a list of filenames that Apache will use when looking for per-directory configuration files.

To determine whether a directive can be overridden in the per-directory configuration file, check whether the Context: field of the directive syntax definition contains .htaccess.

Apache directives belong to different groups, specified in the Override: field in the directive syntax description. Possible values are

▶ AuthConfig—Authorization directives

▶ FileInfo—Directives controlling document types

▶ Indexes—Directives controlling directory indexing

▶ Limit—Directives controlling host access

▶ Options—Directives controlling specific directory features

You can control which of these directive groups can appear in per-directory configuration files by using the AllowOverride directive. AllowOverride can also take an All or a None argument. All means that directives belonging to all groups can appear in the configuration file. None disables per-directory files in a directory and any of its subdirectories. Listing 2.4 shows how to disable per-directory configuration files for the server as a whole. This improves performance and is the default Apache configuration.

LISTING 2.4   Disabling Per-Directory Configuration Files

```
1: <Directory />
2: AllowOverride none
3: </Directory>
```

Apache Log Files

Apache includes two log files by default. The access_log file is used to track client requests. The error_log is used to record important events, such as errors or server restarts. These files don't exist until you start Apache for the first time. The files are named access.log and error.log in Windows platforms.

access_log

When a client requests a file from the server, Apache records several parameters associated with the request, including the IP address of the client, the document requested, the HTTP status code, and the current time. Listing 2.5 shows sample log file entries. Chapter 24, "Logging and Monitoring Server Activity," will show you how to modify which parameters are logged.

LISTING 2.5   Sample access_log Entries

```
1: 127.0.0.1 - - [01/Sep/2003:09:43:37 -0700] "GET / HTTP/1.1" 200 1494
2: 127.0.0.1 - - [01/Sep/2003:09:43:40 -0700] "GET /manual/ HTTP/1.1" 200 10383
```

error_log

This file includes error messages, startup messages, and any other significant events in the life cycle of the server. This is the first place to look when you have a problem with Apache. Listing 2.6 shows sample error_log entries.

LISTING 2.6   Sample error_log Entries

```
1: [Sun Sep 01 09:42:59 2003] [notice] Parent: Created child process -2245
2: [Sun Sep 01 09:42:59 2003] [notice] Child -2242: Child process is running
3: [Sun Sep 01 09:42:59 2003] [notice] Child -2242: Acquired the start mutex.
4: [Sun Sep 01 09:42:59 2003] [notice] Child -2242: Starting 250 worker threads.
```

Additional Files

The httpd.pid file contains the process ID of the running Apache server. You can use this number to send signals to Apache manually, as described in the next section.

The scoreboard file, present on Linux/Unix Apache, is used by the process-based MPMs to communicate with their children.

In general, you do not need to worry about these files.

Apache-Related Commands

The Apache distribution includes several executables. This section covers only the server binary and related scripts. Chapter 23, "Restricting Access to Your Applications," and Chapter 26, "Apache Performance Tuning and Virtual Hosting," cover additional utilities included with the Apache distribution.

Apache Server Binary

The Apache executable is named httpd in Linux/Unix and apache.exe in Windows. It accepts several command-line options, which are described in Table 2.1. You can get a complete listing of options by typing /usr/local/apache2/bin/httpd -h on Linux/Unix, or by typing apache.exe -h from a command prompt on Windows.

TABLE 2.1   httpd Options

Option	Meaning
-D	Allows you to pass a parameter that can be used for <IfDefine> section processing
-l	Lists compiled-in modules
-v	Shows version number and server compilation time
-f	Allows you to pass the location of httpd.conf if it is different from the compile-time default

After Apache is running, you can use the kill command on Linux/Unix to send signals to the parent Apache process. Signals provide a mechanism to send commands to a process. To send a signal, execute the following command:

```
# kill -SIGNAL pid
```

where *pid* is the process ID and *SIGNAL* is one of the following:

- ▶ HUP—Stop the server
- ▶ USR1 or WINCH—Graceful restart; which signal to use depends on the underlying operating system
- ▶ SIGHUP—Restart

If you make some changes to the configuration files and you want them to take effect, you must signal Apache that the configuration has changed. You can do this by stopping and starting the server or by sending a restart signal. This tells Apache to reread its configuration.

A normal restart can result in a momentary pause in service. A graceful restart takes a different approach. Each thread or process serving a client will keep processing the current request, but when it is finished, it will be killed and replaced by a new thread or process with the new configuration. This allows seamless operation of the Web server with no downtime.

On Windows, you can signal Apache using the apache.exe executable:

- ▶ apache.exe -k restart—Tells Apache to restart
- ▶ apache.exe -k graceful—Tells Apache to do a graceful restart
- ▶ apache.exe -k stop—Tells Apache to stop

You can access shortcuts to these commands in the Start menu entries that the Apache installer created. If you installed Apache as a service, you can start or stop Apache by using the Windows service interface: In Control Panel, select Administrative Tasks and then click on the Services icon.

Apache Control Script

Although it is possible to control Apache on Linux/Unix using the httpd binary, it is recommended that you use the apachectl tool. The apachectl support program wraps common functionality in an easy-to-use script. To use apachectl, type

```
# /usr/local/apache2/bin/apachectl command
```

where *command* is stop, start, restart, or graceful. You can also edit the contents of the apachectl script to add extra command-line options.

Some OS distributions provide you with additional scripts to control Apache; please check the documentation included with your distribution.

Starting Apache for the First Time

Before you start Apache, you should verify that the minimal set of information is present in the Apache configuration file, httpd.conf. The following sections describe the basic information needed to configure Apache and how to start the server.

Check Your Configuration File

You can edit the Apache httpd.conf file with your favorite text editor. In Linux/Unix, this probably means vi or emacs. In Windows, you can use Notepad or WordPad. You must remember to save the configuration file in plain text, which is the only format Apache will understand.

There are only two parameters that you might need to change to enable you to start Apache for the first time: the name of the server and the address and port to which it is listening. The name of the server is the one Apache will use when it needs to refer to itself (for example, when redirecting requests).

Apache can usually figure out its server name from the IP address of the machine, but this is not always the case. If the server does not have a valid DNS entry, you might need to specify one of the IP addresses of the machine. If the server is not connected to a network (you might want to test Apache on a stand-alone machine), you can use the value 127.0.0.1, which is the loopback address. The default port value is 80. You might need to change this value if there is already a server running in the machine at port 80, or if you do not have administrator permissions—on Linux/Unix systems, only the root user can bind to privileged ports (those with port numbers lower than 1024).

You can change both the listening address and the port values with the Listen directive. The Listen directive takes either a port number or an IP address and a port, separated by a semicolon. If only the port is specified, Apache will listen on that port at all available IP addresses in the machine. If an additional IP address is provided, Apache will listen at only that address and port combination. For example, Listen 80 tells Apache to listen for requests at all IP addresses on port 80. Listen 10.0.0.1:443 tells Apache to listen only at 10.0.0.1 on port 443.

The ServerName directive enables you to define the name the server will report in any self-referencing URLs. The directive accepts a DNS name and an optional port, separated by a colon. Make sure that ServerName has a valid value. Otherwise, the server will not function properly; for example, it will issue incorrect redirects.

On Linux/Unix platforms, you can use the User and Group directives to specify which user and group IDs the server will run as. The nobody user is a good choice for most platforms. However, there are problems in the HP-UX platform with this user ID, so you must create and use a different user ID, such as www.

Starting Apache

To start Apache on Linux/Unix, change to the directory containing the apachectl script and execute the following command:

```
# /usr/local/apache2/bin/apachectl start
```

To start Apache on Windows, click on the Start Apache in Console link in the Control Apache Server section, within the Apache HTTP Server 2.0.47 program group in the Start menu. If you installed Apache as a service, you must start the Apache service instead.

If everything goes well, you can access Apache using a browser. The default installation page will be displayed, as shown in Figure 2.6. If you cannot start the Web server or an error page appears instead, please consult the "Troubleshooting" section that follows. Make sure that you are accessing Apache in one of the ports specified in the Listen directive—usually 80 or 8080.

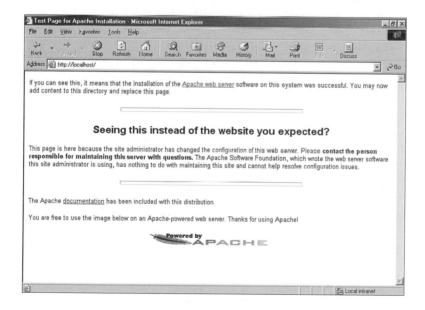

FIGURE 2.6
Apache default installation page.

Troubleshooting

The following subsections describe several common problems that you might encounter the first time you start Apache.

Already an Existing Web Server

If there is already a server running in the machine and listening to the same IP address and port combination, Apache will not be able to start successfully. You will get an entry in the error log file indicating that Apache cannot bind to the port:

```
[crit] (48)Address already in use: make_sock: could not bind to
➥address 10.0.0.2:80
[alert] no listening sockets available, shutting down
```

To solve this problem, you need to stop the running server or change the Apache configuration to listen on a different port.

No Permission to Bind to Port

You will get an error if you do not have administrator permissions and you try to bind to a privileged port (between 0 and 1024):

```
[crit] (13)Permission denied: make_sock: could not bind to address 10.0.0.2:80
[alert] no listening sockets available, shutting down
```

To solve this problem, you must either log on as the administrator before starting Apache or change the port number (8080 is a commonly used nonprivileged port).

Access Denied

You might not be able to start Apache if you do not have permission to read the configuration files or to write to the log files. You will get an error similar to the following:

```
(13)Permission denied: httpd: could not open error log file
    ➥ /usr/local/apache2/logs/error_log.
```

This problem can arise if Apache was built and installed by a different user than the one trying to run it.

Wrong Group Settings

You can configure Apache to run under a certain username and group. Apache has default values for the running server username and group. Sometimes the default value is not valid, and you will get an error containing `setgid: unable to set group id`.

To solve this problem on Linux/Unix, you must change the value of the `Group` directive in the configuration file to a valid value. Check the `/etc/groups` file for existing groups.

Summary

This chapter explained different ways of getting an Apache 2.0 server installed on your Linux/Unix or Windows machine. It covered both binary and source installation and explained the basic build-time options. Additionally, you learned the location of the server configuration files, and the syntax of the commands used to modify your Apache configuration. You learned about the two main log files: `access_log` and `error_log`. Finally, you saw how to start and stop the server using the Apache control scripts or the Apache server binary on Linux/Unix and Windows platforms.

Q&A

Q. *How can I start a clean build?*

If you need to build a new Apache from source and do not want the result of earlier builds to affect the new one, it is always a good idea to run the `make clean` command. That will take care of cleaning up any existing binaries, intermediate object files, and so on.

Q. *Why are per-directory configuration files useful?*

A. Although per-directory configuration files have an effect on server performance, they can be useful for delegated administration. Because per-directory configuration files are read every time a request is made, there is no need to restart the server when a change is made to the configuration.

You can allow users of your Web site to make configuration changes on their own without granting them administrator privileges. In this way, they can password-protect sections of their home pages, for example.

Q. *What do you mean by a valid `ServerName` directive?*

A. The DNS system is used to associate IP addresses with domain names. The value of `ServerName` is returned when the server generates a URL. If you are using a certain domain name, you must make sure that it is included in your DNS system and will be available to clients visiting your site.

Workshop

The workshop is designed to help you anticipate possible questions, review what you've learned, and begin putting your knowledge into practice.

Quiz

1. How can you specify the location where you want to install Apache?

2. What is the main difference between `<Location>` and `<Directory>` sections?

3. What is the difference between a restart and a graceful restart?

Answers

1. Linux/Unix users can use the `--prefix` option of the `configure` script. If an existing installation is present at that location, the configuration files will be preserved but the binaries will be replaced. On Windows, this location is set in the installation wizard.

2. `Directory` sections refer to file system objects; `Location` sections refer to elements in the address bar of the Web page (also called the *URI*).

3. During a normal restart, the server is stopped and then started, causing some requests to be lost. A graceful restart allows Apache children to continue to serve their current requests until they can be replaced with children running the new configuration.

Activities

1. Practice the various types of server shutdown and restart procedures.

2. Make some configuration changes, such as different port assignments and `ServerName` changes.

CHAPTER 3

Installing and Configuring PHP

In the last of the three installation-related chapters, you will acquire, install, and configure PHP and make some basic changes to your Apache installation. In this chapter, you will learn

- ▶ How to install PHP with Apache on Linux/Unix
- ▶ How to install PHP with Apache server on Windows
- ▶ How to test your PHP installation
- ▶ How to find help when things go wrong
- ▶ The basics of the PHP language

Current and Future Versions of PHP

The installation instructions in this chapter refer to PHP version 4.3.3, which is the current version of the software. The PHP Group uses minor release numbers for updates containing security enhancements or bug fixes. Minor releases do not follow a set release schedule; when enhancements or fixes are added to the code and thoroughly tested, the PHP Group will releases a new version, with a new minor version number.

It is possible that by the time you purchase this book, the minor version number will have changed, to 4.3.4 or beyond. If that is the case, you should read the list of changes at http://www.php.net/ChangeLog-4.php for any changes regarding the installation or configuration process, which makes up the bulk of this chapter.

Although it is unlikely that any installation instructions will change between minor version updates, you should get in the habit of always checking the changelog of software that you install and maintain. If a minor version change does occur during the time you are reading this book, but no installation changes are noted in the

changelog, simply make a mental note and substitute the new version number
wherever it appears in the installation instructions and accompanying figures.

> For instructions on installing PHP from the CD, please refer to Appendix A, "Installing
> MySQL, Apache, and PHP from the CD-ROM."

Building PHP on Linux/Unix with Apache

In this section, we will look at one way of installing PHP with Apache on
Linux/Unix. The process is more or less the same for any Unix operating system.
Although you might be able to find pre-built versions of PHP for your system,
compiling PHP from the source gives you greater control.

To download the PHP distribution files, go to the home of PHP, http://www.php.
net/, and follow the link to the Downloads section. Grab the latest version of the
source code—for this example, we are using 4.3.3. Your distribution will be
named something similar to php-*version*.tar.gz, where *version* is the most
recent release number. This archive will be a compressed tar file, so you will need
to unpack it:

```
# gunzip < php-version.tar.gz ¦ tar xvf -
```

Keep the downloaded file in a directory reserved for source files, such as /usr/
src/ or /usr/local/src/. After your distribution is unpacked, you should move to
the PHP distribution directory:

```
# cd php-version
```

Within your distribution directory, you will find a script called configure. This
script accepts additional information that is provided when the configure script
is run from the command line. These command-line arguments control the features that PHP will support. In this example, we will include the basic options you
need to use to install PHP with Apache and MySQL support. We will discuss some
of the available configure options later in the chapter, and throughout the book
as they become relevant.

```
# ./configure  --prefix=/usr/local/php --with-mysql \
--with-apxs2=/usr/local/apache2/bin/apxs
```

Once the configure script has run, you will be returned to the prompt after
receiving informational notes from the PHP Group:

```
+----------------------------------------------------------------+
| License:                                                       |
| This software is subject to the PHP License, available in this |
| distribution in the file LICENSE.  By continuing this installation |
| process, you are bound by the terms of this license agreement. |
| If you do not agree with the terms of this license, you must abort |
| the installation process at this point.                        |
+----------------------------------------------------------------+
|                      *** NOTE ***                              |
|            The default for register_globals is now OFF!         |
|                                                                |
| If your application relies on register_globals being ON, you   |
| should explicitly set it to on in your php.ini file.           |
| Note that you are strongly encouraged to read                  |
| http://www.php.net/manual/en/security.registerglobals.php      |
| about the implications of having register_globals set to on, and |
| avoid using it if possible.                                    |
+----------------------------------------------------------------+

Thank you for using PHP.
```

Next, issue the make command, followed by the make install command. These commands should end the process of PHP compilation and installation and return you to your prompt.

You will need to ensure that two very important files are copied to their correct locations. First, issue the following command to copy the distributed version of php.ini to its default location. You will learn more about php.ini later in this chapter.

```
# cp php.ini-dist /usr/local/lib/php.ini
```

Next, copy the PHP shared object file to its proper place in the Apache installation directory, if it has not already been placed there by the installation process:

```
# cp libs/libphp4.so /usr/local/apache2/modules/
```

You should now be able to configure and run Apache, but let's cover some additional configuration options before heading on to the "Integrating PHP with Apache on Linux/Unix" section.

Additional Configuration Options

When we ran the configure script, we included some command-line arguments that determined some features that the PHP engine will include. The configure script itself gives you a list of available options, including the ones we used. From the PHP distribution directory, type the following:

```
# ./configure  --help
```

This produces a long list, so you might want to add it to a file and read it at your leisure:

```
# ./configure  --help  > configoptions.txt
```

If you discover additional functionality you wish to add to PHP after it has been installed, simply run the configuration and build process again. Doing so will create a new version of libphp4.so and place it in the Apache directory structure. All you have to do is restart Apache in order for the new file to be loaded.

Integrating PHP with Apache on Linux/Unix

To ensure that PHP and Apache get along with one another, you need to check for—and potentially add—a few items to the httpd.conf configuration file. First, look for a line like the following:

```
LoadModule php4_module          modules/libphp4.so
```

If this line is not present, or only appears with a pound sign (#) at the beginning of the line, you must add the line or remove the #. This line tells Apache to use the PHP shared object file that was created by the PHP build process (libphp4.so).

Next, look for this section:

```
#
# AddType allows you to add to or override the MIME configuration
# file mime.types for specific file types.
#
```

Add the following line:

```
AddType application/x-httpd-php .php .phtml .html
```

This ensures that the PHP engine will parse files that end with the .php, .phtml, and .html extensions. Your selection of filenames might differ, and you might want to add .php3 as an extension, for backward compatibility with any very old scripts you may have.

Save this file, and then restart Apache. When you look in your error_log, you should see something like the following line:

```
[Sun Sep 28 10:42:47 2002] [notice] Apache/2.0.47 (Unix) PHP/4.3.3 configured
```

PHP is now part of the Apache Web server. If you want to learn how to install PHP on a Windows platform, keep reading. Otherwise, you can skip ahead to the "Testing Your Installation" section.

Installing PHP Files on Windows

Unlike building and installing PHP on Linux/Unix, installing PHP on Windows requires nothing more than downloading the distribution and moving a few files around. To download the PHP distribution files, go to the home of PHP, http://www.php.net/, and follow the link to the Downloads section. Grab the latest version of the zip package (*not* the installer!) from the Windows Binaries section—for this example, we are using 4.3.3. Your distribution will be named something like to php-version.zip, where *version* is the most recent release number.

Once the file is downloaded to your system, double-click on it to launch your unzipping software. The distribution is packed up with pathnames already in place, so extract the files to the root of your drive, where it will create a directory called php-version-Win32, and place all the files and subdirectories under that new directory.

Now that you have all the basic PHP distribution files, you just need to move a few of them around:

1. In the PHP installation directory, find the php.ini-dist file and rename it php.ini.

2. Copy the php.ini file to C:\WINDOWS\ or wherever you usually put your *.ini files.

3. Copy the php4ts.dll file to C:\WINDOWS\SYSTEM\ or wherever you usually put your *.dll files.

To get a basic version of PHP working with Apache, you'll need to make a few minor modifications to the Apache configuration file.

Integrating PHP with Apache on Windows

To ensure that PHP and Apache get along with one another, you need to add a few items to the httpd.conf configuration file in the Apache directory on your computer. First, find a section that looks like this:

```
# Example:
# LoadModule foo_module modules/mod_foo.so
#
LoadModule access_module modules/mod_access.so
LoadModule actions_module modules/mod_actions.so
LoadModule alias_module modules/mod_alias.so
LoadModule asis_module modules/mod_asis.so
LoadModule auth_module modules/mod_auth.so
#LoadModule auth_anon_module modules/mod_auth_anon.so
```

```
#LoadModule auth_dbm_module modules/mod_auth_dbm.so
#LoadModule auth_digest_module modules/mod_auth_digest.so
LoadModule autoindex_module modules/mod_autoindex.so
#LoadModule cern_meta_module modules/mod_cern_meta.so
LoadModule cgi_module modules/mod_cgi.so
#LoadModule dav_module modules/mod_dav.so
#LoadModule dav_fs_module modules/mod_dav_fs.so
LoadModule dir_module modules/mod_dir.so
LoadModule env_module modules/mod_env.so
#LoadModule expires_module modules/mod_expires.so
#LoadModule file_cache_module modules/mod_file_cache.so
#LoadModule headers_module modules/mod_headers.so
```

At the end of this section, add the following:

```
LoadModule php4_module c:/php-version/sapi/php4apache2.dll
```

Next, look for this section:

```
#
# AddType allows you to add to or override the MIME configuration
# file mime.types for specific file types.
#
```

Add the following lines:

```
AddType application/x-httpd-php .php .phtml .html
```

This ensures that the PHP engine will parse files that end with the .php, .phtml, and .html extensions. Your selection of filenames might differ, and you might want to add .php3 as an extension, for backward compatibility with any very old scripts you might have.

Save this file, and then restart Apache. The server should start without warning, PHP is now part of the Apache Web server.

php.ini **Basics**

After you have compiled or installed PHP, you can still change its behavior with the php.ini file. On Unix systems, the default location for this file is /usr/local/ php/lib, or the lib subdirectory of the PHP installation location you used at configuration time. On a Windows system, this file should be in the Windows directory.

Directives in the php.ini file come in two forms: values and flags. Value directives take the form of a directive name and a value separated by an equal sign. Possible values vary from directive to directive. Flag directives take the form of a directive name and a positive or negative term separated by an equal sign. Positive terms include 1, On, Yes, and True. Negative terms include 0, Off, No, and False. Whitespace is ignored.

You can change your php.ini settings at any time, but after you do, you'll need to restart the server for the changes to take effect. At some point, take time to read through the php.ini file on your own to see the types of things that can be configured.

Testing Your Installation

The simplest way to test your PHP installation is to create a small test script utilizing the phpinfo() function. This function will produce a long list of configuration information. Open a text editor and type the following line:

```
<?php phpinfo(); ?>
```

Save this file as phpinfo.php and place it in the document root of your Web server—the htdocs subdirectory of your Apache installation. Access this file via your Web browser and you should see something like Figure 3.1 or Figure 3.2.

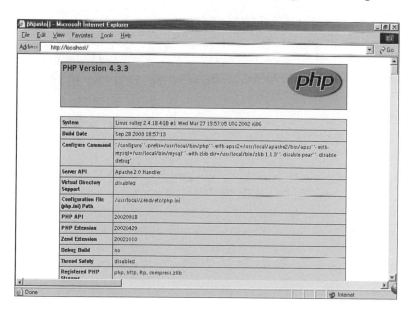

FIGURE 3.1
The results of phpinfo() on a Linux/Unix system.

FIGURE 3.2
The results of
phpinfo() on a
Windows system.

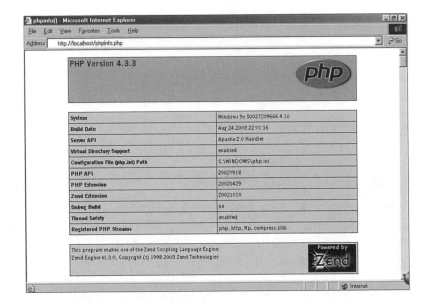

Getting Installation Help

Help is always at hand on the Internet, particularly for problems concerning
open source software. Wait a moment before you click the send button, however.
No matter how intractable your installation, configuration, or programming
problem might seem, chances are you are not alone. Someone has probably
already answered your question.

When you hit a brick wall, your first recourse should be to the official PHP site at
http://www.php.net/ (particularly the annotated manual at http://www.php.
net/manual/).

If you still can't find your answer, don't forget that the PHP site is searchable. The
advice you are seeking may be lurking in a press release or a Frequently Asked
Questions file. You can also search the mailing list archives at http://www.php.
net/search.php. These archives represent a huge information resource with con-
tributions from many of the great minds in the PHP community. Spend some time
trying out a few keyword combinations.

If you are still convinced that your problem has not been addressed, you might
well be doing the PHP community a service by exposing it. You can join the PHP
mailing lists at http://www.php.net/support.php. Although these lists often have
high volume, you can learn a lot from them. If you are serious about PHP

scripting, you should certainly subscribe to at least a digest list. Once you've sub-scribed to the list that matches your concerns, you might consider posting your problem.

When you post a question, it is a good idea to include as much information as possible (without writing a novel). The following items are often pertinent:

- Your operating system
- The version of PHP you are running or installing
- The configuration options you chose
- Any output from the `configure` or `make` commands that preceded an installation failure
- A reasonably complete example of the code that is causing problems

Why all these cautions about posting a question to a mailing list? First, develop-ing research skills will stand you in good stead. A good researcher can generally solve a problem quickly and efficiently. Posting a naive question to a technical list often results in a wait rewarded only by a message or two referring you to the archives where you should have begun your search for answers in the first place.

Second, remember that a mailing list is not analogous to a technical support call center. No one is paid to answer your questions. Despite this, you have access to an impressive pool of talent and knowledge, including that of some of the cre-ators of PHP itself. A good question and its answer will be archived to help other coders. Asking a question that has been answered several times just adds more noise.

Having said this, don't be afraid to post a problem to the list. PHP developers are a civilized and helpful breed, and by bringing a problem to the attention of the community, you might be helping others to solve the same problem.

The Basics of PHP Scripts

Let's jump straight in with a PHP script. To begin, open your favorite text editor. Like HTML documents, PHP files are made up of plain text. You can create them with any text editor, such as Notepad on Windows, Simple Text and BBEdit on Mac OS, or vi and Emacs on Unix operating systems. Most popular HTML editors provide at least some support for PHP.

Did you Know?

Keith Edmunds maintains a handy list of PHP-friendly editors at `http://phpeditors.linuxbackup.co.uk/`.

Type in the example in Listing 3.1 and save the file, calling it something like `first.php`.

LISTING 3.1   A Simple PHP Script

```
1: <?php
2:     echo "Hello Web!";
3: ?>
```

If you are not working directly on the machine that will be serving your PHP script, you will probably need to use an FTP client such as WS-FTP for Windows or Fetch for Mac OS to upload your saved document to the server.

Once the document is in place, you should be able to access it via your browser. If all has gone well, you should see the script's output. Figure 3.3 shows the output from the `first.php` script.

FIGURE 3.3
Success: the output from Listing 3.1.

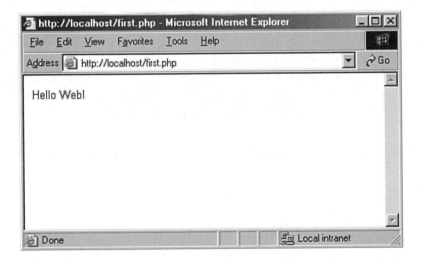

Beginning and Ending a Block of PHP Statements

When writing PHP, you need to inform the PHP engine that you want it to execute your commands. If you don't do this, the code you write will be mistaken for HTML and will be output to the browser. You can designate your code as PHP with special tags that mark the beginning and end of PHP code blocks. Table 3.1 shows four such PHP delimiter tags.

TABLE 3.1   PHP Start and End Tags

Tag Style	Start Tag	End Tag
Standard tags	`<?php`	`?>`
Short tags	`<?`	`?>`
ASP tags	`<%`	`%>`
Script tags	`<SCRIPT LANGUAGE="php">`	`</SCRIPT>`

Of the tags in Table 3.1, only the standard and script tags are guaranteed to work on any configuration. The short and ASP-style tags must be explicitly enabled in your `php.ini`.

To activate recognition for short tags, you must make sure that the `short_open_tag` switch is set to On in `php.ini`:

```
short_opon_tag  =  On,
```

Short tags are enabled by default, so you need to edit `php.ini` only if you want to disable them.

To activate recognition for the ASP-style tags, you must enable the `asp_tags` setting:

```
asp_tags = On;
```

After you have edited `php.ini`, you should be able to use any of the four styles in your scripts. This is largely a matter of preference, although if you intend to include XML in your script, you should disable the short tags (`<? ?>`) and work with the standard tags (`<?php ?>`).

> The character sequence `<?` tells an XML parser to expect a processing instruction and is therefore frequently included in XML documents. If you include XML in your script and have short tags enabled, the PHP engine is likely to confuse XML processing instructions and PHP start tags. Disable short tags if you intend to incorporate XML in your document.

Watch
Out!

Let's run through some of the ways in which you can legally write the code in Listing 3.1. You can use any of the four PHP start and end tags that you have seen:

```
<?
echo"Hello Web!";
?>

<?php
echo "Hello Web!";
?>

<%
echo "Hello Web!";
%>

<SCRIPT LANGUAGE="php">
echo "Hello Web!";
</SCRIPT>
```

You can also put single lines of code in PHP on the same line as the PHP start and end tags:

```
<? echo "Hello Web!"; ?>
```

Now that you know how to define a block of PHP code, let's take a closer look at the code in Listing 3.1 itself.

The echo **Statement and** print() **Function**

Simply, the echo statement is used to output data. In most cases, anything output by echo ends up viewable in the browser. You could also have used the print() function in place of the echo statement. Using echo or print() is a matter of taste; when you look at other people's scripts, you might see either use.

Whereas echo is a statement, print() is a function. A *function* is a command that performs an action, usually modified in some way by data provided for it. Data sent to a function is almost always placed in parentheses after the function name. In this case, you could have sent the print() function a collection of characters, or a *string*. Strings must always be enclosed in quotation marks, either single or double. For example:

```
<?
print("Hello Web!");
?>
```

The only line of code in Listing 3.1 ended with a semicolon. The semicolon informs the PHP engine that you have completed a statement.

A *statement* represents an instruction to the PHP engine. Broadly, it is to PHP what a sentence is to written or spoken English. A sentence should usually end with a period; a statement should usually end with a semicolon. Exceptions to this include statements that enclose other statements, and statements that end a block of code. In most cases, however, failure to end a statement with a semicolon will confuse the PHP engine and result in an error.

Combining HTML and PHP

The script in Listing 3.1 is pure PHP. You can incorporate this into an HTML document by simply adding HTML outside the PHP start and end tags, as shown in Listing 3.2.

LISTING 3.2   A PHP Script Incorporated into HTML

```
 1: <html>
 2: <head>
 3: <title>Listing 3.2 A PHP script including HTML</title>
 4: </head>
 5: <body>
 6: <b>
 7: <?php
 8:     echo "hello world";
 9: ?>
10: </b>
11: </body>
12: </html>
```

As you can see, incorporating PHP code into a predominantly HTML document is simply a matter of typing in the code. The PHP engine ignores everything outside the PHP open and close tags. If you were to view Listing 3.2 with a browser, as shown in Figure 3.4, you would see the string hello world in bold. If you were to view the document source, as shown in Figure 3.5, the listing would look exactly like a normal HTML document.

You can include as many blocks of PHP code as you need in a single document, interspersing them with HTML as required. Although you can have multiple blocks of code in a single document, they combine to form a single script. Any variables defined in the first block will usually be available to subsequent blocks.

FIGURE 3.4
The output of
Listing 3.2 as
viewed in a
browser.

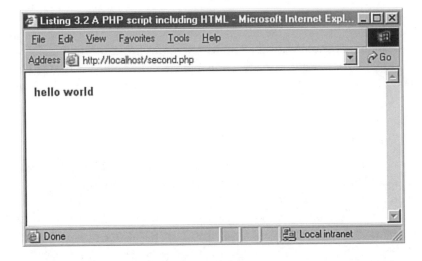

FIGURE 3.5
The output of
Listing 3.2 as
HTML source code.

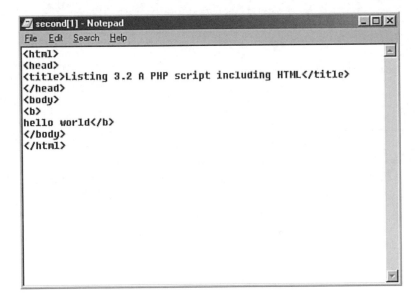

Adding Comments to PHP Code

Code that seems clear at the time of writing can seem like a hopeless tangle when
you try to amend it six months later. Adding comments to your code as you write
can save you time later on and make it easier for other programmers to work
with your code.

A *comment* is text in a script that is ignored by the PHP engine. Comments can be used to make code more readable or to annotate a script.

Single-line comments begin with two forward slashes (//) or a single hash sign (#). The PHP engine ignores all text between these marks and either the end of the line or the PHP close tag:

```
// this is a comment
#  this is another comment
```

Multiline comments begin with a forward slash followed by an asterisk (/*) and end with an asterisk followed by a forward slash (*/):

```
/*
this is a comment
none of this will
be parsed by the
PHP engine
*/
```

Summary

In this chapter, you learned how to install and configure PHP for use with Apache on either Linux/Unix or Windows. You learned that various configure options in the Linux/Unix build script can change the features that are supported. You learned about php.ini and how to change the values of its directives. Using the phpinfo() function, you tested your installation and produced a list of its configuration values. You created a simple PHP script using a text editor. You examined four sets of tags that you can use to begin and end blocks of PHP code. Finally, you learned how to use the echo statement or print() function to send data to the browser, and you brought HTML and PHP together into the same script. In the next chapter, you will use these skills to test some of the fundamental building blocks of the PHP language, including variables, data types, and operators.

Q&A

Q. *You have covered an installation for Linux/Unix or Windows, and the Apache Web server. Does this mean that the material presented in this book will not apply to my server and operating system?*

A. No. One of PHP's great strengths is that it runs on multiple platforms. You can find installation instructions for different Web servers and configuration directives for database support in the PHP manual. Although the examples throughout this book are specifically geared toward the combination of PHP, MySQL, and Apache, only slight modifications would be needed to work with the examples using different Web servers or databases.

Q. *Which are the best start and end tags to use?*

A. It is largely a matter of preference. For the sake of portability, the standard tags (<?php ?>) are probably the safest bet. Short tags are enabled by default and have the virtue of brevity, but with the increasing popularity of XML, it is safest to avoid them.

Q. *What editors should I avoid when creating PHP code?*

A. Do not use word processors that format text for printing (such as Word, for example). Even if you save files created using this type of editor in plain text format, hidden characters are likely to creep into your code.

Q. *When should I comment my code?*

A. Once again, this is a matter of preference. Some short scripts will be self-explanatory, even after a long interval. For scripts of any length or complexity, you should comment your code. This often saves you time and frustration in the long run.

Workshop

The workshop is designed to help you anticipate possible questions, review what you've learned, and begin putting your knowledge into practice.

Quiz

1. From a Linux/Unix operating system, how would you get help on configuration options (the options that you pass to the configure script in your PHP distribution)?

2. What line should you add to the Apache configuration file to ensure that the .php extension is recognized?

3. What is PHP's configuration file called?

4. Can a person browsing your Web site read the source code of PHP script you have successfully installed?

Answers

1. You can get help on configuration options by calling the `configure` script in the PHP distribution folder and passing it the `--help` argument:

```
./configure --help
```

2. The line

```
AddType application/x-httpd-php .php
```

ensures that Apache will treat files ending with the .php extension as PHP scripts.

3. PHP's configuration file is called `php.ini`.

4. No, the user will see only the output of your script

Activities

1. Install PHP on your system. If it is already in place, review your `php.ini` file and check your configuration.

2. Familiarize yourself with the process of creating, uploading, and running PHP scripts. In particular, create your own "hello world" script. Add HTML code to it, and add additional blocks of PHP. Experiment with the different PHP delimiter tags. Which ones are enabled in your configuration? Take a look at your `php.ini` file to confirm your findings. Don't forget to add some comments to your code.

PART II

PHP Language Structure

CHAPTER 4

The Building Blocks of PHP

In this chapter, you will get your hands dirty with some of the nuts and bolts of the PHP scripting language. Those of you new to programming may feel overwhelmed at times, but don't worry—you can always refer back to this chapter later on. Concentrate on understanding the concepts rather than memorizing the features covered.

If you're already an experienced programmer, you should at least skim this chapter, as it covers a few PHP-specific features.

In this chapter, you will learn

▶ About variables—what they are, why you need to use them, and how to use them

▶ How to define and access variables

▶ About data types

▶ About some of the more commonly used operators

▶ How to use operators to create expressions

▶ How to define and use constants

Variables

A variable is a special container that you can define, which will then "hold" a value, such as a number, string, object, array, or a Boolean. Variables are fundamental to programming. Without variables, we would be forced to hard-code all the values in our scripts. By adding two numbers together and printing the result, you can achieve something useful:

```
echo (2 + 4);
```

This snippet of code will only be useful for people who want to know the sum of 2 and 4, however. To get past this, you could write a script for finding the sum of another set of numbers, say 3 and 5. However, this approach to programming is clearly absurd, and this is where variables come into play.

Variables allow us to create templates for operations (adding two numbers, for example), without worrying about what values the variables contain. Values will be given to the variables when the script is run, possibly through user input, through a database query, or from the result of another action earlier in the script. In other words, variables are used whenever the data in your script is liable to change—either during the lifetime of the script, or when it is passed to another script for later use.

A variable consists of a name of your choosing, preceded by a dollar sign ($). Variable names can include letters, numbers, and the underscore character (_), but they cannot include spaces. Names must begin with a letter or an underscore. The following list shows some legal variables:

```
$a;
$a_longish_variable_name;
$2453;
$sleepyZZZZ;
```

By the Way

> Your variable names should be meaningful as well as consistent in style. For example, if your script deals with name and password values, don't create a variable called $n for the name and $p for the password—those are not meaningful names. If you pick up that script weeks later, you might think that $n is the variable for "number" rather than "name" and that $p stands for "page" rather than "password."

A semicolon (;)—also known as the *instruction terminator*—is used to end a PHP statement. The semicolons in the previous fragment of code are not part of the variable names, but are used to end the statement which defines the variables.

As you can see, you have plenty of choices when naming variables. To declare a variable, you need only include it in your script. When you declare a variable, you usually assign a value to it in the same statement, as shown here:

```
$num1 = 8;
$num2 = 23;
```

The preceding lines declare two variables, using the assignment operator (=) to give them values. You will learn about assignment in more detail in the "Operators and Expressions" section later in this chapter. After you assign values to your variables, you can treat them exactly as if they were the values themselves. In other words

```
echo $num1;
```

is equivalent to

```
echo 8;
```

as long as $num1 is assigned a value of 8.

Globals and Superglobals

In addition to the rules for naming variables, there are rules regarding the availability of variables. In general, the assigned value of a variable is present only within the function or script where it resides. For example, if you have scriptA.php which holds a variable called $name with a value of joe, and you want to create scriptB.php that also uses a $name variable, you can assign to it a value of jane without affecting scriptA.php. The value of the $name variable is *local* to each script, and the assigned values are independent of each other.

However, you can also define the $name variable as *global* in a script or function. If this is the case in scriptA.php and scriptB.php, and these scripts are connected, there will only be one value for the now-shared $name variable. Examples of global variable scope will be explained in more detail in Chapter 6, "Working with Functions."

In addition to global variables of your own creation, PHP has several predefined variables called *superglobals*. These variables are always present, and their values available to all of your scripts. Each of the following superglobals is actually an array of other variables:

- ▶ $_GET contains any variables provided to a script through the GET method.
- ▶ $_POST contains any variables provided to a script through the POST method.
- ▶ $_COOKIE contains any variables provided to a script through a cookie.
- ▶ $_FILES contains any variables provided to a script through file uploads.
- ▶ $_SERVER contains information such as headers, file paths, and script locations.
- ▶ $_ENV contains any variables provided to a script as part of the server environment.
- ▶ $_REQUEST contains any variables provided to a script via any user input mechanism.
- ▶ $_SESSION contains any variables that are currently registered in a session.

By the
~~Way~~

> If you're using a version of PHP earlier than 4.1.x and cannot upgrade to a newer
> version, you must adjust the names of the variables when you're following the
> scripts in this book. The old names are $HTTP_GET_VARS (for $_GET),
> $HTTP_POST_VARS (for $_POST), $HTTP_COOKIE_VARS (for $_COOKIE),
> $HTTP_POST_FILES (for $_FILES), $HTTP_ENV_VARS (for $_ENV), and
> $HTTP_SESSION_VARS (for $_SESSION). These old names are simply arrays and not
> superglobals, so if you want the old arrays to be global, you must define them as
> such.

The examples in this book will use superglobals wherever possible. Using superglobals within your scripts is an important in creating secure applications, as it
reduces the likelihood of injected input to your scripts. By coding your scripts to
only accept what you want, in the manner defined by you, you can eliminate
some of the problems created by loosely written scripts.

Data Types

Different types of data take up different amounts of memory and may be treated
differently when they are manipulated in a script. Some programming languages
therefore demand that the programmer declare in advance which type of data a
variable will contain. By contrast, PHP is loosely typed, meaning that it will calculate data types as data is assigned to each variable. This is a mixed blessing.
On the one hand, it means that variables can be used flexibly, holding a string at
one point and an integer at another. On the other hand, this can lead to problems in larger scripts if you expect a variable to hold one data type when in fact
it holds something completely different. For example, suppose you have created
code that is designed to work with an array variable. If the variable in question
instead contains a number value, errors might occur when the code attempts to
perform array-specific operations on the variable.

Table 4.1 shows the six standard data types available in PHP.

TABLE 4.1   Standard Data Types

Type	Example	Description
Integer	5	A whole number
Double	3.234	A floating-point number
String	"hello"	A collection of characters
Boolean	true	One of the special values true or false
Object		An instance of a class
Array		An ordered set of keys and values

PHP also provides two special data types, listed in Table 4.2.

TABLE 4.2 Special Data Types

Type	Description
Resource	Reference to a third-party resource (a database, for example)
NULL	An uninitialized variable

Resource types are often returned by functions that deal with external applications or files. The type NULL is reserved for variables that have not been initialized (that is, variables that have not yet had a value assigned to them).

You can use PHP's built-in function gettype() to test the type of any variable. If you place a variable between the parentheses of the function call, gettype() returns a string representing the relevant type. Listing 4.1 assigns five different data types to a single variable, testing it with gettype() each time. The comments in the code show you where the script is in the process.

> You can read more about calling functions in Chapter 6, "Working with Functions."

By the Way

LISTING 4.1 Testing the Type of a Variable

```
 1: <html>
 2: <head>
 3: <title>Listing 4.1 Testing the type of a variable</title>
 4: </head>
 5: <body>
 6: <?php
 7: $testing; // declare without assigning
 8: echo gettype($testing); // null
 9: echo "<br>";
10: $testing = 5;
11: echo gettype($testing); // integer
12: echo "<br>";
13: $testing = "five";
14: echo gettype($testing); // string
15: echo "<br>";
16: $testing = 5.0;
17: echo gettype($testing); // double
18: echo "<br>";
19: $testing = true;
20: echo gettype($testing); // boolean
21: echo "<br>";
22: ?>
23: </body>
24: </html>
```

Put these lines into a text file called gettype.php, and place this file in your Web server document root. When you access this script through your Web browser, it produces the following:

```
NULL
integer
string
double
boolean
```

When we declare the $testing variable in line 7, we do not assign a value to it, so when we first use the gettype() function to test the variable in line 8, we get the string NULL. After this, we assign values to $testing by using the = sign before passing it to gettype(). An integer, assigned to the $testing variable in line 10, is a whole or real number. In simple terms, you can think of it as a number without a decimal point. A string, assigned to the $testing variable in line 13, is a collection of characters. When you work with strings in your scripts, they should always be surrounded by double or single quotation marks (" or '). A double, assigned to the $testing variable in line 16, is a floating-point number (that is, a number that includes a decimal point). A Boolean, assigned to the $testing variable in line 19, can have one of two special values: true or false.

Changing Type with settype()

PHP provides the function settype() to change the type of a variable. To use settype(), you must place the variable to change and the type to change it to between the parentheses and separate them with a comma. Listing 4.2 converts the value 3.14 (a double) to each of the four types that we are focusing on in this chapter.

LISTING 4.2   Changing the Type of a Variable with settype()

```
 1: <html>
 2: <head>
 3: <title>Listing 4.2 Changing the type of a variable with settype()</title>
 4: </head>
 5: <body>
 6: <?php
 7: $undecided = 3.14;
 8: echo gettype($undecided); // double
 9: echo " is $undecided<br>";  // 3.14
10: settype($undecided, 'string');
11: echo gettype($undecided); // string
12: echo " is $undecided<br>";  // 3.14
13: settype($undecided, 'integer');
14: echo gettype($undecided); // integer
15: echo " is $undecided<br>";  // 3
16: settype($undecided, 'double');
```

LISTING 4.2 Continued

```
17: echo gettype($undecided); // double
18: echo " is $undecided<br>";  // 3
19: settype($undecided, 'boolean');
20: echo gettype($undecided); // boolean
21: echo " is $undecided<br>";  // 1
22: ?>
23: </body>
24: </html>
```

In each case, we use gettype() to confirm that the type change worked and then print the value of the variable $undecided to the browser. When we convert the string "3.14" to an integer in line 13, any information beyond the decimal point is lost forever. That's why $undecided contains 3.0 after we change it back to a double in line 16. Finally, in line 19, we convert $undecided to a Boolean. Any number other than 0 becomes true when converted to a Boolean. When printing a Boolean in PHP, true is represented as 1 and false is represented as an empty string, so in line 21, $undecided is printed as 1.

Put these lines into a text file called settype.php, and place this file in your Web server document root. When you access this script through your Web browser, it produces the following:

```
double is 3.14
string is 3.14
integer is 3
double is 3
boolean is 1
```

Changing Type by Casting

By placing the name of a data type in parentheses in front of a variable, you create a copy of that variable's value converted to the data type specified.

The principal difference between a settype() and a cast is the fact that casting produces a copy, leaving the original variable untouched. Listing 4.3 illustrates this.

LISTING 4.3 Casting a Variable

```
1: <html>
2: <head>
3: <title>Listing 4.3 Casting a variable</title>
4: </head>
5: <body>
6: <?php
7: $undecided = 3.14;
```

LISTING 4.3 Continued

```
 8: $holder = (double) $undecided;
 9: echo gettype($holder) ; // double
10: echo " is $holder<br>";    // 3.14
11: $holder = (string) $undecided;
12: echo gettype($holder);  // string
13: echo " is $holder<br>";    // 3.14
14: $holder = (integer) $undecided;
15: echo gettype($holder);  // integer
16: echo " is $holder<br>";    // 3
17: $holder = (double) $undecided;
18: echo gettype($holder);  // double
19: echo " is $holder<br>";    // 3.14
20: $holder = (boolean) $undecided;
21: echo gettype($holder);  // boolean
22: echo " is $holder<br>";    // 1
23: echo "<hr>";
24: echo "original variable type: ";
25: echo gettype($undecided); // double
26: ?>
27: </body>
28: </html>
```

We never actually change the type of $undecided, which remains a double throughout. This is illustrated on line 25, where we use the gettype() function to output the type of $undecided.

In fact, by casting $undecided, we create a copy that is then converted to the type we specify. This new value is stored in the variable $holder, first in line 8, and also in lines 11, 14, 17, and 20. Because we are working with a copy of $undecided, we never discard any information from it as we did in lines 13 and 19 of Listing 4.2.

Put these lines into a text file called testcast.php, and place this file in your Web server document root. When you access this script through your Web browser, it produces the following:

```
double is 3.14
string is 3.14
integer is 3
double is 3.14
boolean is 1
original variable type: double
```

Now that we can change the contents of a variable from one type to another, using either settype() or a cast, we should consider why this might be useful. It is certainly not a procedure that you will use often because PHP will automatically cast for you when the context requires it. However, an automatic cast is temporary, and you might wish to make a variable persistently hold a particular data type.

Numbers that a user types into an HTML form will be made available to your script as a string. If you try to add two strings containing numbers, PHP will helpfully convert the strings into numbers while the addition is taking place. So

```
"30cm" + "40cm"
```

will give the integer 70. In casting the strings, PHP will ignore the non-numeric characters. However, you might want to clean up the user input yourself. Imagine that the user has been asked to submit a number. We can simulate this by declaring a variable and assigning to it:

```
$test = "30cm";
```

As you can see, the user has added units to the number. We can make sure that the user input is clean by casting it to an integer:

```
$newtest = (integer)$test;
echo "Your imaginary box has a width of $test centimeters";
```

Why Test Type?

Why might it be useful to know the type of a variable? There are often circumstances in programming in which data is passed to you from another source. In Chapter 6, for example, you will learn how to create functions in your scripts. Functions can accept information from calling code in the form of arguments. For the function to work with the data it is given, it is often a good idea to first verify that it has been given values of the correct data type. A function that is expecting a resource, for example, will not work well when passed a string.

Operators and Expressions

With what you have learned so far, you can assign data to variables. You can even investigate and change the data type of a variable. A programming language isn't very useful, though, unless you can manipulate the data you have stored. Operators are symbols that make it possible to use one or more values to produce a new value. A value that is operated on by an operator is referred to as an operand.

An *operator* is a symbol or series of symbols that, when used in conjunction with values, performs an action and usually produces a new value.

An *operand* is a value used in conjunction with an operator. There are usually two operands to one operator.

By the Way

Let's combine two operands with an operator to produce a new value:

```
4 + 5
```

4 and 5 are operands. They are operated on by the addition operator (+) to produce 9. Operators almost always sit between two operands, although you will see a few exceptions later in this chapter.

The combination of operands with an operator to produce a result is called an *expression*. Although most operators form the basis of expressions, an expression need not contain an operator. In fact, an expression in PHP is defined as anything that can be used as a value. This includes integer constants such as 654, variables such as $user, and function calls such as gettype(). (4 + 5), for example, is an expression that consists of two further expressions and an operator. When an expression produces a value, it is often said to *resolve to* that value. That is, when all sub-expressions are taken into account, the expression can be treated as if it were a code for the value itself.

By the Way

An *expression* is any combination of functions, values, and operators that resolve to a value. As a rule of thumb, if you can use it as if it were a value, it is an expression.

Now that we have the principles out of the way, it's time to take a tour of PHP's more common operators.

The Assignment Operator

You have seen the assignment operator each time we have initialized a variable; it consists of the single character =. The assignment operator takes the value of its right-hand operand and assigns it to its left-hand operand:

```
$name = "matt";
```

The variable $name now contains the string "matt". Interestingly, this construct is an expression. It might appear at first glance that the assignment operator simply changes the variable $name without producing a value, but in fact, a statement that uses the assignment operator always resolves to a copy of the value of the right operand. Thus

```
echo $name = "matt";
```

prints the string "matt" to the browser in addition to assigning the value "matt" to the $name variable.

Arithmetic Operators

The arithmetic operators do exactly what you would expect—they perform arithmetic operations. Table 4.3 lists these operators. The addition operator adds the right operand to the left operand. The subtraction operator subtracts the right-hand operand from the left. The division operator divides the left-hand operand by the right. The multiplication operator multiplies the left-hand operand by the right. The modulus operator returns the remainder of the left operand divided by the right.

TABLE 4.3   Arithmetic Operators

Operator	Name	Example	Example Result
+	Addition	10+3	13
-	Subtraction	10-3	7
/	Division	10/3	3.3333333333333
*	Multiplication	10*3	30
%	Modulus	10%3	1

The Concatenation Operator

The concatenation operator is represented by a single period (.). Treating both operands as strings, this operator appends the right-hand operand to the left. So

```
"hello"." world"
```

returns

```
"hello world"
```

Note that the resulting space between the words occurs because there is a leading space in the second operand. The concatenation operator literally smashes together two strings, without adding any of its own padding. So, if you tried to concatenate two strings without leading or trailing spaces, such as

```
"hello"."world"
```

you would get

```
"helloworld"
```

as your result.

Regardless of the data types of the operands, they are treated as strings, and the result is always a string. We will encounter concatenation frequently throughout this book when we need to combine the results of an expression of some kind with a string, as in

```
$centimeters = 212;
echo "the width is ".($centimeters/100)." meters";
```

Combined Assignment Operators

Although there is really only one assignment operator, PHP provides a number of combination operators that transform the left-hand operand and return a result. As a rule, operators use their operands without changing their values, but assignment operators break this rule. A combined assignment operator consists of a standard operator symbol followed by an equal sign. Combination assignment operators save you the trouble of using two operators yourself. For example

```
$x = 4;
$x = $x + 4; // $x now equals 8
```

may instead be written as

```
$x = 4;
$x += 4; // $x now equals 8
```

There is an assignment operator for each of the arithmetic operators and one for the concatenation operator. Table 4.4 lists some of the most common.

TABLE 4.4   Some Combined Assignment Operators

Operator	Example	Equivalent To
+=	$x += 5	$x = $x + 5
-=	$x -= 5	$x = $x - 5
/=	$x /= 5	$x = $x / 5
*=	$x *= 5	$x = $x * 5
%=	$x %= 5	$x = $x % 5
.=	$x .= " test"	$x = $x." test"

Each of the examples in Table 4.4 transforms the value of $x using the value of the right-hand operand.

Automatically Incrementing and Decrementing an Integer Variable

When coding in PHP, you will often find it necessary to increment or decrement an integer variable. You will usually need to do this when you are counting the iterations of a loop. You have already learned two ways of doing this. We can increment the integer contained by $x with the addition operator

```
$x = $x + 1; // $x is incremented
```

or with a combined assignment operator

```
$x += 1; // $x is incremented
```

In both cases, the resultant integer is assigned to $x. Because expressions of this kind are so common, PHP provides some special operators that allow you to add or subtract the integer constant 1 from an integer variable, assigning the result to the variable itself. These are known as the *post-increment* and *post-decrement* operators. The post-increment operator consists of two plus symbols appended to a variable name:

```
$x++; // $x is incremented
```

This expression increments the variable $x by one. Using two minus symbols in the same way decrements the variable:

```
$x--; // $x is decremented
```

If you use the post-increment or post-decrement operators in conjunction with a conditional operator, the operand will only be modified after the test has been completed:

```
$x = 3;
$y = $x++ + 3;
```

In this instance, $y first becomes 6 (3 + 3) and then $x is incremented.

In some circumstances, you might want to increment or decrement a variable in a test expression before the test is carried out. PHP provides the pre-increment and pre-decrement operators for this purpose. These operators behave in exactly the same way as the post-increment and post-decrement operators, but they are written with the plus or minus symbols preceding the variable:

```
++$x; // $x is incremented
--$x; // $x is decremented
```

If these operators are used as part of a test expression, the incrementation occurs before the test is carried out.

```
$x = 3;
++$x < 4; // false
```

In the previous fragment, $x is incremented before it is tested against 4. The test expression returns false because 4 is not smaller than 4.

Comparison Operators

Comparison operators perform tests on their operands. They return the Boolean value true if the test is successful, or false otherwise. This type of expression is useful in control structures, such as if and while statements. We will cover these in Chapter 5, "Flow Control Functions in PHP."

To test whether the value contained in $x is smaller than 5, for example, you can use the less-than operator:

```
$x < 5
```

If $x contains the value 3, this expression has the value true. If $x contains 7, the expression resolves to false.

Table 4.5 lists the comparison operators.

TABLE 4.5   Comparison Operators

Operator	Name	Returns True If...	Example ($x Is 4)	Result
==	Equivalence	Left is equivalent to right	$x == 5	false
!=	Non-equivalence	Left is not equivalent to right	$x != 5	true
===	Identical	Left is equivalent to right and they are the same type	$x === 4	true
	Non-equivalence	Left is equivalent to right but they are not the same type	$x === "4"	false
>	Greater than	Left is greater than right	$x > 4	false
>=	Greater than or equal to	Left is greater than or equal to right	$x >= 4	true
<	Less than	Left is less than right	$x < 4	false
<=	Less than or equal to	Left is less than or equal to right	$x <= 4	true

These operators are most commonly used with integers or doubles, although the equivalence operator is also used to compare strings. Be very sure you understand the difference between the == and = operators. The == operator tests equivalence, whereas the = operator assigns value.

Creating More Complex Test Expressions with the Logical Operators

The logical operators test combinations of Booleans. For example, the or operator, which is indicated by two pipe characters (¦¦) or simply the word or, returns true if either the left or the right operand is true:

```
true ¦¦ false
```

This expression returns true.

The and operator, which is indicated by two ampersand characters (&&) or simply the word and, returns true only if both the left and right operands are true:

```
true && false
```

This expression returns false. It's unlikely that you will use a logical operator to test Boolean constants, as it makes more sense to test two or more expressions that resolve to a Boolean. For example

```
( $x > 2 ) && ( $x < 15 )
```

returns true if $x contains a value that is greater than 2 and smaller than 15. We include the parentheses to make the code easier to read. Table 4.6 lists the logical operators.

TABLE 4.6   Logical Operators

Operator	Name	Returns True If...	Example	Result
¦¦	Or	Left or right is true	true ¦¦ false	true
or	Or	Left or right is true	true or false	true
xor	Xor	Left or right is true but not both	true xor true	false
&&	And	Left and right are true	true && false	false
and	And	Left and right are true	true and false	false
!	Not	The single operand is not true	! true	false

Why are there two versions of both the or and the and operators? The answer lies in operator precedence, which we will look at next.

Operator Precedence

When you use an operator, the PHP engine usually reads your expression from left to right. For complex expressions that use more than one operator, though, the waters can become a little murky. First, consider a simple case:

```
4 + 5
```

There's no room for confusion here. PHP simply adds 4 to 5. But what about the following fragment?

```
4 + 5 * 2
```

This presents a problem. Does it mean the sum of 4 and 5, multiplied by 2, giving the result 18? Or does it mean 4 plus the result of 5 multiplied by 2, resolving to 14? If you were to simply read from left to right, the former would be true. However, PHP attaches different precedence to operators. Because the multiplication operator has higher precedence than the addition operator does, the second solution to the problem is the correct one.

You can use parentheses to force PHP to execute the addition expression before the multiplication expression:

```
(4 + 5) * 2
```

Whatever the precedence of the operators in a complex expression, it is a good idea to use parentheses to make your code clearer and to save you from obscure bugs. The following is a list of the operators covered in this chapter in precedence order (those with highest precedence are listed first):

```
++, --, (cast)

/, *, %

+, -

<, <=, =>, >

==, ===, !=

&&

||

=, +=, -=, /=, *=, %=, .=

and

xor

or
```

As you can see, or has a lower precedence than ¦¦ and and has a lower precedence than &&, so you can use the lower-precedence logical operators to change the way a complex test expression is read. This is not necessarily a good idea. The following two expressions are equivalent, but the second is much easier to read:

```
$x and $y ¦¦ $z
```

```
$x && ($y ¦¦ $z)
```

Taking it one step further, the following example is easier still:

```
$x and ($y or $z)
```

The three examples are all equivalent.

The order of precedence is the only reason that both && and and are present in PHP. The same is true of ¦¦ and or. In most, if not all circumstances, however, use of parentheses will make for clearer code and fewer bugs than code that takes advantage of the difference in precedence of these operators. Throughout this book, we will tend to use the more common ¦¦ and && operators.

Constants

Variables offer a flexible way of storing data. You can change their values and the type of data they store at any time. However, if you want to work with a value that you want to remain unchanged throughout your script's execution, you can define and use a constant. You must use PHP's built-in define() function to create a constant, which subsequently cannot be changed. To use the define() function, you must place the name of the constant and the value you want to give it within parentheses, separated by a comma:

```
define("CONSTANT_NAME", 42);
```

The value you want to set can be a number, a string, or a Boolean. By convention, the name of the constant should be in capital letters. Constants are accessed with the constant name only; no dollar symbol is required. Listing 4.4 shows you how to define and access a constant.

LISTING 4.4   Defining and Accessing a Constant

```
1: <html>
2: <head>
3: <title>Listing 4.4 Defining and accessing a constant</title>
4: </head>
5: <body>
```

LISTING 4.4 Continued

```
 6: <?php
 7: define("USER", "Gerald");
 8: echo "Welcome ".USER;
 9: ?>
10: </body>
11: </html>
```

> When using constants, keep in mind they can be used anywhere in your scripts, including external functions which are included.

Notice that in line 8 we used the concatenation operator to append the value held by our constant to the string "Welcome ". This is because the PHP engine has no way of distinguishing between a constant and a string within quotation marks.

Put these lines into a text file called constant.php, and place this file in your Web server document root. When you access this script through your Web browser, it produces the following:

```
Welcome Gerald
```

The define() function can also accept a third, Boolean argument that determines whether or not the constant name should be case-independent. By default, constants are case-dependent. However, by passing true to the define() function, we can change this behavior, so if we were to set up our USER constant as

```
define("USER", "Gerald", true);
```

we could access its value without worrying about case:

```
echo User;
echo usEr;
echo USER;
```

These expressions are all equivalent, and all would result in an output of Gerald. This feature can make scripts a little friendlier for other programmers who work with our code, as they will not need to consider case when accessing a constant that we have defined. On the other hand, given the fact that other constants *are* case-sensitive, this might make for more rather than less confusion as programmers forget which constants to treat in which way. Unless you have a compelling reason to do otherwise, the safest course is to keep your constants case-sensitive and define them using uppercase characters, which is an easy-to-remember convention.

Predefined Constants

PHP automatically provides some built-in constants for you. For example, the constant __FILE__ returns the name of the file that the PHP engine is currently reading. The constant __LINE__ returns the line number of the file. These constants are useful for generating error messages. You can also find out which version of PHP is interpreting the script with the PHP_VERSION constant. This can be useful if you need version information included in script output when sending a bug report.

Summary

In this chapter, you covered some of the basic features of the PHP language. You learned about variables and how to assign values to them using the assignment operator, as well as received an introduction to variable scope and built-in super-globals. You got an introduction to operators and learned how to combine some of the most common of these into expressions. Finally, you learned how to define and access constants.

Now that you have mastered some of the fundamentals of PHP, the next chapter will really put you in the driver's seat. You will learn how to make scripts that can make decisions and repeat tasks, with help from variables, expressions, and operators.

Q&A

Q. *Why is it useful to know the type of data a variable holds?*

A. Often the data type of a variable constrains what you can do with it. You may want to make sure that a variable contains an integer or a double before using it in a mathematical calculation, for example.

Q. *Should I obey any conventions when naming variables?*

A. Your goal should always be to make your code easy to read and understand. A variable such as $ab123245 tells you nothing about its role in your script and invites typos. Keep your variable names short and descriptive.

A variable named $f is unlikely to mean much to you when you return to your code after a month or so. A variable named $filename, on the other hand, should make more sense.

Q. *Should I learn the operator precedence table?*

A. There is no reason that you shouldn't, but I would save the effort for more useful tasks. By using parentheses in your expressions, you can make your code easy to read while defining your own order of precedence.

Workshop

The workshop is designed to help you anticipate possible questions, review what you've learned, and begin putting your knowledge into practice.

Quiz

1. Which of the following variable names is not valid?

```
$a_value_submitted_by_a_user
$666666xyz
$xyz666666
$_____counter_____
$the first
$file-name
```

2. What will the following code fragment output?

```
$num = 33;
(boolean) $num;
echo $num;
```

3. What will the following statement output?

```
echo gettype("4");
```

4. What will be the output from the following code fragment?

```
$test_val = 5.5466;
settype($test_val, "integer");
echo $test_val;
```

5. Which of the following statements does not contain an expression?

```
4;
gettype(44);
5/12;
```

6. Which of the statements in question 5 contains an operator?

7. What value will the following expression return?

```
5 < 2
```

What data type will the returned value be?

Answers

1. The variable name $666666xyz is not valid because it does not begin with a letter or an underscore character. The variable name $the first is not valid because it contains a space. $file-name is also invalid because it contains a non-alphanumeric character.

2. The fragment will print the integer 33. The cast to Boolean produces a converted copy of the value stored in $num. It does not alter the value actually stored there.

3. The statement will output the string "string".

4. The code will output the value 5. When a double is converted to an integer, any information beyond the decimal point is lost.

5. They are all expressions because they all resolve to values.

6. The statement 5/12; contains a division operator.

7. The expression will resolve to false, which is a Boolean value.

Activities

1. Create a script that contains at least five different variables. Populate them with values of different data types and use the `gettype()` function to print each type to the browser.

2. Assign values to two variables. Use comparison operators to test whether the first value is

   ▶ The same as the second

   ▶ Less than the second

   ▶ Greater than the second

   ▶ Less than or equal to the second

   Print the result of each test to the browser.

   Change the values assigned to your test variables and run the script again.

CHAPTER 5

Flow Control Functions in PHP

The scripts created in the last chapter flow only in a single direction. The same statements are executed in the same order every time a script is run. This does not allow for much flexibility.

You will now look at some structures that enable your scripts to adapt to circumstances. In this chapter, you will learn

- ▶ How to use the if statement to execute code if a test expression evaluates to true
- ▶ How to execute alternative blocks of code when the test expression of an if statement evaluates to false
- ▶ How to use the switch statement to execute code based on the value returned by a test expression
- ▶ How to repeat execution of code using a while statement
- ▶ How to use for statements to make neater loops
- ▶ How to break out of loops
- ▶ How to nest one loop within another
- ▶ How to use PHP start and end tags within control structures

Switching Flow

Most scripts will evaluate conditions and change their behavior accordingly. These decisions are what make your PHP pages dynamic; that is, able to change their output according to circumstances. Like most programming languages, PHP allows you to do this with an if statement.

The if **Statement**

An if statement is a way of controlling the execution of a statement that follows it (that is, a single statement or a block of code inside braces). The if statement evaluates an expression between parentheses. If this expression results in a true value, the statement is executed. Otherwise, the statement is skipped entirely. This enables scripts to make decisions based on any number of factors:

```
if (expression) {
    // code to execute if the expression evaluates to true
}
```

Listing 5.1 executes a block of code only if a variable contains the string "happy".

LISTING 5.1   An if Statement

```
 1: <html>
 2: <head>
 3: <title>Listing 5.1</title>
 4: </head>
 5: <body>
 6: <?php
 7: $mood = "happy";
 8: if ($mood == "happy") {
 9:     echo "Hooray, I'm in a good mood";
10: }
11: ?>
12: </body>
13: </html>
```

You use the comparison operator == to compare the variable $mood with the string "happy". If they match, the expression evaluates to true, and the code block below the if statement is executed.

Put these lines into a text file called testif.php, and place this file in your Web server document root. When you access this script through your Web browser, it produces the following:

```
Hooray, I'm in a good mood
```

If you change the value of $mood to "sad" or any other string besides "happy", then run the script again, the expression in the if statement will evaluate to false, and the code block will be skipped. The script remains silent, which leads us to the else clause.

Using the `else` **Clause with the** `if` **Statement**

When working with the `if` statement, you will often want to define an alternative block of code that should be executed if the expression you are testing evaluates to `false`. You can do this by adding `else` to the `if` statement followed by a further block of code:

```
if (expression) {
    // code to execute if the expression evaluates to true
} else {
    // code to execute in all other cases
}
```

Listing 5.2 amends the example in Listing 5.1 so that a default block of code is executed if $mood is not equivalent to "happy".

LISTING 5.2   An `if` Statement That Uses `else`

```
 1: <html>
 2: <head>
 3: <title>Listing 5.2</title>
 4: </head>
 5: <body>
 6: <?php
 7: $mood = "sad";
 8: if ($mood == "happy") {
 9:     echo "Hooray, I'm in a good mood";
10: } else {
11:     echo "Not happy but $mood";
12: }
13: ?>
14: </body>
15: </html>
```

Put these lines into a text file called `testifelse.php`, and place this file in your Web server document root. When you access this script through your Web browser, it produces the following:

```
Not happy but sad
```

Notice in line 7 that $mood contains the string "sad", which obviously is not equal to "happy", so the expression in the `if` statement in line 8 evaluates to `false`. This results in the first block of code (line 9) being skipped. However, the block of code after `else` is executed, and the message Not happy but sad is printed to the browser. The string "sad" is the value assigned to the variable $mood.

Using the else clause with the if statement allows scripts to make sophisticated decisions, but your options are currently limited to an either-or branch. PHP allows you to evaluate multiple expressions one after another, as you'll learn next.

Using the else if Clause with the if Statement

You can use an if...else if...else construct to test multiple expressions before offering a default block of code:

```
if (expression) {
    // code to execute if the expression evaluates to true
} else if (another expression) {
    // code to execute if the previous expression failed
    // and this one evaluates to true
} else {
    // code to execute in all other cases
}
```

If the first expression does not evaluate to true, the first block of code is ignored. The else if clause then causes another expression to be evaluated. Once again, if this expression evaluates to true, the second block of code is executed. Otherwise, the block of code associated with the else clause is executed. You can include as many else if clauses as you want, and if you don't need a default action, you can omit the else clause.

By the Way

The else if clause can also be written as a single word (else if). The syntax you employ is a matter of taste.

Listing 5.3 adds an else if clause to the previous example.

LISTING 5.3   An if Statement That Uses else and else if

```
 1: <html>
 2: <head>
 3: <title>Listing 5.3</title>
 4: </head>
 5: <body>
 6: <?php
 7: $mood = "sad";
 8: if ($mood == "happy") {
 9:     echo "Hooray, I'm in a good mood";
10: } else if ($mood == "sad") {
11:     echo "Awww. Don't be down!";
12: } else {
13:     echo "Neither happy nor sad but $mood";
14: }
15: ?>
16: </body>
17: </html>
```

Once again, $mood holds a string, "sad", in line 7. This is not equal to "happy", so the first block in line 9 is ignored. The else if clause in line 10 tests for equivalence between the contents of $mood and the value "sad", which evaluates to true. This block of code is therefore executed. In lines 12, 13, and 14, we provide the default behavior which is invoked if none of the test conditions have been fulfilled. In this case, we simply print a message including the actual value of the $mood variable.

Put these lines into a text file called testifelseif.php, and place this file in your Web server document root. When you access this script through your Web browser, it produces the following:

```
Awww. Don't be down!
```

Change the value of $mood to "unknown" and run the script, and it will produce the following:

```
Neither happy nor sad but unknown
```

The switch **Statement**

The switch statement is an alternative way of changing flow according to the evaluation of an expression. Using the if statement in conjunction with else if, you can evaluate multiple expressions. However, a switch statement evaluates only one expression, executing different code according to the result of that expression, for as long as the expression evaluates to a simple type (a number, a string, or a Boolean). The result of an expression evaluated as part of an if statement is read as either true or false, whereas the expression of a switch statement yields a result that is subsequently tested against any number of values:

```
switch (expression) {
    case result1:
        // execute this if expression results in result1
        break;
    case result2:
        // execute this if expression results in result2
        break;
    default:
        // execute this if no break statement
        // has been encountered hitherto
}
```

The expression used in a switch statement is often just a variable. Within the switch statement's block of code, you find a number of case statements. Each of these cases tests a value against the result of the switch expression. If the case is equivalent to the expression result, the code after the case statement is executed.

The break statement ends the execution of the switch statement altogether. If the break statement is left out, the next case statement is evaluated. If the optional default statement is reached, its code is executed.

> It is important to include a break statement at the end of any code that will be executed as part of a case statement. Without a break statement, the program flow will continue to the next case statement and ultimately to the default statement. In most cases, this will result in unexpected behavior, likely incorrect!

Listing 5.4 re-creates the functionality of the if statement example, using the switch statement.

LISTING 5.4   A switch **Statement**

```
 1: <html>
 2: <head>
 3: <title>Listing 5.4</title>
 4: </head>
 5: <body>
 6: <?php
 7: $mood = "sad";
 8: switch ($mood) {
 9:     case "happy":
10:         echo "Hooray, I'm in a good mood";
11:         break;
12:     case "sad":
13:         echo "Awww. Don't be down!";
14:         break;
15:     default:
16:         print "Neither happy nor sad but $mood";
17:         break;
18: }
19: ?>
20: </body>
21: </html>
```

Once again, in line 7, the $mood variable is initialized to "sad". The switch statement in line 8 uses this variable as its expression. The first case statement in line 9 tests for equivalence between "happy" and the value of $mood. There is no match, so script execution moves on to the second case statement in line 12. The string "sad" is equivalent to the value of $mood, so this block of code is executed. The break statement in line 14 ends the process. Lines 15 through 17 provide the default action should neither case evaluate as true.

Put these lines into a text file called testswitch.php, and place this file in your Web server document root. When you access this script through your Web browser, it produces the following:

```
Awww. Don't be down!
```

Change the value of $mood to "happy" and run the script, and it will produce the following:

```
Hooray, I'm in a good mood
```

To emphasize the caution regarding the importance of the break statement, try running this script without the second break statement. Your output will be

```
Awww. Don't be down!Neither happy nor sad but sad
```

This is definitely not the desired output, so be sure to include break statements where appropriate!

Using the ? Operator

The ? or *ternary* operator is similar to the if statement, but returns a value derived from one of two expressions separated by a colon. This construct will provide you with three parts of the whole, hence the name *ternary*. The expression used to generate the returned value depends on the result of a test expression:

```
(expression) ? returned_if_expression_is_true : returned_if_expression_is_false;
```

If the test expression evaluates to true, the result of the second expression is returned; otherwise, the value of the third expression is returned. Listing 5.5 uses the ternary operator to set the value of a variable according to the value of $mood.

LISTING 5.5   Using the ? Operator

```
 1: <html>
 2: <head>
 3: <title>Listing 5.5</title>
 4: </head>
 5: <body>
 6: <?php
 7: $mood = "sad";
 8: $text = ($mood == "happy") ? "I'm in a good mood" : "Not happy but $mood";
 9: echo "$text";
10: ?>
11: </body>
12: </html>
```

In line 7, $mood is set to "sad". In line 8, $mood is tested for equivalence to the string "happy". Because this test returns false, the result of the third of the three expressions is returned.

Put these lines into a text file called `testtern.php`, and place this file in your Web server document root. When you access this script through your Web browser, it produces the following:

```
Not happy but sad
```

The ternary operator can be difficult to read, but is useful if you are dealing with only two alternatives and want to write compact code.

Loops

So far we've looked at decisions that a script can make about what code to execute. Scripts can also decide how many times to execute a block of code. Loop statements are designed to enable you to achieve repetitive tasks. A loop will continue to operate until a condition is achieved, or you explicitly choose to exit the loop.

The while Statement

The while statement looks similar in structure to a basic if statement:

```
while (expression) {
      // do something
}
```

However, unlike an if statement, a while statement will execute for as long as the expression evaluates to true, over and over again if need be. Each execution of a code block within a loop is called an *iteration*. Within the block, you usually change something that affects the while statement's expression; otherwise, your loop continues indefinitely. Listing 5.6 creates a while loop that calculates and prints multiples of 2 up to 24.

LISTING 5.6   A while Statement

```
 1: <html>
 2: <head>
 3: <title>Listing 5.6</title>
 4: </head>
 5: <body>
 6: <?php
 7: $counter = 1;
 8: while ($counter <= 12) {
 9:     echo "$counter times 2 is ".($counter * 2)."<br>";
10:     $counter++;
11: }
12: ?>
13: </body>
14: </html>
```

In this example, we initialize a variable $counter in line 7. The while statement in line 8 tests the $counter variable. As long as the integer that $counter contains is less than or equal to 12, the loop continues to run. Within the while statement's code block, the value contained by $counter is multiplied by two and the result is printed to the browser. Next, the value of $counter is incremented in line 10. This last stage is extremely important. If you were to forget to change the value assigned to the $counter variable, the while expression would never resolve to false, and the loop would never end.

Put these lines into a text file called testwhile.php, and place this file in your Web server document root. When you access this script through your Web browser, it produces the following:

```
1 times 2 is 2
2 times 2 is 4
3 times 2 is 6
4 times 2 is 8
5 times 2 is 10
6 times 2 is 12
7 times 2 is 14
8 times 2 is 16
9 times 2 is 18
10 times 2 is 20
11 times 2 is 22
12 times 2 is 24
```

The do...while Statement

A do...while statement looks a little like a while statement turned on its head. The essential difference between the two is that the code block is executed before the truth test and not after it:

```
do  {
    // code to be executed
} while (expression);
```

> The test expression of a do...while statement should always end with a semi-colon.
>
> **By the Way**

This type of statement is useful when you want the code block to be executed at least once, even if the while expression evaluates to false. Listing 5.7 creates a do...while statement. The code block is executed a minimum of one time.

LISTING 5.7   The do...while **Statement**

```
 1: <html>
 2: <head>
 3: <title>Listing 5.7</title>
 4: </head>
 5: <body>
 6: <?php
 7: $num = 1;
 8: do {
 9:     echo "The number is: $num<br>\n";
10:     $num++;
11: } while (($num > 200) && ($num < 400));
12: ?>
13: </body>
14: </html>
```

The do...while statement tests whether the variable $num contains a value that is greater than 200 and less than 400. In line 7, we have initialized $num to 1, so this expression returns false. Nonetheless, the code block is executed before the expression is evaluated, so the statement will print a single line to the browser.

Put these lines into a text file called testdowhile.php, and place this file in your Web server document root. When you access this script through your Web browser, it produces the following:

```
The number is: 1
```

If you change the value of $num in line 7 to something like 300 and then run the script, the loop will display

```
The number is: 300
```

and will continue to print similar lines, with increasing numbers, through

```
The number is: 399
```

The for **Statement**

Anything you want to do with a for statement, you can also do with a while statement, but a for statement is often a neater and safer way of achieving the same effect. Earlier, Listing 5.6 initialized a variable outside the while statement. The while statement then tested the variable in its expression. The variable was incremented within the code block. The for statement allows you to achieve this on a single line. This allows for more compact code and makes it less likely that you will forget to increment a counter variable, thereby creating an infinite loop:

```
for (initialization expression; test expression; modification expression) {
    // code to be executed
}
```

Infinite loops are, as the name suggests, loops that run without bounds. If your loop is running infinitely, your script is running for an infinite amount of time. This is very stressful on your Web server, and renders the Web page in question unusable.

By the Way

The expressions within the parentheses of the for statement are separated by semicolons. Usually, the first expression initializes a counter variable, the second expression is the test condition for the loop, and the third expression increments the counter. Listing 5.8 shows a for statement that re-creates the example in Listing 5.6, which multiplies 12 numbers by 2.

LISTING 5.8   Using the for Statement

```
 1: <html>
 2: <head>
 3: <title>Listing 5.8</title>
 4: </head>
 5: <body>
 6: <?php
 7: for ($counter=1; $counter<=12; $counter++) {
 8:     echo "$counter times 2 is ".($counter ^ 2)."<br>";
 9: }
10: ?>
11: </body>
12: </html>
```

Put these lines into a text file called testfor.php, and place this file in your Web server document root. When you access this script through your Web browser, it produces the following:

```
1 times 2 is 2
2 times 2 is 4
3 times 2 is 6
4 times 2 is 8
5 times 2 is 10
6 times 2 is 12
7 times 2 is 14
8 times 2 is 16
9 times 2 is 18
10 times 2 is 20
11 times 2 is 22
12 times 2 is 24
```

The results of Listings 5.6 and 5.8 are exactly the same, but the for statement makes the code in Listing 5.8 more compact. Because the $counter variable is initialized and incremented at the beginning of the statement, the logic of the loop is clear at a glance. In line 7, the first expression initializes the $counter variable and sets it to 1. The test expression verifies that $counter contains a value that is less than or equal to 12. The final expression increments the $counter variable.

When program flow reaches the for loop, the $counter variable is initialized, and the test expression is evaluated. If the expression evaluates to true, the code block is executed. The $counter variable is then incremented and the test expression is evaluated again. This process continues until the test expression evaluates to false.

Breaking Out of Loops with the break Statement

Both while and for statements incorporate a built-in test expression with which you can end a loop. However, the break statement enables you to break out of a loop based on the results of additional tests. This can provide a safeguard against error. Listing 5.9 creates a simple for statement that divides a large number by a variable that is incremented, printing the result to the screen.

LISTING 5.9   A for Loop That Divides 4000 by 10 Incremental Numbers

```
 1: <html>
 2: <head>
 3: <title>Listing 5.9</title>
 4: </head>
 5: <body>
 6: <?php
 7: for ($counter=1; $counter <= 10; $counter++) {
 8:     $temp = 4000/$counter;
 9:     echo "4000 divided by $counter is... $temp<br>";
10: }
11: ?>
12: </body>
13: </html>
```

In line 7, this example initializes the variable $counter to 1. The for statement's test expression verifies that $counter is less than or equal to 10. Within the code block, 4000 is divided by $counter, printing the result to the browser.

Put these lines into a text file called testfor2.php, and place this file in your Web server document root. When you access this script through your Web browser, it produces the following:

```
4000 divided by 1 is... 4000
4000 divided by 2 is... 2000
4000 divided by 3 is... 1333.33333333
```

```
4000 divided by 4 is... 1000
4000 divided by 5 is... 800
4000 divided by 6 is... 666.666666667
4000 divided by 7 is... 571.428571429
4000 divided by 8 is... 500
4000 divided by 9 is... 444.444444444
4000 divided by 10 is... 400
```

This seems straightforward enough. But what if the value you place in $counter comes from user input? The value could be a negative number, or even a string. Let's take the first instance. Changing the initial value of $counter from 1 to -4 causes 4000 to be divided by 0 when the code block is executed for the fifth time. It is generally not a good idea for your code to divide by zero, as it results in an answer of "undefined." Listing 5.10 guards against this by breaking out of the loop if the $counter variable equals zero.

LISTING 5.10   Using the break Statement

```
 1: <html>
 2: <head>
 3: <title>Listing 5.10</title>
 4: </head>
 5: <body>
 6: <?php
 7: $counter = -4;
 8: for (; $counter <= 10; $counter++) {
 9:     if ($counter == 0) {
10:         break;
11:     } else {
12:         $temp = 4000/$counter;
13:         echo "4000 divided by $counter is... $temp<br>";
14:     }
15: }
16 ?>
17: </body>
18: </html>
```

> Dividing a number by zero does not cause a fatal error in PHP. Instead, PHP generates a warning and execution continues.

By the Way

We use an if statement, shown in line 9, to test the value of $counter. If it is equal to zero, the break statement immediately halts execution of the code block, and program flow continues after the for statement (line 16).

Put these lines into a text file called testfor3.php, and place this file in your Web server document root. When you access this script through your Web browser, it produces the following:

```
4000 divided by -4 is... -1000
4000 divided by -3 is... -1333.33333333
4000 divided by -2 is... -2000
4000 divided by -1 is... -4000
```

Notice that we initialize the $counter variable in line 7, outside the for statement's parentheses, to simulate a situation in which the value of $counter is set from outside the script.

> You can omit any of the expressions from a for statement, but you must remember to retain the semicolons.

Skipping an Iteration with the continue Statement

The continue statement ends execution of the current iteration but doesn't cause the loop as a whole to end. Instead, the next iteration begins immediately. Using the break statement as we did in Listing 5.10 is a little drastic. With the continue statement in Listing 5.11, you can avoid a divide by zero error without ending the loop completely.

LISTING 5.11   Using the continue **Statement**

```
 1: <html>
 2: <head>
 3: <title>Listing 5.11</title>
 4: </head>
 5: <body>
 6: <?php
 7: $counter = -4;
 8: for (; $counter <= 10; $counter++) {
 9:     if ($counter == 0) {
10:         continue;
11:     }
12:     $temp = 4000/$counter;
13:     echo "4000 divided by $counter is... $temp<br>";
14: }
15: ?>
16: </body>
17: </html>
```

In line 10, we have swapped the break statement for a continue statement. If the $counter variable is equivalent to zero, the iteration is skipped and the next one starts immediately.

Put these lines into a text file called testcontinue.php, and place this file in your Web server document root. When you access this script through your Web browser, it produces the following:

```
4000 divided by -4 is... -1000
4000 divided by -3 is... -1333.33333333
4000 divided by -2 is... -2000
4000 divided by -1 is... -4000
4000 divided by 1 is... 4000
4000 divided by 2 is... 2000
4000 divided by 3 is... 1333.33333333
4000 divided by 4 is... 1000
4000 divided by 5 is... 800
4000 divided by 6 is... 666.666666667
4000 divided by 7 is... 571.428571429
4000 divided by 8 is... 500
4000 divided by 9 is... 444.444444444
```

> The break and continue statements can make code more difficult to read. Because they often add layers of complexity to the logic of the loop statements that contain them, you should use them with care.

Nesting Loops

Loop statements can contain other loop statements. The combination of such statements is particularly useful when working with dynamically created HTML tables. Listing 5.12 uses two for statements to print a multiplication table to the browser.

LISTING 5.12   Nesting Two for Loops

```
 1: <html>
 2: <head>
 3: <title>Listing 5.12</title>
 4: </head>
 5: <body>
 6: <?php
 7: echo "<table border=\"1\"> \n";
 8: for ($y=1; $y<=12; $y++) {
 9:     echo "<tr> \n";
10:     for ($x=1; $x<=12; $x++) {
11:         echo "<td>";
12:         echo ($x * $y);
13:         echo "</td> \n";
14:     }
15:     echo "</tr> \n";
16: }
17: echo "</table>";
18: ?>
19: </body>
20: </html>
```

Before we examine the for loops, let's take a closer look at line 7 in Listing 5.12:

```
echo "<table border=\"1\"> \n";
```

Notice that we have used the backslash character (\) before each of the quotation marks within the string. This is necessary in order to tell the PHP engine that we wish to use the quotation mark character, rather than interpret it as the beginning or end of a string. If we did not do this, the statement would not make sense to the engine, which would read it as a string followed by a number followed by another string. This would generate an error. In this listing, we also use \n to represent a newline character.

The outer for statement (line 8) initializes a variable called $y, setting its starting value to 1. It defines an expression that verifies that $y is less than or equal to 12 and defines the increment for $y. For each iteration, the code block prints a tr (table row) HTML element (line 9) and defines another for statement (line 10). This inner loop initializes a variable called $x and defines expressions along the same lines as for the outer loop. For each iteration, the inner loop prints a td (table cell) element to the browser (line 11), as well as the result of $x multiplied by $y (line 12). In line 13, we close the table cell. After the inner loop has finished, we fall back through to the outer loop, where we close the table row on line 15, ready for the process to begin again. When the outer loop has finished, the result is a neatly formatted multiplication table. We wrap things up by closing the table on line 17.

Put these lines into a text file called testnestfor.php, and place this file in your Web server document root. When you access this script through your Web browser, it should look like Figure 5.1.

FIGURE 5.1
Output of Listing
5.12.

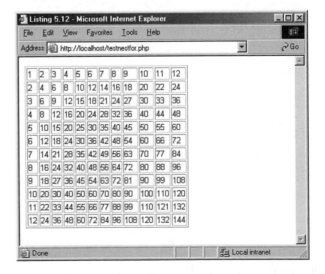

Code Blocks and Browser Output

In Chapter 3, "Installing and Configuring PHP," you learned that you can slip in and out of HTML mode at will, using the PHP start and end tags. In this chapter, you have discovered that you can present distinct output to the user according to a decision-making process that we can control with `if` and `switch` statements. In this section, we will combine these two techniques.

Imagine a script that outputs a table of values only when a variable is set to the Boolean value `true`. Listing 5.13 shows a simplified HTML table constructed with the code block of an `if` statement.

LISTING 5.13   A Code Block Containing Multiple echo Statements

```
 1: <html>
 2: <head>
 3: <title>Listing 5.13</title>
 4: </head>
 5: <body>
 6: <?php
 7: $display_prices = true;
 8: if ($display_prices) {
 9:     echo "<table border=\"1\">";
10:     echo "<tr><td colspan=\"3\">";
11:     echo "today's prices in dollars";
12:     echo "</td></tr>";
13:     echo "<tr><td>14</td><td>32</td><td>71</td></tr>";
14:     echo "</table>";
15: }
16: ?>
17: </body>
18: </html>
```

If `$display_prices` is set to `true` in line 7, the table is printed. For the sake of readability, we split the output into multiple `print()` statements, and once again escape any quotation marks.

Put these lines into a text file called `testmultiprint.php`, and place this file in your Web server document root. When you access this script through your Web browser, it should look like Figure 5.2.

There's nothing wrong with the way this is coded, but we can save ourselves some typing by simply slipping back into HTML mode within the code block. In Listing 5.14 we do just that.

FIGURE 5.2
Output of Listing
5.13.

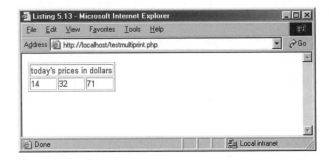

LISTING 5.14   Returning to HTML Mode Within a Code Block

```
 1: <html>
 2: <head>
 3: <title>Listing 5.14</title>
 4: </head>
 5: <body>
 6: <?php
 7: $display_prices = true;
 8: if ($display_prices) {
 9: ?>
10:     <table border="1">
11:     <tr><td colspan="3">today's prices in dollars</td></tr>
12:     <tr><td>14</td><td>32</ld><td>71</td>
13:     </table>
14: <?php
15: }
16: ?>
17: </body>
18: </html>
```

The important thing to note here is that the shift to HTML mode on line 9 occurs only if the condition of the if statement is fulfilled. This can save us the bother of escaping quotation marks and wrapping our output in print() statements. It might, however, affect the readability of the code in the long run, especially if the script grows larger.

Summary

In this chapter, you learned about control structures and the ways in which they can help to make your scripts flexible and dynamic. Most of these structures will reappear regularly throughout the rest of the book.

You learned how to define an if statement and how to provide for alternative actions with the else if and else clauses. You learned how to use the switch statement to change flow according to multiple equivalence tests on the result of an expression. You learned about loops—in particular, the `while` and `for` statements—and you learned how to use `break` and `continue` to prematurely end the execution of a loop or to skip an iteration. You learned how to nest one loop within another and saw a typical use for this structure. Finally, you looked at a technique for using PHP start and end tags in conjunction with conditional code blocks.

You should now know enough of the basics to write scripts of your own that make decisions and perform repetitive tasks. In the next chapter, we will be looking at a way of adding even more power to your applications. You will learn how functions enable you to organize your code, preventing duplication and improving reusability.

Q&A

Q. *Must a control structure's test expression result in a Boolean value?*

A. Ultimately, yes, but in the context of a test expression, zero, an undefined variable, or an empty string will be converted to `false`. All other values will evaluate to `true`.

Q. *Must I always surround a code block in a control statement with brackets?*

A. If the code you want executed as part of a control structure consists of only a single line, you can omit the brackets. However, the habit of always using opening and closing brackets, regardless of structure length, is a good one.

Workshop

The workshop is designed to help you anticipate possible questions, review what you've learned, and begin putting your knowledge into practice.

Quiz

1. How would you use an `if` statement to print the string `"Youth message"` to the browser if an integer variable, $age, is between 18 and 35? If $age contains any other value, the string `"Generic message"` should be printed to the browser.

2. How would you extend your code in question 1 to print the string `"Child message"` if the $age variable is between 1 and 17?

3. How would you create a `while` statement that increments through and prints every odd number between 1 and 49?

4. How would you convert the `while` statement you created in question 3 into a `for` statement?

Answers

1.

```
$age = 22;

if (($age >= 18) && ($age <= 35)) {
    echo "Youth message<br>\n";
} else {
    echo "Generic message<br>\n";
}
```

2.

```
$age = 12;

if (($age >= 18) && ($age <= 35)) {
    echo "Youth message<br>\n";
} elseif (($age >= 1) && ($age <= 17)) {
    echo "Child message<br>\n";
} else {
    echo "Generic message<br>\n";
}
```

3.

```
$num = 1;

while ($num <= 49) {
    echo "$num<br>\n";
    $num += 2;
}
```

4.

```
for ($num = 1; $num <= 49; $num += 2) {
    echo "$num<br>\n";
}
```

Activity

Review the syntax for control structures. Think about how the techniques you've learned will help you in your scripting. Perhaps some of the script ideas you develop will be able to behave in different ways according to user input, or will loop to display an HTML table. Start to build the control structures you will be using. Use temporary variables to mimic user input or database queries for the time being.

CHAPTER 6

Working with Functions

Functions are at the heart of a well-organized script, and will make your code easy to read and reuse. No large project would be manageable without them. Throughout this chapter, we will investigate functions and demonstrate some of the ways in which they can save you from repetitive work. In this chapter, you will learn

- ▶ How to define and call functions
- ▶ How to pass values to functions and receive values in return
- ▶ How to call a function dynamically using a string stored in a variable
- ▶ How to access global variables from within a function
- ▶ How to give a function a "memory"
- ▶ How to pass data to functions by reference
- ▶ How to create anonymous functions
- ▶ How to verify that a function exists before calling it

What Is a Function?

You can think of a function as a machine. A machine takes the raw materials you feed it and works with them to achieve a purpose or to produce a product. A function accepts values from you, processes them, and then performs an action (printing to the browser, for example), returns a new value, or both.

If you needed to bake a single cake, you would probably do it yourself. If you needed to bake thousands of cakes, you would probably build or acquire a cake-baking machine. Similarly, when deciding whether to create a function, the most important factor to consider is the extent to which it can save you from writing repetitive code.

A *function* is a self-contained block of code that can be called by your scripts. When called, the function's code is executed. You can pass values to a function, which will then use them appropriately. When finished, a function can pass a value back to the calling code.

Calling Functions

Functions come in two flavors—those built in to the language and those you define yourself. PHP has hundreds of built-in functions. Take a look at the following snippet for an example of a function use:

```
print ("Hello Web!");
```

In this example, we call the `print()` function, passing it the string `"Hello Web!"`. The function then goes about the business of writing the string. A function call consists of the function name (`print` in this case) followed by parentheses. If you want to pass information to the function, you place it between these parentheses. A piece of information passed to a function in this way is called an *argument*. Some functions require that more than one argument be passed to them, separated by commas:

```
some_function($an_argument, $another_argument);
```

`print()` is typical for a function in that it returns a value. Most functions give you some information back when they've completed their task—they usually at least tell whether their mission was successful. `print()` returns a Boolean.

By the Way

> The `print()` and `echo()` functions are similar in functionality and are used interchangably throughout this book. Whichever one you use is a matter of taste.

The `abs()` function, for example, requires a signed numeric value and returns the absolute value of that number. Let's try it out in Listing 6.1.

LISTING 6.1   Calling the Built-in `abs()` Function

```
 1: <html>
 2: <head>
 3: <title>Listing 6.1</title>
 4: </head>
 5: <body>
 6: <?php
 7: $num = -321;
 8: $newnum = abs( $num );
 9: echo $newnum;
10: //prints "321"
11: ?>
12: </body>
13: </html>
```

In this example, we assign the value -321 to a variable $num. We then pass that variable to the abs() function, which makes the necessary calculation and returns a new value. We assign this to the variable $newnum and display the result.

Put these lines into a text file called abs.php, and place this file in your Web server document root. When you access this script through your Web browser, it produces the following:

```
321
```

In fact, we could have dispensed with temporary variables altogether, passing our number straight to abs(), and directly printing the result:

```
echo abs(-321);
```

We used the temporary variables $num and $newnum, though, to make each step of the process as clear as possible. Sometimes you can make your code more readable by breaking it up into a greater number of simple expressions.

You can call user-defined functions in exactly the same way that we have been calling built-in functions.

Defining a Function

You can define your own functions using the function statement:

```
function some_function($argument1, $argument2) {
    //function code here
}
```

The name of the function follows the function statement and precedes a set of parentheses. If your function requires arguments, you must place comma-separated variable names within the parentheses. These variables will be filled by the values passed to your function. Even if your function doesn't require arguments, you must nevertheless supply the parentheses.

> The naming rules for functions are similar to the naming rules for variables, which you learned in Chapter 4, "The Building Blocks of PHP." Names cannot include spaces, and they must begin with a letter or an underscore.

By the Way

Listing 6.2 declares a function.

LISTING 6.2   Declaring a Function

```
 1: <html>
 2: <head>
 3: <title>Listing 6.2</title>
 4: </head>
 5: <body>
 6: <?php
 7: function bighello() {
 8:      echo "<h1>HELLO!</h1>";
 9: }
10: bighello();
11: ?>
12: </body>
13: </html>
```

The script in Listing 6.2 simply outputs the string "HELLO" wrapped in an HTML h1 element.

Put these lines into a text file called bighello.php, and place this file in your Web server document root. When you access this script through your Web browser, it should look like Figure 6.1.

FIGURE 6.1
Output of
Listing 6.2.

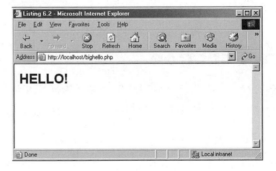

We declared a function, bighello(), that requires no arguments. Because of this, we leave the parentheses empty. Although bighello() is a working function, it is not terribly useful. Listing 6.3 creates a function that requires an argument and actually does something with it.

LISTING 6.3   Declaring a Function That Requires an Argument

```
 1: <html>
 2: <head>
 3: <title>Listing 6.3</title>
 4: </head>
 5: <body>
 6: <?php
 7: function printBR($txt) {
```

LISTING 6.3   Continued

```
 8:       echo "$txt<br> \n";
 9: }
10: printBR("This is a line");
11: printBR("This is a new line");
12: printBR("This is yet another line");
13: ?>
14: </body>
15: </html>
```

> Unlike variable names, function names are not case sensitive. In the example preceding, the printBR() function could have been called as printbr(), PRINTBR(), or any combination thereof, with success.

Put these lines into a text file called printbr.php, and place this file in your Web server document root. When you access this script through your Web browser, it should look like Figure 6.2.

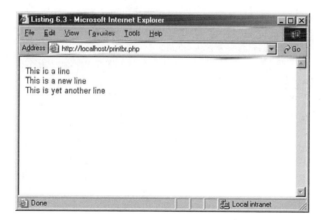

FIGURE 6.2
A function that prints a string with an appended <br> tag.

In line 7, the printBR() function expects a string, so we place the variable name $txt between the parentheses when we declare the function. Whatever is passed to printBR() will be stored in the $txt variable. Within the body of the function, in line 8, we print the $txt variable, appending a <br> element and a newline character to it.

When we want to write a line to the browser, such as in line 10, 11, or 12, we can call printBR() instead of the built-in print(), saving us the bother of typing the <br> element.

Returning Values from User-Defined Functions

In the previous example, we output an amended string to the browser within the printBR() function. Sometimes, however, you will want a function to provide you with a value that you can work with yourself. If your function has transformed a string that you have provided, you may wish to get the amended string back so that you can pass it to other functions. A function can return a value using the return statement in conjunction with a value. The return statement stops the execution of the function and sends the value back to the calling code.

Listing 6.4 creates a function that returns the sum of two numbers.

LISTING 6.4   A Function That Returns a Value

```
 1: <html>
 2: <head>
 3: <title>Listing 6.4</title>
 4: </head>
 5: <body>
 6: <?php
 7: function addNums($firstnum, $secondnum) {
 8:      $result = $firstnum + $secondnum;
 9:      return $result;
10: }
11: echo addNums(3,5);
12: //will print "8"
13: ?>
14: </body>
15: </html>
```

Put these lines into a text file called addnums.php, and place this file in your Web server document root. When you access this script through your Web browser, it produces the following:

8

Notice in line 7 that addNums() should be called with two numeric arguments (line 11 shows those to be 3 and 5 in this case). These are stored in the variables $firstnum and $secondnum. Predictably, addNums() adds the numbers contained in these variables and stores the result in a variable called $result.

The return statement can return a value or nothing at all. How we arrive at a value passed by return can vary. The value can be hard-coded:

```
return 4;
```

It can be the result of an expression:

```
return $a/$b;
```

It can be the value returned by yet another function call:

```
return another_function($an_argument);
```

Variable Scope

A variable declared within a function remains local to that function. In other words, it will not be available outside the function or within other functions. In larger projects, this can save you from accidentally overwriting the contents of a variable when you declare two variables with the same name in separate functions.

Listing 6.5 creates a variable within a function and then attempts to print it outside the function.

LISTING 6.5 Variable Scope: A Variable Declared Within a Function Is Unavailable Outside the Function

```
 1: <html>
 2: <head>
 3: <title>Listing 6.5</title>
 4: </head>
 5: <body>
 6: <?php
 7: function test() {
 8:     $testvariable = "this is a test variable";
 9: }
10: echo "test variable: $testvariable<br>";
11: ?>
12: </body>
13: </html>
```

Put these lines into a text file called scopetest.php, and place this file in your Web server document root. When you access this script through your Web browser, it should look like Figure 6.3.

The value of the variable $testvariable is not printed. This is because no such variable exists outside the test() function. Note that the attempt in line 10 to access a nonexistent variable does not cause an error.

Similarly, a variable declared outside a function will not automatically be available within it.

FIGURE 6.3
Output of
Listing 6.5.

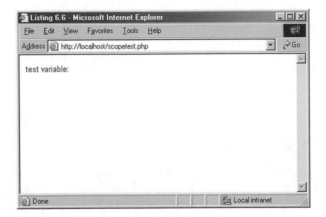

Accessing Variables with the global Statement

From within one function, you cannot (by default) access a variable defined in another function or elsewhere in the script. Within a function, if you attempt to use a variable with the same name, you will only set or access a local variable. Let's put this to the test in Listing 6.6.

LISTING 6.6   Variables Defined Outside Functions Are Inaccessible from Within a Function by Default

```
 1: <html>
 2: <head>
 3: <title>Listing 6.6</title>
 4: </head>
 5: <body>
 6: <?php
 7: $life = 42;
 8: function meaningOfLife() {
 9:     echo "The meaning of life is $life<br>";
10: }
11: meaningOfLife();
12: ?>
13: </body>
14: </html>
```

Put these lines into a text file called scopetest2.php, and place this file in your Web server document root. When you access this script through your Web browser, it should look like Figure 6.4.

As you might expect, the meaningOfLife() function does not have access to the $life variable in line 7; $life is empty when the function attempts to print it. On the whole, this is a good thing; it saves us from potential clashes between identically named variables, and a function can always demand an argument if it needs information about the outside world. Occasionally, you may want to access an important variable from within a function without passing it in as an argument. This is where the `global` statement comes into play. Listing 6.7 uses `global` to restore order to the universe.

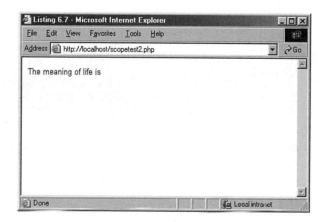

FIGURE 6.4
Attempting to reference a variable from outside the scope of a function.

LISTING 6.7   Accessing Global Variables with the `global` Statement

```
 1: <html>
 2: <head>
 3: <title>Listing 6.7</title>
 4: </head>
 5: <body>
 6: <?php
 7: $life=42;
 8: function meaningOfLife() {
 9:     global $life;
10:     echo "The meaning of life is $life<br>";
11: }
12: meaningOfLife();
13: ?>
14: </body>
15: </html>
```

Put these lines into a text file called `scopetest3.php`, and place this file in your Web server document root. When you access this script through your Web browser, it should look like Figure 6.5.

By placing `global` in front of the `$life` variable when we declare it in the `meaningOfLife()` function (line 9), it now refers to the `$life` variable declared outside the function (line 7).

FIGURE 6.5
Successfully
accessing a global
variable from within
a function using
the global
keyword.

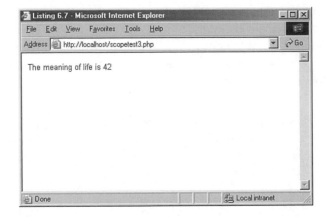

You will need to use the global statement for every function that you want to access for a particular global variable. Be careful, though, because if you manipulate the contents of the variable within the function, $life will be changed for the script as a whole.

You can declare more than one variable at a time with the global statement by simply separating each of the variables you wish to access with commas:

```
global $var1, $var2, $var3;
```

Usually, an argument is a copy of whatever value is passed by the calling code; changing it in a function has no effect beyond the function block. Changing a global variable within a function, on the other hand, changes the original and not a copy. Use the global statement sparingly.

Saving State Between Function Calls with the static Statement

Variables within functions have a short but happy life on the whole. They come into being when the function is called and die when execution is finished, as they should. It is usually best to build a script as a series of self-contained blocks, each with as little knowledge of others as possible. Occasionally, however, you may want to give a function a rudimentary memory.

Let's assume that we want a function to keep track of the number of times it has been called so that numbered headings can be created by a script. We could, of course, use the global statement to do this, as shown in Listing 6.8.

LISTING 6.8   Using the `global` Statement to Remember the Value of a Variable Between Function Calls

```
 1: <html>
 2: <head>
 3: <title>Listing 6.8</title>
 4: </head>
 5: <body>
 6: <?php
 7: $num_of_calls = 0;
 8: function numberedHeading($txt) {
 9:     global $num_of_calls;
10:     $num_of_calls++;
11:     echo "<h1>$num_of_calls. $txt</h1>";
12: }
13: numberedHeading("Widgets");
14: echo "<p>We build a fine range of widgets</p>";
15: numberedHeading("Doodads");
16: echo "<p>Finest in the world</p>";
17: ?>
18: </body>
19: </html>
```

Put these lines into a text file called numberedheading.php, and place this file in your Web server document root. When you access this script through your Web browser, it should look like Figure 6.6.

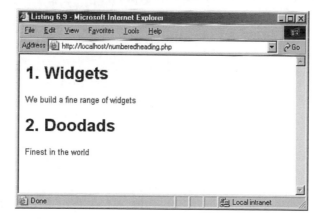

FIGURE 6.6
Using the global statement to keep track of the number of times a function has been called.

This does the job. We declare a variable, $num_of_calls, in line 7, outside the function numberedHeading(). We make this variable available to the function using the global statement in line 9.

Every time numberedHeading() is called, $num_of_calls is incremented (line 10). We can then print out a heading complete with a heading number.

This is not the most elegant solution, however. Functions that use the global statement cannot be read as standalone blocks of code. In reading or reusing them, we need to look out for the global variables that they manipulate.

This is where the static statement can be useful. If you declare a variable within a function in conjunction with the static statement, the variable remains local to the function, and the function "remembers" the value of the variable from execution to execution. Listing 6.9 adapts the code from Listing 6.8 to use the static statement.

LISTING 6.9   Using the static Statement to Remember the Value of a Variable Between Function Calls

```
 1: <html>
 2: <head>
 3: <title>Listing 6.9</title>
 4: </head>
 5: <body>
 6: <?php
 7: function numberedHeading($txt) {
 8:      static $num_of_calls = 0;
 9:      $num_of_calls++;
10:      echo "<h1>$num_of_calls. $txt</h1>";
11: }
12: numberedHeading("Widgets");
13: echo "<p>We build a fine range of widgets</p>";
14: numberedHeading("Doodads");
15: echo "<p>Finest in the world</p>";
16: ?>
17: </body>
18: </html>
```

The numberedHeading() function has become entirely self-contained. When we declare the $num_of_calls variable on line 8, we assign an initial value to it. This assignment is made when the function is first called on line 12. This initial assignment is ignored when the function is called a second time on line 14. Instead, the code remembers the previous value of $num_of_calls. We can now paste the numberedHeading() function into other scripts without worrying about global variables. Although the output of Listing 6.10 is exactly the same as that of Listing 6.9, we have made the code more elegant.

More About Arguments

You've already seen how to pass arguments to functions, but there's plenty more to cover. In this section, you'll look at a technique for giving your arguments default values and explore a method of passing variables by reference rather than by value. This means that the function is given an alias of the original value rather than a copy of it.

Setting Default Values for Arguments

PHP gives you a nifty feature to help build flexible functions. Until now, we've said that some functions require one or more arguments. By making some arguments optional, you can render your functions a little less autocratic.

Listing 6.10 creates a useful little function that wraps a string in an HTML font element. We want to give the user of the function the chance to change the font element's size attribute, so we demand a $size argument in addition to the string (line 7).

LISTING 6.10   A Function Requiring Two Arguments

```
 1: <html>
 2: <head>
 3: <title>Listing 6.10</title>
 4: </head>
 5: <body>
 6: <?php
 7: function fontWrap($txt, $size) {
 8:     echo "<font size=\"$size\"
 9:         face=\"Helvetica, Arial, Sans-Serif\">
10.         $txt</font>";
11: }
12: fontWrap("A heading<br>",5);
13: fontWrap("some body text<br>",3);
14: fontWrap("some more body text<br>",3);
15: fontWrap("yet more body text<br>",3);
16: ?>
17: </body>
18: </html>
```

Put these lines into a text file called fontwrap.php, and place this file in your Web server document root. When you access this script through your Web browser, it should look like Figure 6.7.

Useful though this function is, we really only need to change the font size occasionally. Most of the time we use the default value of 3. By assigning a value to an argument variable within the function definition's parentheses, we can make the $size argument optional. If the function call doesn't define an argument for this, the value we have assigned to the argument is used instead. Listing 6.11 uses this technique to make the $size argument optional.

FIGURE 6.7
A function that for-
mats and outputs
strings.

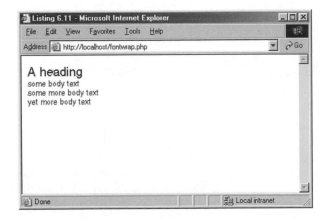

LISTING 6.11 A Function with an Optional Argument

```
 1: <html>
 2: <head>
 3: <title>Listing 6.11</title>
 4: </head>
 5: <body>
 6: <?php
 7: function fontWrap($txt, $size = 3) {
 8:     echo "<font size=\"$size\"
 9:         face=\"Helvetica, Arial, Sans-Serif\">
10:         $txt</font>";
11: }
12: fontWrap("A heading<br>",5);
13: fontWrap("some body text<br>");
14: fontWrap("some more body text<br>");
15: fontWrap("yet more body text<br>");
16: ?>
17: </body>
18: </html>
```

When the `fontWrap()` function is called with a second argument, as in line 12,
this value is used to set the `size` attribute of the `font` element. When we omit this
argument, as in lines 13, 14, and 15, the default value of 3 is used instead. You
can create as many optional arguments as you want, but when you've given an
argument a default value, all subsequent arguments should also be given
defaults.

Passing Variable References to Functions

When you pass arguments to functions, they are stored as copies in parameter
variables. Any changes made to these variables in the body of the function are

local to that function and are not reflected beyond it. This is illustrated in Listing 6.12.

LISTING 6.12   Passing an Argument to a Function by Value

```
 1: <html>
 2: <head>
 3: <title>Listing 6.12</title>
 4: </head>
 5: <body>
 6: <?php
 7: function addFive($num) {
 8:     $num += 5;
 9: }
10: $orignum = 10;
11: addFive($orignum);
12: echo $orignum;
13: ?>
14: </body>
15: </html>
```

Put these lines into a text file called addfive.php, and place this file in your Web server document root. When you access this script through your Web browser, it produces the following:

10

The addFive() function accepts a single numeric value and adds 5 to it. It returns nothing. We assign a value to a variable $orignum in line 10, and then pass this variable to addFive() in line 11. A copy of the contents of $orignum is stored in the variable $num. Although we increment $num by 5, this has no effect on the value of $orignum. When we print $orignum, we find that its value is still 10. By default, variables passed to functions are passed by value. In other words, local copies of the values of the variables are made.

We can change this behavior by creating a reference to our original variable. You can think of a reference as a signpost that points to a variable. In working with the reference, you are manipulating the value to which it points.

Listing 6.13 shows this technique in action. When you pass an argument to a function by reference, as in line 11, the contents of the variable you pass ($orignum) are accessed by the argument variable and manipulated within the function, rather than just a copy of the variable's value (10). Any changes made to an argument in these cases will change the value of the original variable. You can pass an argument by reference by adding an ampersand to the argument name in the function definition, as shown in line 7.

LISTING 6.13 Using a Function Definition to Pass an Argument to a Function by Reference

```
 1: <html>
 2: <head>
 3: <title>Listing 6.13</title>
 4: </head>
 5: <body>
 6: <?php
 7: function addFive(&$num) {
 8:     $num += 5;
 9: }
10: $orignum = 10;
11: addFive($orignum);
12: echo $orignum;
13: ?>
14: </body>
15: </html>
```

Put these lines into a text file called addfive2.php, and place this file in your Web server document root. When you access this script through your Web browser, it produces the following:

15

Testing for the Existence of a Function

We do not always know that a function exists before we try to invoke it. Different builds of the PHP engine may include different functionality, and if you are writing a script that may be run on multiple servers, you might want to verify that key features are available. For instance, you might want to write code that will use MySQL if MySQL-related functions are available, but simply log data to a text file otherwise.

You can use function_exists() to check for the availability of a function. function_exists() requires a string representing a function name. It will return true if the function can be located and false otherwise.

Listing 6.14 shows function_exists() in action, and illustrates some of the other topics we have covered in this chapter.

LISTING 6.14 Testing for a Function's Existence

```
 1: <html>
 2: <head>
 3: <title>Listing 6.14</title>
 4: </head>
 5: <body>
```

LISTING 6.14   Continued

```php
 6: <?php
 7:
 8: function tagWrap($tag, $txt, $func = "") {
 9:     if ((!empty($txt)) && (function_exists($func))) {
10:         $txt = $func($txt);
11:         return "<$tag>$txt</$tag>\n";
12:     }
13: }
14:
15: function underline($txt) {
16:     return "<u>$txt</u>";
17: }
18:
19: echo tagWrap('b', 'make me bold');
20: // will print <b>make me bold</b>
21:
22: echo tagWrap('i', 'underline me too', "underline");
23: // will print <i><u>underline me too</u></i>
24:
25: echo tagWrap('i', 'make me italic and quote me',
26:     create_function('$txt', 'return "&quot;$txt&quot;";'));
27: // will print <i>&quot;make me italic and quote me&quot;</i>
28: ?>
29: </body>
30: </html>
```

We define two functions, tagWrap() (line 8) and underline() (line 15). The tagWrap() function accepts three strings: a tag, the text to be formatted, and an optional function name. It returns a formatted string. underline() requires a single argument—the text to be formatted—and returns the text wrapped in <u> tags.

When we first call tagWrap() on line 19, we pass it the character b and the string make me bold. Because we haven't passed a value for the function argument, the default value (an empty string) is used. On line 9, we check whether the $func variable contains characters and, if it is not empty, we call function_exists() to check for a function by that name. Of course, the $func variable is empty, so we wrap the $txt variable in <b> tags on line 11 and return the result.

We call tagWrap() on line 22 with the string 'i', some text, and a third argument: "underline". function_exists() finds a function called underline() (line 15), so it calls this function and passes the $txt argument variable to it before any further formatting is done. The result is an italicized, underlined string.

Finally, on line 25, we call tagWrap(), which wraps text in quotation entities. Of course, it would be quicker to simply add the entities to the text to be transformed ourselves, but this illustrates the point that function_exists() works as well on anonymous functions as it does on strings representing function names.

Put these lines into a text file called exists.php, and place this file in your Web server document root. When you access this script through your Web browser, it should look like Figure 6.8.

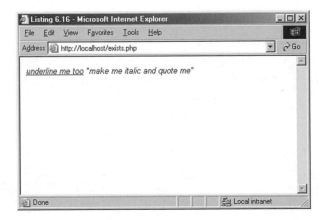

Summary

This chapter taught you about functions and how to deploy them. You learned how to define and pass arguments to a function, how to use the global and static statements, how to pass references to functions, and how to create default values for function arguments. Finally, you learned to test for the existence of functions.

Q&A

Q. *Can you include a function call within a double- or single-quoted string, as you can with a variable?*

A. No. You must call functions outside quotation marks. However, you can break the string apart and place the function call between the parts of the string, using the concatenation operator to tie them together. For example:

```
$newstring = "I purchased".numPurchase($somenum)." items.";
```

Workshop

The workshop is designed to help you anticipate possible questions, review what you've learned, and begin putting your knowledge into practice.

Quiz

1. True or false: If a function doesn't require an argument, you can omit the parentheses in the function call.

2. How do you return a value from a function?

3. What would the following code fragment print to the browser?

```
$number = 50;

function tenTimes() {
    $number = $number * 10;
}

tenTimes();
echo $number;
```

4. What would the following code fragment print to the browser?

```
$number = 50;

function tenTimes() {
    global $number;
    $number = $number * 10;
}

tenTimes();
echo $number;
```

5. What would the following code fragment print to the browser?

```
$number = 50;

function tenTimes( &$n ) {
    $n = $n * 10;
}

tenTimes( $number );
echo $number;
```

Answers

1. The statement is false. You must always include the parentheses in your function calls, whether you are passing arguments to the function or not.

2. You must use the `return` keyword.

3. It would print 50. The `tenTimes()` function has no access to the global `$number` variable. When it is called, it will manipulate its own local `$number` variable.

4. It would print 500. We have used the `global` statement, which gives the `tenTimes()` function access to the `$number` variable.

5. It would print 500. By adding the ampersand to the parameter variable `$n`, we ensure that this argument is passed by reference. `$n` and `$number` point to the same value, so any changes to `$n` will be reflected when you access `$number`.

Activity

Create a function that accepts four string variables and returns a string that contains an HTML table element, enclosing each of the variables in its own cell.

CHAPTER 7

Working with Arrays and Objects

Arrays and objects are used to store and organize data. PHP includes a large number of functions that enable you to create, modify, and manipulate arrays. The object-oriented programming structures found in many programming languages are also evident in PHP.

In this chapter, you learn the basics of working with arrays and objects:

▶ How to create and manipulate arrays using the myriad array-related functions built into PHP

▶ How to create and manipulate objects and the data they contain

What Is an Array?

You've already learned about and used scalar variables in this book, and you know that these variables are used to store values. But scalar variables can store only one value at a time. The $color variable can hold only a value of red or blue, and so forth—it cannot be used to hold a list of colors in the rainbow, for example. But arrays are special types of variables that enable you to store as many values as you want.

Arrays are indexed, which means that each entry is made up of a *key* and a *value*. The key is the index position, beginning with 0. The value is whatever value you associate with that position—a string, an integer, or whatever you want. Think of an array as a filing cabinet and each key/value pair as a file folder. The key is the label written on the top of the folder, and the value is what is inside.

Creating Arrays

You can create an array using either the array() function or the array operator [ ]. The array() function is usually used when you want to create a new array and populate it with more than one element at the same time. The array operator is used when you want to create a new array with just one element (for now), or when you want to add to an existing element.

The following code snippet shows how to create an array called $rainbow, containing all its various colors:

```
$rainbow = array("red", "orange", "yellow", "green", "blue", "indigo", "violet");
```

The following snippet shows the same array being created incrementally using the array operator:

```
$rainbow[] = "red";
$rainbow[] = "orange";
$rainbow[] = "yellow";
$rainbow[] = "green";
$rainbow[] = "blue";
$rainbow[] = "indigo";
$rainbow[] = "violet";
```

Both snippets create a seven-element array called $rainbow, with values starting at index position 0 and ending at index position 6. If you wanted to be literal about it, you could have specified the index positions, such as in this code:

```
$rainbow[0] = "red";
$rainbow[1] = "orange";
$rainbow[2] = "yellow";
$rainbow[3] = "green";
$rainbow[4] = "blue";
$rainbow[5] = "indigo";
$rainbow[6] = "violet";
```

However, PHP does this for you when positions are not specified, and that eliminates the possibility that you will misnumber your elements, as in this example:

```
$rainbow[0] = "red";
$rainbow[1] = "orange";
$rainbow[2] = "yellow";
$rainbow[5] = "green";
$rainbow[6] = "blue";
$rainbow[7] = "indigo";
$rainbow[8] = "violet";
```

Regardless of whether you initially create your array with the array() function or the array operator, you can still add to it using the array operator:

```
$rainbow = array("red", "orange", "yellow", "green", "blue", "indigo");
$rainbow[] = "violet";
```

The examples used in this section were of numerically indexed arrays, arguably the most common type you'll see. In the next two sections, you learn about two other types of arrays: associative and multidimensional.

Creating Associative Arrays

Whereas numerically indexed arrays use an index position as the key—0, 1, 2, and so forth—associative arrays utilize actual named keys. The following example demonstrates this by creating an array called $character with four elements:

```
$character = array(
            "name" => "Bob",
            "occupation" => "superhero",
            "age" => 30,
            "special power" => "x-ray vision"
            );
```

The four keys in the $character array are called name, occupation, age, and special power. The associated values are Bob, superhero, 30, and x-ray vision. You can reference specific elements of an associative array using the specific key, such as in this example:

```
<?php
echo $character['occupation'];
?>
```

The output of this snippet is this:

```
superhero
```

As with numerically indexed arrays, you can use the array operator to add to an associative array:

```
$character['supername'] = "Mega X-Ray Guy";
```

This example adds a key called supername with a value of Mega X-Ray Guy.

Creating Multidimensional Arrays

The first two types of arrays hold strings and integers, whereas this third type holds other arrays. If each set of key/value pairs constitutes a dimension, a multidimensional array holds more than one series of these key/value pairs. For example, Listing 7.1 defines a multidimensional array called $characters, each element of which contains an associative array.

LISTING 7.1   Defining a Multidimensional Array

```
 1:  <?php
 2:  $characters = array(
 3:               array(
 4:                 "name" => "Bob",
 5:                 "occupation" => "superhero",
 6:                 "age" => 30,
 7:                 "special power" => "x-ray vision"
 8:                 ),
 9:               array(
10:                 "name" => "Sally",
11:                 "occupation" => "superhero",
12:                 "age" => 24,
13:                 "special power" => "superhuman strength"
14:                 ),
15:               array(
16:                 "name" => "Jane",
17:                 "occupation" => "arch villain",
18:                 "age" => 45,
19:                 "special power" => "nanotechnology"
20:                 )
21:             );
22:  ?>
```

In line 2, the $characters array is initialized using the array() function. Lines 3–8 represent the first element, lines 9–14 represent the second element, and lines 15–20 represent the third element. These elements can be referenced as $characters[0], $characters[1], and $characters[2].

However, if you attempt to print these elements:

```
<?php
echo $character[2];
?>
```

the output will be this:

```
Array
```

To access specific information found within the array element, you need to access the element index position and the associative name of the value you want to view. Take a look at this example:

```
<?php
echo $character[2]['occupation'];
?>
```

It will print this:

```
superhero
```

Some Array-Related Functions

Approximately 60 array-related functions are built into PHP, which you can read about in detail at http://www.php.net/array. Some of the more common (and useful) functions are explained in this section.

▶ count() and sizeof()—Each counts the number of elements in an array. Given the following array:

```
$colors = array("blue", "black", "red", "green");
```

both count($colors); and sizeof($colors); return a value of 4.

▶ each() and list()—These usually appear together, in the context of stepping through an array and returning its keys and values. The following example steps through an associative array called $character, printing its key, the text has a value of, and the value, followed by an HTML break.

```
while (list($key, $val) = each($character)) {
    echo "$key has a value of $val <br>";
}
```

▶ foreach()—This is also used to step through an array, assigning the value of an element to a given variable. The following example steps through an associative array called $character, prints some text, the value, and finally an HTML break.

```
foreach($character as $c) {
    echo "The value is $c <br>";
}
```

▶ reset()—This rewinds the pointer to the beginning an array, as in this example:

```
reset($character);
```

This function is useful when you are performing multiple manipulations on an array, such as sorting, extracting values, and so forth.

▶ array_push()—This adds one or more elements to the end of an existing array, as in this example:

```
array_push($existingArray, "element 1", "element 2", "element 3");
```

▶ array_pop()—This removes (and returns) the last element of an existing array, as in this example:

```
$last_element = array_pop($existingArray);
```

▶ `array_unshift()`—This adds one or more elements to the beginning of an existing array, as in this example:

```
array_unshift($existingArray, "element 1", "element 2", "element 3");
```

▶ `array_shift()`—This removes (and returns) the first element of an existing array, as in this example:

```
$first_element = array_shift($existingArray);
```

▶ `array_merge()`—This combines two or more existing arrays, as in this example:

```
$newArray = array_merge($array1, $array2);
```

▶ `array_keys()`—This returns an array containing all the key names within a given array, as in this example:

```
$keysArray = array_keys($existingArray);
```

▶ `array_values()`—This returns an array containing all the values within a given array, as in this example:

```
$valuesArray = array_values($existingArray);
```

▶ `shuffle()`—This randomizes the elements of a given array. The syntax of this function is simply as follows:

```
shuffle($existingArray);
```

This brief rundown of array-related functions only scratches the surface of using arrays. However, arrays and array-related functions are used in the code examples throughout this book.

Creating an Object

Explaining the concept of an object is a little difficult: It's a sort of theoretical box of things—variables, functions, and so forth—that exists in a templated structure called a *class*. Although it's easy to visualize a scalar variable, such as $color, with a value of red, or an array called $character with three or four different elements inside it, some people have a difficult time visualizing objects. For now, try to think of an object like a little box, with inputs and outputs on either side. The input mechanisms are called *methods*, and methods have properties. Throughout this section, we look at how classes, methods, and properties all work together to product various outputs.

The section opened with saying that the object has a structure called a class. In a class, you define a set of characteristics. For example, say that you have created an automobile class. In the automobile class, you might have color, make, and model characteristics. Each automobile object uses all the characteristics, but they are initialized to different values, such as silver, Mazda, and Protege5, or red, Porsche, and Boxter.

The whole purpose of using objects is to create a reusable section of code. Because classes are so tightly structured but self-contained and independent of one another, they can be reused from one application to another. For example, suppose you write a text-formatting class on one project and decide you can use that class in another project. Because it's just a set of characteristics, you can pick up the code and use it in the second project, reaching into it with methods specific to the second application but using the inner workings of the existing code to achieve new results.

> If the concept of classes is completely foreign to you, you can supplement your knowledge by reading the chapter called "Classes and Objects" of the PHP manual. You can find it at `http://www.php.net/manual/en/language.oop.php`.

By the Way

Creating an object is quite simple. You simply declare it to be in existence:

```
class myClass {
     //code will go here
}
```

Now that you have a class, you can create a new instance of an object:

```
$object1 = new myClass();
```

In Listing 7.2, you have proof that your object exists.

LISTING 7.2 Proof That Your Class Exists

```
1:  <?php
2:  class myClass {
3:      //code will go here
4:  }
5:  $object1 = new myClass();
6:  echo "\$object1 is an ".gettype($object1);
7:  ?>
```

If you save this code as listing7.2.php, place it in your document root, and access it with your Web browser, you will see the following on your screen:

```
$object1 is an object
```

This is not a particularly useful class because it does absolutely nothing, but it is valid and shows you how the template works. Next, you'll learn about object properties and methods.

Properties of Objects

The variables declared inside an object are called *properties*. It is standard practice to declare your variables at the top of the class. These properties can be values, arrays, or even other objects. The following snippet uses simple scalar variables inside the class, prefaced with the var keyword:

```
class myCar {
    var $color = "silver";
    var $make = "Mazda";
    var $model = "Protege5";
}
```

Now, when you create a myCar object, it will always have these three properties. Listing 7.3 shows you how to access these properties.

LISTING 7.3   Showing Object Properties

```
1:  <?php
2:  class myCar {
3:      var $color = "silver";
4:      var $make = "Mazda";
5:      var $model = "Protege5";
6:  }
7:  $car = new myCar();
8:  echo "I drive a ".$car -> color." ".$car -> make." ".$car -> model;
9:  ?>
```

If you save this code as listing7.3.php, place it in your document root, and access it with your Web browser, you will see the following on your screen:

```
I drive a silver Mazda Protege5
```

Because the odds are low that you also will drive a silver Mazda Protege5, you'll want to change the properties of the myCar object. Listing 7.4 shows you how to do just that.

LISTING 7.4   Changing Object Properties

```
1:  <?php
2:  class myCar {
3:      var $color = "silver";
4:      var $make = "Mazda";
5:      var $model = "Protege5";
6:  }
```

LISTING 7.4   Continued

```
7:  $car = new myCar();
8:  $car -> color = "red";
9:  $car -> make = "Porsche";
10: $car -> model = "Boxter";
11: echo "I drive a ".$car -> color." ".$car -> make." ".$car -> model;
12: ?>
```

If you save this code as listing7.4.php, place it in your document root, and access it with your Web browser, you will see the following on your screen:

```
I drive a red Porsche Boxter
```

The purpose of Listing 7.4 is to show that regardless of whether you have a well-defined class with properties, you can easily change the values of these properties to fit your own needs.

Object Methods

Methods add functionality to your objects. No longer will they be sitting there, just holding on to their properties for dear life—they'll actually do something! Listing 7.5 shows just that.

LISTING 7.5   A Class with a Method

```
1:  <?php
2:  class myClass {
3:      function sayHello() {
4:          echo "HELLO!";
5:      }
6:  }
7:  $object1 = new myClass();
8:  $object1 -> sayHello();
9:  ?>
```

Although it's not the most thrilling example of action, if you save this code as listing7.5.php, place it in your document root, and access it with your Web browser, you will see the following on your screen:

```
HELLO!
```

So, a method looks and acts like a normal function but is defined within the framework of a class. The -> operator is used to call the object method in the context of your script. Had there been any variables stored in the object, the method would have been capable of accessing them for its own purposes. This is illustrated in Listing 7.6.

LISTING 7.6   Accessing Class Properties Within a Method

```
1:  <?php
2:  class myClass {
3:      var $name = "Matt";
4:      function sayHello() {
5:          echo "HELLO! My name is ".$this->name;
6:      }
7:  }
8:  $object1 = new myClass();
9:  $object1 -> sayHello();
10: ?>
```

If you save this code as listing7.6.php, place it in your document root, and access it with your Web browser, you will see the following on your screen:

```
HELLO! My name is Matt
```

The special variable $this is used to refer to the currently instantiated object, as you see on line 5. Anytime an object refers to itself, you must use the $this variable. Using the $this variable in conjunction with the -> operator enables you to access any property or method in a class, within the class itself.

One final tidbit regarding the basics of working with an object's properties is how to change a property from within a method. Previously, a property was changed outside the method in which it was contained. Listing 7.7 shows how this is done.

LISTING 7.7   Changing the Value of a Property from Within a Method

```
1:  <?php
2:  class myClass {
3:      var $name = "Matt";
4:      function setName($n) {
5:          $this->name = $n;
6:      }
7:      function sayHello() {
8:          echo "HELLO! My name is ".$this->name;
9:      }
10: }
11: $object1 = new myClass();
12: $object1 -> setName("Julie");
13: $object1 -> sayHello();
14: ?>
```

If you save this code as listing7.7.php, place it in your document root, and access it with your Web browser, you will see the following on your screen:

```
HELLO! My name is Julie
```

Why? Because in lines 4–6, a new function called setName() was created. When it is called in line 12, it changes the value of $name to Julie. Thus, when the sayHello() function is called in line 13 and it looks for $this->name, it uses Julie, which is the new value that was just set by the setName() function.

In other words, an object is capable of modifying its own property—in this case, the $name variable.

Constructors

A *constructor* is a function that lives within a class and, given the same name as the class, is automatically called when a new instance of the class is created using new *classname*. Using constructors enables you to provide arguments to your class, to be processed immediately when it is first called. You see constructors in action in the next section, on object inheritance.

Object Inheritance

Having learned the absolute basics of objects, properties, and methods, you can start to look at object inheritance. Inheritance with regard to classes is just what it sounds like: One class inherits the functionality from its parent class. An example is shown in Listing 7.8.

LISTING 7.8 A Class Inheriting from Its Parent

```
1:  <?php
2:  class myClass {
3:      var $name = "Matt";
4:      function myClass($n) {
5:          $this->name = $n;
6:      }
7:      function sayHello() {
8:          echo "HELLO! My name is ".$this->name;
9:      }
10: }
11: class childClass extends myClass {
12: //code goes here
13: }
14: $object1 = new childClass("Baby Matt");
15: $object1 -> sayHello();
16: ?>
```

If you save this code as listing7.8.php, place it in your document root, and access it with your Web browser, you will see the following on your screen:

```
HELLO! My name is Baby Matt
```

Lines 4–6 make up a constructor. Notice that this function is named the same as the class in which it is contained: myClass. Lines 11–13 define a second class, childClass, that contains no code. That's fine because, in this example, it's meant to demonstrate only inheritance from the parent class. The inheritance occurs through the use of the extends clause, shown in line 11. The second class inherits the elements of the first class because this clause is used.

One last example shows you how a child class can override the methods of the parent class—see Listing 7.9.

LISTING 7.9   The Method of a Child Class Overriding That of Its Parent

```
1:   <?php
2:   class myClass {
3:        var $name = "Matt";
4:        function myClass($n) {
5:             $this->name = $n;
6:        }
7:        function sayHello() {
8:             echo "HELLO! My name is ".$this->name;
9:        }
10:  }
11:  class childClass extends myClass {
12:       function sayHello() {
13:            echo "I will not tell you my name";
14:       }
15:  }
16:  $object1 = new childClass("Baby Matt");
17:  $object1 -> sayHello();
18:  ?>
```

The only changes in this code from Listing 7.8 are the new lines 12–14. In these lines, a function is created called sayHello() that, instead of printing HELLO! My name is..., prints the message I will not tell you my name. Now, because the sayHello() function exists in childClass, and childClass is the class that is called in line 16, its version of sayHello() is the one used.

If you save this code as listing7.9.php, place it in your document root, and access it with your Web browser, you will see the following on your screen:

```
I will not tell you my name
```

Like most elements of object-oriented programming, inheritance is useful when attempting to make your code flexible. Suppose you created a text-formatting class that organized and stored data, formatted it in HTML, and output the result to a browser—your own personal masterpiece. Now suppose you had a client who wanted to use that concept, but instead of formatting the content into HTML and sending it to a browser, he wanted to format it for plain text and save it to a text file. No problem—you just add a few methods and properties, and away you go. Finally, the client comes back and says that he really wants the data to be formatted and sent as an email—and then, what the heck, why not create XML-formatted files as well?

Although you might want to pull your hair out in frustration, you're really not in a bad situation. If you separate the compilation and storage classes from the formatting classes—one for each of the various delivery methods (HTML, text, email, XML)—you essentially have a parent-child relationship. Consider the parent class the one that holds the compilation and storage methods. The formatting classes are the children—they inherit the information from the parent and output the result based on their own functionality.

Summary

This chapter introduced you to the concepts of arrays and objects. First, you learned about a few different types of arrays and how they are created and referenced. These array types were the numerically indexed array, associative array, and multidimensional array. Additionally, you saw examples of some of the numerous array-related functions already built into PHP. These functions can be used to manipulate and modify existing arrays, sometimes even creating entirely new ones.

In the second part of the hour, you were given a foundation for working with object-oriented code. In no way does this hour cover all the aspects of object-oriented programming—universities teach entire series of classes (no pun intended) devoted to this topic, so you can imagine that these pages are a little light. However, you did learn to create classes and instantiate objects from them. You learned how to create and access the properties and methods of a class, how to build new classes, and how to inherit features from parent classes. That's not too shabby!

Q&A

Q. *Do I have to understand object-oriented programming to become a good PHP programmer, or even to finish this book?*

A. Not at all. In fact, the vast majority of this book does *not* contain object-oriented (OO) programming! Object-oriented programming is an organizational approach that is intended to improve the reusability and extensibility of the code that makes up a given application. You might not know enough about your project in the beginning stages of development to fully plan for an OO design. When it is complete—or, at least, approaching a solid state—you might start to see areas in which an OO approach can be taken, and you might start to combine your code into classes, properties, and methods. But for the most part, simple scripts performing particular duties are not written in OO fashion unless it is your background and comes naturally to you.

Workshop

The workshop is designed to help you anticipate possible questions, review what you've learned, and begin learning how to put your knowledge into practice.

Quiz

1. What construct can you use to define an array?

2. What function would you use to join two arrays?

3. How would you declare a class called `emptyClass` that has no methods or properties?

4. How would you choose a name for a constructor method?

Answers

1. `array()`

2. `array_merge()`

3. Use the `class` keyword:

```
class emptyClass {
}
```

4. You don't—a constructor is named for the class in which it resides.

Activities

1. Create a multidimensional array of movies organized by genre. This should take the form of an associative array with genres as keys, such as `Science Fiction`, `Action`, `Adventure`, and so forth. Each of the array's elements should be an array containing movie names, such as `Alien`, `Terminator 3`, `Star Wars`, and so on. When your arrays are created, loop through them, printing the name of each genre and its associated movie(s).

2. Create a class called `baseCalc()` that stores two numbers as properties. Next, create a `calculate()` method that prints the numbers to the browser. Finally, create classes called `addCalc()`, `subCalc()`, `mulCalc()`, and `divCalc()` that inherit functionality from `baseCalc()` but override the `calculate()` method and print appropriate totals to the browser.

PART III

Getting Involved with the Code

CHAPTER 8

Working with Strings, Dates, and Times

The World Wide Web is very much a plain text environment. No matter how rich Web content becomes, HTML lies behind it all. It is no accident, then, that PHP provides many functions with which you can format, investigate, and manipulate strings. Similarly, dates and times are so much a part of everyday life that it becomes easy to work with them without thinking. However, the quirks of the Gregorian calendar can be difficult to work with in programs. Fortunately, PHP provides powerful tools for date arithmetic that make date manipulation an easy task.

In this chapter, you will learn

- ▶ How to format strings
- ▶ How to determine the length of a string
- ▶ How to find a substring within a string
- ▶ How to break a string down into component parts
- ▶ How to remove white space from the beginning or end of a string
- ▶ How to replace substrings
- ▶ How to change the case of a string
- ▶ How to acquire the current date and time
- ▶ How to get information about a date
- ▶ How to format date information
- ▶ How to test dates for validity
- ▶ How to set dates

Formatting Strings with PHP

Until now, we have simply printed any strings that we want to display directly to the browser. PHP provides two functions that allow you first to apply formatting, whether to round doubles to a given number of decimal places, define alignment within a field, or display data according to different number systems. In this section, you will look at a few of the formatting options provided by printf() and sprintf().

Working with printf()

If you have any experience with a C-like programming language, you will be familiar with the printf() function. The PHP version is similar but not identical to the C function. The PHP printf() function requires a string argument, known as a *format control string*. It also accepts additional arguments of different types. The format control string contains instructions as to how to display these additional arguments. The following fragment, for example, uses printf() to output an integer as a decimal:

```
printf("This is my number: %d", 55 );
// prints "This is my number: 55"
```

Within the format control string (the first argument), we have included a special code, known as a *conversion specification*.

A conversion specification begins with a percent (%) symbol and defines how to treat the corresponding argument to printf(). You can include as many conversion specifications as you want within the format control string, as long as you send an equivalent number of arguments to printf().

The following fragment outputs two numbers using printf():

```
printf("First number: %d<br>\nSecond number: %d<br>\n", 55, 66 );
// Output:
// First number: 55
// Second number: 66
```

The first conversion specification corresponds to the first of the additional arguments to printf(), which is 55. The second conversion specification corresponds to 66. The d following the percent symbol requires that the data be treated as a decimal integer. This part of a conversion specification is a type specifier.

`printf()` **and Type Specifiers**

You have already come across one type specifier, d, which displays data in decimal format. Table 8.1 lists the other type specifiers that are available.

TABLE 8.1 Type Specifiers

Specifier	Description
d	Display an argument as a decimal number
b	Display an integer as a binary number
c	Display an integer as an ASCII equivalent
f	Display an integer as a floating-point number (double)
o	Display an integer as an octal number (base 8)
s	Display an argument as a string
x	Display an integer as a lowercase hexadecimal number (base 16)
X	Display an integer as an uppercase hexadecimal number (base 16)

Listing 8.1 uses printf() to display a single number according to some of the type specifiers listed in Table 8.1.

Notice that we do not only add conversion specifications to the format control string. Any additional text we include will be printed.

LISTING 8.1   Demonstrating Some Type Specifiers

```
 1: <html>
 2: <head>
 3: <title>Listing 8.1 Demonstrating some type specifiers</title>
 4: </head>
 5: <body>
 6: <?php
 7: $number = 543;
 8: printf("Decimal: %d<br>", $number);
 9: printf("Binary: %b<br>", $number);
10: printf("Double: %f<br>", $number);
11: printf("Octal: %o<br>", $number);
12: printf("String: %s<br>", $number);
13: printf("Hex (lower): %x<br>", $number);
14: printf("Hex (upper): %X<br>", $number);
15: ?>
16: </body>
17: </html>
```

Put these lines into a text file called listing8.1.php, and place this file in your Web server document root. When you access this script through your Web browser, it should look something like Figure 8.1. As you can see, printf() is a quick way of converting data from one number system to another and outputting the result.

FIGURE 8.1
Demonstrating conversion specifiers.

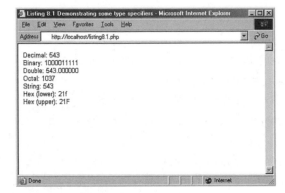

When you specify a color in HTML, you combine three hexadecimal numbers between 00 and FF, representing the values for red, green, and blue. You can use printf() to convert three decimal numbers between 0 and 255 to their hexadecimal equivalents:

```
$red = 204;
$green = 204;
$blue = 204;
printf("#%X%X%X", $red, $green, $blue);
// prints "#CCCCCC"
```

Although you can use the type specifier to convert from decimal to hexadecimal numbers, you can't use it to determine how many characters the output for each argument should occupy. Within an HTML color code, each hexadecimal number should be padded to two characters, which would become a problem if we changed our $red, $green, and $blue variables in the previous fragment to contain 1, for example. We would end up with the output "#111". You can force the output of leading zeroes by using a padding specifier.

Padding Output with the Padding Specifier

You can require that output be padded by leading characters. The padding specifier should directly follow the percent sign that begins a conversion specification. To pad output with leading zeroes, the padding specifier should consist of a zero followed by the number of characters you want the output to take up. If the output occupies fewer characters than this total, the difference will be filled with zeroes:

```
printf( "%04d", 36 );
// prints "0036"
```

To pad output with leading spaces, the padding specifier should consist of a space character followed by the number of characters that the output should occupy:

```
printf("% 4d", 36)
// prints "  36"
```

A browser will not display multiple spaces in an HTML document. You can force the display of spaces and newlines by placing <PRE> tags around your output.

```
<pre>
<?php
echo "The          spaces          will be visible";
?>
</pre>
```

If you wish to format an entire document as text, you can use the header() function to change the Content-Type header.

```
header("Content-Type: text/plain");
```

Remember that your script must not have sent any output to the browser for the header() function to work as desired.

You can specify any character other than a space or a zero in your padding specifier with a single quotation mark followed by the character you want to use:

```
printf ("%'x4d", 36);
// prints "xx36"
```

We now have the tools we need to complete our HTML code example. Until now, we could convert three numbers, but we could not pad them with leading zeroes:

```
$red = 1;
$green = 1;
$blue = 1;
printf("#%02X%02X%02X", $red, $green, $blue);
// prints "#010101"
```

Each variable is output as a hexadecimal number. If the output occupies fewer than two spaces, leading zeroes will be added.

Specifying a Field Width

You can specify the number of spaces within which your output should sit. The field width specifier is an integer that should be placed after the percent sign that begins a conversion specification (assuming that no padding specifier is defined).

The following fragment outputs a list of four items, all of which sit within a field of 20 spaces. To make the spaces visible on the browser, we place all our output within a PRE element.

```
echo "<pre>";
printf("%20s\n", "Books");
printf("%20s\n", "CDs");
printf("%20s\n", "Games");
printf("%20s\n", "Magazines");
echo "</pre>";
```

Figure 8.2 shows the output of this fragment.

FIGURE 8.2
Aligning with field
width specifiers.

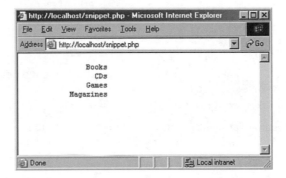

By default, output is right-aligned within the field you specify. You can make it left-aligned by prepending a minus (–) symbol to the field width specifier:

```
printf("%-20s\n", "Left aligned");
```

Note that alignment applies to the decimal portion of any number that you output. In other words, only the portion before the decimal point of a double will sit flush to the end of the field width when right aligned.

Specifying Precision

If you want to output data in floating-point format, you can specify the precision to which you want to round your data. This is particularly useful when dealing with currency. The precision identifier should be placed directly before the type specifier. It consists of a dot followed by the number of decimal places to which you want to round. This specifier only has an effect on data that is output with the f type specifier:

```
printf("%.2f", 5.333333);
// prints "5.33"
```

> In the C language, it is possible to use a precision specifier with `printf()` to specify padding for decimal output. The precision specifier will have no effect on decimal output in PHP. Use the padding specifier to add leading zeroes to integers.

By the Way

Conversion Specifications: A Recap

Table 8.2 lists the specifiers that can make up a conversion specification in the order that they would be included. Note that it is difficult to use both a padding specifier and a field width specifier. You should choose to use one or the other, but not both.

TABLE 8.2 Components of Conversion Specification

Name	Description	Example
Padding specifier	Determines the number of characters that output should occupy, and the characters to add otherwise	`' 4'`
Field width specifier	Determines the space within which output should be formatted	`'20'`
Precision specifier	Determines the number of decimal places to which a double should be rounded	`'.4'`
Type specifier	Determines the data type that should be output	`'d'`

Listing 8.2 uses `printf()` to output a list of products and prices.

LISTING 8.2 Using `printf()` to Format a List of Product Prices

```
 1: <html>
 2: <head>
 3: <title>Listing 8.2 Using printf() to format a list of product prices</title>
 4: </head>
 5: <body>
 6: <?php
 7: $products = array("Green armchair"=>"222.4",
 8: "Candlestick"=>"4",
 9: "Coffee table"=>80.6
10:);
11: echo "<pre>";
12: printf("%-20s%23s\n", "Name", "Price");
13: printf("%'-43s\n", "");
14: foreach ($products as $key=>$val) {
15:     printf( "%-20s%20.2f\n", $key, $val );
16: }
17: echo "</pre>";
18: ?>
19: </body>
20: </html>
```

We first define an associative array containing product names and prices on line 7. We open print a PRE element, so that the browser will recognize our spaces and newlines. Our first `printf()` call on line 12 defines the following format control string:

```
"%-20s%23s\n"
```

The first conversion specification (`"%-20s"`) uses a field width specifier of 20 characters, with the output left-justified. We use a string type specifier. The second conversion specification (`"%23s"`) sets up a right-aligned field width. This `printf()` call will output our field headers.

Our second `printf()` function call on line 13 draws a line of - characters across a field of 43 characters. We achieve this with a padding specifier, which adds padding to an empty string.

The final `printf()` call on line 15 is part of a `foreach` statement that loops through our product array. We use two conversion specifications. The first (`"%-20s"`) prints the product name as a string left-justified within a 20-character field. The second conversion specification (`"%20.2f"`) uses a field width specifier to ensure that output will be right-aligned within a 20-character field, and a precision specifier to ensure that the double we output is rounded to two decimal places.

Put these lines into a text file called `listing8.2.php`, and place this file in your Web server document root. When you access this script through your Web browser, it should look like Figure 8.3.

FIGURE 8.3
Products and prices formatted with `printf()`.

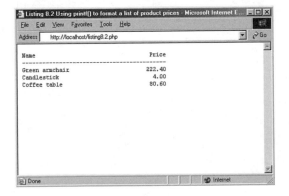

Argument Swapping

Imagine that you are printing dates to the browser. You have the dates in a multi-dimensional array and you are using `printf()` to format the output.

```php
<?php
$dates = array(
            array('mon'=> 12, 'mday'=>25, 'year'=>2002),
            array('mon'=>  5, 'mday'=>23, 'year'=>2003),
            array('mon'=> 10, 'mday'=>29, 'year'=>2002)
            );

$format = include("local_format.php");

foreach($dates as $date) {
    printf("$format", $date['mon'], $date['mday'], $date['year']);
}
?>
```

In the preceding snippet, we are getting our format control string from an include file called `local_format.php`. Assuming that this file contains only

```php
<?php
return "%02d/%02d/%d<br>";
?>
```

Our output will be in the format mm/dd/yyyy.

```
12/25/2002
05/23/2003
10/29/2002
```

Imagine now that we are installing our script for a British site. In the United Kingdom, dates are commonly presented with days before months (dd/mm/yyyy). The core code cannot be changed, but configuration files such as `local_format.php` can. Luckily we can now alter the order in which the arguments are presented from within the format control code.

```php
return "%2\$02d/%1\$02d/%3\$d<br>";
```

We can insert the argument number we are interested in after the initial percentage character that marks each conversion specification, followed by an escaped dollar ($) character. So, in our fragment, we are demanding that the second argument be presented, followed by the first, followed by the third. The result is a list of dates in British format.

```
25/12/2002
23/05/2003
29/10/2002
```

Storing a Formatted String

The `printf()` function outputs data to the browser, which means that the results are not available to your scripts. You can, however, use the function `sprintf()`, which works in exactly the same way as `printf()` except that it returns a string that you can then store in a variable for later use. The following fragment uses `sprintf()` to round a double to two decimal places, storing the result in `$dosh`:

```
$dosh = sprintf("%.2f", 2.334454);
echo "You have $dosh dollars to spend";
```

A particular use of `sprintf()` is to write formatted data to a file. You can call `sprintf()` and assign its return value to a variable that can then be printed to a file with `fputs()`.

Investigating Strings in PHP

You do not always know everything about the data that you are working with. Strings can arrive from many sources, including user input, databases, files, and Web pages. Before you begin to work with data from an external source, you often will need to find out more about it. PHP provides many functions that enable you to acquire information about strings.

A Note About Indexing Strings

We will frequently use the word *index* in relation to strings. You will have come across the word more frequently in the context of arrays, such as in Chapter 7, "Working with Arrays and Objects." In fact, strings and arrays are not as different as you might imagine. You can think of a string as an array of characters. So, you can access individual characters of a string as if they were elements of an array:

```
$test = "scallywag";
echo $test[0]; // prints "s"
echo $test[2]; // prints "a"
```

It is important to remember, therefore, that when we talk about the position or index of a character within a string, characters, like array elements, are indexed from 0.

Finding the Length of a String with `strlen()`

You can use `strlen()` to determine the length of a string. `strlen()` requires a string and returns an integer representing the number of characters in the variable you have passed it. `strlen()` might typically be used to check the length of user input. The following fragment tests a membership code to ensure that it is four digits long:

```
if (strlen($membership) == 4) {
    echo "<p>Thank you!</p>";
} else {
    echo "<p>Your membership number must have 4 digits</p>";
}
```

The user is thanked for his input only if the global variable `$membership` contains four characters; otherwise, an error message is generated.

Finding a Substring Within a String with `strstr()`

You can use `strstr()` to test whether a string exists embedded within another string. `strstr()` requires two arguments: a source string and the substring you want to find within it. The function returns `false` if the substring is absent. Otherwise, it returns the portion of the source string beginning with the substring. For the following example, imagine that we want to treat membership codes that contain the string `AB` differently from those that do not:

```
$membership = "pAB7";
if (strstr($membership, "AB")) {
    echo "<p>Thank you. Don't forget that your membership expires soon!</p>";
} else {
    echo "<p>Thank you!</p>";
}
```

Because our test variable `$membership` does contain the string `AB`, `strstr()` returns the string `AB7`. This resolves to `true` when tested, so we print a special message. What happens if our user enters `"pab7"`? Because `strstr()` is case sensitive, `AB` will not be found. The `if` statement's test will fail, and the default message will be printed to the browser. If we want search for either `AB` or `ab` within the string, we must use `stristr()`, which works in exactly the same way but is not case sensitive.

Finding the Position of a Substring with `strpos()`

The `strpos()` function tells you both whether a string exists within a larger string and where it is to be found. `strpos()` requires two arguments: the source string and the substring you are seeking. The function also accepts an optional third argument, an integer representing the index from which you want to start searching. If the substring does not exist, `strpos()` returns `false`; otherwise, it returns the index at which the substring begins. The following fragment uses `strpos()` to ensure that a string begins with the string `mz`:

```
$membership = "mz00xyz";
if (strpos($membership, "mz") === 0) {
    echo "hello mz";
}
```

Notice the trick we had to play to get expected results. `strpos()` finds mz in our string, but it finds it at the first element of the string. This means that it will return zero, which will resolve to `false` in our test. To work around this, we use PHP's equivalence operator `===`, which returns `true` if the left- and right-hand operands are equivalent and of the same type.

Extracting Part of a String with `substr()`

The `substr()` function returns a portion of a string based on the start index and length of the portion you are looking for. This function demands two arguments: a source string and the starting index. It returns all characters from the starting index to the end of the string you are searching. It optionally accepts a third argument, which should be an integer representing the length of the string you want returned. If this argument is present, `substr()` returns only the number of characters specified from the start index onwards.

```
$test = "scallywag";
echo substr($test,6);  // prints "wag"
echo substr($test,6,2) // prints "wa"
```

If you pass `substr()` a negative number as its second (starting index) argument, it will count from the end rather than the beginning of the string. The following fragment writes a specific message to people who have submitted an email address ending in `.uk`:

```
$test = "matt@corrosive.co.uk";
if ($test = substr($test, -3) == ".uk") {
    echo "<p>Don't forget our special offers for British customers!</p>";
} else {
    echo "<p>Welcome to our shop!</p>";
}
```

Tokenizing a String with `strtok()`

You can parse a string word by word using `strtok()`. The `strtok()` function initially requires two arguments: the string to be tokenized and the delimiters by which to split the string. The delimiter string can include as many characters as you want, and the function will return the first token found. After `strtok()` has been called for the first time, the source string will be cached. For subsequent calls, you should only pass `strtok()` the delimiter string. The function will return the next found token every time it is called, returning `false` when the end of the string is reached. `strtok()` will usually be called repeatedly within a loop. Listing 8.3 uses `strtok()` to tokenize a URL, splitting the host and path from the query string, and further dividing the name/value pairs of the query string.

LISTING 8.3   Dividing a String into Tokens with `strtok()`

```
 1: <html>
 2: <head>
 3: <title>Listing 8.3 Dividing a string into tokens with strtok()</title>
 4: </head>
 5: <body>
 6: <?php
 7: $test  = "http://www.deja.com/qs.xp?";
 8: $test .= "OP=dnquery.xp&ST=MS&DBS=2&QRY=developer+php";
 9: $delims = "?&";
10. $word = strtok($test, $delims);
11: while (is_string($word)) {
12:     if ($word) {
13:         echo "$word<br>";
14:     }
15:     $word = strtok($delims);
16: }
17: ?>
18: </body>
19: </html>
```

Put these lines into a text file called `listing8.3.php`, and place this file in your Web server document root. When you access this script through your Web browser, it should look like Figure 8.4.

The `strtok()` function is something of a blunt instrument, and a few tricks are required to work with it. We first store the delimiters that we want to work with in a variable, `$delims`, on line 9. We call `strtok()` on line 10, passing it the URL we want to tokenize and the `$delims` string. We store the first result in `$word`. Within the conditional expression of the `while` loop on line 11, we test that `$word` is a string. If it isn't, we know that end of the string has been reached and no further action is required.

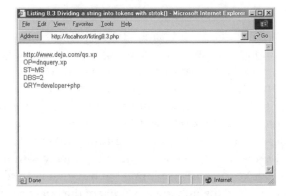

We are testing the return type because a string containing two delimiters in a row would cause strtok() to return an empty string when it reaches the first of these delimiters. So, a more conventional test such as

```
while ($word) {
     $word = strtok($delims);
}
```

would fail if $word is an empty string, even if the end of the source string has not yet been reached.

Having established that $word contains a string, we can go on to work with it. If $word does not contain an empty string, we print it to the browser on line 13. We must then call strtok() again on line 15 to repopulate the $word variable for the next test. Notice that we don't pass the source string to strtok() a second time. If we were to do this, the first word of the source string would be returned once again, and we would find ourselves in an infinite loop.

Manipulating Strings with PHP

PHP provides many functions that will transform a string argument, subtly or radically, as you'll soon see.

Cleaning Up a String with trim() and ltrim() and strip_tags()

When you acquire text from the user or a file, you can't always be sure that you haven't also picked up white space at the beginning and end of your data. The trim() function shaves any white space characters, including newlines, tabs, and spaces, from both the start and end of a string. It accepts the string to be modified, returning the cleaned-up version.

```
$text = "\t\tlots of room to breathe      ";
echo "<pre>$text</pre>";
// prints "            lots of room to breathe      ";
$text = trim($text);
echo "<pre>$text</pre>";
// prints "lots of room to breathe";
```

Of course this might be more work than you require. You might want to keep white space at the beginning of a string but remove it from the end. You can use PHP's rtrim() function exactly the same as you would use trim(). Only white space at the end of the string argument will be removed, however:

```
$text = "\t\tlots of room to breathe      ";
echo "<pre>$text</pre>";
// prints "            lots of room to breathe      ";
$text = rtrim($text);
echo $test;
// prints "            lots of room to breathe";
```

PHP provides the ltrim() function to strip white space only from the beginning of a string. Once again, this is called with the string you want to transform and returns a new string, shorn of tabs, newlines, and spaces:

```
$text = "\t\tlots of room to breathe      ";
echo "<pre>$text</pre>";
// prints "            lots of room to breathe      ";
$text = ltrim($text);
echo "<pre>$text</pre>";
// prints "lots of room to breathe      ";
```

It is not unusual to have to remove tags from a block in order to present it without HTML formatting. PHP provides the strip_tags() function for this purpose. The strip_tags() function accepts two arguments. The first is the text to transform. The second argument is optional and should be a list of HTML tags that strip_tags() can leave in place. The tags in the exception list should not be separated by any characters.

```
$string = "<p>I <i>simply</i> will not have it, <br>said Mr Dean</p><p><b>The
end</b></p>";
echo strip_tags($string, "<br><p>");
```

In the previous code fragment, we create an HTML-formatted string. When we call strip_tags(), we pass it the $string variable and a list of exceptions. The result is that the <p> and <br> tags are left in place and all other tags are stripped out. Also, the matching tag for <p>—</p>—is removed as well.

Replacing a Portion of a String Using `substr_replace()`

The `substr_replace()` function works similarly to `substr()` except that it allows you replace the portion of a string that you extract. The function requires three arguments: the string you are transforming, the text you want to add to it, and the starting index. It also accepts an optional length argument. The `substr_replace()` function finds the portion of a string specified by the starting index and length arguments, replacing this portion with the string provided in the replace string argument and returning the entire transformed string.

In the following code fragment used to renew a user's membership code, we must change its second two characters:

```php
<?php
$membership = "mz02xyz";
$membership = substr_replace($membership, "03", 2, 2);
echo "New membership number: $membership";
// prints "New membership number: mz03xyz"
?>
```

The result of this code is that the old membership number, `mz02xyz`, becomes the new membership number, `mz03xyz`.

Replacing Substrings Using `str_replace`

The `str_replace()` function replaces all instances of a string within another string. It requires three arguments: a search string, the replacement string, and the string on which this transformation is to be effected. The function returns the transformed string. The following example uses `str_replace()` to change all references to 2002 to 2003 within a string:

```php
$string  = "Site contents copyright 2002. ";
$string .= "The 2002 Guide to All Things Good in Europe";
echo str_replace("2002","2003",$string);
```

The `str_replace()` function accepts arrays as well as strings for all of its arguments. This allows us to perform multiple search and replace operations on a subject string, and even on more than one subject string. Take the following snippet for instance:

```php
<?php
$source = array(
    "The package which is at version 4.2 was released in 2002",
    "The year 2002 was an excellent period for PointyThing 4.2" );
$search  = array("4.2", "2002");
$replace = array("5.0", "2003");
```

```
$source = str_replace($search, $replace, $source);
foreach($source as $str) {
    echo "$str<br>";
}
// prints:
// The package which is at version 5.0 was released in 2003
// The year 2003 was an excellent period for PointyThing 5.0
?>
```

When str_replace() is passed an array of strings for its first and second arguments, it will attempt to switch each search string with its corresponding replace string in the text to be transformed. When the third argument is an array, str_replace() will return an array of strings. The search and replace operation will have been executed upon each string in the array.

Converting Case

PHP provides several functions that allow you to convert the case of a string. Changing case is often useful for string comparisons. To get an uppercase version of a string, use the function strtoupper(). This function requires only the string that you want to convert and returns the converted string:

```
$membership = "mz03xyz";
$membership = strtoupper($membership);
echo "$membership"; // prints "MZ03XYZ"
```

To convert a string to lowercase characters, use the function strtolower(). Once again, this requires the string you want to convert and returns a converted version:

```
$membership = "MZ03XYZ";
$membership = strtolower($membership);
echo "$membership"; // prints "mz03xyz"
```

PHP also provides a case function that has a useful cosmetic purpose. The ucwords() function makes the first letter of every word in a string uppercase. In the following fragment, we make the first letter of every word in a user-submitted string uppercase:

```
$full_name = "violet elizabeth bott";
$full_name = ucwords($full_name);
echo $full_name; // prints "Violet Elizabeth Bott"
```

Although this function makes the first letter of each word uppercase, it does not touch any other letters. So, if the user had had problems with her Shift key in the previous example and submitted VIolEt eLIZaBeTH bOTt, our approach would not have done much to fix the string. We would have ended up with VIolEt

ELIZaBeTH BOTt, which isn't much of an improvement. We can deal with this by making the submitted string lowercase with strtolower() before invoking ucwords():

```
$full_name = "VIolEt eLIZaBeTH bOTt";
$full_name = ucwords(strtolower($full_name));
echo $full_name; // prints "Violet Elizabeth Bott"
```

Finally, the ucfirst() function will capitalize only the first letter in a string. In the following fragment, we capitalize the first letter in a user-submitted string:

```
$myString = "this is my string";
$myString = ucfirst($myString);
echo $myString; // prints "This is my string"
```

Wrapping Text with wordwrap() and nl2br()

When you present plain text within a Web page, you are often faced with the problem that newlines are not displayed, and your text runs together into a featureless blob. The nl2br() function is a convenience method that converts every newline into an HTML break. So

```
$string  = "one line\n";
$string .= "another line\n";
$string .= "a third for luck\n";
echo nl2br($string);
```

will print

```
one line<br />
another line<br />
a third for luck<br />
```

Notice that the <br> tags are output in XHTML-compliant form.

The nl2br() function is great for honoring newlines that are already in the text you are converting. Occasionally, you may wish to add arbitrary linebreaks in order to format a column of text. The wordwrap() function is perfect for this. wordwrap() requires one argument, the string to be transformed. By default, wordwrap() will wrap lines every 75 characters, and will use \n as its linebreak character. So, the code fragment

```
$string  = "Given a long line, wordwrap() is useful as a means of ";
$string .= "breaking it into a column and thereby making it easier to read";
echo wordwrap($string);
```

would output

```
Given a long line, wordwrap() is useful as a means of breaking it into a
column and thereby making it easier to read
```

Because the lines are broken with the character \n, the formatting will not show up in HTML code, of course. wordwrap() has two more optional arguments: a number representing the maximum number of characters per line, and a string representing the end of line string you would like to use. So, applying the function call

```
echo wordwrap($string, 24, "<br>\n");
```

to our $string variable, our output would be

```
Given a long line,<br>
wordwrap() is useful as<br>
a means of breaking it<br>
into a column and<br>
thereby making it easier<br>
to read
```

The wordwrap() function won't automatically break at your line limit if a word has more characters than the limit. You can, however, use an optional fourth argument to enforce this. The argument should be a positive integer. So, using wordwrap() in conjunction with the fourth argument, we can now wrap a string, even where it contains words that extend beyond the limit we are setting. This fragment

```
$string  = "As usual you will find me at http://www.witteringonaboutit.com/";
$string .= "chat/eating_green_cheese/forum.php. Hope to see you there!";
echo wordwrap($string, 24, "<br>\n", 1);
```

will output

```
As usual you will find<br>
me at<br>
http://www.witteringonab<br>
outit.com/chat/eating_gr<br>
een_cheese/forum.php.<br>
Hope to see you there!
```

Instead of

```
As usual you will find<br>
me at<br>
http://www.witteringonaboutit.com/chat/eating_green_cheese/forum.php. <br>
Hope to see you there!
```

Breaking Strings into Arrays with explode()

The delightfully named explode() function is similar in some ways to strtok().
But explode() will break up a string into an array, which you can then store,
sort, or examine as you want. The explode() function requires two arguments:
the delimiter string that you want to use to break up the source string and the
source string itself. The function optionally accepts a third argument, which will
determine the maximum number of pieces the string can be broken into. The
delimiter string can include more than one character, all of which will form a single delimiter (unlike multiple delimiter characters passed to strtok(), each of
which will be a delimiter in its own right). The following fragment breaks up a
date and stores the result in an array:

```
$start_date = "2003-08-12";
$date_array = explode("-", $start_date);
// $date[0] == "2003"
// $date[1] == "08"
// $date[2] == "12"
```

Now that your head is filled with PHP string functions, let's move on to date and
time functions.

Using Date and Time Functions in PHP

The sections that follow introduce you to the date- and time-related functions
specifically in PHP. Try out each listing for yourself, to see how simple and powerful these functions can be.

Getting the Date with time()

PHP's time() function gives you all the information that you need about the current date and time. It requires no arguments and returns an integer. For us
humans, the returned number is a little hard on the eyes, but it's extremely useful
nonetheless.

```
echo time();
// sample output: 1060751270
//this represents August 12th, 2003 at 10:07PM
```

The integer returned by time() represents the number of seconds elapsed since
midnight GMT on January 1, 1970. This moment is known as the *Unix epoch*, and
the number of seconds that have elapsed since then is referred to as *a timestamp*.
PHP offers excellent tools to convert a timestamp into a form that humans are
comfortable with. Even so, isn't a timestamp a needlessly convoluted way of

storing a date? In fact, the opposite is true. From just one number, you can extract enormous amounts of information. Even better, a timestamp can make date arithmetic much easier than you might imagine.

Think of a homegrown date system in which you record days of the month as well as months and years. Now imagine a script that must add one day to a given date. If this date happened to be 31 December 1999, rather than adding 1 to the date, you'd have to write code to set the day of the month to 1, the month to January, and the year to 2000. Using a timestamp, you need only add a day's worth of seconds (60 * 60 * 24, or 86400) to your current figure and you're done. You can convert this new figure into something more friendly at your leisure.

Converting a Timestamp with getdate()

Now that you have a timestamp to work with, you must convert it before you present it to the user. getdate() optionally accepts a timestamp and returns an associative array containing information about the date. If you omit the timestamp, getdate() works with the current timestamp as returned by time(). Table 8.3 lists the elements contained in the array returned by getdate().

TABLE 8.3 The Associative Array Returned by getdate()

Key	Description	Example
seconds	Seconds past the minute (0–59)	28
minutes	Minutes past the hour (0–59)	7
hours	Hours of the day (0–23)	12
mday	Day of the month (1–31)	20
wday	Day of the week (0–6)	4
mon	Month of the year (1–12)	1
year	Year (4 digits)	2000
yday	Day of year (0–365)	19
weekday	Day of the week (name)	Thursday
month	Month of the year (name)	January
0	Timestamp	948370048

Listing 8.4 uses getdate() in line 7 to extract information from a timestamp, employing a foreach statement to print each element (line 8). You can see typical output in Figure 8.5. The getdate() function returns the date according to the local time zone.

LISTING 8.4   Acquiring Date Information with `getdate()`

```
1: <html>
2: <head>
3: <title>Listing 8.4 Acquiring date information with getdate()</title>
4: </head>
5: <body>
6: <?php
7: $date_array = getdate(); // no argument passed so today's date will be used
8: foreach ($date_array as $key => $val) {
9:     echo "$key = $val<br>";
10: }
11: ?>
12: <hr>
13: <?
14: echo "Today's date: ".$date_array['mon']."/".$date_array['mday']."/".
15:     $date_array['year']."<p>";
16: ?>
17: </body>
18: </html>
```

FIGURE 8.5
Using `getdate()`.

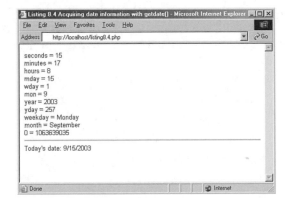

Converting a Timestamp with `date()`

You can use `getdate()` when you want to work with the elements that it outputs. Sometimes, though, you want to display the date as a string. The `date()` function returns a formatted string that represents a date. You can exercise an enormous amount of control over the format that `date()` returns with a string argument that you must pass to it. In addition to the format string, `date()` optionally accepts a timestamp. Table 8.4 lists some of the codes that a format string can contain. You can find the complete list at `http://www.php.net/date`. Any other data you include in the format string passed to `date()` is included in the return value.

TABLE 8.4 Some Format Codes for Use with `date()`

Format	Description	Example
a	am or pm (lowercase)	pm
A	AM or PM (uppercase)	PM
d	Day of month (number with leading zeroes)	20
D	Day of week (three letters)	Thu
F	Month name	January
h	Hour (12-hour format—leading zeroes)	12
H	Hour (24-hour format—leading zeroes)	12
g	Hour (12-hour format—no leading zeroes)	12
G	Hour (24-hour format—no leading zeroes)	12
i	Minutes	47
j	Day of the month (no leading zeroes)	20
l	Day of the week (name)	Thursday
L	Leap year (1 for yes, 0 for no)	1
m	Month of year (number—leading zeroes)	09
M	Month of year (three letters)	Sep
n	Month of year (number—no leading zeroes)	9
s	Seconds of hour	24
S	Ordinal suffix for the day of the month	th
r	Full date standardized to RFC 822 (http://www.faqs.org/rfcs/rfc822.html)	Mon, 15 Sep 2003 08:25:55 -0700
U	Timestamp	1063639555
y	Year (two digits)	00
Y	Year (four digits)	2003
z	Day of year (0–365)	257
Z	Offset in seconds from GMT	0

Listing 8.5 puts a few of these format codes to the test.

LISTING 8.5 Formatting a Date with `date()`

```
1: <html>
2: <head>
3: <title>Listing 8.5 Formatting a date with date()</title>
4: </head>
5: <body>
6: <?php
```

LISTING 8.5   Continued

```
 7: $time = time(); //stores the exact timestamp to use in this script
 8: echo date("m/d/y G.i:s", $time);
 9: echo "<br>";
10: echo "Today is ";
11: echo date("j of F Y, \a\\t g.i a", $time);
12: ?>
13: </body>
14: </html>
```

Listing 8.5 calls date() twice: the first time on line 8 to output an abbreviated date format, and the second time on line 11 for a longer format. Save the text of this listing in a file called listing8.5.php and open it in your Web browser. Your date will differ from the following, obviously, but here's some sample output:

```
08/12/03 22.12:53
Today is 12 of August 2003, at 10.12 pm
```

Although the format string looks arcane, it's easy to build. If you want to add a string that contains letters that are also format codes to the format, you can escape them by placing a backslash (\) in front of them. For characters that become control characters when escaped, you must escape the backslash that precedes them. For example, \t is a format code for a tab, so to ensure that the tab prints, use \\t as in the previous example.

Another example would be in the context of a word you are adding to a string; for example, *the*. The word *the* is made up of three format codes, so all must be escaped:

```
<?php
echo date("l \\t\h\e jS");
//prints Monday the 15th
?>
```

Also note that the date() function returns information according to your local time zone. If you want to format a date in GMT, you use the gmdate() function, which works in exactly the same way.

Creating Timestamps with mktime()

You can already get information about the current time, but you cannot yet work with arbitrary dates. mktime() returns a timestamp that you can then use with date() or getdate(). mktime() accepts up to six integer arguments in the following order:

Hour

Minute

Second

Month

Day of month

Year

Listing 8.6 uses mktime() to get a timestamp that we then use with the date() function.

LISTING 8.6 Creating a Timestamp with mktime()

```
1: <html>
2: <head>
3: <title>Listing 8.6 Creating a timestamp with mktime()</title>
4: </head>
5: <body>
6: <?php
7: // make a timestamp for Aug 23 2003 at 4.15 am
8: $ts = mktime(4, 15, 0, 8, 23, 2003);
9: echo date("m/d/y G.i:s", $ts);
10: echo "<br>";
11: echo "The date is ";
12: echo date("j of F Y, \a\\t g.i a", $ts );
13: ?>
14: </body>
15: </html>
```

We call mktime() on line 8 and assign the returned timestamp to the $ts variable. We then use date() on lines 9 and 12 to output formatted versions of the date using $ts. You can choose to omit some or all the arguments to mktime(), and the value appropriate to the current time is used instead. mktime() also adjusts for values that go beyond the relevant range, so an hour argument of 25 translates to 1:00 a.m. on the day after that specified in the month, day, and year arguments.

Save the text of this listing in a file called listing8.6.php and open it in your Web browser. You should see

```
08/23/03 4.15:00
```

```
The date is 23 of August 2003, at 4.15 am
```

Testing a Date with checkdate()

You might need to accept date information from user input. Before you work with a user-entered date or store it in a database, you should check that the date is valid. `checkdate()` accepts three integers: month, day, and year. `checkdate()` returns `true` if the month is between 1 and 12, the day is acceptable for the given month and year (accounting for leap years), and the year is between 0 and 32767. Be careful, though: A date might be valid but not acceptable to other date functions. For example, the following line returns `true`:

```
checkdate(4, 4, 1066)
```

If you were to attempt to build a date with `mktime()` using these values, you'd end up with a timestamp of `-1`. As a rule of thumb, don't use `mktime()` with years before 1902, and be cautious of using date functions with any date before 1970, as negative numbers are not valid dates. Because the epoch began January 1, 1970, anything before that is an invalid (negative) timestamp.

Summary

In this chapter, you have covered some of the functions that enable you to take control of the strings in your PHP scripts. You learned how to format strings with `printf()` and `sprint()`. You should be able to use these functions both to create strings that transform data and lay it out. You learned about functions that investigate strings. You should be able to discover the length of a string with `strlen()`, determine the presence of a substring with `strpos()`, or extract a substring with `substr()`. You should be able to tokenize a string with `strtok()`.

You also learned about functions that transform strings. You can now remove white space from the beginning or end of a string with `trim()`, `ltrim()`, or `rtrim()`. You can change case with `strtoupper()`, `strtolower()`, or `ucwords()`. You can replace all instances of a string with `str_replace()`.

You also learned how to use various PHP functions to perform date- and time-related actions. The `time()` function gets a date stamp for the current date and time, and you can use `getdate()` to extract date information from a timestamp and `date()` to convert a timestamp into a formatted string. You learned how to create a timestamp using `mktime()`, and how to test a date for validity with `checkdate()`. You will learn many more powerful date-related functions in Chapter 15, "Learning Basic SQL Commands," so much so that you may find yourself using MySQL and not PHP for many of your date-related needs.

Workshop

The workshop is designed to help you anticipate possible questions, review what you've learned, and begin putting your knowledge into practice.

Q&A

Q. *Are there any other string functions that might be useful to me?*

A. Yes. PHP has more than 60 string functions! You can read about them all in the PHP online manual at `http://www.php.net/manual/ref.strings.php`.

Quiz

1. What conversion specifier would you use with `printf()` to format an integer as a double? Indicate the full syntax required to convert the integer 33.

2. How would you pad the conversion you effected in question 1 with zeroes so that the part before the decimal point is four characters long?

3. How would you specify a precision of two decimal places for the floating-point number we have been formatting in the previous questions?

4. What function would you use to extract a substring from a string?

5. How might you remove white space from the beginning of a string?

6. How would you break up a delimited string into an array of substrings?

7. Using PHP, how do you acquire a Unix timestamp that represents the current date and time?

8. Which PHP function accepts a timestamp and returns an associative array that represents the given date?

9. Which PHP function do you use to format date information?

10. Which PHP function could you use to check the validity of a date?

Answers

1. The conversion specifier f is used to format an integer as a double:

   ```
   printf("%f", 33 );
   ```

2. You can pad the output from printf() with the padding specifier—that is, a space or a zero followed by a number representing the number of characters you want to pad by.

   ```
   printf("%04f", 33 );
   ```

3. The precision specifier consists of dot (.) followed by a number representing the precision you want to apply. It should be placed before the conversion specifier:

   ```
   printf("%04.2f", 33 );
   ```

4. The substr() function extracts and returns a substring.

5. The ltrim() function removes white space from the start of a string.

6. The explode() function will split up a string into an array.

7. Use time().

8. The getdate() function returns an associative array whose elements contain aspects of the given date.

9. Use date().

10. You can check a date with the checkdate() function.

Activities

1. Create a feedback form that accepts a user's full name and an email address. Use case conversion functions to capitalize the first letter of each name the user submits and print the result back to the browser. Check that the user's email address contains the @ symbol and print a warning otherwise.

2. Create an array of doubles and integers. Loop through the array, converting each element to a floating-point number with a precision of 2. Right-align the output within a field of 20 characters.

3. Create a birthday countdown script. Given form input of month, day, and year, output a message that tells the user how many days, hours, minutes, and seconds until the big day.

CHAPTER 9

Working with Forms

Until now, the PHP examples in this book have been missing a crucial dimension. Sure, you know the basics, can set variables and arrays, create and call functions, and work with strings. But that's all meaningless if users can't reach into a language's environment to offer it information. In this chapter, you look at strategies for acquiring and working with user input. On the World Wide Web, HTML forms are the principal means by which substantial amounts of information pass from the user to the server.

In this chapter, you will learn

- ▶ How to access information from form fields
- ▶ How to work with form elements that allow multiple selections
- ▶ How to create a single document that contains both an HTML form and the PHP code that handles its submission
- ▶ How to save state with hidden fields
- ▶ How to redirect the user to a new page
- ▶ How to build HTML forms and PHP code that send mail
- ▶ How to build HTML forms that upload files and how to write the PHP code to handle them

Creating a Simple Input Form

For now, let's keep our HTML separate from our PHP code. Listing 9.1 builds a simple HTML form.

LISTING 9.1 A Simple HTML Form

```
1: <html>
2: <head>
3: <title>Listing 9.1 A simple HTML form</title>
4: </head>
5: <body>
6: <form action="listing9.2.php" method="POST">
```

LISTING 9.1   Continued

```
 7: <p><strong>Name:</strong><br>
 8. <input type="text" name="user"></p>
 9: <p><strong>Address:</strong><br>
10. <textarea name="address" rows="5" cols="40"></textarea></p>
11: <p><input type="submit" value="send"></p>
12: </form>
13: </body>
14: </html>
```

Put these lines into a text file called listing9.1.html, and place that file in your Web server document root. This listing defines a form that contains a text field with the name "user" on line 8, a text area with the name "address" on line 10, and a submit button on line 12. The FORM element's ACTION argument points to a file called listing9.2.php, which processes the form information. The method of this form is POST, so the variables are stored in the $_POST superglobal.

Listing 9.2 creates the code that receives our users' input.

LISTING 9.2   Reading Input from a Form

```
 1: <html>
 2: <head>
 3: <title>Listing 9.2 Reading input from a form </title>
 4: </head>
 5: <body>
 6: <?php
 7: echo "<p>Welcome <b>$_POST[user]</b></p>";
 8: echo "<p>Your address is:<br><b>$_POST[address]</b></p>";
 9: ?>
10: </body>
11: </html>
```

Put these lines into a text file called listing9.2.php, and place that file in your Web server document root. Now access the form itself with your Web browser, and you should see something like Figure 9.1.

The script in Listing 9.2 is the first script in this book that isn't designed to be called by clicking a link or typing directly into the browser's location field. Instead, this file is called when a user submits the form created in Listing 9.1.

In the code, we access two variables: $_POST[user] and $_POST[address]. These are references to the variables in the $_POST superglobal, which contain the values that the user entered in the user text field and the address text area. Forms in PHP really are as simple as that.

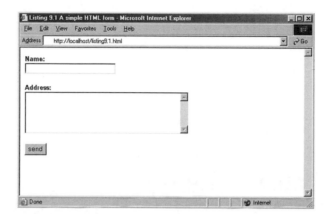

FIGURE 9.1
Form created in
Listing 9.1.

Enter some information in the form fields, and click the send button. You should see your input echoed to the screen.

You could also use the GET method in this form (and others). POST can handle more data than GET and does not pass the data in the query string. If you use the GET method, be sure to change your superglobal to $_GET and not $_POST.

By the
Way

Accessing Form Input with User-Defined Arrays

The previous example showed how to gather information from HTML elements that submit a single value per element name. This leaves us with a problem when working with SELECT elements, when it possible for the user to choose one or more items. If we name the SELECT element with a plain name, like so

```
<select name="products" multiple>
```

the script that receives this data has access to only a single value corresponding to this name. We can change this behavior by renaming an element of this kind so that its name ends with an empty set of square brackets. We do this in Listing 9.3.

LISTING 9.3   An HTML Form Including a SELECT Element

```
1: <html>
2: <head>
3: <title>Listing 9.3 An HTML form including a SELECT element</title>
4: </head>
5: <body>
```

LISTING 9.3 Continued

```
 6: <form action="listing9.4.php" method="POST">
 7: <p><strong>Name:</strong><br>
 8: <input type="text" name="user">
 9:
10: <p><strong>Address:</strong><br>
11: <textarea name="address" rows="5" cols="40"></textarea>
12:
13: <p><strong>Select Some Products:</strong> <br>
14: <select name="products[]" multiple>
15: <option value="Sonic Screwdriver">Sonic Screwdriver</option>
16: <option value="Tricoder">Tricorder</option>
17: <option value="ORAC AI">ORAC AI</option>
18: <option value="HAL 2000">HAL 2000</option>
19: </select>
20:
21: <p><input type="submit" value="send"></p>
22: </form>
23: </body>
24: </html>
```

Put these lines into a text file called listing9.3.html, and place that file in your
Web server document root. Next, in the script that processes the form input, we
find that input from the "products[]" form element created on line 14 is available in an array called $_POST[products]. Because products[] is a SELECT ele-
ment, we offer the user multiple choices using the option elements on lines 15
through 18. We demonstrate that the user's choices are made available in an
array in Listing 9.4.

LISTING 9.4 Reading Input from the Form in Listing 9.3

```
 1: <html>
 2: <head>
 3: <title>Listing 9.4 Reading input from the form in Listing 9.3</title>
 4: </head>
 5: <body>
 6: <?php
 7: echo "<p>Welcome <b>$_POST[user]</b></p>";
 8:   echo "<p>Your address is:<br><b>$_POST[address]</b></p>";
 9:   echo "<p>Your product choices are:<br>";
10: if (!empty($_POST[products])) {
11:      echo "<ul>";
12:      foreach ($_POST[products] as $value) {
13:          echo "<li>$value";
14:      }
15:      echo "</ul>";
16: }
17: ?>
18: </body>
19: </html>
```

Put these lines into a text file called `listing9.4.php`, and place that file in your Web server document root. Now access the form in Listing 9.3 with your Web browser and fill out the fields. Figure 9.2 shows an example.

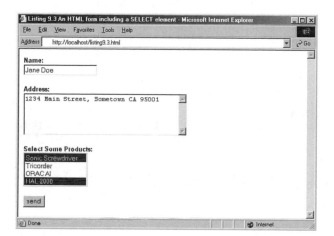

FIGURE 9.2
Form created in
Listing 9.3.

On line 7 of the script in Listing 9.4, we access the $_POST[user] variable, which is derived from the user form element. On line 10, we test for the $_POST[products] variable. If $_POST[products] is present, we loop through it on line 12, and output each choice to the browser on line 13. The text within the value attribute of the selected OPTION element becomes one of the stored values in the array.

Submit the form and you might see something like that shown in Figure 9.3.

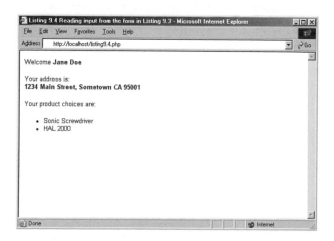

FIGURE 9.3
Sample output of
Listing 9.4.

Although the looping technique is particularly useful with the SELECT element, it can work with other types of form elements. For example, by giving a number of check boxes the same name, you can enable a user to choose many values within a single field name. As long as the name you choose ends with empty square brackets, PHP compiles the user input for this field into an array. We can replace the SELECT elements from lines 15–18 in Listing 9.3 with a series of check boxes to achieve the same effect:

```
<input type="checkbox" name="products[]"
       value="Sonic Screwdriver">Sonic Screwdriver<br>
<input type="checkbox" name="products[]" value="Tricorder">Tricorder<br>
<input type="checkbox" name="products[]" value="ORAC AI">ORAC AI<br>
<input type="checkbox" name="products[]" value="HAL 2000">HAL 2000<br>
```

Combining HTML and PHP Code on a Single Page

In some circumstances, you might want to include form-parsing code on the same page as a hard-coded HTML form. Such a combination can be useful if you need to present the same form to the user more than once. You would have more flexibility if you were to write the entire page dynamically, of course, but you would miss out on one of the great strengths of PHP. The more standard HTML you can leave in your pages, the easier they are for designers and page builders to amend without reference to you. You should avoid scattering substantial chunks of PHP code throughout your documents, however. Doing so makes them hard to read and maintain. Where possible, you should create functions that can be called from within your HTML code and can be reused in other projects.

For the following examples, imagine that we're creating a site that teaches basic math to preschool children, and have been asked to create a script that takes a number from form input and tells the user whether it's larger or smaller than a predefined integer.

Listing 9.5 creates the HTML. For this example, we need only a single text field, but even so, we'll include a little PHP.

LISTING 9.5   An HTML Form That Calls Itself

```
1: <html>
2: <head>
3: <title>Listing 9.5 An HTML form that calls itself</title>
4: </head>
5: <body>
6: <form action="<?php echo $_SERVER[PHP_SELF] ?>" method="POST">
```

LISTING 9.5   Continued

```
 7: <p><strong>Type your guess here:</strong> <input type="text" name="guess"></p>
 8: <p><input type="submit" value="submit your guess"></p>
 9: </form>
10: </body>
11: </html>
```

The action of this script is $_SERVER[PHP_SELF]. This variable is the equivalent of the name of the current script. In other words, the action tells the script to reload itself. The script in Listing 9.5 doesn't produce any output. However, if you upload the script to your Web server, access the page, and view the source of the page, you will notice that the form action now contains the name of the script itself.

In Listing 9.6, we begin to build up the PHP element of the page. First, we must define the number that the user guesses. In a fully working version, we'd probably randomly generate this number, but for now, we keep it simple. We assign 42 to the $num_to_guess variable on line 2. Next, we must determine whether the form has been submitted; otherwise, we'd attempt to assess variables that aren't yet made available. We can test for submission by testing for the existence of the variable $_POST[guess], which is made available if your script has been sent a guess parameter. If $_POST[guess] isn't present, we can safely assume that the user arrived at the page without submitting a form. If the value *is* present, we can test the value it contains. The test for the presence of the $_POST[guess] variable takes place on line 4.

LISTING 9.6   A PHP Number-Guessing Script

```
 1: <?php
 2: $num_to_guess = 42;
 3: $message = "";
 4: if (!isset($_POST[guess])) {
 5:     $message = "Welcome to the guessing machine!";
 6: } else if ($_POST[guess] > $num_to_guess) {
 7:     $message = "$_POST[guess] is too big! Try a smaller number";
 8: } else if ($_POST[guess] < $num_to_guess) {
 9:     $message = "$_POST[guess] is too small! Try a larger number";
10: } else { // must be equivalent
11:     $message = "Well done!";
12: }
13: ?>
14: <html>
15: <head>
16: <title>Listing 9.6 A PHP number guessing script</title>
17: </head>
18: <body>
19: <h1>
20: <?php echo $message ?>
21: </h1>
```

LISTING 9.6   Continued

```
22: <form action="<?php echo $_SERVER[PHP_SELF] ?>" method="POST">
23: <p><strong>Type your guess here:</strong> <input type="text" name="guess"></p>
24: <p><input type="submit" value="submit your guess"></p>
25: </form>
26: </body>
27: </html>
```

Put these lines into a text file called listing9.6.php, and place this file in your Web server document root. Now access the script with your Web browser, and you should see something like Figure 9.4.

FIGURE 9.4
Form created in
Listing 9.6.

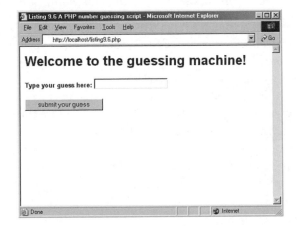

The bulk of this script consists of an if statement that determines which string to assign to the variable $message. If the $_POST[guess] variable hasn't been set, we assume that the user has arrived for the first time and assign a welcome string to the $message variable on line 5.

Otherwise, we test the $_POST[guess] variable against the number we stored in $num_to_guess, and assign advice to $message accordingly. We test whether $_POST[guess] is larger than $num_to_guess on line 6, and whether it's smaller than $num_to_guess on line 8. If $_POST[guess] is neither larger nor smaller than $num_to_guess, we can assume that it's equivalent and assign a congratulations message to the variable (line 11). Now all we must do is print the $message variable within the body of the HTML.

There are still a few more additions you could make, but you can probably see how easy it would be to hand this page over to a designer. He can make it beautiful without having to disturb the programming in any way.

Using Hidden Fields to Save State

The script in Listing 9.6 has no way of knowing how many guesses a user has made, but we can use a hidden field to keep track of this. A hidden field behaves exactly the same as a text field, except that the user cannot see it unless he views the HTML source of the document that contains it. Listing 9.7 adds a hidden field to the number-guessing script and some PHP to work with it.

LISTING 9.7   Saving State with a Hidden Field

```
1:  <?php
2:  $num_to_guess = 42;
3:  $num_tries = (isset($_POST[num_tries])) ? $num_tries  + 1 : 0;
4:  $message = "";
5:  if (!isset($_POST[guess])) {
6:      $message = "Welcome to the guessing machine!";
7:  } else if ($_POST[guess] > $num_to_guess) {
8:      $message = "$_POST[guess] is too big! Try a smaller number";
9:  } else if ($_POST[guess] < $num_to_guess) {
10:     $message = "$_POST[guess] is too small! Try a larger number";
11: } else { // must be equivalent
12:     $message = "Well done!";
13: }
14: $guess = $_POST[guess];
15: ?>
16: <html>
17: <head>
18: <title>Listing 9.7 Saving state with a hidden field</title>
19: </head>
20: <body>
21: <h1>
22: <?php echo $message ?>
23: </h1>
24: <p><strong>Guess number:</strong> <?php echo $num_tries ?></p>
25: <form action="<?php echo $_SERVER[PHP_SELF] ?>" method="POST">
26: <p><strong>Type your guess here:</strong>
27: <input type="text" name="guess" value="<?php echo $guess ?>">
28: <input type="hidden" name="num_tries" value="<?php echo $num_tries ?>">
29: <p><input type="submit" value="submit your guess"></p>
30: </form>
31: </body>
32: </html>
```

The hidden field on line 28 is given the name "num_tries". We also use PHP to write its value. While we're at it, we do the same for the guess field on line 27 so that the user can always see his last guess. This technique is useful for scripts that parse user input. If we reject a form submission for some reason, we can at least allow our user to edit his previous query.

Within the main PHP code, we use a ternary operator to increment the $num_tries variable. If the $num_tries variable is set, we add one to it and reassign this incremented value; otherwise, we initialize $num_tries to 0. Within the body of the HTML, we can now report to the user how many guesses he's made.

Put these lines into a text file called listing9.7.php, and place that file in your Web server document root. Access the form a few times with your Web browser, and try to guess the number (pretend you don't already know it).

Redirecting the User

Our simple script still has one major drawback. The form is reloaded whether or not the user guesses correctly. The fact that the HTML is hard-coded makes it difficult to avoid writing the entire page. We can, however, redirect the user to a congratulations page, thereby sidestepping the issue altogether.

When a server script communicates with a client, it must first send some headers that provide information about the document to follow. PHP usually handles this for you automatically, but you can choose to send your own header lines with PHP's header() function.

To call the header() function, you must be sure that absolutely no output has been sent to the browser. The first time content is sent to the browser, PHP sends out headers and it's too late for you to send your own. Any output from your document, even a line break or a space outside of your script tags, causes headers to be sent. If you intend to use the header() function in a script, you must make certain that nothing precedes the PHP code that contains the function call. You should also check any libraries that you might be using.

Listing 9.8 shows typical headers sent to the browser by PHP, beginning with line 3, in response to the request in line 1.

LISTING 9.8   Typical Server Headers Sent from a PHP Script

```
1: HTTP/1.1 200 OK
2: Date: Mon,  11 Aug 2003 12:32:28 GMT
3: Server: Apache/2.0.44 (Unix) mod_ssl/2.0.44 OpenSSL/0.9.7a PHP/4.3.2
4: X-Powered-By: PHP/4.3.2
5: Connection: close
6: Content-Type: text/html
```

By sending a Location header instead of PHP's default header, you can cause the browser to be redirected to a new page, such as

```
header("Location: http://www.samspublishing.com");
```

Assuming that we've created a suitably upbeat page called `congrats.html`, we can amend our number-guessing script to redirect the user if she guesses correctly, as shown in Listing 9.9.

LISTING 9.9 Using `header()` to Send Raw Headers

```
1: <?php
2: $num_to_guess = 42;
3: $num_tries = (isset($_POST[num_tries])) ? $num_tries + 1: 0;
4: $message = "";
5: if (!isset($_POST[guess])) {
6:     $message = "Welcome to the guessing machine!";
7: } elseif ($_POST[guess] > $num_to_guess) {
8:     $message = "$_POST[guess] is too big! Try a smaller number";
9: } elseif ($_POST[guess] < $num_to_guess) {
10:     $message = "$_POST[guess] is too small! Try a larger number";
11: } else { // must be equivalent
12:     header("Location: congrats.html");
13:     exit;
14: }
15: $guess = $_POST[guess];
16: ?>
17: <html>
18: <head>
19: <title>Listing 9.0 Using header() to Send Raw Headers</title>
20: </head>
21: <body>
22: <h1>
23: <?php echo $message ?>
24: </h1>
25: <p><strong>Guess number:</strong> <?php echo $num_tries ?></p>
26: <form action="<?php echo $_SERVER[PHP_SELF] ?>" method="POST">
27: <p><strong>Type your guess here:</strong>
28: <input type="text" name="guess" value="<?php echo $guess ?>">
29: <input type="hidden" name="num_tries" value="<?php echo $num_tries ?>">
30: <p><input type="submit" value="submit your guess"></p>
31: </form>
32: </body>
33: </html>
```

The `else` clause of our `if` statement on line 11 now causes the browser to request `congrats.html`. We ensure that all output from the current page is aborted with the `exit` statement on line 13, which immediately ends execution and output, whether HTML or PHP.

Sending Mail on Form Submission

You've already seen how to take form responses and print the results to the screen. You're only one step away from sending those responses in an email message, as you'll soon see. Before learning about sending mail, however, read through the next section to make sure that your system is properly configured.

System Configuration for the `mail()` Function

Before you can use the `mail()` function to send mail, a few directives must be set up in the `php.ini` file so that the function works properly. Open `php.ini` with a text editor and look for these lines:

```
[mail function]
; For Win32 only.
SMTP = localhost

; For Win32 only.
sendmail_from = me@localhost.com

; For Unix only.  You may supply arguments as well (default: "sendmail -t -i").
;sendmail_path =
```

If you're using Windows as your Web server platform, the first two directives apply to you. For the `mail()` function to send mail, it must be able to access a valid outgoing mail server. If you plan to use the outgoing mail server of your ISP (in the following example, we use EarthLink), the entry in `php.ini` should look like this:

```
SMTP = mail.earthlink.net
```

The second configuration directive is `sendmail_from`, which is the email address used in the `From` header of the outgoing email. It can be overwritten in the mail script itself, but normally operates as the default value. For example:

```
sendmail_from = youraddress@yourdomain.com
```

A good rule of thumb for Windows users is that whatever outgoing mail server you've set up in your email client on that machine, you should also use as the value of SMTP in `php.ini`.

If your Web server is running on a Linux/Unix platform, you use the `sendmail` functionality of that particular machine. In this case, only the last directive applies to you: `sendmail_path`. The default is `sendmail -t -i`, but if `sendmail` is in an odd place or if you need to specify different arguments, feel free to do so, as in the following example, which does not use real values:

```
sendmail_path = /opt/sendmail -odd –arguments
```

After making any changes to `php.ini` on any platform, you must restart the Web server process for the changes to take effect.

Creating the Form

In Listing 9.10, you see the basic HTML for creating a simple feedback form. This form has an action of listing9.11.php, which we create in the next section. The fields are very simple: Line 7 contains a name field, line 8 contains the return email address field, and line 10 contains the text area for the user's message.

LISTING 9.10   Creating a Simple Feedback Form

```
 1: <HTML>
 2: <HEAD>
 3: <TITLE>E-Mail Form</TITLE>
 4: </HEAD>
 5: <BODY>
 6: <FORM action="listing9.11.php" method="POST">
 7: <p><strong>Your Name:</strong><br> <INPUT type="text" size="25"
    name="name"></p>
 8: <p><strong>Your E-Mail Address:</strong><br> <INPUT type="text" size="25"
    name="email"></p>
 9: <p><strong>Message:</strong><br>
10: <textarea name="message" cols=30 rows=5></textarea></p>
11: <p><INPUT type="submit" value="send"></p>
12: </FORM>
13: </BODY>
14: </HTML>
```

Put these lines into a text file called listing9.10.html, and place this file in your Web server document root. Now access the script with your Web browser, and you should see something like Figure 9.5.

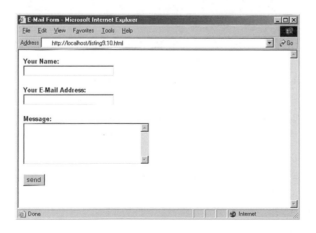

FIGURE 9.5
Form created in
Listing 9.10.

In the next section, you create the script that sends this form to a recipient.

Creating the Script to Send the Mail

The script in Listing 9.11 is only slightly different in concept from the script in Listing 9.4, which simply printed form responses to the screen. In this script, in addition to printing the responses to the screen, you send them to an email address as well.

LISTING 9.11 Sending the Simple Feedback Form

```
 1: <html>
 2: <head>
 3: <title>Listing 9.11 Sending mail from the form in Listing 9.10</title>
 4: </head>
 5: <body>
 6: <?php
 7: echo "<p>Thank you, <b>$_POST[name]</b>, for your message!</p>";
 8: echo "<p>Your e-mail address is: <b>$_POST[email]</b></p>";
 9: echo "<p>Your message was:<br>";
10: echo "$_POST[message] </p>";
11: //start building the mail string
12: $msg = "Name:    $_POST[name]\n";
13: $msg .= "E-Mail:  $_POST[email]\n";
14: $msg .= "Message: $_POST[message]\n";
15: //set up the mail
16: $recipient = "you@yourdomain.com";
17: $subject = "Form Submission Results";
18: $mailheaders = "From: My Web Site <defaultaddress@yourdomain.com> \n";
19: $mailheaders .= "Reply-To: $_POST[email]";
20: //send the mail
21: mail($recipient, $subject, $msg, $mailheaders);
22: ?>
23: </body>
24: </html>
```

The variables you use in lines 7–9 are $_POST[name], $_POST[email], and $_POST[message]—the names of the fields in the form, as part of the $_POST superglobal. That's all well and good for printing the information to the screen, but in this script, you also want to create a string that's sent in email. For this task, you essentially build the email by concatenating strings to form one long message string, using the newline (\n) character to add line breaks where appropriate.

Lines 12 through 14 create the $msg string, which contains the values typed by the user in the form fields. This string is the one sent in the email. Note the use of the concatenation operator (.=) when adding to the variable $msg, in lines 13 and 14.

Lines 16 and 17 are hard-coded variables for the email recipient and the subject of the email message. Replace you@yourdomain.com with your own email address, obviously. If you want to change the subject, feel free!

Lines 18 and 19 set up some mail headers, namely From: and Reply-to: headers. You could put any value in the From: header; this is the information that displays in the From or Sender column of your email application when you receive this mail.

If your outbound mail server is a Windows machine, the \n newline character should be replaced with \r\n.

By the Way

The mail() function takes four parameters: the recipient, the subject, the message, and any additional mail headers. The order of these parameters is shown in line 21, and your script is complete after you close up your PHP block and your HTML elements in lines 22–24.

Put these lines into a text file called listing9.11.php, and place that file in your Web server document root. Use your Web browser and go back to the form, enter some information, and click the submission button. You should see something like Figure 9.6 in your browser.

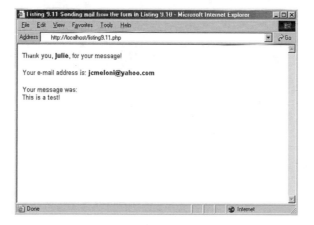

FIGURE 9.6
Sample results from Listing 9.11.

If you then check your email, you should have a message waiting for you. It might look something like Figure 9.7.

FIGURE 9.7
Email sent from
Listing 9.11.

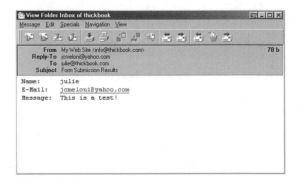

FIGURE 9.7
Email sent from
Listing 9.11.

Formatting Your Mail with HTML

The "trick" to sending HTML-formatted email is not a trick at all. In fact, it only involves writing the actual HTML and modifying the headers sent by the mail() function. In Listing 9.12, a variation of Listing 9.11, you can see the changes made in lines 12–14 and lines 18–19.

LISTING 9.12　Sending the Simple Feedback Form – HTML Version

```
 1: <html>
 2: <head>
 3: <title>Listing 9.12 Sending the Simple Feedback Form – HTML Version</title>
 4: </head>
 5: <body>
 6: <?php
 7: echo "<p>Thank you, <b>$_POST[name]</b>, for your message!</p>";
 8: echo "<p>Your e-mail address is: <b>$_POST[email]</b></p>";
 9: echo "<p>Your message was:<br>";
10: echo "$_POST[message] </p>";
11: //start building the mail string
12: $msg = "<p><strong>Name:</strong> $_POST[name]</p>";
13: $msg .= "<p><strong>E-Mail:</strong> $_POST[email]</p>";
14: $msg .= "<p><strong>Message:</strong> $_POST[message]</p>";
15: //set up the mail
16: $recipient = "you@yourdomain.com";
17: $subject = "Form Submission Results";
18: $mailheaders = "MIME-Version: 1.0\r\n";
19: $mailheaders .= "Content-type: text/html; charset=ISO-8859-1\r\n";
20: $mailheaders .= "From: My Web Site <defaultaddress@yourdomain.com> \n";
21: $mailheaders .= "Reply-To: $_POST[email]";
22: //send the mail
23: mail($recipient, $subject, $msg, $mailheaders);
24: ?>
25: </body>
26: </html>
```

In lines 12–14, the message string now contains HTML code. Additional headers are created in lines 18–19, which set the Mime Version header to 1.0 and the Content-type header to text/html with a character set of ISO-8859-1. When opened in an HTML-enabled mail client, the HTML in the message string will appear as intended, as shown in Figure 9.8.

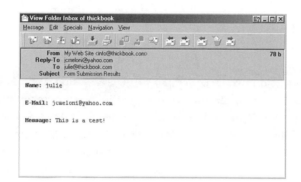

FIGURE 9.8
Email sent from
Listing 9.12.

Working with File Uploads

So far, we've looked at simple form input. However, all popular Web browsers support file uploads, and so, of course, does PHP. In this section, you examine the features that PHP makes available to deal with this kind of input.

Information about the uploaded file becomes available to you in the $_FILES superglobal, which is indexed by the name of the upload field (or fields) in the form. The corresponding value for each of these keys is an associative array. These fields are described in Table 9.1, using fileupload as the name of the form field used for the upload.

TABLE 9.1   File Upload Global Variables

Element	Contains	Example
$_FILES['fileupload']['name']	Original name of uploaded file	test.gif
$_FILES['fileupload']['tmp_name']	Path to temporary file	/tmp/phprDfZvN
$_FILES['fileupload']['size']	Size (in bytes) of uploaded file	6835
$_FILES['fileupload']['type']	MIME type of uploaded file (where given by client)	image/gif

Keep these elements in the back of your mind for a moment, while we create the upload form in the next section.

Creating the File Upload Form

First, we must create the HTML form to handle the upload. HTML forms that include file upload fields must include an ENCTYPE argument:

```
ENCTYPE="multipart/form-data"
```

PHP also works with an optional hidden field that can be inserted before the file upload field. This field must be called MAX_FILE_SIZE and should have a value representing the maximum size in bytes of the file that you're willing to accept. This size cannot override the maximum size set in the upload_max_filesize field in your php.ini file that defaults to 2MB. The MAX_FILE_SIZE field is obeyed at the browser's discretion, so you should rely on the php.ini setting to cap unreasonable uploads. After the MAX_FILE_SIZE field has been entered, you're ready to add the upload field itself. This is simply an INPUT element with a TYPE argument of "file". You can give it any name you want. Listing 9.13 brings all this together into an HTML upload form.

LISTING 9.13   A Simple File Upload Form

```
 1: <html>
 2: <head>
 3: <title>Listing 9.13 A simple file upload form</title>
 4: </head>
 5: <body>
 6: <form action="listing9.14.php" enctype="multipart/form-data" method="POST">
 7: <input type="hidden" name="MAX_FILE_SIZE" value="51200">
 8: <p><strong>File to Upload:</strong> <input type="file" name="fileupload"></p>
 9: <p><input type="submit" value="upload!"></p>
10: </form>
11: </body>
12: </html>
```

As you can see, file uploads are limited to 50KB on line 7, and the name of the file upload field is fileupload, as shown on line 8. Save this listing in a text file called listing9.13.html, and place that file in your Web server document root. Use your Web browser to access this form and you should see something like Figure 9.9.

This form calls the listing9.14.php script, which we will create next.

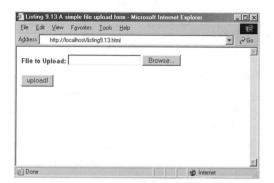

FIGURE 9.9
Form created by
Listing 9.13.

Creating the File Upload Script

If you remember the information regarding the $_FILES superglobal, you have all
the information you need to write a simple file upload script. This script is the
backend for the form created in Listing 9.13.

LISTING 9.14 A File Upload Script

```
 1: <html>
 2: <head>
 3: <title>Listing 9.14 A file upload script</title>
 4: </head>
 5: <body>
 6: <h1>File Upload Results</h1>
 7: <?php
 8: $file_dir = "/path/to/upload/directory";
 9:
10: foreach($_FILES as $file_name => $file_array) {
11:     echo "path: ".$file_array['tmp_name']."<br>\n";
12:     echo "name: ".$file_array['name']."<br>\n";
13:     echo "type: ".$file_array['type']."<br>\n";
14:     echo "size: ".$file_array['size']."<br>\n";
15:
16:     if (is_uploaded_file($file_array['tmp_name'])) {
17:         move_uploaded_file($file_array['tmp_name'],
18:             "$file_dir/$file_array[name]") or die ("Couldn't copy");
19:         echo "file was moved!<br><br>";
20:     }
21: }
22: ?>
23: </body>
24: </html>
```

In Listing 9.14, we first create the $file_dir variable on line 8 to store path infor-
mation. This path should be one that exists on your system, and the Web server
user (for example, httpd, www, nobody) must have write permissions for it.

By the
Way

> The path used in line 8 is a Linux/Unix path. Windows users would use backslash-es, such as \My Documents\.

Line 10 begins a foreach statement that loops through every element in the $_FILES array. A loop is used rather than an if statement to make our script capable of scaling to deal with multiple uploads on the same page. The foreach loop on line 10 stores the upload file's name in the $file_name variable and the file information in the $file_array variable. We can then output the information we have about the upload.

Before moving the uploaded file from its temporary position to the location specified in line 8, first check that it exists. We do so on line 16, using the is_uploaded_file() function. This function accepts a path to an uploaded file and returns true only if the file in question is a valid upload file. This function therefore enhances the security of your scripts.

Assuming that all is well, the file is copied from its temporary home to a new directory on lines 17 and 18. We use another function, move_uploaded_file(), for this purpose. This function copies a file from one place to another, first performing the same security checks as those performed by is_uploaded_file(). The move_uploaded_file() function requires a path to the source file and a path to the destination. It returns true if the move is successful and false if the file isn't a valid upload file or if the file couldn't be found.

Watch
Out!

> Beware of the names of uploaded files. Operating systems such as Mac OS and Windows are pretty relaxed when it comes to file naming, so expect uploaded files to come complete with spaces, quotation marks, and all manner of other unexpected characters. Therefore, it's a good idea to filter filenames.

Put these lines into a text file called listing9.14.php, and place that file in your Web server document root. Use your Web browser to go back to the form, and try to upload a file. If successful, you should see something like Figure 9.10 in your browser.

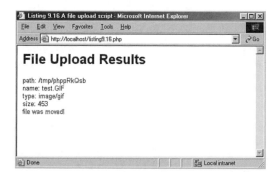

FIGURE 9.10
Sample results
from Listing 9.14.

Summary

Things are really getting exciting now! A few things are still missing, of course. Now that you can get information from the user, it would be nice to be able to do something with it. Write it to a file, perhaps. That's the subject of an upcoming chapter.

Throughout this chapter, you learned how to work with various superglobals and form input. You also learned how to send raw headers to the client to redirect a browser. You learned how to acquire list information from form submissions and how to pass information from script call to script call using hidden fields. Finally, you learned how to send your form results in email, and also how to upload files through your Web browser via a PHP script.

Workshop

The workshop is designed to help you anticipate possible questions, review what you've learned, and begin putting your knowledge into practice.

Quiz

1. Which predefined variable do you use to find the name of the script?

2. Which built-in associative array contains all values submitted as part of a POST request?

3. Which built-in associative array contains all values submitted as part of a file upload?

4. What function do you use to redirect the browser to a new page?

5. What are the four arguments used by the mail() function?

6. On the client side, how do you limit the size of a file that a user can submit via a particular upload form?

Answers

1. The variable $_SERVER['PHP_SELF'] holds the name of the script.

2. The $_POST superglobal.

3. The $_FILES superglobal.

4. The header() function, along with a location.

5. The recipient, the subject, the message string, and additional headers.

6. Use a hidden field called MAX_FILE_SIZE in your form.

Activities

1. Create a calculator script that enables the user to submit two numbers and choose an operation (addition, multiplication, division, or subtraction) to perform on them.

2. Use hidden fields with the script you created in activity 1 to store and display the number of requests that the user submitted.

## CHAPTER 10

Working with User Sessions

PHP contains numerous functions for managing user sessions, which can be stored in the $_SESSION superglobal. Sessions use techniques built into the PHP language, making the act of saving state as easy as calling a function.

In this chapter, you will learn

- ▶ What session variables are and how they work
- ▶ How to start or resume a session
- ▶ How to store variables in a session
- ▶ How to destroy a session
- ▶ How to unset session variables

Session Function Overview

Session functions provide a unique identifier to a user, which can then be used to store and acquire information linked to that ID. When a visitor accesses a session-enabled page, she is either allocated a new identifier or re-associated with one that was already established in a previous access. Any variables that have been associated with the session will become available to your code through the $_SESSION superglobal.

When you use sessions, cookies are used by default to store the session identifier, but you can ensure success for all clients by encoding the session ID into all links in your session-enabled pages.

Session state is usually stored in a temporary file, although you can implement database storage using a function called session_set_save_handler(). The use of session_set_save_handler() is beyond the scope of this book, but you can find more information at http://www.php.net/session-set-save-handler.

Starting a Session

To work with a session, you need to explicitly start or resume that session *unless* you have changed your php.ini configuration file. By default, sessions do not start automatically. If you want to start a session this way, you will have to find the following line in your php.ini file and change the value from 0 to 1 (and restart the Web server):

```
session.auto_start = 0
```

By changing the value of session.auto_start to 1, you ensure that a session is initiated for every PHP document. If you don't change this setting, you need to call the session_start() function in each script.

After a session is started, you instantly have access to the user's session ID via the session_id() function. session_id() allows you to either set or get a session ID. Listing 10.1 starts a session and prints the session ID to the browser.

LISTING 10.1   Starting or Resuming a Session

```
 1: <?php
 2: session_start();
 3: ?>
 4: <html>
 5: <head>
 6: <title>Listing 10.1 Starting or resuming a session</title>
 7: </head>
 8: <body>
 9: <?php
10: echo "<p>Your session ID is ".session_id()."</p>";
11: ?>
12: </body>
13: </html>
```

When this script is run for the first time from a browser, a session ID is generated by the session_start() function call on line 2. If the page is later reloaded or revisited, the same session ID is allocated to the user. This action assumes that the user has cookies enabled. For example, when I run this script the first time, the output is

```
Your session ID is fa963e3e49186764b0218e82d050de7b
```

When I reload the page, the output is still

```
Your session ID is fa963e3e49186764b0218e82d050de7b
```

because I have cookies enabled and the session ID still exists.

Because start_session() attempts to set a cookie when initiating a session for the first time, it is imperative that you call this function before you output anything else at all to the browser. If you do not follow this rule, your session will not be set, and you will likely see warnings on your page.

Sessions remain current as long as the Web browser is active. When the user restarts the browser, the cookie is no longer stored. You can change this behavior by altering the session.cookie_lifetime setting in your php.ini file. The default value is 0, but you can set an expiry period in seconds.

Working with Session Variables

Accessing a unique session identifier in each of your PHP documents is only the start of session functionality. When a session is started, you can store any number of variables in the $_SESSION superglobal and then access them on any session-enabled page.

> If you are using a pre-4.1.x version of PHP, the $_SESSION superglobal is not present, and session functionality is much different. If you cannot upgrade to the current version of PHP, read the PHP manual section on sessions at http://www.php.net/session, which includes notes for previous releases.

By the Way

Listing 10.2 adds two variables into the $_SESSION superglobal: product1 and product2 (lines 10 and 11).

LISTING 10.2   Storing Variables in a Session

```
 1: <?php
 2: session_start();
 3: ?>
 4: <html>
 5: <head>
 6: <title>Listing 10.2 Storing variables in a session</title>
 7: </head>
 8: <body>
 9: <?php
10: $_SESSION[product1] = "Sonic Screwdriver";
11: $_SESSION[product2] = "HAL 2000";
12: echo "The products have been registered.";
13: ?>
14: </body>
15: </html>
```

The magic in Listing 10.2 will not become apparent until the user moves to a new page. Listing 10.3 creates a separate PHP script that accesses the variables stored in the $_SESSION superglobal in Listing 10.2.

LISTING 10.3 Accessing Stored Session Variables

```
 1: <?php
 2: session_start();
 3: ?>
 4: <html>
 5: <head>
 6: <title>Listing 10.3 Accessing stored session variables</title>
 7: </head>
 8: <body>
 9: <?php
10: echo "Your chosen products are:";
11: echo "<ul><li>$_SESSION[product1] <li>$_SESSION[product2]\n</ul>\n";
12: ?>
13: </body>
14: </html>
```

Figure 10.1 shows the output from Listing 10.3. As you can see, we have access to the $_SESSION[product1] and $_SESSION[product2] variables in an entirely new page.

FIGURE 10.1
Accessing stored
session variables.

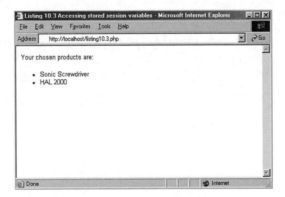

Although not a terribly interesting or useful example, the script does show how to access stored session variables. Behind the scenes, PHP writes information to a temporary file. You can find out where this file is being written on your system by using the session_save_path() function. This function optionally accepts a path to a directory and then writes all session files to it. If you pass it no arguments, it returns a string representing the current directory to which session files are saved. On my system,

```
echo session_save_path();
```

prints /tmp. A glance at my /tmp directory reveals a number of files with names like the following:

```
sess_fa963e3e49186764b0218e82d050de7b
sess_76cae8ac1231b11afa2c69935c11dd95
sess_bb50771a769c605ab77424d59c784ea0
```

Opening the file that matches the session ID I was allocated when I first ran Listing 10.1, I can see how the registered variables have been stored:

```
product1¦s:17:"Sonic Screwdriver";product2¦s:8:"HAL 2000";
```

When a value is placed in the $_SESSION superglobal, PHP writes the variable name and value to a file. This information can be read and the variables resurrected later—as you have already seen. After you add a variable to the $_SESSION superglobal, you can still change its value at any time during the execution of your script, but the altered value won't be reflected in the global setting until you reassign the variable to the $_SESSION superglobal.

The example in Listing 10.2 demonstrates the process of adding variables to the $_SESSION superglobal. This example is not very flexible, however. Ideally, you should be able to register a varying number of values. You might want to let users pick products from a list, for example. In this case, you can use the serialize() function to store an array in your session.

Listing 10.4 creates a form that allows a user to choose multiple products. You should then be able to use session variables to create a rudimentary shopping cart.

LISTING 10.4 Adding an Array Variable to a Session Variable

```
 1: <?php
 2: session_start();
 3: ?>
 4: <html>
 5: <head>
 6: <title>Listing 10.4 Storing an array with a session</title>
 7: </head>
 8: <body>
 9: <h1>Product Choice Page</h1>
10: <?php
11: if (isset($_POST[form_products])) {
12:     if (!empty($_SESSION[products])) {
13:         $products = array_unique(
14:         array_merge(unserialize($_SESSION[products]),
15:         $_POST[form_products]));
16:         $_SESSION[products] = serialize($products);
17:     } else {
18:         $_SESSION[products] = serialize($_POST[form_products]);
19:     }
20:     echo "<p>Your products have been registered!</p>";
```

LISTING 10.4   Continued

```
21: }
22: ?>
23: <form method="POST" action="<?php $_SERVER[PHP_SELF] ?>">
24: <P><strong>Select some products:</strong><br>
25: <select name="form_products[]" multiple size=3>
26: <option value="Sonic Screwdriver">Sonic Screwdriver</option>
27: <option value="Hal 2000">Hal 2000</option>
28: <option value="Tardis">Tardis</option>
29: <option value="ORAC">ORAC</option>
30: <option value="Transporter bracelet">Transporter bracelet</option>
31: </select>
32:
33: <P><input type="submit" value="choose"></p>
34: </form>
35:
36: <p><a href="listing10.5.php">go to content page</a></p>
37: </body>
38: </html>
```

We start or resume a session by calling session_start() on line 2. This should give us access to any previously set session variables. We begin an HTML form on line 23 and, on line 25, create a SELECT element named form_products[], which contains OPTION elements for a number of products. Remember that HTML form elements that allow multiple selections should have square brackets appended to the value of their NAME arguments. This makes the user's choices available in an array.

Within the block of PHP code beginning on line 10, we test for the presence of the $_POST[form_products] array (line 11). If the variable is present, we can assume that the form has been submitted and information has already been stored in the $_SESSION superglobal. We then test for an array called $_SESSION[products] on line 12. If the array exists, it was populated on a previous visit to this script, so we merge it with the $_POST[form_products] array, extract the unique elements, and assign the result back to the $products array (lines 13–15). We then add the $products array to the $_SESSION superglobal on line 16.

Line 36 contains a link to another script, which we will use to demonstrate our access to the products the user has chosen. We create this new script in Listing 10.5.

LISTING 10.5   Accessing Session Variables

```
1: <?php
2: session_start();
3: ?>
4: <html>
5: <head>
6: <title>Listing 10.5 Accessing session variables</title>
```

LISTING 10.5   Continued

```
 7: </head>
 8: <body>
 9: <h1> Content Page</h1>
10: <?php
11: if (isset($_SESSION[products])) {
12:     echo "<strong>Your cart:</strong><ol>";
13:     foreach (unserialize($_SESSION[products]) as $p) {
14:         echo "<li>$p";
15:     }
16:     echo "</ol>";
17: }
18: ?>
19: <p><a href="listing10.4.php">return to product choice page</a></p>
20: </body>
21: </html>
```

Once again, we use `session_start()` to resume the session on line 2. We test for the presence of the `$_SESSION[products]` variable on line 11. If it exists, we unserialize it and loop through it on lines 13–15, printing each of the user's chosen items to the browser. An example is shown in Figure 10.2.

FIGURE 10.2
Accessing an array of session variables.

For a real shopping cart program, of course, you would keep product details in a database and test user input, rather than blindly store and present it, but Listings 10.4 and 10.5 demonstrate the ease with which you can use session functions to access array variables set in other pages.

Passing Session IDs in the Query String

So far you have relied on a cookie to save the session ID between script requests. On its own, this method is not the most reliable way of saving state because you cannot be sure that the browser will accept cookies. You can build in a failsafe, however, by passing the session ID from script to script embedded in a query string. PHP makes a name/value pair available in a constant named SID if a cookie value for a session ID cannot be found. You can add this string to any HTML links in session-enabled pages:

```
<a href="anotherpage.html?<?php echo SID; ?>">Another page</a>
```

It will reach the browser as

```
<a href="anotherpage.html?PHPSESSID=08ecedf79fe34561fa82591401a01da1">Another
page</a>
```

The session ID passed in this way will automatically be recognized in the target page when session_start() is called, and you will have access to session variables in the usual way.

Destroying Sessions and Unsetting Variables

You can use session_destroy() to end a session, erasing all session variables. The session_destroy() function requires no arguments. You should have an established session for this function to work as expected. The following code fragment resumes a session and abruptly destroys it:

```
session_start();
session_destroy();
```

When you move on to other pages that work with a session, the session you have destroyed will not be available to them, forcing them to initiate new sessions of their own. Any registered variables will be lost.

The session_destroy() function does not instantly destroy registered variables, however. They remain accessible to the script in which session_destroy() is called (until it is reloaded). The following code fragment resumes or initiates a session and registers a variable called test, which we set to 5. Destroying the session does not destroy the registered variable.

```
session_start();
$_SESSION[test] = 5;
session_destroy();
print $_SESSION[test]; // prints 5
```

To remove all registered variables from a session, you simply unset the variable:

```
session_start();
$_SESSION[test] = 5;
session_destroy();
unset($_SESSION[test]);
print $_SESSION[test]; // prints nothing.
```

Summary

In this chapter, you looked at different ways of saving state in a stateless protocol. All methods use some combination of cookies and query strings, sometimes combined with the use of files or databases. These approaches all have their benefits and problems.

You learned that a cookie alone is not intrinsically reliable and cannot store much information. On the other hand, it can persist over a long period of time. Approaches that write information to a file or database involve some cost to speed and might become a problem on a popular site. Nonetheless, a simple ID can unlock large amounts of data stored on disk. To ensure that as many users as possible get the benefit of your session-enabled environment, you can use the SID constant to pass a session ID to the server as part of a query string.

With regards to sessions themselves, you learned how to initiate or resume a session with session_start(). When in a session, you learned how to add variables to the $_SESSION superglobal, check that they exist, unset them if you want, and destroy the entire session.

Q&A

Q. *Should I be aware of any pitfalls with session functions?*

A. The session functions are generally reliable. However, remember that cookies cannot be read across multiple domains, so if your project uses more than one domain name on the same server (perhaps as part of an e-commerce environment), you might need to consider disabling cookies for sessions by setting the

`session.use_cookies`

directive to 0 in the `php.ini` file.

Workshop

The workshop is designed to help you anticipate possible questions, review what you've learned, and begin learning how to put your knowledge into practice.

Quiz

1. Which function would you use to start or resume a session?

2. Which function contains the current session's ID?

3. How would you end a session and erase all traces of it for future visits?

4. What does the `SID` constant return?

Answers

1. You can start a session by using the `session_start()` function.

2. You can access the session's ID by using the `session_id()` function.

3. The `session_destroy()` function removes all traces of a session for future requests.

4. If cookies are not available, the `SID` constant contains a name/value pair that can be incorporated in a query string. It will pass the session ID from script request to script request.

Activity

Create a script that uses session functions to remember which pages in your environment the user has visited. Provide the user with a list of links on each page to make it easy for her to retrace her steps.

CHAPTER 11

Working with Files and Directories

Testing, reading, and writing to files are staple activities for any full-featured programming language. PHP is no exception, providing you with functions that make the process straightforward. In this chapter, you will learn

- ► How to include files in your documents
- ► How to test files and directories
- ► How to open a file before working with it
- ► How to read data from files
- ► How to write or append to a file
- ► How to lock a file
- ► How to work with directories

Including Files with `include()`

The `include()` statement enables you to incorporate files into your PHP documents. PHP code in these files can be executed as if it were part of the main document. This can be useful for including library code in multiple pages.

Having created a really useful function, your only option until now would have been to paste it into every document that needs to use it. Of course, if you discover a bug or want to add a feature, you would have to find every page that uses the function to make the change. The `include()` statement can save you from this chore. You can add the function to a single document and, at runtime, read it into any page that needs it. The `include()` statement requires a single argument: a relative path to the file to be included. Listing 11.1 creates a simple PHP script that uses `include()` to incorporate and output the contents of a file.

LISTING 11.1   Using include()

```
 1: <html>
 2: <head>
 3: <title>Listing 11.1 Using include()</title>
 4: </head>
 5: <body>
 6: <?php
 7: include("listing11.2.php");
 8: ?>
 9: </body>
10: </html>
```

The include() statement in Listing 11.1 incorporates the document listing11.2.php, the contents of which you can see in Listing 11.2.

LISTING 11.2   The File Included in Listing 11.1

```
1: I have been included!!
```

Put the contents of Listing 11.1 in a file named listing11.1.php, and the contents of Listing 11.2 in a file named listing11.2.php. Place both files in your Web server document root. When you access listing11.1.php through your Web browser, the output on the screen is

```
I have been included!!
```

This might seem strange to you, given that we've included plain text within a block of PHP code. In fact, the contents of an included file are displayed as text by default. If you want to execute PHP code in an included file, you must enclose it in PHP start and end tags. In Listings 11.3 and 11.4, we amend the previous example so that code is executed in the included file.

LISTING 11.3   Using the include() Statement to Execute PHP in Another File

```
 1: <html>
 2: <head>
 3: <title>Listing 11.3 Using include to execute PHP in another file</title>
 4: </head>
 5: <body>
 6: <?php
 7: include("listing11.4.php");
 8: ?>
 9: </body>
10: </html>
```

LISTING 11.4   An Include File Containing PHP Code

```
1: <?php
2: echo "I have been included!!<BR>";
3: echo "But now I can add up...  4 + 4 = ".(4 + 4);
4: ?>
```

Put the contents of Listing 11.3 in a file named listing11.3.php, and the contents of Listing 11.4 in a file named listing11.4.php. Place both these files in your Web server document root. When you access listing11.3.php through your Web browser, the output on the screen is

I have been included!!

But now I can add up... 4 + 4 = 8

Returning a Value from an Included Document

Included files in PHP can return a value in the same way that functions do. As in a function, using the return statement ends the execution of code within the included file. Additionally, no further HTML is included. In Listings 11.5 and 11.6, we include a file and assign its return value to a variable.

LISTING 11.5   Using include() to Execute PHP and Assign the Return Value

```
 1: <html>
 2: <head>
 3: <title>Listing 11.5 Using include() to execute PHP and
 4:     assign the return value</title>
 5: </head>
 6: <body>
 7: <?php
 8: $addResult = include("listing11.6.php");
 9: echo "The include file returned $addResult";
10: ?>
11: </body>
12: </html>
```

LISTING 11.6   An Include File That Returns a Value

```
1: <?php
2: $retval = ( 4 + 4 );
3: return $retval;
4: ?>
5: This HTML will never be displayed because it comes after a return statement!
```

Put the contents of Listing 11.5 in a file named `listing11.5.php`, and the contents of Listing 11.6 in a file named `listing11.6.php`. Place both of these files in your Web server document root. When you access `listing11.5.php` through your Web browser, the output is

```
The include file returned 8
```

Using `include()` Within Control Structures

You can use an `include()` statement in a conditional statement, and the referenced file is read only if the condition is met. For example, the `include()` statement in the following fragment will never be called:

```
$test = false;
if ($test) {
    include("a_file.txt"); // won't be included
}
```

If you use an `include()` statement within a loop, it's replaced with the contents of the referenced file each time the `include()` statement is called. This content is executed for every call. Listing 11.7 illustrates this concept by using an `include()` statement in a `for` loop. The `include()` statement references a different file for each iteration.

LISTING 11.7   Using `include()` Within a Loop

```
1:  <html>
2:  <head>
3:  <title>Listing 11.7 Using include() within a loop</title>
4:  </head>
5:  <body>
6:  <?php
7:  for ($x = 1; $x<=3; $x++) {
8:      $incfile = "incfile$x".".txt";
9:      echo "Attempting include $incfile<br>";
10:     include("$incfile");
11:     echo "<br>";
12: }
13: ?>
14: </body>
15: </html>
```

When Listing 11.7 is run, it includes the content of three different files: `incfile1.txt`, `incfile2.txt`, and `incfile3.txt`. Assuming that each of these files simply contains a confirmation of its own name, the output should look like Figure 11.1.

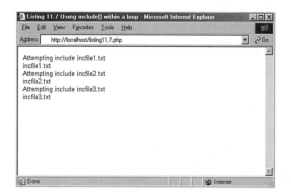

FIGURE 11.1
Output of
Listing 11.7.

include_once()

One of the problems caused by using multiple libraries within your code is the danger of calling include() twice on the same file. This can occur in larger projects when different library files call include() on a common file. Including the same file twice often results in repeated declarations of functions and classes, thereby causing the PHP engine great unhappiness.

The situation is saved by the include_once() statement. include_once() requires the path to an include file and behaves the same way as include() the first time it's called. However, if include_once() is called again for the same file during script execution, the file is *not* included again. This makes include_once() an excellent tool for the creation of reusable code libraries!

The include_path **Directive**

Using include() and include_once() to access libraries can increase the flexibility and reusability of your projects. However, there are still headaches to overcome. Portability in particular can suffer if you hard-code the paths to included files. Imagine that you create a lib directory and reference it throughout your project:

```
include_once("/home/user/bob/htdocs/project4/lib/mylib.inc.php");
```

When you move your project to a new server, you might find that you have to change a hundred or more include paths. You can escape this fate by setting the include_path directive in your php.ini file:

```
include_path    .:/home/user/bob/htdocs/project4/lib/
```

The `include_path` can include as many directories as you want, separated by colons (semicolons in Windows). The order of the items in the `include_path` directive determines the order in which the directories are searched for the named file. The first dot (.) before the first colon indicates "current directory." You can then reference your library file by only its name:

```
include_once("mylib.inc.php");
```

When you move your project, you need to change only the `include_path` directive.

> PHP has both a `require()` statement, which performs a similar function to `include()`, and a `require_once()` statement.
>
> `require()` is executed regardless of a script's flow, and therefore shouldn't be used as part of conditional or loop structures.
>
> A file included as a result of a `require()` statement cannot return a value.

Testing Files

Before you work with a file or directory, it's often a good idea to learn more about it. PHP provides many functions to help you to discover information about files on your system. This section briefly covers some of the most useful functions.

Checking for Existence with `file_exists()`

You can test for the existence of a file with the `file_exists()` function. This function requires a string representing an absolute or relative path to a file that might or might not be there. If the file is found, `file_exists()` returns true; otherwise, it returns false.

```
if (file_exists("test.txt")) {
        echo "The file exists!";
}
```

A File or a Directory?

You can confirm that the entity you're testing is a file, as opposed to a directory, with the `is_file()` function. `is_file()` requires the file path and returns a Boolean value.

```
if (is_file("test.txt")) {
        echo "test.txt is a file!";
}
```

Conversely, you might want to check that the entity you're testing is a directory. You can do this with the is_dir() function. is_dir() requires the path to the directory and returns a Boolean value.

```
if (is_dir("/tmp")) {
        echo "/tmp is a directory";
}
```

Checking the Status of a File

When you know that a file exists, and it's what you expect it to be, you can find out some things that you can do with it. Typically, you might want to read, write to, or execute a file. PHP can help you with all of these operations.

The is_readable() function tells you whether you can read a file. On Unix systems, you might be able to see a file but still be barred from reading its contents. This function accepts the file path as a string and returns a Boolean value.

```
if (is_readable("test.txt")) {
        echo "test.txt is readable";
]
```

The is_writable() function tells you whether you can write to a file. As with is_readable(), the is_writable() function requires the file path and returns a Boolean value.

```
if (is_writable("test.txt")) {
        echo "test.txt is writable";
}
```

The is_executable() function tells you whether you can run a file, relying on either the file's permissions or its extension depending on your platform. It accepts the file path and returns a Boolean value.

```
if (is_executable("test.txt")) {
        echo "test.txt is executable";
}
```

Determining File Size with filesize()

Given the path to a file, the filesize() function attempts to determine and return its size in bytes. It returns false if it encounters problems.

```
echo "The size of test.txt is.. ";
echo filesize("test.txt");
```

Getting Date Information About a File

Sometimes you need to know when a file was last written to or accessed. PHP provides several functions that can provide this information.

You can find out when a file was last accessed with `fileatime()`. This function requires the file path and returns the date that the file was last accessed. To *access* a file means either to read or write to it. Dates are returned from all the date information functions in timestamp—that is, the number of seconds since January 1, 1970. In our examples, we use the `date()` function to translate this into human-readable form.

```
$atime = fileatime("test.txt");
echo "test.txt was last accessed on ";
echo date("D d M Y g:i A", $atime);
// Sample output: Mon 11 Aug 2003 9:54 PM
```

You can discover the modification date of a file with the function `filemtime()`, which requires the file path and returns the date in Unix epoch format. To *modify* a file means to change its contents in some way.

```
$mtime = filemtime("test.txt");
echo "test.txt was last modified on ";
echo date("D d M Y g:i A", $mtime);
// Sample output: Mon 11 Aug 2003 9:54 PM
```

PHP also enables you to test the change time of a document with the `filectime()` function. On Unix systems, the change time is set when a file's contents are modified or changes are made to its permissions or ownership. On other platforms, the `filectime()` returns the creation date.

```
$ctime = filectime("test.txt");
echo "test.txt was last changed on ";
echo date("D d M Y g:i A", $ctime);
// Sample output: Mon 11 Aug 2003 9:54 PM
```

Creating a Function That Performs Multiple File Tests

Listing 11.8 creates a function that brings together the file test functions we've looked at into one script.

LISTING 11.8   A Function to Output the Results of Multiple File Tests

```
1: <html>
2: <head>
3: <title>Listing 11.8 A function to output the results of
4:     multiple file tests</title>
5: </head>
```

LISTING 11.8 Continued

```
 6: <body>
 7: <?php
 8: $file = "test.txt";
 9: outputFileTestInfo($file);
10:
11: function outputFileTestInfo($f) {
12:    if (!file_exists( $f)) {
13:        echo "<p>$f does not exist</p>";
14:        return;
15:    }
16:    echo "<p>$f is ".(is_file($f)?"":"not ")."a file</p>";
17:    echo "<p>$f is ".(is_dir($f)?"":"not ")."a directory</p>";
18:    echo "<p>$f is ".(is_readable($f)?"":"not ")."readable</p>";
19:    echo "<p>$f is ".(is_writable($f)?"":"not ")."writable</p>";
20:    echo "<p>$f is ".(is_executable($f)?"":"not ")."executable</p>";
21:    echo "<p>$f is ".(filesize($f))." bytes</p>";
22:    echo "<p>$f was accessed on ".date( "D d M Y g:i A",fileatime($f))."</p>";
23:    echo "<p>$f was modified on ".date( "D d M Y g:i A",filemtime($f))."</p>";
24:    echo "<p>$f was changed on ".date( "D d M Y g:i A",filectime($f) )."</p>";
25: }
26: ?>
27: </body>
28: </html>
```

If this code were saved to the document root of your Web server and run through your Web browser, the output would look something like Figure 11.2.

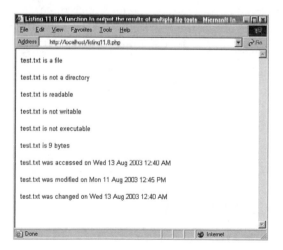

FIGURE 11.2
Output of
Listing 11.8.

Notice that we used the ternary operator as a compact way of working with some of these tests. Let's look at one such test, found in line 16, in more detail:

```
echo "<p>$f is ".(is_file($f)?"":"not ")."a file</p>";
```

We use the is_file() function as the left-side expression of the ternary operator. If it returns true, an empty string is returned. Otherwise, the string "not " is returned. The return value of the ternary expression is added to the string to be printed with concatenation operators. This statement could be made clearer, but less compact, as follows:

```
$is_it = is_file($f)?"":"not ";
echo $f." is ".$is_it." a file";
```

We could, of course, be even clearer with an if statement, but imagine how large the function would become if we used the following:

```
if (is_file($f)) {
        echo "$f is a file<br>";
} else {
        echo "$f is not a file<br>";
}
```

Because the result of these three approaches is the same, the approach you take becomes a matter of preference.

Creating and Deleting Files

If a file does not yet exist, you can create it with the touch() function. Given a string representing a file path, touch() attempts to create an empty file of that name. If the file already exists, the contents aren't disturbed, but the modification date is updated to the time at which the function executed.

```
touch("myfile.txt");
```

You can remove an existing file with the unlink() function. As did the touch() function, unlink() accepts a file path:

```
unlink("myfile.txt");
```

All functions that create, delete, read, write, and modify files on Unix systems require the correct file or directory permissions to be set.

Opening a File for Writing, Reading, or Appending

Before you can work with a file, you must first open it for reading, writing, or both. PHP provides the fopen() function for doing so. fopen() requires a string that contains the file path followed by a string that contains the mode in which the file is to be opened. The most common modes are read (r), write (w), and append (a). fopen() returns a file resource you'll use later to work with the open file. To open a file for reading, you use the following:

```
$fp = fopen("test.txt", "r");
```

You use the following to open a file for writing:

```
$fp = fopen("test.txt", "w");
```

To open a file for *appending* (that is, to add data to the end of a file), you use this:

```
$fp = fopen("test.txt", "a");
```

The fopen() function returns false if the file cannot be opened for any reason. Therefore, it's a good idea to test the function's return value before proceeding to work with it. You can do so with an if statement:

```
if ($fp = fopen("test.txt", "w")) {
   // do something with $fp
}
```

Or you can use a logical operator to end execution if an essential file can't be opened:

```
($fp = fopen("test.txt", "w")) or die ("Couldn't open file, sorry");
```

If the fopen() function returns true, the rest of the expression won't be parsed, and the die() function (which writes a message to the browser and ends the script) is never reached. Otherwise, the right side of the or operator is parsed and the die() function is called.

Assuming that all is well and you go on to work with your open file, you should remember to close it when you finish. You can do so by calling fclose(), which requires the file resource returned from a successful fopen() call as its argument:

```
fclose($fp);
```

Reading from Files

PHP provides a number of functions for reading data from files. These enable you to read by the byte, the line, and even by the character.

Reading Lines from a File with `fgets()` and `feof()`

After you open a file for reading, you often need to access it line by line. To read a line from an open file, you can use `fgets()`, which requires the file resource returned from `fopen()` as an argument. You must also pass `fgets()` an integer as a second argument. The integer argument specifies the number of bytes that the function should read if it doesn't first encounter a line end or the end of the file. The `fgets()` function reads the file until it reaches a newline character (`"\n"`), the number of bytes specified in the length argument, or the end of the file.

```
$line = fgets($fp, 1024); // where $fp is the file resource returned by fopen()
```

Although you can read lines with `fgets()`, you need some way to tell when you reach the end of the file. The `feof()` function does this by returning `true` when the end of the file has been reached and `false` otherwise. `feof()` requires a file resource as its argument.

```
feof($fp); // where $fp is the file resource returned by fopen()
```

You now have enough information to read a file line by line, as shown in Listing 11.9.

LISTING 11.9   Opening and Reading a File Line by Line

```
 1: <html>
 2: <head>
 3: <title>Listing 11.9 Opening and reading a file line by line</title>
 4: </head>
 5: <body>
 6: <?php
 7: $filename = "test.txt";
 8: $fp = fopen($filename, "r") or die("Couldn't open $filename");
 9: while (!feof($fp)) {
10:     $line = fgets($fp, 1024);
11:     echo "$line<br>";
12: }
13: ?>
14: </body>
15: </html>
```

If this code were saved to the document root of your Web server and run through your Web browser, the output would look something like Figure 11.3 (the contents of your sample text file might be different).

We call `fopen()` on line 8 with the name of the file that we want to read, using the or operator to ensure that script execution ends if the file cannot be read. This usually occurs if the file does not exist, or (on a Unix system) if the file's permissions don't allow the script read access to the file. The actual reading takes place in the `while` statement on line 9. The `while` statement's test expression calls `feof()` for each iteration, ending the loop when it returns `true`. In other words, the loop continues until the end of the file is reached. Within the code block, we use `fgets()` on line 10 to extract a line (or 1024 bytes) of the file. We assign the result to `$line` and print it to the browser on line 11, appending a `<BR>` tag for the sake of readability.

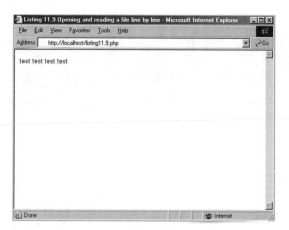

FIGURE 11.3
Output of
Listing 11.9.

Reading Arbitrary Amounts of Data from a File with `fread()`

Rather than reading text by the line, you can choose to read a file in arbitrarily defined chunks. The `fread()` function accepts a file resource as an argument, as well as the number of bytes you want to read. `fread()` returns the amount of data you requested, unless the end of the file is reached first.

```
$chunk = fread($fp, 16);
```

Listing 11.10 amends our previous example so that it reads data in chunks of 16 bytes rather than by the line.

LISTING 11.10   Reading a File with `fread()`

```
1: <html>
2: <head>
3: <title>Listing 11.10 Reading a file with fread()</title>
4: </head>
5: <body>
6: <?php
7: $filename = "test.txt";
```

LISTING 11.10 Continued

```
 8: $fp = fopen($filename, "r") or die("Couldn't open $filename");
 9: while (!feof($fp)) {
10:     $chunk = fread($fp, 16);
11:     echo "$chunk<br>";
12: }
13: ?>
14: </body>
15: </html>
```

If this code were saved to the document root of your Web server and run through your Web browser, the output could look something like Figure 11.4.

FIGURE 11.4
Output of
Listing 11.10.

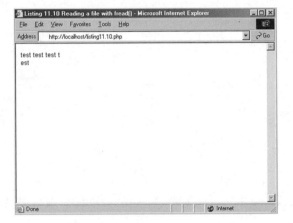

Although `fread()` enables you to define the amount of data acquired from a file, it doesn't let you decide the position from which the acquisition begins. You can set this manually with the `fseek()` function. `fseek()` enables you to change your current position within a file. It requires a file resource and an integer that represents the offset from the start of the file (in bytes) to which you want to jump:

```
fseek($fp, 64);
```

Listing 11.11 uses `fseek()` and `fread()` to output the second half of a file to the browser.

LISTING 11.11 Moving Around a File with `fseek()`

```
1: <html>
2: <head>
3: <title>Listing 11.11 Moving around a file with fseek()</title>
4: </head>
5: <body>
```

LISTING 11.11   Continued

```
 6: <?php
 7: $filename = "test.txt";
 8: $fp = fopen($filename, "r") or die("Couldn't open $filename");
 9: $fsize = filesize($filename);
10: $halfway = (int)($fsize / 2);
11: echo "Halfway point: $halfway <BR>\n";
12: fseek($fp, $halfway);
13: $chunk = fread($fp, ($fsize - $halfway));
14: echo $chunk;
15: ?>
16: </body>
17: </html>
```

If this code were saved to the document root of your Web server and run through
your Web browser, the output could look something like Figure 11.5.

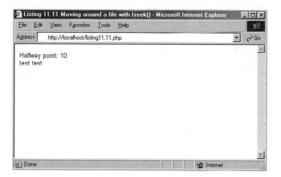

FIGURE 11.5
Output of
Listing 11.11.

We calculate the halfway point of our file by dividing the return value of
filesize() by 2 on line 10. We use this as the second argument to fseek() on
line 12, jumping to the halfway point. Finally, we call fread() on line 13 to
extract the second half of the file and then print the result to the browser.

Reading Characters from a File with fgetc()

The fgetc() function is similar to fgets() except that it returns only a single
character from a file every time it is called. Because a character is always one
byte in size, fgetc() doesn't require a length argument. You must simply pass it a
file resource:

```
$char = fgetc($fp);
```

Listing 11.12 creates a loop that reads the file test.txt one character at a time,
outputting each character to the browser on its own line.

LISTING 11.12   Moving Around a File with `fgetc()`

```
 1: <html>
 2: <head>
 3: <title>Listing 11.12 Moving around a file with fgetc()</title>
 4: </head>
 5: <body>
 6: <?php
 7: $filename = "test.txt";
 8: $fp = fopen($filename, "r") or die("Couldn't open $filename");
 9: while (!feof($fp)) {
10:    $char = fgetc($fp);
11:    echo "$char<BR>";
12: }
13: ?>
14: </body>
15: </html>
```

If this code were saved to the document root of your Web server and run through your Web browser, the output could look something like Figure 10.6.

FIGURE 11.6
Output of
Listing 11.12.

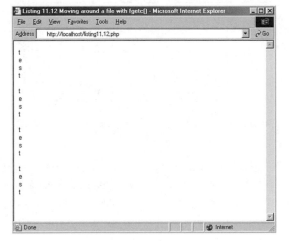

Writing or Appending to a File

The processes for writing to and appending to a file are the same. The difference lies in the `fopen()` call. When you write to a file, you use the mode argument `"w"` when you call `fopen()`:

```
$fp = fopen("test.txt", "w");
```

All subsequent writing occurs from the start of the file. If the file doesn't already exist, it is created. If the file already exists, any prior content is destroyed and replaced by the data you write.

When you append to a file, you use the mode argument "a" in your fopen() call:

```
$fp = fopen("test.txt", "a");
```

Any subsequent writes to your file are added to the existing content, but if you attempt to append content to a nonexistent file, the file is first created.

Writing to a File with fwrite() or fputs()

The fwrite() function accepts a file resource and a string, and then writes the string to the file. fputs() works in exactly the same way.

```
fwrite($fp, "hello world");
fputs($fp, "hello world");
```

Writing to files is as straightforward as that. Listing 11.13 uses fwrite() to print to a file. We then append a further string to the same file using fputs().

LISTING 11.13   Writing and Appending to a File

```
 1: <html>
 2: <head>
 3: <title>Listing 10.13 Writing and appending to a file</title>
 4: </head>
 5: <body>
 6: <?php
 7: $filename = "test.txt";
 8: echo "<p>Writing to $filename ... </p>";
 9: $fp = fopen($filename, "w") or die("Couldn't open $filename");
10: fwrite($fp, "Hello world\n");
11: fclose($fp);
12: echo "<p>Appending to $filename ...</p>";
13: $fp = fopen($filename, "a") or die("Couldn't open $filename");
14: fputs($fp, "And another thing\n");
15: fclose($fp);
16: ?>
17: </body>
18: </html>
```

The screen output of this script, when run from your Web browser, is

```
Writing to test.txt ...

Appending to test.txt ...
```

If you open the `test.txt` file or use `listing11.9.php` to read its contents, you'll find the file now contains:

```
Hello world
```

```
And another thing
```

Locking Files with `flock()`

The techniques you learned for reading and amending files work fine if you're presenting your script to only a single user. In the real world, however, you'd expect many users to access your projects at more or less the same time. Imagine what would happen if two users were to execute a script that writes to one file at the same moment. The file would quickly become corrupt.

PHP provides the `flock()` function to forestall this eventuality. `flock()` locks a file to warn other processes against writing to or reading from that file while the current process is working with it. `flock()` requires a valid file resource and an integer representing the kind of lock you want to set. PHP provides predefined constants for each of the integers you're likely to need. Table 11.1 lists three kinds of locks you can apply to a file.

TABLE 11.1   Integer Arguments to the `flock()` Function

Constant	Integer	Lock Type	Description
LOCK_SH	1	Shared	Allows other processes to read the file but prevents writing (used when reading a file)
LOCK_EX	2	Exclusive	Prevents other processes from either reading from or writing to a file (used when writing to a file)
LOCK_UN	3	Release	Releases a shared or exclusive lock

You should call `flock()` directly after calling `fopen()` and call it again to release the lock before closing the file. If the lock is not released, you will not be able to read from or write to the file.

```
$fp = fopen("test.txt", "a") or die("couldn't open");
flock($fp, LOCK_EX); // exclusive lock
// write to the file
flock($fp, LOCK_UN); // release the lock
fclose($fp);
```

For more information on file locking, see the PHP manual entry for the `flock()` function at `http://www.php.net/flock`.

Did you Know?

Working with Directories

Now that you can test, read, and write to files, let's turn our attention to directories. PHP provides many functions for working with directories. Let's look at how to create, remove, and read them.

Creating Directories with `mkdir()`

The `mkdir()` function enables you to create a directory. The `mkdir()` function requires a string that represents the path to the directory you want to create, and an octal number integer that represents the mode you want to set for the directory. You specify an octal (base 8) number with a leading 0. The mode argument has an effect only on Unix systems. The mode should consist of three numbers between 0 and 7, representing permissions for the directory owner, group, and everyone, respectively. The `mkdir()` function returns `true` if it successfully creates a directory, or `false` if it doesn't. If `mkdir()` fails, it's usually because the containing directory has permissions that preclude processes with the script's user ID from writing. If you're not comfortable setting Unix directory permissions, you should find that one of the following examples fits your needs. Unless you really need your directory to be world-writable, you should probably use 0755, which allows the world to read your directory but not to write to it.

```
mkdir("testdir", 0777); // global read/write/execute permissions
mkdir("testdir", 0755); // world and group: read/execute only
                        // owner: read/write/execute
```

Removing a Directory with `rmdir()`

The `rmdir()` function enables you to remove a directory from the file system if the process running your script has the right to do so and if the directory is empty. The `rmdir()` function requires only a string representing the path to the directory you want to create.

```
rmdir("testdir");
```

Opening a Directory for Reading with opendir()

Before you can read the contents of a directory, you must first obtain a directory resource. You can do so with the opendir() function. The opendir() function requires a string that represents the path to the directory you want to open. The opendir() function returns a directory handle unless the directory isn't present or readable; in that case, it returns false.

```
$dh = opendir("testdir");
```

Reading the Contents of a Directory with readdir()

Just as you use gets() to read a line from a file, you can use readdir() to read a file or directory name from a directory. The readdir() function requires a directory handle and returns a string containing the item name. If the end of the directory is reached, readdir() returns false. Note that readdir() returns only the names of its items, rather than full paths. Listing 11.14 shows the contents of a directory.

LISTING 11.14   Listing the Contents of a Directory with readdir()

```
 1: <html>
 2: <head>
 3: <title>Listing 11.14 Listing the contents
 4: of a directory with readdir()</title>
 5: </head>
 6: <body>
 7: <?php
 8: $dirname = ".";
 9: $dh = opendir($dirname) or die("couldn't open directory");
10:
11: while (!(($file = readdir($dh)) === false ) ) {
12:     if (is_dir("$dirname/$file")) {
13:             echo "(D) ";
14:     }
15:     echo "$file<br>";
16: }
17: closedir($dh);
18: ?>
19: </body>
20: </html>
```

If this code were saved to the document root of your Web server and run through your Web browser, the output could look something like Figure 11.7.

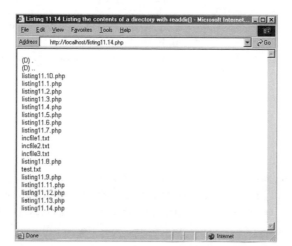

FIGURE 11.7
Output of
Listing 11.14.

We open our directory for reading with the opendir() function on line 9 and use a while statement to loop through each of its elements on line 11. We call readdir() as part of the while statement's test expression and assign its result to the $file variable. Within the body of the while statement, we use the $dirname variable in conjunction with the $file variable to create a full file path, which we can then test on line 12. If the path leads to a directory, we print (D) to the browser on line 13. Finally, we print the filename on line 15.

We used a cautious construction in the test of the while statement. Most PHP programmers (myself included) would use something like the following:

```
while ($file = readdir($dh)) {
        echo "$file<BR>\n";
}
```

The value returned by readdir() is tested. Because any string other than "0" resolves to true, there should be no problem. Imagine, however, a directory that contains four files: 0, 1, 2, and 3. On my system, the output from the preceding code is as follows:

```
.
..
```

When the loop reaches the file named 0, the string returned by readdir() resolves to false, which causes the loop to end. The approach in Listing 10.14 uses === to check that the return value returned by readdir() is not *exactly* equivalent to false. 0 only *resolves* to false in the test, so we circumvent the problem.

By the Way

If you find the ordering of items in a directory listing to be arbitrary, it's because the order is determined by the file system. If you want the items ordered in a specific fashion, you must read the contents into an array, which can then be sorted to your liking and subsequently displayed.

Summary

In this chapter, you learned how to use `include()` to incorporate files into your documents and to execute any PHP code contained in include files. You learned how to use some of PHP's file test functions. You explored functions for reading files by the line, by the character, and in arbitrary chunks. You learned how to write to files, either replacing or appending to existing content. Finally, you learned how to create, remove, and read directories.

Now that we can work with files, we can save and access substantial amounts of data. If we need to look up data from large files, however, our scripts begin to slow down quite considerably. What we need is some kind of database.

Q&A

Q. *Does the* `include()` *statement slow down my scripts?*

A. Because an included file must be opened and parsed by the engine, it adds some overhead. However, the benefits of reusable code libraries often outweigh the relatively low performance overhead.

Q. *Should I always end script execution if a file cannot be opened for writing or reading?*

A. You should always allow for this possibility. If your script absolutely depends on the file you want to work with, you might want to use the `die()` function, writing an informative error message to the browser. In less critical situations, you still need to allow for the failure, perhaps by adding it to a log file.

Workshop

The workshop is designed to help you anticipate possible questions, review what you've learned, and begin putting your knowledge into practice.

Quiz

1. What functions do you use to add library code to the currently running script?

2. What function do you use to find out whether a file is present on your file system?

3. How do you determine the size of a file?

4. What function do you use to open a file for reading or writing?

5. What function do you use to read a line of data from a file?

6. How can you tell when you've reached the end of a file?

7. What function do you use to write a line of data to a file?

8. How do you open a directory for reading?

9. What function do you use to read the name of a directory item after you've opened a directory for reading?

Answers

1. You can use the `require()` or `include()` statement to incorporate PHP files into the current document. You could also use `include_once()` or `require_once()`.

2. You can test for the existence of a file with the `file_exists()` function.

3. The `filesize()` function returns a file's size in bytes.

4. The `fopen()` function opens a file. It accepts the path to a file and a character representing the mode. It returns a file resource.

5. The `fgets()` function reads data up to the buffer size you pass it, the end of the line, or the end of the document, whichever comes first.

6. The `feof()` function returns `true` when the file resource it's passed reaches the end of the file.

7. You can write data to a file with the `fputs()` function.

8. The `opendir()` function enables you to open a directory for reading.

9. The `readdir()` function returns the name of a directory item from an opened directory.

Activities

1. Create a form that accepts a user's first and second name. Create a script that saves this data to a file.

2. Create a script that reads the data file you created in activity 1. In addition to writing its contents to the browser (adding a <BR> tag to each line), print a summary that includes the number of lines in the file and the file's size.

CHAPTER 12

Working with the Server Environment

PHP, Apache, and MySQL are not the only applications on your machine. In this chapter, you'll learn some techniques for running some of those programs from within your PHP scripts. While the examples in this chapter are best suited for Linux/Unix users, the same principles hold true for Windows users.

In this chapter, you'll learn

▶ How to pipe data to and from external applications

▶ How to send shell commands and display results in the browser

Opening Pipes to and from Processes Using popen()

In Chapter 11, "Working with Files and Directories," you learned how to open a file for reading and writing, using the fopen() function. Now, you'll see that you can open a pipe to a process using the popen() function.

The popen() function is used like this:

```
$file_pointer = popen("some command", mode)
```

The *mode* is either r (read) or w (write).

Listing 12.1 is designed to produce an error—it will attempt to open a file for reading, which does not exist.

LISTING 12.1   Using popen() to Read a File

```
1: <?php
2: $file_handle = popen("/path/to/fakefile 2>&1", "r");
3: $read = fread($file_handle, 2096);
4: echo $read;
5: pclose($file_handle);
6: ?>
```

Line 2 utilizes the popen() function, attempting to open a file for reading. In line 3, any error message stored in the $file_handle pointer is read, and printed to the screen in line 4. Finally, line 5 closes the file pointer opened in line 2.

If you save this code as listing12.1.php, place it in your document root and access it with your Web browser, you will see the following error message displayed on your screen:

```
sh: /path/to/fakefile: No such file or directory
```

LISTING 12.2   Using popen() to Read the Output of the Unix who Command

```
1:  <?php
2:  $handle = popen("who", "r");
3:  while (!feof($handle)) {
4:    $line = fgets($handle,1024);
5:    if (strlen($line) >= 1) {
6:        echo "$line <br>";
7:    }
8:  }
9:  pclose($handle);
10: ?>
```

In line 2, a file pointer is returned when we use popen() for reading. Line 3 begins a while loop which will read each line of output from the process and eventually print the line—if it contains information—in line 6. The connection is closed in line 9.

If you save this code as listing12.1.php, place it in your document root, and access it with your Web browser, you may see something like the following (with your actual information, not mine, of course):

```
julie pts/0 Sep 30 21:06 (adsl-67-125-85-212.dsl.snfc21.pacbell.net)
```

Listing 12.3 shows how to use popen() in write mode, to pass data to an external application, in this case column. The goal of the script is to take the elements of a multidimensional array and output them in table format, in an ASCII file.

LISTING 12.3   Using popen() to Pass Data to the Unix column Command

```
1:  <?php
2:  $products = array(
3:              array("HAL 2000", 2, "red"),
4:              array("Tricorder", 3, "blue"),
5:              array("ORAC AI", 1, "pink"),
6:              array("Sonic Screwdriver", 1, "orange")
```

LISTING 12.3   Continued

```
7:                 );
8:
9: $handle = popen("column -lc 3 -s / > /somepath/purchases.txt", "w");
10: foreach ($products as $p) {
11:     fputs($handle, join('/',$p)."\n");
12: }
13: pclose($handle);
14: echo "done";
15: ?>
```

In lines 2–7, a multidimensional array called $products is defined. In line 9, popen() is used in write format to send a command to the column application. The command sends parameters to the column application, telling it to format the input as a three-column table, using / as a field delimiter. The output will be sent to a file called purchases.txt. Lines 10–12 use foreach to loop through the $products array and send each element to the open file pointer. The join() function is used to convert the arrays to a string, with the delimiter appended to it. Line 13 closes the open file pointer, and line 14 prints a status to the screen.

If you save this code as listing12.3.php, place it in your document root, and access it with your Web browser, it should create a file in the specified location. Looking at the file created on my machine, I see the following:

```
HAL 2000          2  red
Tricorder         3  blue
ORAC AI           1  pink
Sonic Screwdriver 1  orange
```

Running Commands with exec()

The exec() function is one of several functions you can use to pass commands to the shell. The exec() function requires a string representing the path to the command you want to run, and optionally accepts an array variable which will contain the output of the command, and a scalar variable which will contain the return value (1 or 0). For example:

```
exec("/path/to/somecommand", $output_array, $return_val);
```

Listing 12.4 uses the exec() function to produce a directory listing with the shell-based ls command.

LISTING 12.4   Using `exec()` and `ls` to Produce a Directory Listing

```
1: <?php
2: exec("ls -al .", $output_array, $return_val);
3: echo "Returned $return_val<br>";
4: foreach ($output_array as $o) {
5:    echo "$o <br>";
6: }
7: ?>
```

In line 2, the `exec()` function issues the `ls` command, with the output of the command placed in the `$output_array` array and the return value placed in the `$return_val` variable. Line 3 simply prints the return value, while the `foreach` loop in lines 4–6 prints out each element in `$output_array`.

If you save this code as `listing12.4.php`, place it in your document root, and access it with your Web browser, you may see something like Figure 12.1 (with your actual information, not mine, of course).

FIGURE 12.1
Output of a script that uses `exec()` to list directory contents.

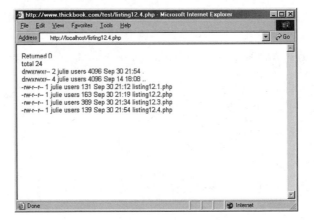

In the previous chapter, you learned to use `opendir()` and `readdir()` to display a directory listing, but this was a simple example of using `exec()` to perform a task using system tools. There will be times when running a command on your system will achieve an effect that may take a great deal of code to reproduce in PHP. For example, you may have already created a shell script or Perl script that performs a complex task in a short period of time; rather than reinvent the wheel using PHP, you can simply use `exec()` to access the existing script. However, remember that calling an external process will always add some amount of additional overhead to your script, in terms of both time and memory usage.

Running Commands with `system()` or `passthru()`

The `system()` function is similar to the `exec()` function in that it launches an external application, and it utilizes a scalar variable for storing a return value:

```
system("/path/to/somecommand", $return_val);
```

The `system()` function differs from `exec()` in that it outputs information directly to the browser, without programmatic intervention. The following snippet of code uses `system()` to print a man page for the man command, formatted with the `<pre></pre>` tag pair:

```
<?php
echo "<pre>";
system("man man ¦ col -b", $return_val);
echo "</pre>";
?>
```

Similarly, the `passthru()` function follows the syntax of the `system()` function, but it behaves differently. When using `passthru()`, any output from the shell command is not buffered on its way back to you; this is suitable for running commands the produce binary data instead of simple text data. An example of this would be to use shell tools to locate an image and send it back to the browser, as seen in Listing 12.5.

LISTING 12.5 Using `passthru()` to Output Binary Data

```
1: <?php
2: if ((isset($_GET[imagename])) && (file_exists($_GET[imagename]))) {
3:     header("Content-type: image/gif");
4:     passthru("giftopnm $_GET[imagename] ¦ pnmscale -xscale .5 -yscale .5 ¦
       ppmtogif");
5: } else {
6:     echo "The image $_GET[imagename] could not be found";
7: }
8: ?>
```

> **By the Way**
>
> The shell utilities used in this script, `giftopnm`, `pnmscale` and `ppmtogif` may or may not be installed on your system. If they are not, don't worry about it; just use this listing to understand the concept of using the `passthru()` function.

This script would be called from HTML like the following:

```
<img src="listing12.5.php?imagename=<?php echo urlencode("test.gif;") ?>">
```

In line 2 of Listing 12.5, the user input is tested to ensure that the file in question (test.gif, according to the HTML snippet) exists. Because the script will be outputting GIF data to the browser, the appropriate header is set on line 3. On line 4, the passthru() function consecutively executes three different commands—giftopnm, pnmscale, and ppmtogif, which scales the image to 50% of its original height and width. The output of the passthru() command—that is, the new image data—is sent to the browser.

By the
~~Way~~

> In this and other system-related examples, you could have used the escapeshellcmd() or escapeshellarg() function to escape elements in the user input. Doing so ensures that the user cannot trick the system into executing arbitrary commands such as deleting important system files or resetting passwords. These functions go around the first instance of the user input, such as
>
> `$new_input = escapeshellcmd($_GET[someinput]);`
>
> You would then reference $new_input throughout the remainder of your script, instead of $_GET[someinput]. Using these two commands, plus ensuring that your script is written so as to only perform tasks *you* want it to do, and not your users, is a way to keep your system secure.

Summary

In this short chapter, you were introduced to various methods of communicating with your system and its external applications. Although PHP is a very fast and robust language, you may find it more cost- and time-effective to simply utilize pre-existing scripts in other languages such as C or Perl. You can access these external applications using popen(), exec(), system(), and passthru() functions.

You learned how to pipe data to a command using popen(), which is useful for applications that accept data from standard input, and when you want to parse data as it is sent to you by an application. You also learned to use exec() and system() to pass commands to the shell and acquire user input. You also learned to use the passthru() function to accept binary data that is the result of a shell command.

Q&A

Q. *Where can I get more information about security on the Web?*

A. One authoritative introduction to Web security is "The World Wide Web Security FAQ" document written by Lincoln Stein, found at http://www.w3.org/Security/Faq/.

Workshop

The workshop is designed to help you anticipate possible questions, review what you've learned, and begin learning how to put your knowledge into practice.

Quiz

1. Which function is used to open a pipe to a process?

2. How can you read data from a process after you have opened a connection? What about writing data?

3. How can you escape user input to make it a little safer before passing it to a shell command?

Answers

1. popen()

2. You can read and write to and from a process just as you can with an open file, namely with feof() and fgets() for reading and fputs() for writing.

3. You can use the escapeshellcmd() or escapeshellarg() functions, if you must accept user input.

CHAPTER 13

Working with Images

A standard installation of PHP has many built-in functions for dynamically creating and manipulating images. With a few adjustments, you can expand the functionality even more. In this chapter, you learn the basics of creating and manipulating images using PHP functions:

- ▶ How to modify PHP to increase image-related functionality
- ▶ How to create a new image
- ▶ How to modify existing images

Understanding the Image-Creation Process

Creating an image with PHP is not like creating an image with a drawing program: There's no pointing and clicking or dragging buckets of color into a predefined space to fill your image. Similarly, there's no Save As functionality, in which your drawing program automatically creates a GIF or JPEG or PNG (and so on) just because you ask it to do so.

Instead, you have to become the drawing application. As the programmer, you must create each step along the way in your PHP script. You are responsible for using the individual PHP functions to define colors, draw and fill shapes, size and resize the image, and save the image as a specific file type. It's not as difficult as it might seem, however, if you understand each step along the way and complete the tasks in order.

A Word About Color

When defining colors in your image-related scripts, you will be using the RGB color system. Using decimal values from 0 to 255 for each of the red, green, and blue (R, G, and B) entries, you can define a specific color. A value of 0 indicates no amount of that specific color, while a value of 255 indicates the highest amount of that color.

For example, the RGB value for pure red is (255,0,0) or the entire allocation of red values, no green, and no blue. Similarly, pure green has a value of (0,255,0), and pure blue has a value of (0,0,255). White, on the other hand, has an RGB value of (255,255,255), while black has an RGB value of (0,0,0). A nice shade of purple has an RGB value of (153,51,153), and a light gray has an RGB value of (204,204,204).

Necessary Modifications to PHP

Beginning with version 4.3.0, the PHP distribution includes a bundled version of Thomas Boutell's GD graphics library. The inclusion of this library eliminates the need to download and install many different third-party libraries, but this library will need to be activated at installation time.

By the Way

> If you cannot install PHP as directed in Chapter 3, "Installing and Configuring PHP," and are stuck with a version of PHP earlier than 4.3.0, you will have to go to http://www.boutell.com/gd/ and download the source of the GD library. Follow the instructions included with that software, and consult its manual for difficulties with installation.

To enable the use of the GD library at installation time, Linux/Unix users must add the following to the configure parameters when preparing to build PHP:

--with-gd

By the Way

> If you download your own version of GD, you must specify the path, as in --with-gd=/path/to/gd.

After running the configure program again, you must go through the make and make install process as you did in Chapter 3. Windows users who want to enable GD simply have to activate php_gd2.dll as an extension in the php.ini file, as you learned in Chapter 3.

When using the GD library, you are limited to working with files in GIF format. However, by installing additional libraries, you can work with JPEG and PNG files as well.

Obtaining Additional Libraries

Working with GIF files might suit your needs perfectly, but if you want to create JPEG or PNG files, you will need to download and install a few libraries, and make some modifications to your PHP installation.

▶ JPEG libraries and information can be found at `ftp://ftp.uu.net/graphics/jpeg/`.

▶ PNG libraries and information can be found at `http://www.libpng.org/pub/png/libpng.html`.

▶ If you are working with PNG files, you should also install the zlib library, found at `http://www.gzip.org/zlib/`.

Follow the instructions at these sites to install the libraries. After installation, Linux/Unix users must again reconfigure and rebuild PHP by first adding the following to the `configure` parameters (assuming that you want to use all three):

```
--with-jpeg-dir=[path to jpeg directory]
--with-png-dir=[path to PNG directory]
--with-zlib-[path to zlib directory]
```

After running the `configure` program again, you need to go through the `make` and `make install` process as you did in Chapter 3. Your libraries should then be activated and ready for use.

Drawing a New Image

The basic PHP function used to create a new image is called `ImageCreate()`, but creating an image is not as simple as just calling the function. Creating an image is a stepwise process and includes the use of several different PHP functions.

Creating an image begins with the `ImageCreate()` function, but all this function does is set aside a canvas area for your new image. The following line creates a drawing area that is 150 pixels wide by 150 pixels high:

```
$myImage = ImageCreate(150,150);
```

With a canvas now defined, you should next define a few colors for use in that new image. The following examples define five such colors, using the `ImageColorAllocate()` function and RGB values:

```
$black = ImageColorAllocate($myImage, 0, 0, 0);
$white = ImageColorAllocate($myImage, 255, 255, 255);
$red   = ImageColorAllocate($myImage, 255, 0, 0);
```

```
$green = ImageColorAllocate($myImage, 0, 255, 0);
$blue = ImageColorAllocate($myImage, 0, 0, 255);
```

In your script, the first color you allocate is used as the background color of the image. In this case, the background color will be black.

Now that you know the basics of setting up your drawing canvas and allocated colors, you can move on to learning to draw shapes and actually output the image to a Web browser.

Drawing Shapes and Lines

Several PHP functions can assist you in drawing shapes and lines on your canvas:

▶ ImageEllipse() is used to draw an ellipse.

▶ ImageArc() is used to draw a partial ellipse.

▶ ImagePolygon() is used to draw a polygon.

▶ ImageRectangle() is used to draw a rectangle.

▶ ImageLine() is used to draw a line.

Using these functions requires a bit of thinking ahead because you must set up the points where you want to start and stop the drawing that occurs. Each of these functions uses x-axis and y-axis coordinates as indicators of where to start drawing on the canvas. You must also define how far along the x-axis and y-axis you want the drawing to occur.

For example, the following line will draw a rectangle on the canvas beginning at point (15,15) and continuing on for 25 pixels horizontally and 40 pixels vertically, so that the lines end at point (40,55). Additionally, the lines will be drawn with the color red, which has already been defined in the variable $red.

```
ImageRectangle($myImage, 15, 15, 40, 55, $red);
```

If you want to draw another rectangle of the same size but with white lines, beginning at the point where the previous rectangle stopped, you would use this code:

```
ImageRectangle($myImage, 40, 55, 65, 95, $white);
```

Listing 13.1 shows the image-creation script so far, with a few more lines added to output the image to the Web browser.

LISTING 13.1   Creating a New Image

```
1:  <?
2:  //create the canvas
3:  $myImage = ImageCreate(150,150);
4:
5:  //set up some colors
6:  $black = ImageColorAllocate($myImage, 0, 0, 0);
7:  $white = ImageColorAllocate($myImage, 255, 255, 255);
8:  $red  = ImageColorAllocate($myImage, 255, 0, 0);
9:  $green = ImageColorAllocate($myImage, 0, 255, 0);
10: $blue = ImageColorAllocate($myImage, 0, 0, 255);
11:
12: //draw some rectangles
13: ImageRectangle($myImage, 15, 15, 40, 55, $red);
14: ImageRectangle($myImage, 40, 55, 65, 95, $white);
15:
16: //output the image to the browser
17: header ("Content-type: image/jpeg");
18: ImageJpeg($myImage);
19:
20: //clean up after yourself
21: ImageDestroy($myImage);
21: ?>
```

Lines 17–18 output the stream of image data to the Web browser by first sending
the appropriate header() function, using the MIME type of the image being created. Then you use the ImageGif(), ImageJpeg(), or ImagePng() functions as appropriate to output the data stream; this example outputs a JPEG. Line 21 uses the
ImageDestroy() function just to clear up the memory used by the ImageCreate()
function.

Save this listing as imagecreate.php, and place it in the document root of your
Web server. When accessed, it should look something like Figure 13.1, but in
color.

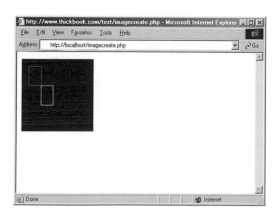

FIGURE 13.1
A canvas with two
drawn rectangles.

Using a Color Fill

The output of Listing 13.1 produced only outlines of rectangles. PHP has image functions designed to fill areas as well:

▶ ImageFilledEllipse() is used to fill an ellipse.

▶ ImageFilledArc() is used to fill a partial ellipse.

▶ ImageFilledPolygon() is used to fill a polygon.

▶ ImageFilledRectangle() is used to fill a rectangle.

These functions are used just like their nonfill counterparts. In Listing 13.2, the nonfill functions are replaced with functions designed to fill an area.

LISTING 13.2   Creating a New Image with Color Fills

```
 1: <?
 2: //create the canvas
 3: $myImage = ImageCreate(150,150);
 4:
 5: //set up some colors
 6: $black = ImageColorAllocate($myImage, 0, 0, 0);
 7: $white = ImageColorAllocate($myImage, 255, 255, 255);
 8: $red  = ImageColorAllocate($myImage, 255, 0, 0);
 9: $green = ImageColorAllocate($myImage, 0, 255, 0);
10: $blue = ImageColorAllocate($myImage, 0, 0, 255);
11:
12: //draw some rectangles
13: ImageFilledRectangle($myImage, 15, 15, 40, 55, $red);
14: ImageFilledRectangle($myImage, 40, 55, 65, 95, $white);
15:
16: //output the image to the browser
17: header ("Content-type: image/jpeg");
18: ImageJpeg($myImage);
19:
20: //clean up after yourself
21: ImageDestroy($myImage);
21: ?>
```

Save this listing as imagecreatefill.php, and place it in the document root of your Web server. When accessed, it should look something like Figure 13.2, but in color.

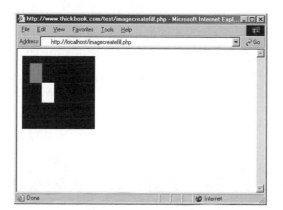

FIGURE 13.2
A canvas with two
drawn and filled
rectangles.

Getting Fancy with Pie Charts

The previous examples were a little boring, but they introduced you to the process of creating images—define the canvas, define the colors, and then draw and fill. You can use this same sequence of events to expand your scripts to create charts and graphs, using either static or dynamic data for the data points. Listing 13.3 draws a basic pie chart.

LISTING 13.3   A Basic Pie Chart

```
1:  <?
2:  //create the canvas
3:  $myImage = ImageCreate(150,150);
4:
5:  //set up some colors
6:  $white = ImageColorAllocate($myImage, 255, 255, 255);
7:  $red   = ImageColorAllocate($myImage, 255, 0, 0);
8:  $green = ImageColorAllocate($myImage, 0, 255, 0);
9:  $blue  = ImageColorAllocate($myImage, 0, 0, 255);
10:
11: //draw a pie
12: ImageFilledArc($myImage, 50, 50, 100, 50, 0, 90, $red, IMG_ARC_PIE);
13: ImageFilledArc($myImage, 50, 50, 100, 50, 91, 180 , $green, IMG_ARC_PIE);
14: ImageFilledArc($myImage, 50, 50, 100, 50, 181, 360 , $blue, IMG_ARC_PIE);
15:
16: //output the image to the browser
17: header ("Content-type: image/jpeg");
18: ImageJpeg($myImage);
19:
20: //clean up after yourself
21: ImageDestroy($myImage);
22: ?>
```

With the exception of lines 12–14, this script is almost identical to the previous listings. Additionally, the definition of the color black has been removed, leaving the color white as the first to be defined and, therefore, the color of the canvas.

In lines 12–14, the function in use is `ImageFilledArc()`, which has several attributes:

- ▶ The image identifier
- ▶ The partial ellipse centered at x
- ▶ The partial ellipse centered at y
- ▶ The partial ellipse width
- ▶ The partial ellipse height
- ▶ The partial ellipse start point
- ▶ The partial ellipse end point
- ▶ Color
- ▶ Style

Look at line 14 from Listing 13.3:

```
14: ImageFilledArc($myImage, 50, 50, 100, 50, 181, 360 , $blue, IMG_ARC_PIE);
```

This line of code says to begin the arc at point (50,50) and give it a width of 100 and height of 50. The start point (think degrees) is 181, and the end is 360. The arc should be filled with the defined color $blue and should use the IMG_ARC_PIE style. IMG_ARC_PIE is one of several built-in styles that are used in the display; this one says to create a rounded edge. You can learn about all the various styles in the PHP manual, at http://www.php.net/image.

Save this listing as imagecreatepie.php, and place it in the document root of your Web server. When accessed, it should look something like Figure 13.3, but in color.

You can extend the code in Listing 13.3 and give your pie a 3D appearance. To do so, define three more colors for the edge. These colors can be either lighter or darker than the base colors, as long as they provide some contrast. The following examples define lighter colors:

```
$lt_red = ImageColorAllocate($myImage, 255, 150, 150);
$lt_green = ImageColorAllocate($myImage, 150, 255, 150);
$lt_blue = ImageColorAllocate($myImage, 150, 150, 255);
```

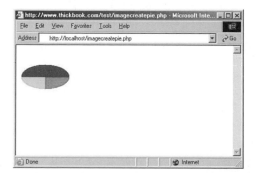

FIGURE 13.3
A simple pie, with slices.

To create the shading effect, you use a for loop to add a series of small arcs at the points (50,60) to (50,51), using the lighter colors as fill colors:

```
for ($i = 60;$i > 50;$i--) {
    ImageFilledArc($myImage, 50, $i, 100, 50, 0, 90, $lt_red, IMG_ARC_PIE);
    ImageFilledArc($myImage, 50, $i, 100, 50, 91, 180, $lt_green, IMG_ARC_PIE);
    ImageFilledArc($myImage, 50, $i, 100, 50, 181, 360, $lt_blue, IMG_ARC_PIE);
}
```

Listing 13.4 shows the code used for a 3D pie:

LISTING 13.4 A 3D Pie Chart

```
 1: <?
 2: //create the canvas
 3: $myImage = ImageCreate(150,150);
 4:
 5: //set up some colors
 6: $white = ImageColorAllocate($myImage, 255, 255, 255);
 7: $red  = ImageColorAllocate($myImage, 255, 0, 0);
 8: $green = ImageColorAllocate($myImage, 0, 255, 0);
 9: $blue = ImageColorAllocate($myImage, 0, 0, 255);
10: $lt_red = ImageColorAllocate($myImage, 255, 150, 150);
11: $lt_green = ImageColorAllocate($myImage, 150, 255, 150);
12: $lt_blue = ImageColorAllocate($myImage, 150, 150, 255);
13:
14: //draw the shaded area
15: for ($i = 60;$i > 50;$i--) {
16:     ImageFilledArc($myImage, 50, $i, 100, 50, 0, 90, $lt_red, IMG_ARC_PIE);
17:     ImageFilledArc($myImage, 50, $i, 100, 50, 91, 180, $lt_green,
    IMG_ARC_PIE);
18:     ImageFilledArc($myImage, 50, $i, 100, 50, 181, 360, $lt_blue,
    IMG_ARC_PIE);
19: }
20:
21: //draw a pie
22: ImageFilledArc($myImage, 50, 50, 100, 50, 0, 90, $red, IMG_ARC_PIE);
23: ImageFilledArc($myImage, 50, 50, 100, 50, 91, 180 , $green, IMG_ARC_PIE);
24: ImageFilledArc($myImage, 50, 50, 100, 50, 181, 360 , $blue, IMG_ARC_PIE);
```

LISTING 13.4   Continued

```
25:
26: //output the image to the browser
27: header ("Content-type: image/jpeg");
28: ImageJpeg($myImage);
29:
30: //clean up after yourself
31: ImageDestroy($myImage);
32: ?>
```

Save this listing as imagecreate3dpie.php, and place it in the document root of your Web server. When accessed, it should look something like Figure 13.4, but in color.

FIGURE 13.4
A 3D pie, with slices.

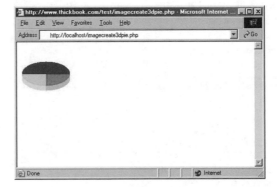

These are just very basic examples that show the power of some of the image-drawing and filling functions. In the next section, you learn how to manipulate existing images.

Modifying Existing Images

The process of creating images from other images follows the same essential steps as creating a new image—the difference lies in what acts as the image canvas. Previously, you created a new canvas using the ImageCreate() function. When creating an image from a new image, you use the ImageCreateFrom*() family of functions.

You can create images from existing GIFs, JPEGs, PNGs, and plenty of other image types. The functions used to create images from these formats are called

ImageCreateFromGif(), ImageCreateFromJpg(), ImageCreateFromPng(), and so forth. In the next example, you can see how easy it is to create a new image from an existing one. The base image is shown in Figure 13.5.

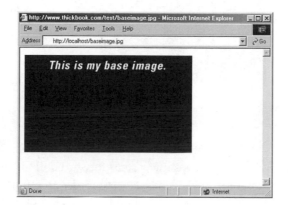

FIGURE 13.5
The base image.

Listing 13.5 shows how to use an existing image as the canvas, which then has ellipses drawn on it.

LISTING 13.5 Creating a New Image from an Existing Image

```
1:  <?
2:  //use existing image as a canvas
3:  $myImage = ImageCreateFromJpeg("baseimage.jpg");
4:
5:  //allocate the color white
6:  $white = ImageColorAllocate($myImage, 255, 255, 255);
7:
8:  //draw on the new canvas
9:  ImageFilledEllipse($myImage, 75, 70, 20, 20, $white);
10: ImageFilledEllipse($myImage, 150, 70, 20, 20, $white);
11: ImageFilledEllipse($myImage, 225, 70, 20, 20, $white);
12:
13: //output the image to the browser
14: header ("Content-type: image/jpeg");
15: ImageJpeg($myImage);
16:
17: //clean up after yourself
18: ImageDestroy($myImage);
19: ?>
```

Save this listing as imagefrombase.php, and place it in the document root of your Web server. When accessed, it should look something like Figure 13.6.

FIGURE 13.6
Drawing on an
existing image.

The next example takes this process a few steps forward and utilizes some different image-modification functions. In this case, the existing images are four PNG images, each with a differently colored triangular slice on a gray background. In Listing 13.6, you stack these images on top of each other and blend them at each step so that the gray background becomes transparent and the image beneath it shows through.

LISTING 13.6   Stacking Images and Making Them Transparent

```
1:  <?
2:  //select an image to start with
3:  $baseimage = ImageCreateFromPng("img1.png");
4:
5:  //loop through images #2 through the end
6:  for($i=2; $i <5; $i++) {
7:      //allocate the transparent color, and stack
8:      $myImage = ImageCreateFromPng("img".$i.".png");
9:      $gray = ImageColorAllocate($myImage, 185, 185, 185);
10:     ImageColorTransparent($myImage, $gray);
11:     ImageCopyMerge($baseimage,$myImage,0,0,0,0,150,150,100);
12: }
13:
14: //output the image to the browser
15: header ("Content-type: image/png");
16: ImagePng($baseimage);
17:
18: //clean up after yourself
19: ImageDestroy($baseimage);
20: ?>
```

In line 3, one of the images is selected to be the base image. In this case, it's img1.png. The for loop in lines 8–11 handles the bulk of the work. Knowing that you have four images and that the first one is already used as the base, three more images are left to be stacked and made transparent. After the new layer is created on line 8, its gray areas are indicated as transparent and it is merged on top of the base image. As the layers are stacked, the base image contains an increasing number of layers, until the total number of four layers is reached. At that point, the image is sent to the browser, in lines 15–16.

Save this listing as imagestacker.php, and place it in the document root of your Web server. When accessed, it should look something like Figure 13.7.

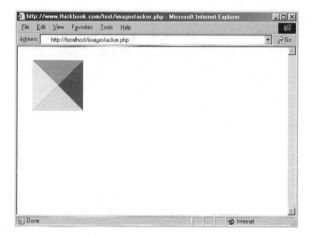

FIGURE 13.7
Stacked transparent images produce a composite.

Summary

This chapter provided you with a brief introduction to what you can do with images and PHP. The "Image Functions" section of the PHP manual, at http://www.php.net/image, is highly recommended not only for a complete list of image-related functions, but also for examples and discussion about their use in your applications.

In this hour, you learned about installing and using additional libraries for working with images—namely, for working with JPEGs and PNGs. You learned the basic steps for creating an image canvas and allocating color, and for drawing and filling shapes. You learned that your drawing canvas can consist of an existing image and that you can merge layers so that a final image is a composite of the layers that have been merged.

Q&A

Q. *How do I use dynamic data to create the slices of a pie chart?*

A. When creating any image, the start points and drawing lengths do not need to be statically indicated—they can be variables whose values are determined by a database, user input, or calculations within the script. For example, this code creates a red, filled arc of 90[dg]:

```
ImageFilledArc($myImage, 50, 50, 100, 50, 0, 90, $red, IMG_ARC_PIE);
```

You could set this up so that the red filled arc at the top of the pie will hold the percentage of the total for May Sales in a variable called `$may_sales_pct`. The line then becomes something like this:

```
ImageFilledArc($myImage, 50, 50, 100, 50, 0, $may_sales_pct, $red,
IMG_ARC_PIE);
```

The number then is filled in from the calculations or database queries in your script. Be sure to add code to verify that all of your arcs add up to 360.

Workshop

The workshop is designed to help you anticipate possible questions, review what you've learned, and begin learning how to put your knowledge into practice.

Quiz

1. What RGB values would you use for pure black and pure white?

2. How do you create a new, blank canvas that is 300 pixels wide and 200 pixels tall?

3. What function is used to draw a polygon? A filled polygon?

Answers

1. (0,0,0) and (255,255,255)

2. `$new_image = ImageCreate(300,200);`

3. `ImagePolygon()` and `ImageFilledPolygon()`

Activity

Instead of creating a pie chart, use your drawing skills to create a bar chart with either vertical or horizontal bars, each 30 pixels wide and filled with the same color, but of different lengths. Ensure that there are 10 pixels of space between each bar.

PART IV

PHP and MySQL Integration

CHAPTER 14

Learning the Database Design Process

In this chapter, you'll learn the thought processes behind designing a relational database. After this theory-focused chapter, you'll jump headlong into creating learning the basic MySQL commands in preparation for integrating MySQL in your own applications.

Topics covered in this chapter are

- ▶ Some advantages to good database design
- ▶ Three types of table relationships
- ▶ How to normalize your database
- ▶ How to implement a good database design process

The Importance of Good Database Design

A good database design is crucial for a high performance application, just like an aerodynamic body is important to a race car. If the car doesn't have smooth lines, it will produce drag and go slower. The same holds true for databases. If a database doesn't have optimized relationships—normalization—it won't be able to perform as efficiently as possible.

Beyond performance is the issue of maintenance. Your database should be easy to maintain. This includes storing a limited amount (if any) of repetitive data. If you have a lot of repetitive data and one instance of that data undergoes a change (such as a name change), that change has to be made for all occurrences of the data. To eliminate duplication and enhance your ability to maintain the data, you would create a table of possible values and use a key to refer to the value. That way, if the value changes names, the change occurs only once—in the master table. The reference remains the same throughout other tables.

For example, suppose you are responsible for maintaining a database of students and the classes in which they're enrolled. If 35 of these students are in the same class, called Advanced Math, this class name would appear 35 times in the table. Now, if the instructor decides to change the name of the class to Mathematics IV, you must change 35 records, to reflect the new name of the class. If the database were designed so that class names appeared in one table and just the class ID number was stored with the student record, you would only have to change 1 record—not 35—in order to update the name change.

The benefits of a well-planned and designed database are numerous, and it stands to reason that the more work you do up front, the less you'll have to do later. A really bad time for a database redesign is after the public launch of the application using it—although it does happen, and the results are costly.

So, before you even start coding an application, spend a lot of time designing your database. Throughout the rest of this chapter, you'll learn more about relationships and normalization, two important pieces to the design puzzle.

Types of Table Relationships

Table relationships come in several forms:

- ▶ One-to-one relationships

- ▶ One-to-many relationships

- ▶ Many-to-many relationships

For example, suppose you have a table called employees that contains each person's Social Security number, name, and the department in which he or she works. Suppose you also have a separate table called departments, containing the list of all available departments, made up of a Department ID and a name. In the employees table, the Department ID field matches an ID found in the departments table. You can see this type of relationship in Figure 14.1. The PK next to the field name indicates the primary key.

In the following sections, you will take a closer look at each of the relationship types.

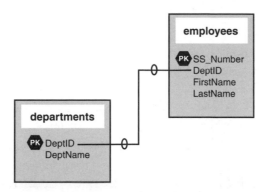

FIGURE 14.1
The employees and departments tables are related through the DeptID key.

One-to-One Relationships

In a one-to-one relationship, a key appears only once in a related table. The employees and departments tables do not have a one-to-one relationship because many employees undoubtedly belong to the same department. A one-to-one relationship exists, for example, if each employee is assigned one computer within a company. Figure 14.2 shows the one-to-one relationship of employees to computers.

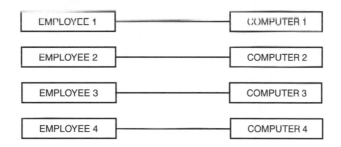

FIGURE 14.2
One computer is assigned to each employee.

The employees and computers tables in your database would look something like Figure 14.3, which represents a one-to-one relationship.

FIGURE 14.3
One-to-one
relationship in the
data model.

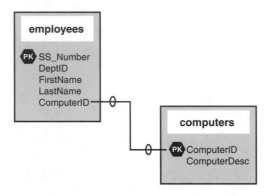

One-to-Many Relationships

In a one-to-many relationship, keys from one table appear multiple times in a related table. The example shown in Figure 14.1, indicating a connection between employees and departments, illustrates a one-to-many relationship. A real-world example would be an organizational chart of the department, as shown in Figure 14.4.

FIGURE 14.4
One department
contains many
employees.

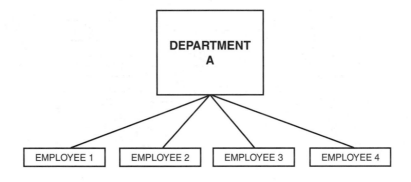

The one-to-many relationship is the most common type of relationship. Another practical example is the use of a state abbreviation in an address database; each state has a unique identifier (CA for California, PA for Pennsylvania, and so on), and each address in the United States has a state associated with it.

If you have eight friends in California and five in Pennsylvania, you will use only two distinct abbreviations in your table. One abbreviation represents a one-to-eight relationship (CA), and the other represents a one-to-five (PA) relationship.

Many-to-Many Relationships

The many-to-many relationship often causes problems in practical examples of normalized databases, so much so that it is common to simply break many-to-many relationships into a series of one-to-many relationships. In a many-to-many relationship, the key value of one table can appear many times in a related table. So far, it sounds like a one-to-many relationship, but here's the curveball: The opposite is also true, meaning that the primary key from that second table can also appear many times in the first table.

Think of such a relationship this way, using the example of students and classes. A student has an ID and a name. A class has an ID and a name. A student usually takes more than one class at a time, and a class always contains more than one student, as you can see in Figure 14.5.

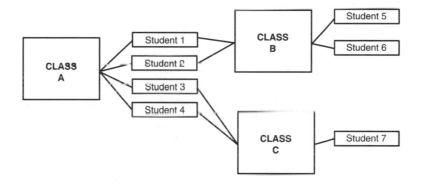

FIGURE 14.5
Students take classes, and classes contain students.

As you can see, this sort of relationship doesn't present an easy method for relating tables. Your tables could look like Figure 14.6, seemingly unrelated.

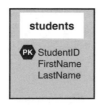
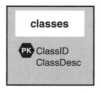

FIGURE 14.6
The students table and the classes table, unrelated.

To make the theoretical many-to-many relationship, you would create an intermediate table, one that sits between the two tables and essentially maps them together. You might build one similar to the table in Figure 14.7.

FIGURE 14.7
The students_
classes_map table
acts as an
intermediary.

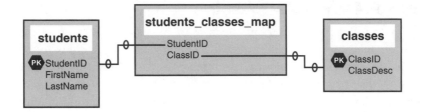

If you take the information in Figure 14.5 and put it into the intermediate table, you would have something like Figure 14.8.

FIGURE 14.8
The students_
classes_map table
populated with
data.

STUDENTID	CLASSID
STUDENT 1	CLASS A
STUDENT 2	CLASS A
STUDENT 3	CLASS A
STUDENT 4	CLASS A
STUDENT 5	CLASS B
STUDENT 6	CLASS B
STUDENT 7	CLASS C
STUDENT 1	CLASS B
STUDENT 2	CLASS B
STUDENT 3	CLASS C
STUDENT 4	CLASS C

As you can see, many students and many classes happily coexist within the students_classes_map table.

With this introduction to the types of relationships, learning about normalization should be a snap.

Understanding Normalization

Normalization is simply a set of rules that will ultimately make your life easier when you're acting as a database administrator. It's the art of organizing your database in such a way that your tables are related where appropriate and flexible for future growth.

The sets of rules used in normalization are called *normal forms*. If your database design follows the first set of rules, it's considered in the *first normal form*. If the first three sets of rules of normalization are followed, your database is said to be in the *third normal form*.

Throughout this chapter, you'll learn about each rule in the first, second, and third normal forms and, we hope, will follow them as you create your own applications. You'll be using a sample set of tables for a students and courses database and taking it to the third normal form.

Problems with the Flat Table

Before launching into the first normal form, you have to start with something that needs to be fixed. In the case of a database, it's the *flat table*. A flat table is like a spreadsheet—it has many, many columns. There are no relationships between multiple tables; all the data you could possibly want is right there in that flat table. This scenario is inefficient and consumes more physical space on your hard drive than a normalized database.

In your students and courses database, assume that you have the following fields in your flat table:

- ▶ StudentName—The name of the student.
- ▶ CourseID1—The ID of the first course taken by the student.
- ▶ CourseDescription1—The description of the first course taken by the student.
- ▶ CourseInstructor1—The instructor of the first course taken by the student.
- ▶ CourseID2—The ID of the second course taken by the student.
- ▶ CourseDescription2—The description of the second course taken by the student.
- ▶ CourseInstructor2—The instructor of the second course taken by the student.
- ▶ Repeat CourseID, CourseDescription, and CourseInstructor columns many more times to account for all the classes students can take during their academic career.

With what you've learned so far, you should be able to identify the first problem area: CourseID, CourseDescription, and CourseInstructor columns are repeated groups.

Eliminating redundancy is the first step in normalization, so next you'll take this flat table to first normal form. If your table remained in its flat format, you could have a lot of unclaimed space and a lot of space being used unnecessarily—not an efficient table design.

First Normal Form

The rules for the first normal form are as follows:

▶ Eliminate repeating information

▶ Create separate tables for related data

If you think about the flat table design with many repeated sets of fields for the students and courses database, you can identify two distinct topics: students and courses. Taking your students and courses database to the first normal form would mean that you create two tables: one for students and one for courses, as shown in Figure 14.9.

FIGURE 14.9
Breaking the flat table into two tables.

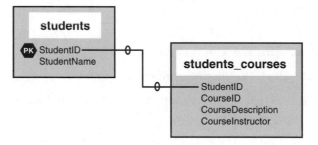

Your two tables now represent a one-to-many relationship of one student to many courses. Students can take as many courses as they want and are not limited to the number of CourseID/CourseDescription/CourseInstructor groupings that existed in the flat table.

The next step is to put the tables into second normal form.

Second Normal Form

The rule for the second normal form is

▶ No non-key attributes depend on a portion of the primary key.

In plain English, this means that if fields in your table are not entirely related to a primary key, you have more work to do. In the students and courses example, you need to break out the courses into their own table and modify the students_courses table.

CourseID, CourseDescription, and CourseInstructor can become a table called courses with a primary key of CourseID. The students_courses table should then just contain two fields: StudentID and CourseID. You can see this new design in Figure 14.10.

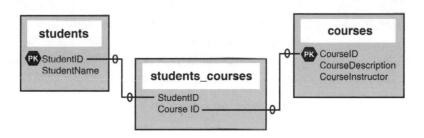

FIGURE 14.10
Taking your tables to second normal form.

This structure should look familiar to you as a many-to-many relationship using an intermediary mapping table. The third normal form is the last form we'll look at, and you'll find it's just as simple to understand as the first two.

Third Normal Form

The rule for the third normal form is

▶ No attributes depend on other non-key attributes.

This rule simply means that you need to look at your tables and see whether you have more fields that can be broken down further and that aren't dependent on a key. Think about removing repeated data and you'll find your answer—instructors. Inevitably, an instructor will teach more than one class. However, CourseInstructor is not a key of any sort. So, if you break out this information and create a separate table purely for the sake of efficiency and maintenance (as shown in Figure 14.11), that's the third normal form.

Third normal form is usually adequate for removing redundancy and allowing for flexibility and growth. The next section will give you some pointers for the thought process involved in database design and where it fits in the overall design process of your application.

FIGURE 14.11
Taking your tables
to third normal
form.

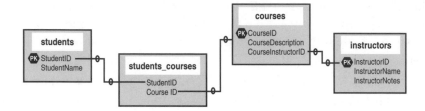

Following the Design Process

The greatest problem in application design is a lack of forethought. As it applies to database-driven applications, the design process must include a thorough evaluation of your database—what it should hold, how data relates to each other, and most importantly, whether it is scalable.

The general steps in the design process are

- ▶ Define the objective
- ▶ Design the data structures (tables, fields)
- ▶ Discern relationships
- ▶ Define and implement business rules
- ▶ Create the application

Creating the application is the last step—not the first! Many developers take an idea for an application, build it, and then go back and try to make a set of database tables fit into it. This approach is completely backward, inefficient, and will cost a lot of time and money.

Before you start any application design process, sit down and talk it out. If you can't describe your application—including the objectives, audience, and target market—then you're not ready to build it, let alone model the database.

After you can describe the actions and nuances of your application to other people and have it make sense to them, you can start thinking about the tables you want to create. Start with big flat tables because after you write them down, your newfound normalization skills will take over. You will be able to find your redundancies and visualize your relationships.

The next step is to do the normalization. Go from flat table to first normal form and so on up to the third normal form if possible. Use paper, pencils, sticky notes, or whatever helps you to visualize the tables and relationships. There's no shame in data modeling on sticky notes until you're ready to create the tables themselves. Plus, using them is a lot cheaper than buying software to do it for you; modeling software ranges from one hundred to several thousands of dollars!

After you have a preliminary data model, look at it from the application's point of view. Or look at it from the point of view of the person using the application you're building. This is the point where you define business rules and see whether your data model will break. An example of a business rule for an online registration application is, "Each user must have one email address, and it must not belong to any other user." If EmailAddress wasn't a unique field in your data model, your model would be broken based on the business rule.

After your business rules have been applied to your data model, only then can application programming begin. You can rest assured that your data model is solid and you will not be programming yourself into a brick wall. The latter event is all too common.

Summary

Following proper database design is the only way your application will be efficient, flexible, and easy to manage and maintain. An important aspect of database design is to use relationships between tables instead of throwing all your data into one long flat file. Types of relationships include one-to-one, one-to-many, and many-to-many.

Using relationships to properly organize your data is called *normalization*. There are many levels of normalization, but the primary levels are the first, second, and third normal forms. Each level has a rule or two that you must follow. Following all the rules helps ensure that your database is well organized and flexible.

To take an idea from inception through to fruition, you should follow a design process. This process essentially says "think before you act." Discuss rules, requirements, and objectives; then create the final version of your normalized tables.

Q&A

Q. *Are there only three normal forms?*

A. No, there are more than three normal forms. Additional forms are the Boyce-Codd normal form, fourth normal form, and fifth normal form/Join-Projection normal form. These forms are not often followed because the benefits of doing so are outweighed by the cost in man-hours and database efficiency.

Workshop

The workshop is designed to help you anticipate possible questions, review what you've learned, and begin learning how to put your knowledge into practice.

Quiz

1. Name three types of data relationships.

2. Because many-to-many relationships are difficult to represent in an efficient database design, what should you do?

Answers

1. One-to-one, one-to-many, many-to-many.

2. Create a series of one-to-many relationships using intermediary mapping tables.

Activity

Explain each of the three normal forms to a person who works with spreadsheets and flat tables.

CHAPTER 15

Learning Basic SQL Commands

Having just learned the basics of the database design process, this chapter provides a primer on the core SQL syntax, which you will use to create and manipulate your MySQL database tables. This is a very hands-on chapter, and it assumes that you are able to issue queries through the MySQL monitor on Windows or Linux/Unix. Alternatively, if you use a GUI to MySQL, this chapter assumes you know the methods for issuing queries through those interfaces.

In this chapter, you will learn

- ▶ The basic MySQL datatypes
- ▶ How to use the CREATE TABLE command to create a table
- ▶ How to use the INSERT command to enter records
- ▶ How to use the SELECT command to retrieve records
- ▶ How to use basic functions, the WHERE clause, and the GROUP BY clause in SELECT expressions
- ▶ How to select from multiple tables, using JOIN
- ▶ How to use the UPDATE and REPLACE commands to modify existing records
- ▶ How to use the DELETE command to remove records
- ▶ How to use string functions built into MySQL
- ▶ How to use date and time functions built into MySQL

Learning the MySQL Data Types

Properly defining the fields in a table is important to the overall optimization of your database. You should use only the type and size of field you really need to use; don't define a field as 10 characters wide if you know you're only going to use 2 characters. These types of fields (or columns) are also referred to as *data types*, after the "type of data" you will be storing in those fields.

MySQL uses many different data types, broken into three categories: numeric, date and time, and string types. Pay close attention because defining the data type is more important than any other part of the table creation process.

Numeric Data Types

MySQL uses all the standard ANSI SQL numeric data types, so if you're coming to MySQL from a different database system, these definitions will look familiar to you. The following list shows the common numeric data types and their descriptions.

By the Way

> The terms *signed* and *unsigned* will be used in the list of numeric data types. If you remember your basic algebra, you'll recall that a signed integer is a positive or negative integer, whereas an unsigned integer is a non-negative integer.

▶ INT—A normal-sized integer that can be signed or unsigned. If signed, the allowable range is from –2147483648 to 2147483647. If unsigned, the allowable range is from 0 to 4294967295. You can specify a width of up to 11 digits.

▶ TINYINT—A very small integer that can be signed or unsigned. If signed, the allowable range is from –128 to 127. If unsigned, the allowable range is from 0 to 255. You can specify a width of up to 4 digits.

▶ SMALLINT—A small integer that can be signed or unsigned. If signed, the allowable range is from –32768 to 32767. If unsigned, the allowable range is from 0 to 65535. You can specify a width of up to 5 digits.

▶ MEDIUMINT—A medium-sized integer that can be signed or unsigned. If signed, the allowable range is from –8388608 to 8388607. If unsigned, the allowable range is from 0 to 16777215. You can specify a width of up to 9 digits.

▶ BIGINT—A large integer that can be signed or unsigned. If signed, the allowable range is from – 9223372036854775808 to 9223372036854775807. If unsigned, the allowable range is from 0 to 18446744073709551615. You can specify a width of up to 11 digits.

▶ FLOAT(M,D)—A floating-point number that cannot be unsigned. You can define the display length (M) and the number of decimals (D). This is not required and will default to 10,2, where 2 is the number of decimals and 10 is the total number of digits (including decimals). Decimal precision can go to 24 places for a FLOAT.

▶ DOUBLE(M,D)—A double precision floating-point number that cannot be unsigned. You can define the display length (M) and the number of decimals (D). This is not required and will default to 16,4, where 4 is the number of decimals. Decimal precision can go to 53 places for a DOUBLE. REAL is a synonym for DOUBLE.

▶ DECIMAL(M,D)—An unpacked floating-point number that cannot be unsigned. In unpacked decimals, each decimal corresponds to one byte. Defining the display length (M) and the number of decimals (D) is required. NUMERIC is a synonym for DECIMAL.

Of all the MySQL numeric data types, you will likely use INT most often. You can run into problems if you define your fields to be smaller than you actually need; for example, if you define an ID field as an unsigned TINYINT, you won't be able to successfully insert that 256th record if ID is a primary key (and thus required).

Date and Time Types

MySQL has several data types available for storing dates and times, and these data types are flexible in their input. In other words, you can enter dates that are not really days, such as February 30—February has only 28 or 29 days, never 30. Also, you can store dates with missing information. If you know that someone was born sometime in November of 1980, you can use 1980-11-00, where "00" would have been for the day, if you knew it.

The flexibility of MySQL's date and time types also means that the responsibility for date checking falls on the application developer. MySQL checks only two elements for validity: that the month is between 0 and 12 and the day is between 0 and 31. MySQL does not automatically verify that the 30th day of the second month (February 30th) is a valid date.

The MySQL date and time datatypes are

▶ DATE—A date in YYYY-MM-DD format, between 1000-01-01 and 9999-12-31. For example, December 30th, 1973 would be stored as 1973-12-30.

▶ DATETIME—A date and time combination in YYYY-MM-DD HH:MM:SS format, between 1000-01-01 00:00:00 and 9999-12-31 23:59:59. For example, 3:30 in the afternoon on December 30th, 1973 would be stored as 1973-12-30 15:30:00.

▶ TIMESTAMP—A timestamp between midnight, January 1, 1970 and sometime in 2037. You can define multiple lengths to the TIMESTAMP field, which directly correlates to what is stored in it. The default length for TIMESTAMP is

14, which stores YYYYMMDDHHMMSS. This looks like the previous DATETIME format, only without the hyphens between numbers; 3:30 in the afternoon on December 30th, 1973 would be stored as 19731230153000. Other definitions of TIMESTAMP are 12 (YYMMDDHHMMSS), 8 (YYYYMMDD), and 6 (YYMMDD).

▶ TIME—Stores the time in HH:MM:SS format.

▶ YEAR(M)—Stores a year in 2-digit or 4-digit format. If the length is specified as 2 (for example, YEAR(2)), YEAR can be 1970 to 2069 (70 to 69). If the length is specified as 4, YEAR can be 1901 to 2155. The default length is 4.

You will likely use DATETIME or DATE more often than any other date- or time-related data type.

String Types

Although numeric and date types are fun, most data you'll store will be in string format. This list describes the common string datatypes in MySQL.

▶ CHAR(M)—A fixed-length string between 1 and 255 characters in length (for example, CHAR(5)), right-padded with spaces to the specified length when stored. Defining a length is not required, but the default is 1.

▶ VARCHAR(M)—A variable-length string between 1 and 255 characters in length; for example, VARCHAR(25). You must define a length when creating a VARCHAR field.

▶ BLOB or TEXT—A field with a maximum length of 65535 characters. BLOBs are "Binary Large Objects" and are used to store large amounts of binary data, such as images or other types of files. Fields defined as TEXT also hold large amounts of data; the difference between the two is that sorts and comparisons on stored data are case sensitive on BLOBs and are not case sensitive in TEXT fields. You do not specify a length with BLOB or TEXT.

▶ TINYBLOB or TINYTEXT—A BLOB or TEXT column with a maximum length of 255 characters. You do not specify a length with TINYBLOB or TINYTEXT.

▶ MEDIUMBLOB or MEDIUMTEXT—A BLOB or TEXT column with a maximum length of 16777215 characters. You do not specify a length with MEDIUMBLOB or MEDIUMTEXT.

▶ LONGBLOB or LONGTEXT—A BLOB or TEXT column with a maximum length of 4294967295 characters. You do not specify a length with LONGBLOB or LONGTEXT.

▶ ENUM—An enumeration, which is a fancy term for *list*. When defining an ENUM, you are creating a list of items from which the value must be selected (or it can be NULL). For example, if you wanted your field to contain "A" or "B" or "C", you would define your ENUM as ENUM ('A', 'B', 'C') and only those values (or NULL) could ever populate that field. ENUMs can have 65535 different values. ENUMs use an index for storing items.

> The SET type is similar to ENUM in that it is defined as a list. However, the SET type is stored as a full value rather than an index of a value, as with ENUMs.

By the Way

You will probably use VARCHAR and TEXT fields more often than other field types, and ENUMs are useful as well.

Learning the Table Creation Syntax

The table creation command requires

▶ Name of the table

▶ Names of fields

▶ Definitions for each field

The generic table creation syntax is

```
CREATE TABLE table_name (column_name column_type);
```

The table name is up to you of course, but should be a name that reflects the usage of the table. For example, if you have a table that holds the inventory of a grocery store, you wouldn't name the table s. You would probably name it something like grocery_inventory. Similarly, the field names you select should be as concise as possible and relevant to the function they serve and data they hold. For example, you might call a field holding the name of an item item_name, not n.

This example creates a generic grocery_inventory table with fields for ID, name, description, price, and quantity:

```
mysql> CREATE TABLE grocery_inventory (
    -> id int not null primary key auto_increment,
    -> item_name varchar (50) not null,
    -> item_desc text,
    -> item_price float not null,
    -> curr_qty int not null
    -> );
Query OK, 0 rows affected (0.02 sec)
```

> The id field is defined as a primary key. You will learn more about keys in later chapters, in the context of creating specific tables as parts of sample applications. By using auto_increment as an attribute of the field, you are telling MySQL to go ahead and add the next available number to the id field for you.

The MySQL server will respond with Query OK each time a command, regardless of type, is successful. Otherwise, an error message will be displayed.

Using the INSERT Command

After you have created some tables, you'll use the SQL command INSERT for adding new records to these tables. The basic syntax of INSERT is

```
INSERT INTO table_name (column list) VALUES (column values);
```

Within the parenthetical list of values, you must enclose strings within quotation marks. The SQL standard is single quotes, but MySQL enables the usage of either single or double quotes. Remember to escape the type of quotation mark used, if it's within the string itself.

> Integers do not require quotation marks around them.

Here is an example of a string where escaping is necessary:

```
O'Connor said "Boo"
```

If you enclose your strings in double quotes, the INSERT statement would look like this:

```
INSERT INTO table_name (column_name) VALUES ("O'Connor said \"Boo\"");
```

If you enclose your strings in single quotes instead, the INSERT statement would look like this:

```
INSERT INTO table_name (column_name) VALUES ('O\'Connor said "Boo"');
```

A Closer Look at INSERT

Besides the table name, there are two main parts of the INSERT statement: the column list and the value list. Only the value list is actually required, but if you omit the column list, you must specifically provide for each column in your value list—in order.

Using the grocery_inventory table as an example, you have five fields: id, item_name, item_desc, item_price, and curr_qty. To insert a complete record, you could use either of these statements:

- A statement with all columns named:

```
insert into grocery_inventory (id, item_name, item_desc, item_price,
curr_qty)
values ('1', 'Apples', 'Beautiful, ripe apples.', '0.25', 1000);
```

- A statement that uses all columns but does not explicitly name them:

```
insert into grocery_inventory values ('2', 'Bunches of Grapes',
'Seedless grapes.', '2.99', 500);
```

Give both of them a try and see what happens. You should get results like this:

```
mysql> insert into grocery_inventory
    -> (id, item_name, item_desc, item_price, curr_qty)
    -> values
    -> (1, 'Apples', 'Beautiful, ripe apples.', 0.25, 1000);
Query OK, 1 row affected (0.01 sec)

mysql> insert into grocery_inventory values (2, 'Bunches of Grapes',
    -> 'Seedless grapes.', 2.99, 500);
Query OK, 1 row affected (0.01 sec)
```

Now for some more interesting methods of using INSERT. Because id is an auto-incrementing integer, you don't have to put it in your value list. However, if there's a value you specifically don't want to list (such as id), you then must list the remaining columns in use. For example, the following statement does not list the columns and also does not give a value for id, and it will produce an error:

```
mysql> insert into grocery_inventory values
    -> ('Bottled Water (6-pack)', '500ml spring water.', 2.29, 250);
ERROR 1136: Column count doesn't match value count at row 1
```

Because you didn't list any columns, MySQL expects all of them to be in the value list, causing an error on the previous statement. If the goal was to let MySQL do the work for you by auto-incrementing the id field, you could use either of these statements:

- A statement with all columns named except id:

```
insert into grocery_inventory (item_name, item_desc, item_price, curr_qty)
values ('Bottled Water (6-pack)', '500ml spring water.', '2.29', 250);
```

- A statement that uses all columns, but does not explicitly name them and indicates a NULL entry for id (so one is filled in for you):

```
insert into grocery_inventory values ('NULL', 'Bottled Water (6-pack)',
'500ml spring water.', 2.29, 250);
```

Go ahead and pick one to use so that your grocery_inventory table has three records in total. It makes no different to MySQL, but as with everything based on user preferences, be consistent in your application development. Consistent structures will be easier for you to debug later because you'll know what to expect.

Using the SELECT Command

SELECT is the SQL command used to retrieve records. This command syntax can be totally simplistic or very complicated. As you become more comfortable with database programming, you will learn to enhance your SELECT statements, ultimately making your database do as much work as possible and not overworking your programming language.

The most basic SELECT syntax looks like this:

```
SELECT expressions_and_columns FROM table_name
[WHERE some_condition_is_true]
[ORDER BY some_column [ASC ¦ DESC]]
[LIMIT offset, rows]
```

Look at the first line:

```
SELECT expressions_and_columns FROM table_name
```

One handy expression is the * symbol, which stands for *everything*. So, to select everything (all rows, all columns) from the grocery_inventory table, your SQL statement would be

```
SELECT * FROM grocery_inventory;
```

Depending on how much data found in the grocery_inventory table, your results will vary, but the results might look something like this:

```
mysql> select * from grocery_inventory;
+---+--------------------+----------------------+----------+--------+
¦ id¦ item_name          ¦ item_desc            ¦ item_price¦ curr_qty¦
+---+--------------------+----------------------+----------+--------+
¦  1¦ Apples             ¦ Beautiful, ripe apples.¦      0.25¦    1000¦
¦  2¦ Bunches of Grapes  ¦ Seedless grapes.     ¦      2.99¦     500¦
¦  3¦ Bottled Water (6-pack)¦ 500ml spring water.  ¦      2.29¦     250¦
+---+--------------------+----------------------+----------+--------+
3 rows in set (0.00 sec)
```

As you can see, MySQL creates a lovely table with the names of the columns along the first row as part of the result set. If you only want to select specific columns, replace the * with the names of the columns, separated by commas.

The following statement selects just the id, item_name, and curr_qty fields from the grocery_inventory table:

```
mysql> select id, item_name, curr_qty from grocery_inventory;
+----+------------------------+----------+
| id | item_name              | curr_qty |
+----+------------------------+----------+
|  1 | Apples                 |     1000 |
|  2 | Bunches of Grapes      |      500 |
|  3 | Bottled Water (6-pack) |      250 |
+----+------------------------+----------+
3 rows in set (0.00 sec)
```

Ordering SELECT Results

Results of SELECT queries are ordered as they were inserted into the table, and shouldn't be relied upon as a meaningful ordering system. If you want to order results a specific way, such as by date, ID, name, and so on, specify your requirements using the ORDER BY clause. In the following statement, results are ordered by item_name:

```
mysql> select id, item_name, curr_qty from grocery_inventory
    -> order by item_name;
+----+------------------------+----------+
| id | item_name              | curr_qty |
+----+------------------------+----------+
|  1 | Apples                 |     1000 |
|  3 | Bottled Water (6-pack) |      250 |
|  2 | Bunches of Grapes      |      500 |
+----+------------------------+----------+
3 rows in set (0.04 sec)
```

> When selecting results from a table without specifying a sort order, the results may or may not be ordered by their key value. This occurs because MySQL reuses the space taken up by previously deleted rows. In other words, if you add records with ID values of 1 through 5, delete the record with ID number 4, and then add another record (ID number 6), the records might appear in the table in this order: 1, 2, 3, 6, 5.

Did you Know?

The default sorting of ORDER BY results is ascending (ASC); strings sort from A to Z, integers start at 0, dates sort from oldest to newest. You can also specify a descending sort, using DESC:

```
mysql> select id, item_name, curr_qty from grocery_inventory
    -> order by item_name desc;
```

```
+----+-------------------------+----------+
¦ id ¦ item_name               ¦ curr_qty ¦
+----+-------------------------+----------+
¦  2 ¦ Bunches of Grapes       ¦      500 ¦
¦  3 ¦ Bottled Water (6-pack)  ¦      250 ¦
¦  1 ¦ Apples                  ¦     1000 ¦
+----+-------------------------+----------+
3 rows in set (0.00 sec)
```

You're not limited to sorting by just one field—you can specify as many fields as you want, separated by a comma. The sorting priority is the order in which you list the fields.

Limiting Your Results

You can use the LIMIT clause to return only a certain number of records from your SELECT query result. There are two requirements when using the LIMIT clause: offset and number of rows. The offset is the starting position, and the number of rows should be self-explanatory.

Suppose you had more than two or three records in the grocery_inventory table, and you wanted to select the ID, name, and quantity of the first three, ordered by curr_qty. In other words, you want to select the three items with the least inventory. The following single-parameter limit will start at the 0 position and go to the third record:

```
mysql> select id, item_name, curr_qty from grocery_inventory
    -> order by curr_qty limit 3;
+----+-------------------------+----------+
¦ id ¦ item_name               ¦ curr_qty ¦
+----+-------------------------+----------+
¦  4 ¦ Bananas                 ¦      150 ¦
¦  3 ¦ Bottled Water (6-pack)  ¦      250 ¦
¦  2 ¦ Bunches of Grapes       ¦      500 ¦
+----+-------------------------+----------+
3 rows in set (0.00 sec)
```

The LIMIT clause can be quite useful in an actual application. For example, you can use the LIMIT clause within a series of SELECT statements to travel through results in steps:

1. SELECT * FROM grocery_inventory ORDER BY curr_qty LIMIT 0, 3;

2. SELECT * FROM grocery_inventory ORDER BY curr_qty LIMIT 3, 3;

3. SELECT * FROM grocery_inventory ORDER BY curr_qty LIMIT 6, 3;

If you specify an offset and number of rows in your query and no results are found, you won't see an error—just an empty result set. For example, if the grocery_inventory table contains only six records, a query with a LIMIT offset of 6 will produce no results:

```
mysql> select id, item_name, curr_qty from grocery_inventory
    -> order by curr_qty limit 6, 3;
Empty set (0.00 sec)
```

In Web-based applications, when lists of data are displayed with links such as "previous 10" and "next 10," it's a safe bet that a LIMIT clause is at work.

Using WHERE in Your Queries

You have learned numerous ways to retrieve particular columns from your tables, but not specific rows. This is when the WHERE clause comes in to play. From the example SELECT syntax, you see that WHERE is used to specify a particular condition:

```
SELECT expressions_and_columns FROM table_name
[WHERE some_condition_is_true]
```

An example would be to retrieve all the records for items with a quantity of 500:

```
mysql> select * from grocery_inventory where curr_qty = 500;
+----+------------------+------------------------+------------+----------+
| id | item_name        | item_desc              | item_price | curr_qty |
+----+------------------+------------------------+------------+----------+
|  2 | Bunches of Grapes | Seedless grapes.       |       2.99 |      500 |
|  5 | Pears            | Anjou, nice and sweet. |        0.5 |      500 |
+----+------------------+------------------------+------------+----------+
2 rows in set (0.00 sec)
```

As shown previously, if you use an integer as part of your WHERE clause, quotation marks are not required. Quotation marks are required around strings, and the same rules apply with regard to escaping characters, as you learned in the section on INSERT.

Using Operators in WHERE Clauses

You've used the equal sign (=) in your WHERE clauses to determine the truth of a condition—that is, whether one thing is equal to another. You can use many types of operators, with comparison operators and logical operators being the most popular types (see Table 15.1).

TABLE 15.1   Basic Comparison Operators and Their Meanings

Operator	Meaning
=	Equal to
!=	Not equal to
<=	Less than or equal to
<	Less than
>=	Greater than or equal to
>	Greater than

There's also a handy operator called BETWEEN, which is useful with integer or data comparisons because it searches for results between a minimum and maximum value. For example

```
mysql> select * from grocery_inventory
    -> where item_price  between 1.50 and 3.00;
+----+----------------------+----------------------+------------+-----------+
| id | item_name            | item_desc            | item_price | curr_qty  |
+----+----------------------+----------------------+------------+-----------+
|  2 | Bunches of Grapes    | Seedless grapes.     |       2.99 |       500 |
|  3 | Bottled Water (6-pack) | 500ml spring water. |       2.29 |       250 |
|  4 | Bananas              | Bunches, green.      |       1.99 |       150 |
+----+----------------------+----------------------+------------+-----------+
3 rows in set (0.00 sec)
```

Other operators include logical operators, which enable you to use multiple comparisons within your WHERE clause. The basic logical operators are AND and OR. When using AND, all comparisons in the clause must be true to retrieve results, whereas using OR allows a minimum of one comparison to be true. Also, you can use the IN operator to specify a list of items that you want to match.

String Comparison Using LIKE

You were introduced to matching strings within a WHERE clause by using = or !=, but there's another useful operator for the WHERE clause comes in to play. From string comparisons: LIKE. This operator uses two characters as wildcards in pattern matching.

▶ %—Matches multiple characters

▶ _—Matches exactly one character

If you want to find records in the grocery_inventory table where the first name of the item starts with the letter A, use

```
mysql> select * from grocery_inventory where item_name like 'A%';
+----+-----------+------------------------+------------+----------+
| id | item_name | item_desc              | item_price | curr_qty |
+----+-----------+------------------------+------------+----------+
|  1 | Apples    | Beautiful, ripe apples.|       0.25 |     1000 |
|  6 | Avocado   | Large Haas variety.    |       0.99 |      750 |
+----+-----------+------------------------+------------+----------+
```

> Unless performing a LIKE comparison on a binary string, the comparison is not case sensitive. You can force a case-sensitive comparison using the BINARY keyword.

By the Way

Selecting from Multiple Tables

You're not limited to selecting only one table at a time. That would certainly make application programming a long and tedious task! When you select from more than one table in one SELECT statement, you are really joining the tables together.

Suppose you have two tables: fruit and color. You can select all rows from each of the two tables, using two separate SELECT statements:

```
mysql> select * from fruit;
+----+-----------+
| id | fruitname |
+----+-----------+
|  1 | apple     |
|  2 | orange    |
|  3 | grape     |
|  4 | banana    |
+----+-----------+
4 rows in set (0.00 sec)

mysql> select * from color;
+----+-----------+
| id | colorname |
+----+-----------+
|  1 | red       |
|  2 | orange    |
|  3 | purple    |
|  4 | yellow    |
+----+-----------+
4 rows in set (0.00 sec)
```

When you want to select from both tables at once, there are a few differences in the syntax of the SELECT statement. First, you must ensure that all the tables you're using in your query appear in the FROM clause of the SELECT statement.

Using the `fruit` and `color` example, if you simply want to select all columns and rows from both tables, you might think you would use the following SELECT statement:

```
mysql> select * from fruit, color;
+----+-----------+----+-----------+
| id | fruitname | id | colorname |
+----+-----------+----+-----------+
|  1 | apple     |  1 | red       |
|  2 | orange    |  1 | red       |
|  3 | grape     |  1 | red       |
|  4 | banana    |  1 | red       |
|  1 | apple     |  2 | orange    |
|  2 | orange    |  2 | orange    |
|  3 | grape     |  2 | orange    |
|  4 | banana    |  2 | orange    |
|  1 | apple     |  3 | purple    |
|  2 | orange    |  3 | purple    |
|  3 | grape     |  3 | purple    |
|  4 | banana    |  3 | purple    |
|  1 | apple     |  4 | yellow    |
|  2 | orange    |  4 | yellow    |
|  3 | grape     |  4 | yellow    |
|  4 | banana    |  4 | yellow    |
+----+-----------+----+-----------+
16 rows in set (0.00 sec)
```

Sixteen rows of repeated information is probably not what you were looking for! What this query did is literally join a row in the `color` table to each row in the `fruit` table. Because there are four records in the `fruit` table and four entries in the `color` table, that's 16 records returned to you.

When you select from multiple tables, you must build proper WHERE clauses to ensure you really get what you want. In the case of the `fruit` and `color` tables, what you really want is to see the `fruitname` and `colorname` records from these two tables where the IDs of each match up. This brings us to the next nuance of the query—how to indicate exactly which field you want when the fields are named the same in both tables!

Simply, you append the table name to the field name, like this:

```
tablename.fieldname
```

So, the query for selecting `fruitname` and `colorname` from both tables where the IDs match would be

```
mysql> select fruitname, colorname from fruit, color where fruit.id = color.id;
+-----------+-----------+
| fruitname | colorname |
+-----------+-----------+
| apple     | red       |
| orange    | orange    |
| grape     | purple    |
| banana    | yellow    |
+-----------+-----------+
4 rows in set (0.00 sec)
```

However, if you attempt to select a column that appears in both tables with the same name, you will get an ambiguity error:

```
mysql> select id, fruitname, colorname from fruit, color
    -> where fruit.id = color.id;
ERROR 1052: Column: 'id' in field list is ambiguous
```

If you mean to select the ID from the fruit table, you would use

```
mysql> select fruit.id, fruitname, colorname from fruit,
    -> color where fruit.id = color.id;
+------+-----------+-----------+
| id   | fruitname | colorname |
+------+-----------+-----------+
|    1 | apple     | red       |
|    2 | orange    | orange    |
|    3 | grape     | purple    |
|    4 | banana    | yellow    |
+------+-----------+-----------+
4 rows in set (0.00 sec)
```

This was a basic example of joining two tables together for use in a single SELECT query. The JOIN keyword is an actual part of SQL, which enables you to build more complex queries.

Using JOIN

Several types of JOINs can be used in MySQL, all of which refer to the order in which the tables are put together and the results are displayed. The type of JOIN used with the fruit and color tables is called an INNER JOIN, although it wasn't written explicitly as such. To rewrite the SQL statement using the proper INNER JOIN syntax, you would use

```
mysql> select fruitname, colorname from fruit
    -> inner join color on fruit.id = color.id;
+-----------+-----------+
| fruitname | colorname |
+-----------+-----------+
| apple     | red       |
| orange    | orange    |
| grape     | purple    |
| banana    | yellow    |
+-----------+-----------+
4 rows in set (0.00 sec)
```

The ON clause replaces the WHERE clause, in this instance telling MySQL to join together the rows in the tables where the IDs match each other. When joining tables using ON clauses, you can use any conditions that you would use in a WHERE clause, including all the various logical and arithmetic operators.

Another common type of JOIN is the LEFT JOIN. When joining two tables with LEFT JOIN, all rows from the first table will be returned, no matter whether there are matches in the second table or not. Suppose you have two tables in an address book, one called master_name, containing basic records, and one called email, containing email records. Any records in the email table would be tied to a particular ID of a record in the master_name table. For example

```
mysql> select name_id, firstname, lastname from master_name;
+---------+-----------+----------+
| name_id | firstname | lastname |
+---------+-----------+----------+
|       1 | John      | Smith    |
|       2 | Jane      | Smith    |
|       3 | Jimbo     | Jones    |
|       4 | Andy      | Smith    |
|       7 | Chris     | Jones    |
|      45 | Anna      | Bell     |
|      44 | Jimmy     | Carr     |
|      43 | Albert    | Smith    |
|      42 | John      | Doe      |
+---------+-----------+----------+
9 rows in set (0.00 sec)

mysql> select name_id, email from email;
+---------+------------------+
| name_id | email            |
+---------+------------------+
|      42 | jdoe@yahoo.com   |
|      45 | annabell@aol.com |
+---------+------------------+
2 rows in set (0.00 sec)
```

Using LEFT JOIN on these two tables, you can see that if a value from the email table doesn't exist, NULL will appear in place of an email address:

```
mysql> select firstname, lastname, email fom master_name
    -> left join email on master_name.name_id = email.name_id;
+-----------+----------+-------------------+
| firstname | lastname | email             |
+-----------+----------+-------------------+
| John      | Smith    | NULL              |
| Jane      | Smith    | NULL              |
| Jimbo     | Jones    | NULL              |
| Andy      | Smith    | NULL              |
| Chris     | Jones    | NULL              |
| Anna      | Bell     | annabell@aol.com  |
| Jimmy     | Carr     | NULL              |
| Albert    | Smith    | NULL              |
| John      | Doe      | jdoe@yahoo.com    |
+-----------+----------+-------------------+
9 rows in set (0.01 sec)
```

A RIGHT JOIN works like LEFT JOIN, but with the table order reversed. In other
words, when using a RIGHT JOIN, all rows from the second table will be returned,
no matter whether there are matches in the first table or not. However, in the case
of the master_name and email tables, there are only two rows in the email table,
whereas there are nine rows in the master_name table. This means that only two
of the nine rows will be returned:

```
mysql> select firstname, lastname, email from master_name
    -> right join email on master_name.name_id = email.name_id;
+-----------+----------+-------------------+
| firstname | lastname | email             |
+-----------+----------+-------------------+
| John      | Doe      | jdoe@yahoo.com    |
| Anna      | Bell     | annabell@aol.com  |
+-----------+----------+-------------------+
2 rows in set (0.00 sec)
```

Several different types of JOINs are available in MySQL, and you've learned about
the most common types. To learn more about JOINs such as CROSS JOIN,
STRAIGHT JOIN and NATURAL JOIN, please visit the MySQL manual at
http://www.mysql.com/doc/J/O/JOIN.html.

Using the UPDATE Command to Modify Records

UPDATE is the SQL command used to modify the contents of one or more columns
in an existing record. The most basic UPDATE syntax looks like this:

```
UPDATE table_name
SET column1='new value',
column2='new value2'
[WHERE some_condition_is_true]
```

The guidelines for updating a record are similar to those used when inserting a record: The data you're entering must be appropriate to the data type of the field, and you must enclose your strings in single or double quotes, escaping where necessary.

For example, assume you have a table called `fruit` containing an ID, a fruit name, and the status of the fruit (`ripe` or `rotten`):

```
mysql> SELECT * FROM fruit;
+----+------------+--------+
| id | fruit_name | status |
+----+------------+--------+
|  1 | apple      | ripe   |
|  2 | pear       | rotten |
|  3 | banana     | ripe   |
|  4 | grape      | rotten |
+----+------------+--------+
4 rows in set (0.00 sec)
```

To update the status of the fruit to `ripe`, use

```
mysql> update fruit set status = 'ripe';
Query OK, 2 rows affected (0.00 sec)
Rows matched: 4   Changed: 2  Warnings: 0
```

Take a look at the result of the query. It was successful, as you can tell from the Query OK message. Also note that only two rows were affected—if you try to set the value of a column to the value it already is, the update won't occur for that column.

The second line of the response shows that four rows were matched, and only two were changed. If you're wondering what matched, the answer is simple: Because you did not specify a particular condition for matching, the match would be all rows.

You must be very careful and use a condition when updating a table, unless you really intend to change all the columns for all records to the same value. For the sake of argument, assume that "grape" is spelled incorrectly in the table, and you want to use UPDATE to correct this mistake. This query would have horrible results:

```
mysql> update fruit set fruit_name = 'grape';
Query OK, 4 rows affected (0.00 sec)
Rows matched: 4   Changed: 4  Warnings: 0
```

When you read the result, you should be filled with dread: 4 of 4 records were changed, meaning your `fruit` table now looks like this:

```
mysql> SELECT * FROM fruit;
+----+------------+--------+
| id | fruit_name | status |
+----+------------+--------+
|  1 | grape      | ripe   |
|  2 | grape      | ripe   |
|  3 | grape      | ripe   |
|  4 | grape      | ripe   |
+----+------------+--------+
4 rows in set (0.00 sec)
```

All your fruit records are now grapes. While attempting to correct the spelling of one field, all fields were changed because no condition was specified! When doling out UPDATE privileges to your users, think about the responsibility you're giving to someone—one wrong move and your entire table could be grapes.

Conditional UPDATEs

Making a conditional UPDATE means that you are using WHERE clauses to match specific records. Using a WHERE clause in an UPDATE statement is just like using a WHERE clause in a SELECT statement. All the same comparison and logical operators can be used, such as equal to, greater than, OR, AND.

Assume your fruit table has not been completely filled with grapes, but instead contains four records, one with a spelling mistake (grappe instead of grape). The UPDATE statement to fix the spelling mistake would be

```
mysql> update fruit set fruit_name = 'grape' where fruit_name = 'grappe';
Query OK, 1 row affected (0.00 sec)
Rows matched: 1  Changed: 1  Warnings: 0
```

In this case, only one row was matched and one row was changed. Your fruit table should be intact, and all fruit names should be spelled properly:

```
mysql> select * from fruit;
+----+------------+--------+
| id | fruit_name | status |
+----+------------+--------+
|  1 | apple      | ripe   |
|  2 | pear       | ripe   |
|  3 | banana     | ripe   |
|  4 | grape      | ripe   |
+----+------------+--------+
4 rows in set (0.00 sec)
```

Using Existing Column Values with UPDATE

Another feature of UPDATE is the capability to use the current value in the record as the base value. For example, go back to the grocery_inventory table used earlier in this chapter:

```
mysql> select * from grocery_inventory;
+----+-----------------------+----------------------+------------+----------+
| id | item_name             | item_desc            | item_price | curr_qty |
+----+-----------------------+----------------------+------------+----------+
|  1 | Apples                | Beautiful, ripe apples.|     0.25 |     1000 |
|  2 | Bunches of Grapes     | Seedless grapes.     |       2.99 |      500 |
|  3 | Bottled Water (6-pack)| 500ml spring water.  |       2.29 |      250 |
|  4 | Bananas               | Bunches, green.      |       1.99 |      150 |
|  5 | Pears                 | Anjou, nice and sweet.|      0.5  |      500 |
|  6 | Avocado               | Large Haas variety.  |       0.99 |      750 |
+----+-----------------------+----------------------+------------+----------+
6 rows in set (0.00 sec)
```

When someone purchases an apple, the inventory table should be updated accordingly. However, you won't know exactly what number to enter in the curr_qty column, just that you sold one. In this case, use the current value of the column and subtract one:

```
mysql> update grocery_inventory set curr_qty = curr_qty - 1 where id = 1;
Query OK, 1 row affected (0.00 sec)
Rows matched: 1  Changed: 1  Warnings: 0
```

This should give you a new value of 999 in the curr_qty column, and indeed it does:

```
mysql> select * from grocery_inventory;
+----+-----------------------+----------------------+------------+----------+
| id | item_name             | item_desc            | item_price | curr_qty |
+----+-----------------------+----------------------+------------+----------+
|  1 | Apples                | Beautiful, ripe apples.|     0.25 |      999 |
|  2 | Bunches of Grapes     | Seedless grapes.     |       2.99 |      500 |
|  3 | Bottled Water (6-pack)| 500ml spring water.  |       2.29 |      250 |
|  4 | Bananas               | Bunches, green.      |       1.99 |      150 |
|  5 | Pears                 | Anjou, nice and sweet.|      0.5  |      500 |
|  6 | Avocado               | Large Haas variety.  |       0.99 |      750 |
+----+-----------------------+----------------------+------------+----------+
6 rows in set (0.00 sec)
```

Using the REPLACE Command

Another method for modifying records is to use the REPLACE command, which is remarkably similar to the INSERT command.

```
REPLACE INTO table_name (column list) VALUES (column values);
```

The REPLACE statement works like this: If the record you are inserting into the table contains a primary key value that matches a record already in the table, the record in the table will be deleted and the new record inserted in its place.

By the Way

> The REPLACE command is a MySQL-specific extension to ANSI SQL. This command mimics the action of a DELETE and re-INSERT of a particular record. In other words, you get two commands for the price of one.

Using the grocery_inventory table, the following command will replace the entry for Apples:

```
mysql> replace into grocery_inventory values
    -> (1, 'Granny Smith Apples', 'Sweet!', '0.50', 1000);
Query OK, 2 rows affected (0.00 sec)
```

In the query result, notice that the result states, 2 rows affected. In this case because id is a primary key that had a matching value in the grocery_inventory table, the original row was deleted and the new row inserted—2 rows affected.

Select the records to verify that the entry is correct, which it is

```
mysql> select * from grocery_inventory;
+----+-----------------------+--------------------+------------+----------+
| id | item_name             | item_desc          | item_price | curr_qty |
+----+-----------------------+--------------------+------------+----------+
|  1 | Granny Smith Apples   | Sweet!             |        0.5 |     1000 |
|  2 | Bunches of Grapes     | Seedless grapes.   |       2.99 |      500 |
|  3 | Bottled Water (6-pack)| 500ml spring water.|       2.29 |      250 |
|  4 | Bananas               | Bunches, green.    |       1.99 |      150 |
|  5 | Pears                 | Anjou, nice and sweet.|    0.5 |      500 |
|  6 | Avocado               | Large Haas variety.|       0.99 |      750 |
+----+-----------------------+--------------------+------------+----------+
6 rows in set (0.00 sec)
```

If you use a REPLACE statement, and the value of the primary key in the new record does not match a value for a primary key already in the table, the record would simply be inserted and only one row would be affected.

Using the DELETE Command

The basic DELETE syntax is

```
DELETE FROM table_name
[WHERE some_condition_is_true]
[LIMIT rows]
```

Notice there is no column specification in the DELETE command—when you use DELETE, the entire record is removed. You might recall the fiasco earlier in this chapter, regarding grapes in the fruit table, when updating a table without specifying a condition caused all records to be updated. You must be similarly careful when using DELETE.

Assuming the structure and data in a table called fruit:

```
mysql> select * from fruit;
+----+------------+--------+
| id | fruit_name | status |
+----+------------+--------+
|  1 | apple      | ripe   |
|  2 | pear       | rotten |
|  3 | banana     | ripe   |
|  4 | grape      | rotten |
+----+------------+--------+
4 rows in set (0.00 sec)
```

This statement will remove all records in the table:

```
mysql> delete from fruit;
Query OK, 0 rows affected (0.00 sec)
```

You can always verify the deletion by attempting to SELECT data from the table:

```
mysql> select * from fruit;
Empty set (0.00 sec)
```

All your fruit is gone.

Conditional DELETE

A conditional DELETE statement, just like a conditional SELECT or UPDATE statement, means you are using WHERE clauses to match specific records. You have the full range of comparison and logical operators available to you, so you can pick and choose which records you want to delete.

A prime example would be to remove all records for rotten fruit from the fruit table:

```
mysql> delete from fruit where status = 'rotten';
Query OK, 2 rows affected (0.00 sec)
```

Two records were deleted, and only ripe fruit remains:

```
mysql> select * from fruit;
+----+------------+--------+
| id | fruit_name | status |
+----+------------+--------+
|  1 | apple      | ripe   |
|  3 | banana     | ripe   |
+----+------------+--------+
2 rows in set (0.00 sec)
```

For users of MySQL 4.0 (and later versions), you can also use ORDER BY clauses in your DELETE statements. Take a look at the basic DELETE syntax with the ORDER BY clause added to its structure:

```
DELETE FROM table_name
[WHERE some_condition_is_true]
[ORDER BY some_column [ASC | DESC]]
[LIMIT rows]
```

At first glance, you might wonder, "Why does it matter in what order I delete records?" The ORDER BY clause isn't for the deletion order, it's for the sorting order of records.

In this example, a table called access_log shows access time and username:

```
mysql> select * from access_log;
+----+---------------------+----------+
| id | date_accessed       | username |
+----+---------------------+----------+
|  1 | 2001-11-06 06:09:13 | johndoe  |
|  2 | 2001-11-06 06:09:22 | janedoe  |
|  3 | 2001-11-06 06:09:39 | jsmith   |
|  4 | 2001-11-06 06:09:44 | mikew    |
+----+---------------------+----------+
4 rows in set (0.00 sec)
```

To remove the oldest record, first use ORDER BY to sort the results appropriately, and then use LIMIT to remove just one record:

```
mysql> delete from access_log order by date_accessed desc limit 1;
Query OK, 1 row affected (0.01 sec)
```

Select the record from access_log and verify that only three records exist:

```
mysql> select * from access_log;
+----+---------------------+----------+
| id | date_accessed       | username |
+----+---------------------+----------+
|  2 | 2001-11-06 06:09:22 | janedoe  |
|  3 | 2001-11-06 06:09:39 | jsmith   |
|  4 | 2001-11-06 06:09:44 | mikew    |
+----+---------------------+----------+
3 rows in set (0.00 sec)
```

Frequently Used String Functions in MySQL

MySQL's built-in string-related functions can be used several ways. You can use functions in SELECT statements without specifying a table to retrieve a result of the function. Or you can use functions to enhance your SELECT results by concatenating two fields to form a new string.

Length and Concatenation Functions

The group of length and concatenation functions focuses on the length of strings and concatenating strings together. Length-related functions include LENGTH(), OCTET_LENGTH(), CHAR_LENGTH(), and CHARACTER_LENGTH(), which do virtually the same thing: count characters in a string.

```
mysql> select length('This is cool!');
+-----------------------+
| LENGTH('This is cool!') |
+-----------------------+
|                    13 |
+-----------------------+

1 row in set (0.00 sec)
```

The fun begins with the CONCAT() function, which is used to concatenate two or more strings:

```
mysql> select concat('My', 'S', 'QL');
+-----------------------+
| CONCAT('My', 'S', 'QL') |
+-----------------------+
| MySQL                 |
+-----------------------+
1 row in set (0.00 sec)
```

Imagine using this function with a table containing names, split into firstname and lastname fields. Instead of using two strings, use two field names to concatenate the firstname and the lastname fields. By concatenating the fields, you reduce the lines of code necessary to achieve the same result in your application:

```
mysql> select concat(firstname, lastname) from table_name;
+----------------------------+
| CONCAT(firstname, lastname) |
+----------------------------+
| JohnSmith                  |
| JaneSmith                  |
| JimboJones                 |
| AndySmith                  |
```

```
¦ ChrisJones                   ¦
¦ AnnaBell                      ¦
¦ JimmyCarr                     ¦
¦ AlbertSmith                   ¦
¦ JohnDoe                       ¦
+------------------------------+
9 rows in set (0.00 sec)
```

If you're using a field name and not a string in a function, don't enclose the field name within quotation marks. If you do, MySQL will interpret the string literally. In the CONCAT() example, you would get the following result:

```
mysql> select concat('firstname', 'lastname') FROM table_name;
+----------------------------------+
¦ CONCAT('firstname', 'lastname') ¦
+----------------------------------+
¦ firstnamelastname               ¦
¦ firstnamelastname               ¦
¦ firstnamelastname               ¦
¦ firstnamelastname               ¦
¦ firstnamelastname               ¦
¦ firstnamelastname               ¦
¦ firstnamelastname               ¦
¦ firstnamelastname               ¦
¦ firstnamelastname               ¦
+----------------------------------+
9 rows in set (0.00 sec)
```

The CONCAT() function would be useful if there were some sort of separator between the names, and that's where the next function comes in: CONCAT_WS().

As you may have figured out, CONTACT_WS() stands for *concatenate with separator*. The separator can be anything you choose, but the following example uses whitespace:

```
mysql> select concat_ws(' ', firstname, lastname) FROM table_name;
+----------------------------------+
¦ CONCAT_WS(' ', firstname, lastname) ¦
+----------------------------------+
¦ John Smith                      ¦
¦ Jane Smith                      ¦
¦ Jimbo Jones                     ¦
¦ Andy Smith                      ¦
¦ Chris Jones                     ¦
¦ Anna Bell                       ¦
¦ Jimmy Carr                      ¦
¦ Albert Smith                    ¦
¦ John Doe                        ¦
+----------------------------------+
9 rows in set (0.00 sec)
```

If you want to shorten the width of your result table, you can use AS to name the custom result field:

```
mysql> select concat_ws(' ', firstname, lastname) AS fullname FROM table_name;
+--------------+
| fullname     |
+--------------+
| John Smith   |
| Jane Smith   |
| Jimbo Jones  |
| Andy Smith   |
| Chris Jones  |
| Anna Bell    |
| Jimmy Carr   |
| Albert Smith |
| John Doe     |
+--------------+
9 rows in set (0.00 sec)
```

Trimming and Padding Functions

MySQL provides several functions for adding and removing extra characters (including whitespace) from strings. The RTRIM() and LTRIM() functions remove whitespace from either the right or left side of a string:

```
mysql> select rtrim('stringstring    ');
+-------------------------+
| RTRIM('stringstring   ') |
+-------------------------+
| stringstring            |
+-------------------------+
1 row in set (0.00 sec)

mysql> select ltrim('  stringstring');
+-----------------------+
| LTRIM('  stringstring') |
+-----------------------+
| stringstring          |
+-----------------------+
1 row in set (0.00 sec)
```

You may have padded strings to trim if the string is coming out of a fixed-width field, and either doesn't need to carry along the additional padding or is being inserted into a varchar or other non–fixed-width field. If your strings are padded with a character besides whitespace, use the TRIM() function to name the characters you want to remove. For example, to remove the leading X characters from the string XXXneedleXXX, use

```
mysql> select trim(leading 'X' from 'XXXneedleXXX');
+-------------------------------------+
| TRIM(LEADING 'X' from 'XXXneedleXXX') |
+-------------------------------------+
| needleXXX                             |
+-------------------------------------+
1 row in set (0.00 sec)
```

Use TRAILING to remove the characters from the end of the string:

```
mysql> select trim(trailing 'X' from 'XXXneedleXXX');
+--------------------------------------+
| TRIM(TRAILING 'X' from 'XXXneedleXXX') |
+--------------------------------------+
| XXXneedle                              |
+--------------------------------------+
1 row in set (0.00 sec)
```

If neither LEADING nor TRAILING is indicated, both are assumed:

```
mysql> select trim('X' from 'XXXneedleXXX');
+----------------------------+
| TRIM('X' from 'XXXneedleXXX') |
+----------------------------+
| needle                       |
+----------------------------+
1 row in set (0.00 sec)
```

Just like RTRIM() and LTRIM() remove padding characters, RPAD() and LPAD() add characters to a string. For example, you may want to add specific identification characters to a string that is part of an order number, in a database used for sales. When you use the padding functions, the required elements are the string, the target length, and the padding character. For example, pad the string needle with the X character until the string is 10 characters long:

```
mysql> select rpad('needle', 10, 'X');
+------------------------+
| RPAD('needle', 10, 'X') |
+------------------------+
| needleXXXX              |
+------------------------+
1 row in set (0.00 sec)

mysql> select lpad('needle', 10, 'X');
+------------------------+
| LPAD('needle', 10, 'X') |
+------------------------+
| XXXXneedle              |
+------------------------+
1 row in set (0.00 sec)
```

Location and Position Functions

The group of location and position functions is useful for finding parts of strings within other strings. The LOCATE() function returns the position of the first occurrence of a given substring within the target string. For example, you can look for a needle in a haystack:

```
mysql> select locate('needle', 'haystackneedlehaystack');
+-------------------------------------------+
¦ LOCATE('needle', 'haystackneedlehaystack') ¦
+-------------------------------------------+
¦                                         9 ¦
+-------------------------------------------+
1 row in set (0.00 sec)
```

The substring needle begins at position 9 in the target string. If the substring cannot be found in the target string, MySQL returns 0 as a result.

> **By the Way**
>
> Unlike position counting within most programming languages, which starts at 0, position counting using MySQL starts at 1.

An extension of the LOCATE() function is to use a third argument for starting position. If you start looking for needle in haystack before position 9, you'll receive a result. Otherwise, because needle starts at position 9, you'll receive a 0 result if you specify a greater starting position:

```
mysql> select locate('needle', 'haystackneedlehaystack',6);
+-------------------------------------------+
¦ LOCATE('needle', 'haystackneedlehaystack',9) ¦
+-------------------------------------------+
¦                                         9 ¦
+-------------------------------------------+
1 row in set (0.00 sec)
```

```
mysql> select locate('needle', 'haystackneedlehaystack',12);
+-------------------------------------------+
¦ LOCATE('needle', 'haystackneedlehaystack',12) ¦
+-------------------------------------------+
¦                                         0 ¦
+-------------------------------------------+
1 row in set (0.00 sec)
```

Substring Functions

If your goal is to extract a substring from a target string, several functions fit the bill. Given a string, starting position, and length, you can use the SUBSTRING()

function. This example gets three characters from the string MySQL, starting at position 2:

```
mysql> select substring("MySQL", 2, 3);
+--------------------------+
| SUBSTRING("MySQL", 2, 3) |
+--------------------------+
| ySQ                      |
+--------------------------+
1 row in set (0.00 sec)
```

If you just want a few characters from the left or right ends of a string, use the LEFT() and RIGHT() functions:

```
mysql> select left("MySQL", 2);
+------------------+
| LEFT("MySQL", 2) |
+------------------+
| My               |
+------------------+
1 row in set (0.00 sec)
```

```
mysql> select right("MySQL", 3);
+-------------------+
| RIGHT("MySQL", 3) |
+-------------------+
| SQL               |
+-------------------+
1 row in set (0.00 sec)
```

One of the many common uses of substring functions is to extract parts of order numbers, to find out who placed the order. In some applications, the system is designed to automatically generate an order number, containing a date, customer identification, and other information. If this order number always follows a particular pattern, such as XXXX-YYYYY-ZZ, you can use substring functions to extract the individual parts of the whole. For example, if ZZ always represents the state to which the order was shipped, you can use the RIGHT() function to extract these characters and report the number of orders shipped to a particular state.

String Modification Functions

Your programming language of choice likely has functions to modify the appearance of strings, but if you can perform the task as part of the SQL statement, all the better.

The MySQL LCASE() and UCASE() functions transform a string into lowercase or uppercase:

```
mysql> select lcase('MYSQL');
+----------------+
| LCASE('MYSQL') |
+----------------+
| mysql          |
+----------------+
1 row in set (0.00 sec)

mysql> select ucase('mysql');
+----------------+
| UCASE('mysql') |
+----------------+
| MYSQL          |
+----------------+
1 row in set (0.00 sec)
```

Remember, if you use the functions with field names, don't use quotation marks:

```
mysql> select ucase(lastname) from table_name;
+-----------------+
| UCASE(lastname) |
+-----------------+
| BELL            |
| CARR            |
| DOE             |
| JONES           |
| JONES           |
| SMITH           |
| SMITH           |
| SMITH           |
| SMITH           |
+-----------------+
9 rows in set (0.00 sec)
```

Another fun string-manipulation function is REPEAT(), which does just what it sounds like—repeats a string for a given number of times:

```
mysql> select repeat("bowwow", 4);
+----------------------------+
| REPEAT("bowwow", 4)        |
+----------------------------+
| bowwowbowwowbowwowbowwow   |
+----------------------------+
1 row in set (0.00 sec)
```

The REPLACE() function replaces all occurrences of a given string with another string:

```
mysql> select replace('bowwowbowwowbowwowbowwow', 'wow', 'WOW');
+---------------------------------------------------+
| REPLACE('bowwowbowwowbowwowbowwow', 'wow', 'WOW') |
+---------------------------------------------------+
| bowWOWbowWOWbowWOWbowWOW                           |
+---------------------------------------------------+
1 row in set (0.00 sec)
```

Using Date and Time Functions in MySQL

MySQL's built-in date-related functions can be used in SELECT statements, with or without specifying a table, to retrieve a result of the function. Or you can use the functions with any type of date field: date, datetime, timestamp, and year. Depending on the type of field in use, the results of the date-related functions are more or less useful.

Working with Days

The DAYOFWEEK() and WEEKDAY() functions do similar things with slightly different results. Both functions are used to find the weekday index of a date, but the difference lies in the starting day and position.

If you use DAYOFWEEK(), the first day of the week is Sunday, at position 1, and the last day of the week is Saturday, at position 7. For example:

```
mysql> select dayofweek('2003-08-25');
+------------------------+
| dayofweek('2003-08-25') |
+------------------------+
|                      2 |
+------------------------+
1 row in set (0.00 sec)
```

The result shows that August 25, 2003 was weekday index 2, or Monday. Using the same date with WEEKDAY() gives you a different result with the same meaning:

```
mysql> select weekday('2003-08-25');
+----------------------+
| WEEKDAY('2003-08-25') |
+----------------------+
|                    0 |
+----------------------+
1 row in set (0.00 sec)
```

The result shows that August 25, 2003 was weekday index 0. Because WEEKDAY() uses Monday as the first day of the week at position 0 and Sunday as the last day at position 6, 0 is accurate: Monday.

The DAYOFMONTH() and DAYOFYEAR() functions are more straightforward, with only one result and a range that starts at 1 and ends at 31 for DAYOFMONTH() and 366 for DAYOFYEAR(). Some examples follow:

```
mysql> select dayofmonth('2003-08-25');
+--------------------------+
| DAYOFMONTH('2003-08-25') |
+--------------------------+
|                       25 |
+--------------------------+
1 row in set (0.00 sec)

mysql> select dayofyear('2003-08-25');
+-------------------------+
| DAYOFYEAR('2003-08-25') |
+-------------------------+
|                     237 |
+-------------------------+
1 row in set (0.00 sec)
```

It might seem odd to have a function that returns the day of the month on a particular date because the day is right there in the string. But think about using these types of functions in WHERE clauses to perform comparisons on records. If you have a table that holds online orders with a field containing the date the order was placed, you can quickly get a count of the orders placed on any given day of the week, or see how many orders were placed during the first half of the month versus the second half.

The following two queries show how many orders were placed during the first three days of the week (throughout all months) and then the remaining days of the week:

```
mysql> select count(id) from orders where dayofweek(date_ordered) < 4;
+-----------+
| COUNT(id) |
+-----------+
|         3 |
+-----------+
1 row in set (0.00 sec)

mysql> select count(id) from orders where dayofweek(date_ordered) > 3;
+-----------+
| COUNT(id) |
+-----------+
|         5 |
+-----------+
1 row in set (0.00 sec)
```

Using DAYOFMONTH(), the following examples show the number of orders placed during the first half of any month versus the second half:

```
mysql> select count(id) from orders where dayofmonth(date_ordered) < 16;
+-----------+
| COUNT(id) |
+-----------+
|         6 |
+-----------+
1 row in set (0.00 sec)

mysql> select count(id) from orders where dayofmonth(date_ordered) > 15;
+-----------+
| COUNT(id) |
+-----------+
|         2 |
+-----------+
1 row in set (0.00 sec)
```

You can use the DAYNAME() function to add more life to your results because it returns the name of the weekday for any given date:

```
mysql> select dayname(date_ordered) from orders;
+-----------------------+
| DAYNAME(date_ordered) |
+-----------------------+
| Thursday              |
| Monday                |
| Thursday              |
| Thursday              |
| Wednesday             |
| Thursday              |
| Sunday                |
| Sunday                |
+-----------------------+
8 rows in set (0.00 sec)
```

Functions aren't limited to WHERE clauses—you can use them in ORDER BY clauses as well:

```
mysql> select dayname(date_ordered) from orders
    -> order by dayofweek(date_ordered);
+-----------------------+
| DAYNAME(date_ordered) |
+-----------------------+
| Sunday                |
| Sunday                |
| Monday                |
| Wednesday             |
| Thursday              |
| Thursday              |
| Thursday              |
| Thursday              |
+-----------------------+
8 rows in set (0.00 sec)
```

Working with Months and Years

Days of the week aren't the only parts of the calendar, and MySQL has functions specifically for months and years as well. Just like the DAYOFWEEK() and DAYNAME() functions, MONTH() and MONTHNAME() return the number of the month in a year and the name of the month for a given date. For example:

```
mysql> select month('2003-08-25'), monthname('2003-08-25');
+---------------------+-------------------------+
| month('2003-08-25') | monthname('2003-08-25') |
+---------------------+-------------------------+
|                   8 | August                  |
+---------------------+-------------------------+
1 row in set (0.00 sec)
```

Using MONTHNAME() on the orders table shows the proper results but a lot of repeated data:

```
mysql> select monthname(date_ordered) from orders;
+-------------------------+
| MONTHNAME(date_ordered) |
+-------------------------+
| November                |
| November                |
| November                |
| November                |
| November                |
| November                |
| November                |
| October                 |
+-------------------------+
8 rows in set (0.00 sec)
```

You can use DISTINCT to get nonrepetitive results:

```
mysql> select distinct monthname(date_ordered) from orders;
+-------------------------+
| MONTHNAME(date_ordered) |
+-------------------------+
| November                |
| October                 |
+-------------------------+
2 rows in set (0.00 sec)
```

For work with years, the YEAR() function will return the year of a given date:

```
mysql> select distinct year(date_ordered) from orders;
+--------------------+
| YEAR(date_ordered) |
+--------------------+
|               2003 |
+--------------------+
1 row in set (0.00 sec)
```

Working with Weeks

Weeks can be tricky things—there can be 53 weeks in a year if Sunday is the first day of the week and December hasn't ended. For example, December 30th of 2001 was a Sunday:

```
mysql> select dayname('2001-12-30');
+-----------------------+
| DAYNAME('2001-12-30') |
+-----------------------+
| Sunday                |
+-----------------------+
1 row in set (0.00 sec)
```

That fact made December 30 of 2001 part of the 53rd week of the year:

```
mysql> select week('2001-12-30');
+--------------------+
| WEEK('2001-12-30') |
+--------------------+
|                 53 |
+--------------------+
1 row in set (0.00 sec)
```

The 53rd week contains December 30 and 31, and is only two days long; the first week of 2002 begins with January 1.

If you want your weeks to start on Mondays but still want to find the week of the year, the optional second argument enables you to change the start day. A 1 indicates a week that starts on Monday. In the following examples, a Monday start day makes December 30 part of the 52nd week of 2001, but December 31 is still part of the 53rd week of 2001.

```
mysql> select week('2001-12-30',1);
+----------------------+
| WEEK('2001-12-30',1) |
+----------------------+
|                   52 |
+----------------------+
1 row in set (0.00 sec)

mysql> select week('2001-12-31',1);
+----------------------+
| WEEK('2001-12-31',1) |
+----------------------+
|                   53 |
+----------------------+
1 row in set (0.00 sec)
```

Working with Hours, Minutes, and Seconds

If you're using a date that includes the exact time, such as datetime or timestamp, or even just a time field, there are functions to find the hours, minutes, and seconds from that string. Not surprisingly, these functions are called HOUR(), MINUTE(), and SECOND(). HOUR() returns the hour in a given time, which is between 0 and 23. The range for MINUTE() and SECOND() is 0 to 59.

Here are some examples:

```
mysql> select hour('2003-08-25 07:27:49') as hour,minute('2003-08-25 07:27:49')
    -> as minute,second('2003-08-25 07:27:49') as second;
+------+--------+--------+
| hour | minute | second |
+------+--------+--------+
|    7 |     27 |     49 |
+------+--------+--------+
1 row in set (0.00 sec)
```

That's a lot of queries to get at one time from a datetime field—you can put the hour and minute together and even use CONCAT_WS() to put the : between the results and get a representation of the time:

```
mysql> select concat_ws(':',hour('2003-08-25 07:27:49'),
    -> minute('2003-08-25 07:27:49')) as sample_time;
+-------------+
| sample_time |
+-------------+
| 7:27        |
+-------------+
1 row in set (0.00 sec)
```

If you use field names instead of strings, remember not to use quotation marks. Here's an example that uses the dateadded field from the sometable table:

```
mysql> select concat_ws(':',hour(dateadded), minute(dateadded))
    -> as sample_time from sometable;
+-------------+
| sample_time |
+-------------+
| 13:11       |
| 13:11       |
| 13:11       |
| 13:11       |
| 14:16       |
| 10:12       |
| 10:12       |
| 10:12       |
| 10:12       |
+-------------+
9 rows in set (0.00 sec)
```

This is cheating because it's not the actual time—it's just two numbers stuck together to look like a time. If you used the concatenation trick on a time such as 02:02, the result would be 2:2, as shown here:

```
mysql> select concat_ws(':',hour('02:02'), minute('02:02')) as sample_time;
+-------------+
| sample_time |
+-------------+
| 2:2         |
+-------------+
1 row in set (0.00 sec)
```

This result is obviously not the intended result. In the next section, you learn how to use the DATE_FORMAT() function to properly format dates and times.

Formatting Dates and Times with MySQL

The DATE_FORMAT() function formats a date, datetime, or timestamp field into a string by using options that tell it exactly how to display the results. The syntax of DATE_FORMAT() is

```
DATE_FORMAT(date,format)
```

There are many formatting options, as shown in Table 15.2.

TABLE 15.2 DATE_FORMAT() Format String Options

Option	Result
%M	Month name (January through December)
%b	Abbreviated month name (Jan through Dec)
%m	Month, padded digits (01 through 12)
%c	Month (1 through 12)
%W	Weekday name (Sunday through Saturday)
%a	Abbreviated weekday name (Sun through Sat)
%D	Day of the month using the English suffix, such as first, second, third, and so on
%d	Day of the month, padded digits (00 through 31)
%e	Day of the month (0 through 31)
%j	Day of the year, padded digits (001 through 366)
%Y	Year, four digits
%y	Year, two digits
%X	Four-digit year for the week where Sunday is the first day; used with %V

TABLE 15.2　Continued

Option	Result
%X	Four-digit year for the week where Monday is the first day; used with %v
%w	Day of the week (0=Sunday...6=Saturday)
%U	Week (0 through 53) where Sunday is the first day of the week
%u	Week (0 through 53) where Monday is the first day of the week
%V	Week (1 through 53) where Sunday is the first day of the week; used with %X
%v	Week (1 through 53) where Monday is the first day of the week; used with %x
%H	Hour, padded digits (00 through 23)
%k	Hour (0 through 23)
%h	Hour, padded digits (01 through 12)
%l	Hour (1 through 12)
%i	Minutes, padded digits (00 through 59)
%S	Seconds, padded digits (00 through 59)
%s	Seconds, padded digits (00 through 59)
%r	Time, 12-hour clock (hh:mm:ss [AP]M)
%T	Time, 24-hour clock (hh:mm:ss)
%p	AM or PM

By the Way

Any other characters used in the DATE_FORMAT() option string appear literally.

To display the 02:02 result that we rigged in the previous section, you'd use the %h and %i options to return the hour and minute from the date with a : between the two options. For example:

```
mysql> select date_format('2003-08-25 02:02:00', '%h:%i') as sample_time;
+-------------+
| sample_time |
+-------------+
| 02:02       |
+-------------+
1 row in set (0.00 sec)
```

The following are just a few more examples of the DATE_FORMAT() function in use, but this function is best understood by practicing it yourself.

```
mysql> select date_format('2003-08-25', '%W, %M %D, %Y') as sample_time;
+----------------------------+
| sample_time                |
+----------------------------+
| Monday, August 25th, 2003  |
+----------------------------+
1 row in set (0.00 sec)

mysql> select date_format(now(),'%W the %D of %M, %Y around %l o\'clock %p')
    -> as sample_time;
+-------------------------------------------------------+
| sample_time                                           |
+-------------------------------------------------------+
| Monday the 25th of August, 2003 around 8 o'clock AM   |
+-------------------------------------------------------+
1 row in set (0.00 sec)
```

If you're working specifically with time fields, the TIME_FORMAT() function works just like the DATE_FORMAT() function. Only the format options for hours, minutes, and seconds are allowed:

```
mysql> select time_format('02:02:00', '%h:%i') as sample_time;
+-------------+
| sample_time |
+-------------+
| 02:02       |
+-------------+
1 row in set (0.00 sec)
```

Performing Date Arithmetic with MySQL

MySQL has several functions to help perform date arithmetic, and this is one of the areas where it might be quicker to allow MySQL to do the math than your PHP script. The DATE_ADD() and DATE_SUB() functions return a result given a starting date and an interval. The syntax for both functions is

```
DATE_ADD(date,INTERVAL value type)

DATE_SUB(date,INTERVAL value type)
```

Table 15.3 shows the possible types and their expected value format.

TABLE 15.3 Values and Types in Date Arithmetic

Value	Type
Number of seconds	SECOND
Number of minutes	MINUTE
Number of hours	HOUR

TABLE 15.3 Continued

Value	Type
Number of days	DAY
Number of months	MONTH
Number of years	YEAR
"minutes:seconds"	MINUTE_SECOND
"hours:minutes"	HOUR_MINUTE
"days hours"	DAY_HOUR
"years-months"	YEAR_MONTH
"hours:minutes:seconds"	HOUR_SECOND
"days hours:minutes"	DAY_MINUTE
"days hours:minutes:seconds"	DAY_SECOND

For example, to find the date of the current day plus 21 days, use the following:

```
mysql> select date_add(now(), interval 21 day);
+----------------------------------+
| date_add(now(), interval 21 day) |
+----------------------------------+
| 2003-09-14 16:22:27              |
+----------------------------------+
1 row in set (0.00 sec)
```

To subtract 21 days, use

```
mysql> select date_sub(now(), interval 21 day);
+----------------------------------+
| date_sub(now(), interval 21 day) |
+----------------------------------+
| 2003-08-03 16:22:38              |
+----------------------------------+
1 row in set (0.00 sec)
```

Use the expression as it's shown in Table 15.3, despite what might be a natural tendency to use DAYS instead of DAY. Using DAYS results in an error:

```
mysql> select date_add(now(), interval 21 days);
ERROR 1064: You have an error in your SQL syntax near 'days)' at line 1
```

If you're using DATE_ADD() or DATE_SUB() with a date value instead of a datetime value, the result will be shown as a date value unless you use expressions related to hours, minutes, and seconds. In that case, your result will be a datetime result.

For example, the result of the first query remains a date field, whereas the second becomes a datetime:

```
mysql> select date_add("2001-12-31", interval 1 day);
+----------------------------------------+
| DATE_ADD("2001-12-31", INTERVAL 1 DAY) |
+----------------------------------------+
| 2002-01-01                             |
+----------------------------------------+
1 row in set (0.00 sec)

mysql> select date_add("2001-12-31", interval 12 hour);
+------------------------------------------+
| DATE_ADD("2001-12-31", INTERVAL 12 HOUR) |
+------------------------------------------+
| 2001-12-31 12:00:00                      |
+------------------------------------------+
1 row in set (0.00 sec)
```

Beginning with MySQL version 3.23, you can also perform date arithmetic using the + and - operators instead of DATE_ADD() and DATE_SUB() functions:

```
mysql> select "2001-12-31" + interval 1 day;
+------------------------------+
| "2001-12-31" + INTERVAL 1 DAY |
+------------------------------+
| 2002-01-01                   |
+------------------------------+
1 row in set (0.00 sec)

mysql> select "2001-12-31" - interval 14 hour;
+---------------------------------+
| "2001-12-31" - INTERVAL 14 HOUR |
+---------------------------------+
| 2001-12-30 10:00:00             |
+---------------------------------+
1 row in set (0.00 sec)
```

Special Functions and Conversion Features

The MySQL NOW() function returns a current datetime result, and is useful for timestamping login or access times, as well as numerous other tasks. MySQL has a few other functions that perform similarly.

The CURDATE() and CURRENT_DATE() functions are synonymous, and each returns the current date in YYYY-MM-DD format:

```
mysql> select curdate(), current_date();
+------------+----------------+
| curdate()  | current_date() |
+------------+----------------+
| 2003-08-25 | 2003-08-25     |
+------------+----------------+
1 row in set (0.01 sec)
```

Similarly, the CURTIME() and CURRENT_TIME() functions return the current time in HH:MM:SS format:

```
mysql> select curtime(), current_time();
+-----------+----------------+
| curtime() | current_time() |
+-----------+----------------+
| 09:14:26  | 09:14:26       |
+-----------+----------------+
1 row in set (0.00 sec)
```

The NOW(), SYSDATE(), and CURRENT_TIMESTAMP() functions return values in full datetime format (YYYY-MM-DD HH:MM:SS):

```
mysql> select now(), sysdate(), current_timestamp();
+---------------------+---------------------+---------------------+
| now()               | sysdate()           | current_timestamp() |
+---------------------+---------------------+---------------------+
| 2003-08-25 09:14:50 | 2003-08-25 09:14:50 | 2003-08-25 09:14:50 |
+---------------------+---------------------+---------------------+
1 row in set (0.00 sec)
```

The UNIX_TIMESTAMP() function returns the current date in—or converts a given date to—Unix timestamp format. Unix timestamp format is in seconds since the epoch, or seconds since midnight, January 1, 1970. For example:

```
mysql> select unix_timestamp();
+------------------+
| UNIX_TIMESTAMP() |
+------------------+
|       1061767446 |
+------------------+
1 row in set (0.00 sec)
```

```
mysql> select unix_timestamp('1973-12-30');
+-----------------------------+
| UNIX_TIMESTAMP('1973-12-30') |
+-----------------------------+
|                   126086400 |
+-----------------------------+
1 row in set (0.00 sec)
```

The FROM_UNIXTIME() function performs a conversion of a Unix timestamp to a full datetime format when used without any options:

```
mysql> select from_unixtime('1061767446');
+-----------------------------+
| from_unixtime('1061767446') |
+-----------------------------+
| 2003-08-24 16:24:06         |
+-----------------------------+
1 row in set (0.00 sec)
```

You can use the format options from the DATE_FORMAT() functions to display a timestamp in a more appealing manner:

```
mysql> select from_unixtime(unix_timestamp(), '%D %M %Y at %h:%i:%s');
+---------------------------------------------------------+
¦ from_unixtime(unix_timestamp(), '%D %M %Y at %h:%i:%s') ¦
+---------------------------------------------------------+
¦ 24th August 2003 at 04:24:54                            ¦
+---------------------------------------------------------+
1 row in set (0.00 sec)
```

If you're working with a number of seconds and want to convert the seconds to a time-formatted result, you can use SEC_TO_TIME() and TIME_TO_SEC() to convert values back and forth.

For example, 1440 seconds is equal to 24 minutes and vice versa:

```
mysql> select sec_to_time('1440'), time_to_sec('00:24:00');
+---------------------+-------------------------+
¦ SEC_TO_TIME('1440') ¦ TIME_TO_SEC('00:24:00') ¦
+---------------------+-------------------------+
¦ 00:24:00            ¦                    1440 ¦
+---------------------+-------------------------+
1 row in set (0.01 sec)
```

Summary

In this chapter, you learned the basics of SQL, from table creation to manipulating records. The table creation command requires three important pieces of information: the table name, the field name, and the field definitions. Field definitions are important because a well-designed table will help speed along your database. MySQL has three different categories of data types: numeric, date and time, and string.

The INSERT command, used to add records to a table, names the table and columns you want to populate, and then defines the values. When placing values in the INSERT statement, strings must be enclosed with single or double quotes. The SELECT SQL command is used to retrieve records from specific tables. The * character enables you to easily select all fields for all records in a table, but you can also specify particular column names. If the result set is too long, the LIMIT clause provides a simple method for extracting slices of results if you indicate a starting position and the number of records to return. To order the results, use the ORDER BY clause to select the columns to sort. Sorts can be performed on integers, dates, and strings, in either ascending or descending order. The default order is ascending. Without specifying an order, results are displayed in the order they appear in the table.

You can pick and choose which records you want to return using WHERE clauses to test for the validity of conditions. Comparison or logical operators are used in WHERE clauses, and sometimes both types are used for compound statements. Selecting records from multiple tables within one statement is as advanced as it gets, as this type of statement—called JOIN—requires forethought and planning to produce correct results. Common types of JOIN are INNER JOIN, LEFT JOIN, and RIGHT JOIN, although MySQL supports many different kinds of JOIN.

The UPDATE and REPLACE commands are used to modify existing data in your MySQL tables. UPDATE is good for changing values in specific columns and for changing values in multiple records based on specific conditions. REPLACE is a variation of INSERT that deletes, and then reinserts a record with a matching primary key. Be very careful when using UPDATE to change values in a column because failure to add a condition will result in the given column being updated throughout all records in the table.

The DELETE command is a simple one—it simply removes whole records from tables. This also makes it very dangerous, so be sure you give DELETE privileges only to users who can handle the responsibility. You can specify conditions when using DELETE so that records are removed only if a particular expression in a WHERE clause is true. Also, you can delete smaller portions of the records in your table using a LIMIT clause. If you have an exceptionally large table, deleting portions is less resource-intensive than deleting each record in a huge table.

You were introduced to MySQL functions that perform actions on strings, dates and times. If you have strings in MySQL you want to concatenate or for which you want to count characters, you can use functions such as CONCAT(), CONCAT_WS(), and LENGTH(). To pad or remove padding from strings, use RPAD(), LPAD(), TRIM(), LTRIM(), and RRIM() to get just the strings you want. You can also find the location of a string within another, or to return a part of a given string, using the LOCATE(), SUBSTRING(), LEFT(), and RIGHT() functions. Functions such as LCASE(), UCASE(), REPEAT(), and REPLACE() also return variations of the original strings. MySQL's built-in date and time functions can definitely take some of the load off your application by internally formatting dates and times and performing the date and time arithmetic. The formatting options used for the DATE_FORMAT() function provide a simple method to produce a custom display string from any sort of date field. The DATE_ADD() and DATE_SUB() functions and their numerous available interval types help you determine dates and times in the past or future. Additionally, functions such as DAY(), WEEK(), MONTH(), and YEAR() are useful for extracting parts of dates for use in WHERE or ORDER BY clauses.

Q&A

Q. *What characters can I use to name my tables and fields, and what is the character limit?*

A. The maximum length of database, table, or field names is 64 characters. Any character that you can use in a directoryname or filename, you can use in database and table names—except / and .. These limitations are in place because MySQL creates directories and files in your file system, which correspond to database and table names. There are no character limitations (besides length) in field names.

Q. *Can I use multiple functions in one statement, such as making a concatenated string all uppercase?*

A. Sure—just be mindful of your opening and closing parentheses. This example shows how to uppercase the concatenated first and last names from the master name table:

```
mysql> SELECT UCASE(CONCAT_WS(' ', firstname, lastname)) FROM table_name;
+--------------------------------------------+
| UCASE(CONCAT_WS(' ', firstname, lastname)) |
+--------------------------------------------+
| JOHN SMITH                                 |
| JANE SMITH                                 |
| JIMBO JONES                                |
| ANDY SMITH                                 |
| CHRIS JONES                                |
| ANNA BELL                                  |
| JIMMY CARR                                 |
| ALBERT SMITH                               |
| JOHN DOE                                   |
+--------------------------------------------+
9 rows in set (0.00 sec)
```

If you want to uppercase just the last name, use

```
mysql> SELECT CONCAT_WS(' ', firstname, UCASE(lastname)) FROM master_name;
+--------------------------------------------+
| CONCAT_WS(' ', firstname, UCASE(lastname)) |
+--------------------------------------------+
| John SMITH                                 |
| Jane SMITH                                 |
| Jimbo JONES                                |
| Andy SMITH                                 |
| Chris JONES                                |
| Anna BELL                                  |
| Jimmy CARR                                 |
| Albert SMITH                               |
| John DOE                                   |
+--------------------------------------------+
9 rows in set (0.00 sec)
```

Workshop

The workshop is designed to help you anticipate possible questions, review what you've learned, and begin learning how to put your knowledge into practice.

Quiz

1. The integer 56678685 could be which datatype(s)?

2. How would you define a field that could only contain the following strings: apple, pear, banana, cherry?

3. What would be the `LIMIT` clauses for selecting the first 25 records of a table? Then the next 25?

4. How would you formulate a string comparison using `LIKE` to match first names of "John" or "Joseph"?

5. How would you explicitly refer to a field called `id` in a table called `table1`?

6. Write a SQL statement that joins two tables, orders, and `items_ordered`, with a primary key in each of `order_id`. From the `orders` table, select the following fields: `order_name` and `order_date`. From the `items_ordered` table, select the `item_description` field.

7. Write a SQL query to find the starting position of a substring `"grape"` in a string `"applepearbananagrape"`.

8. Write a query that selects the last five characters from the string `"applepearbananagrape"`.

Answers

1. `MEDIUMINT, INT,` or `BIGINT`.

2. `ENUM ('apple', 'pear', 'banana', 'cherry')` or `SET ('apple', 'pear', 'banana', 'cherry')`

3. `LIMIT 0, 25` and `LIMIT 25, 25`

4. `LIKE 'Jo%'`

5. Use `table1.id` instead of `id` in your query.

6. `SELECT orders.order_name, orders.order_date, items_ordered.item_description FROM orders LEFT JOIN items_ordered ON orders.order_id = items_ordered.id;`

7. `SELECT LOCATE('grape', 'applepearbananagrape');`

8. `SELECT RIGHT("applepearbananagrape", 5);`

Activity

Take the time to create some sample tables, and practice using basic `INSERT` and `SELECT` commands.

CHAPTER 16

Interacting with MySQL Using PHP

Now that you've learned the basics of the PHP as well as the basics of working with MySQL, you're ready to make the two interact. Think of PHP as a conduit to MySQL—the commands you learned in the previous chapter are the same commands that you will send to MySQL in this chapter, only this time you'll send them with PHP. In this chapter, you will learn

- ▶ How to connect to MySQL using PHP
- ▶ How to insert and select data through PHP scripts

Connecting to MySQL with PHP

To successfully use the PHP functions to talk to MySQL, you must have MySQL running at a location to which your Web server can connect (not necessarily the same machine as your Web server). You also must have created a user (with a password), and you must know the name of the database to which you want to connect. If you followed the instructions in Chapter 1, "Installing and Configuring MySQL," and Chapter 3, "Installing and Configuring PHP," you should already have taken care of this.

In all sample scripts in this chapter, the sample database name is testDB, the sample user is joeuser, and the sample password is somepass. Substitute your own information when you use these scripts.

> You can find the section of the PHP manual that covers all MySQL-related functions at http://www.php.net/mysql. Use it!

By the Way

Using mysql_connect()

The mysql_connect() function is the first function you must call when utilizing a PHP script to connect to MySQL—without an open connection to MySQL, you won't get very far! The basic syntax for the connection is

```
mysql_connect("hostname", "username", "password");
```

Using actual sample values, the connection function looks like this:

```
mysql_connect("localhost", "joeuser", "somepass");
```

This function returns a connection index if the connection is successful or returns false if the connection fails. Listing 16.1 is a working example of a connection script. It assigns the value of the connection index to a variable called $conn, and then prints the value of $conn as proof of a connection.

LISTING 16.1 A Simple Connection Script

```
1: <?php
2: $conn = mysql_connect("localhost", "joeuser", "somepass");
3: echo $conn;
4: ?>
```

Save this script as mysqlconnect.php and place it in the document area of your Web server. Access the script with your Web browser and you will see something like this:

```
Resource id #1
```

Connecting to MySQL using the mysql_connect() function is pretty straightforward. The connection closes when the script finishes its execution, but if you would like to explicitly close the connection, simply add the mysql_close() function at the end of the script, as in Listing 16.2.

LISTING 16.2 The Modified Simple Connection Script

```
1: <?php
2: $conn = mysql_connect("localhost", "joeuser", "somepass");
3: echo $conn;
4: mysql_close($conn);
5: ?>
```

That's all there is to it. The next section will cover the query execution functions, which are far more interesting than simply opening a connection and letting it sit there!

Executing Queries

Half the battle in executing MySQL queries using PHP is knowing how to write the SQL. The mysql_query() function in PHP is used to send your SQL query to MySQL. If it does so successfully, a result index is returned. If a failure occurs, the function returns false.

When you use the mysql_query() function, you'll notice that one piece of the puzzle is missing: picking the database to use. When you connect to MySQL through the command-line interface, the database is specified in the connection string or changed manually after you log in. With PHP, this is done via a separate function called mysql_select_db() with the following syntax:

```
mysql_select_db(database name, connection index);
```

To connect to a database named testDB, first use mysql_connect(), and then use mysql_select_db(), as shown in Listing 16.3.

LISTING 16.3 Connecting and Selecting a Database

```
1: <?php
2: $conn = mysql_connect("localhost", "joeuser", "somepass");
3: mysql_select_db("testDB",$conn);
4: ?>
```

You now have two important pieces of information: the connection index ($conn) and the knowledge that PHP will use testDB as the database throughout the life of this particular script. The connection index is used in mysql_query() syntax:

```
mysql_query(query, connection index);
```

In your script, first make the connection, and then execute a query. The script in Listing 16.4 creates a simple table called testTable.

LISTING 16.4 A Script to Create a Table

```
1: <?php
2: // open the connection
3: $conn = mysql_connect("localhost", "joeuser", "somepass");
4: // pick the database to use
5: mysql_select_db("testDB",$conn);
6: // create the SQL statement
7: $sql = "CREATE TABLE testTable (id int not null primary key auto_increment,
8: testField varchar (75))";
9: // execute the SQL statement
10: $result = mysql_query($sql, $conn);
11: // echo the result identifier
12: echo $result;
13: ?>
```

> When issuing queries using `mysql_query()`, the semicolon at the end of the SQL statement is not required. The only semicolon in that line should be at the end of the PHP command.

Because the `mysql_query` function only returns a `true` or `false` result, the boring output of this script is

```
1
```

The 1 indicates `true`, and indicates that the query was successfully executed. A `0` would have indicated failure. Access MySQL through the command-line interface to verify the creation of the `testTable` table:

```
mysql> describe testTable;
+-----------+-------------+------+-----+---------+----------------+
| Field     | Type        | Null | Key | Default | Extra          |
+-----------+-------------+------+-----+---------+----------------+
| id        | int(11)     |      | PRI | NULL    | auto_increment |
| testField | varchar(75) | YES  |     | NULL    |                |
+-----------+-------------+------+-----+---------+----------------+
2 rows in set (0.00 sec)
```

Congratulations—you have successfully created a table in your MySQL database using PHP!

Retrieving Error Messages

Take some time to familiarize yourself with the `mysql_error()` function—it will become your friend. When used in conjunction with the PHP `die()` function, which simply exits the script at the point at which it appears, the `mysql_error()` function will return a helpful error message when you make a mistake.

For example, now that you have created a table called `testTable`, you won't be able to execute that script again without an error. Let's try to execute the script again, but modify it first to utilize the `mysql_error()` function (see Listing 16.5).

LISTING 16.5 The Script to Create a Table, with Error Messages

```
 1: <?php
 2: // open the connection
 3: $conn = mysql_connect("localhost", "joeuser", "somepass");
 4: // pick the database to use
 5: mysql_select_db("testDB",$conn);
 6: // create the SQL statement
 7: $sql = "CREATE TABLE testTable (id int not null primary key auto_increment,
 8: testField varchar (75))";
 9: // execute the SQL statement
10: $result = mysql_query($sql, $conn) or die(mysql_error());
```

LISTING 16.5 Continued

```
11: // echo the result identifier
12: echo $result;
13: ?>
```

When you execute the script, you should see something like the following in your
Web browser:

```
Table 'testTable' already exists
```

How exciting! Move on to the next section to start inserting data into your table,
and soon you'll be retrieving and formatting it via PHP.

Working with MySQL Data

Inserting, updating, deleting, and retrieving data all revolve around the use of
the mysql_query() function to execute the basic SQL queries. For INSERT, UPDATE,
and DELETE, no additional scripting is required after the query has been executed
because you're not displaying any results (unless you want to). For SELECT, you
have a few options for displaying the data retrieved by your query. Let's start with
the basics and insert some data, so you'll have something to retrieve later on.

Inserting Data with PHP

The easiest method for inserting data is to simply hard-code the INSERT statement, as shown in Listing 16.6.

LISTING 16.6 A Script to Insert a Record

```
 1: <?php
 2: // open the connection
 3: $conn = mysql_connect("localhost", "joeuser", "somepass");
 4: // pick the database to use
 5: mysql_select_db("testDB",$conn);
 6: // create the SQL statement
 7: $sql = "INSERT INTO testTable values ('', 'some value')";
 8: // execute the SQL statement
 9: $result = mysql_query($sql, $conn) or die(mysql_error());
10: // echo the result identifier
11: echo $result;
12: ?>
```

You might wonder why you need to echo the result identifier if you're just inserting data. Well, you don't have to; it's just there for kicks. You can clean this script

up a bit by replacing the query execution line so that it simply executes and prints a relevant statement if successful, as shown in Listing 16.7.

LISTING 16.7   The Modified Insert Script

```
1: <?php
2: // open the connection
3: $conn = mysql_connect("localhost", "joeuser", "somepass");
4: // pick the database to use
5: mysql_select_db("testDB",$conn);
6: // create the SQL statement
7: $sql = "INSERT INTO testTable values ('', 'some value')";
8: // execute the SQL statement
9: if (mysql_query($sql, $conn)) {
10:     echo "record added!";
11: } else {
12:     echo "something went wrong";
13: }
14: ?>
```

Running this script will result in the addition of a row to the testTable table. To enter more records than just the one shown in the script, you can either make a long list of hard-coded SQL statements and use mysql_query() multiple times to execute these statements, or you can create a form-based interface to the record addition script.

To create the form for this script, you really only need one field because the id field can automatically increment. The action of the form is the name of the record-addition script; let's call it insert.php. Your HTML form might look something like Listing 16.8.

LISTING 16.8   An Insert Form

```
1: <HTML>
2: <HEAD>
3: <TITLE>Insert Form</TITLE>
4: </HEAD>
5: <BODY>
6: <FORM ACTION="insert.php" METHOD=POST>
7: <P>Text to add:<br>
8: <input type=text name="testField" size=30>
9: <p><input type=submit name="submit" value="Insert Record"></p>
10: </FORM>
11: </BODY>
12: </HTML>
```

Save this file as insert_form.html, and put it in the document root of your Web server. Next, create the insert.php script shown in Listing 16.9. The value entered in the form will replace the hard-coded values in the SQL query with a variable called $_POST[testField].

LISTING 16.9   An Insert Script Used with the Form

```
 1: <?php
 2: // open the connection
 3: $conn = mysql_connect("localhost", "joeuser", "somepass");
 4: // pick the database to use
 5: mysql_select_db("testDB",$conn);
 6: // create the SQL statement
 7: $sql = "INSERT INTO testTable values ('', '$_POST[testField]')";
 8: // execute the SQL statement
 9: if (mysql_query($sql, $conn)) {
10:     echo "record added!";
11: } else {
12:     echo "something went wrong";
13: }
14: ?>
```

Save the script as insert.php, and put it in the document root of your Web server. In your Web browser, access the HTML form that you created. It should look something like Figure 16.1.

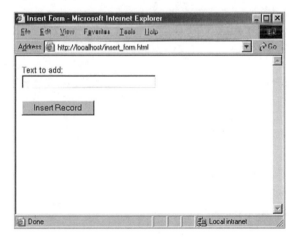

FIGURE 16.1
The HTML form for adding a record.

Enter a string in the Text to Add field, as shown in Figure 16.2.

Finally, click the Insert Record button to execute the insert.php script and insert the record. If successful, you will see results similar to Figure 16.3.

FIGURE 16.2
Text typed in the
form field.

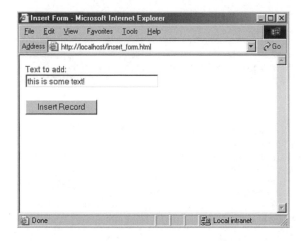

FIGURE 16.3
The record has
been successfully
added.

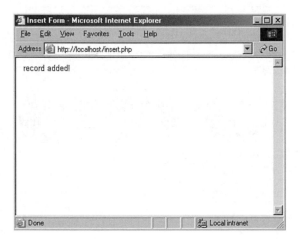

To verify your work, you can use the MySQL command-line interface to view the
records in the table:

```
mysql> select * from testTable;
+----+-------------------+
| id | testField         |
+----+-------------------+
|  1 | some value        |
|  2 | this is some text!|
+----+-------------------+
2 rows in set (0.00 sec)
```

Next, you'll learn how to retrieve and format results with PHP.

Retrieving Data with PHP

Because you have a few rows in your testTable table, you can write a PHP script to retrieve that data. Starting with the basics, write a script that issues a SELECT query but doesn't overwhelm you with result data; let's just get the number of rows. To do this, use the mysql_num_rows() function. This function requires a result, so when you execute the query, put the result index in $result (see Listing 16.10).

LISTING 16.10 A Script to Retrieve Data

```
 1: <?php
 2: // open the connection
 3: $conn = mysql_connect("localhost", "joeuser", "somepass");
 4: // pick the database to use
 5: mysql_select_db("testDB",$conn);
 6: // create the SQL statement
 7: $sql = "SELECT * FROM testTable";
 8: // execute the SQL statement
 9: $result = mysql_query($sql, $conn) or die(mysql_error());
10: //get the number of rows in the result set
11: $number_of_rows = mysql_num_rows($result);
12: echo "The number of rows is $number_of_rows";
13: ?>
```

Save this script as count.php, place it in your Web server document directory, and access it through your Web browser. You should see a message like this:

```
The number of rows is 2
```

The number should be equal to the number of records you inserted during testing. Now that you know there are some records in the table, you can get fancy and fetch the actual contents of those records. You can do this in a few ways, but the easiest method is to retrieve each row as an array.

What you'll be doing is using a while statement to go through each record in the resultset, placing the values of each field into a specific variable, and then displaying the results onscreen. The syntax of mysql_fetch_array() is

```
$newArray = mysql_fetch_array($result);
```

Follow along using the sample script in Listing 16.11.

LISTING 16.11   A Script to Retrieve Data and Display Results

```
 1: <?php
 2: // open the connection
 3: $conn = mysql_connect("localhost", "joeuser", "somepass");
 4: // pick the database to use
 5: mysql_select_db("testDB",$conn);
 6: // create the SQL statement
 7: $sql = "SELECT * FROM testTable";
 8: // execute the SQL statement
 9: $result = mysql_query($sql, $conn) or die(mysql_error());
10: //go through each row in the result set and display data
11: while ($newArray = mysql_fetch_array($result)) {
12:      // give a name to the fields
13:      $id  = $newArray['id'];
14:      $testField = $newArray['testField'];
15:      //echo the results onscreen
16:      echo "The ID is $id and the text is $testField <br>";
17: }
18: ?>
```

Save this script as `select.php`, place it in your Web server document directory, and access it through your Web browser. You should see a message for each record entered into `testTable`, as shown in Figure 16.4.

FIGURE 16.4
Selecting records from MySQL.

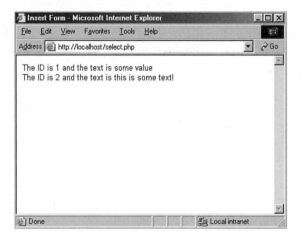

Essentially, you can create an entire database-driven application using just four or five MySQL functions. This chapter has barely scratched the surface of using PHP with MySQL; there are many more MySQL functions in PHP.

Additional MySQL Functions in PHP

There are approximately 40 MySQL-specific functions in PHP. Most of these functions are simply alternate methods of retrieving data or are used to gather information about the table structure in question.

For a complete list of functions, with practical examples, visit the MySQL section of the PHP Manual at `http://www.php.net/ mysql`.

Summary

Using PHP and MySQL to create dynamic, database-driven Web sites is a breeze. Just remember that the PHP functions are essentially a gateway to the database server; anything you'd enter using the MySQL command-line interface, you can use with `mysql_query()`.

To connect to MySQL with PHP, you need to know your MySQL username, password, and database name. Using `mysql_connect()` and `mysql_select_db()`, you can connect to and select a database to use throughout the life of the script.

Once connected, you can issue standard SQL commands with the `mysql_query()` function. If you have issued a SELECT command, you can use `mysql_numrows()` to count the records returned in the result set. If you want to display the data found, you can use `mysql_fetch_array()` to get all the results during a loop and display them onscreen.

Workshop

The workshop is designed to help you anticipate possible questions, review what you've learned, and begin to put your knowledge into practice.

Quiz

1. What is the primary function used to make the connection between PHP and MySQL, and what information is necessary?

2. Which PHP function retrieves a MySQL error message?

3. Which PHP function is used to count the number of records in a result set?

Answers

1. The `mysql_connect()` function creates a connection to MySQL and requires the hostname, username, and password.

2. The `mysql_error()` function returns a MySQL error message.

3. The `mysql_numrows()` function counts the number of records in a resultset.

PART V

Basic Projects

CHAPTER 17

Managing a Simple Mailing List

This chapter provides the first of several hands-on, small projects designed to pull together your PHP and MySQL knowledge. In this chapter, you'll learn the methods for creating a managed distribution list, which can be used to send out newsletters or anything else that you want to send, to a list of email addresses in a database.

The mailing mechanism you'll use in this chapter is not meant to be a replacement for mailing list software, which is specifically designed for bulk messages. The type of system you'll build in this lesson should be used for only small lists of fewer than a few hundred email addresses.

In this chapter, you will learn how to

- ▶ Create a subscribe/unsubscribe form and script
- ▶ Create a front end for sending your message
- ▶ Create the script that sends your message

Developing the Subscription Mechanism

You learned in earlier lessons that planning is the most important aspect of creating any product. In this case, think of the elements you will need for your subscription mechanism:

- ▶ A table to hold email addresses
- ▶ A way for users to add or remove their email addresses
- ▶ A form and script for sending the message

The following sections will describe each item individually.

Creating the subscribers Table

You really need only one field in the subscribers table: to hold the email address of the user. However, you should have an ID field just for consistency among your tables, and also because referencing an ID is a lot simpler than referencing a long email address in where clauses. So, in this case, your MySQL query would look something like

```
mysql> create table subscribers (
    -> id int not null primary key auto_increment,
    -> email varchar (150) unique not null
    -> );
Query OK, 0 rows affected (0.00 sec)
```

Note the use of unique in the field definition for email. This means that although id is the primary key, duplicates should not be allowed in the email field either. The email field is a unique key, and id is the primary key.

```
mysql> desc subscribers;
+-------+--------------+------+-----+---------+----------------+
| Field | Type         | Null | Key | Default | Extra          |
+-------+--------------+------+-----+---------+----------------+
| id    | int(11)      |      | PRI | NULL    | auto_increment |
| email | varchar(150) |      | UNI |         |                |
+-------+--------------+------+-----+---------+----------------+
2 rows in set (0.00 sec)
```

Now that you have a table, you can create the form and script that place values in there.

Creating the Subscription Form

The subscription form will actually be an all-in-one form and script called manage.php, which will handle both subscribe and unsubscribe requests. Listing 17.1 shows the code for manage.php, which uses a few user-defined functions to eliminate repetitive code.

LISTING 17.1 Subscribe and Unsubscribe with manage.php

```
1: <?php
2: //set up a couple of functions
3: function doDB() {
4:     global $conn;
5:     //connect to server and select database; you may need it
6:     $conn = mysql_connect("localhost", "joeuser", "somepass")
7:         or die(mysql_error());
8:     mysql_select_db("testDB",$conn)  or die(mysql_error());
9: }
10:
11: function emailChecker($email) {
```

LISTING 17.1 Continued

```
12:     global $conn, $check_result;
13:     //check that email is not already in list
14:     $check = "select id from subscribers where email = '$email'";
15:     $check_result - mysql_query($check,$conn) or die(mysql_error());
16: }
17:
18: //determine if they need to see the form or not
19: if ($_POST[op] != "ds") {
20:     //they do, so create form block
21:     $display_block = "
22:     <form method=POST action=\"$_SERVER[PHP_SELF]\">
23:
24:     <p><strong>Your E-Mail Address:</strong><br>
25:     <input type=text name=\"email\" size=40 maxlength=150>
26:
27:     <p><strong>Action:</strong><br>
28:     <input type=radio name=\"action\" value=\"sub\" checked> subscribe
29:     <input type=radio name=\"action\" value=\"unsub\"> unsubscribe
30:
31:     <input type=\"hidden\" name=\"op\" value=\"ds\">
32:
33:     <p><input type=submit name=\"submit\" value=\"Submit Form\"></p>
34:     </form>";
35:
36: } else if (($_POST[op] == "ds") && ($_POST[action] -- "sub")) {
37:     //trying to subscribe; validate email address
38:     if ($_POST[email] == "") {
39:         header("Location: manage.php");
40:         exit;
41:     }
42:     //connect to database
43:     doDB();
44:     //check that email is in list
45:     emailChecker($_POST[email]);
46:
47:     //get number of results and do action
48:     if (mysql_num_rows($check_result) < 1) {
49:         //add record
50:         $sql = "insert into subscribers values('', '$_POST[email]')";
51:         $result = mysql_query($sql,$conn) or die(mysql_error());
52:         $display_block = "<P>Thanks for signing up!</P>";
53:     } else {
54:         //print failure message
55:         $display_block = "<P>You're already subscribed!</P>";
56:     }
57: } else if (($_POST[op] == "ds") && ($_POST[action] == "unsub")) {
58:     //trying to unsubscribe; validate email address
59:     if ($_POST[email] == "") {
60:     header("Location: manage.php");
61:         exit;
62:     }
63:     //connect to database
64:     doDB();
65:     //check that email is in list
66:     emailChecker($_POST[email]);
```

LISTING 17.1   Continued

```
67:
68:     //get number of results and do action
69:     if (mysql_num_rows($check_result) < 1) {
70:         //print failure message
71:         $display_block = "<P>Couldn't find your address!</P>
72:         <P>No action was taken.</P>";
73:     } else {
74:         //unsubscribe the address
75:         $id = mysql_result($check_result, 0, "id");
76:         $sql = "delete from subscribers where id = '$id'";
77:         $result = mysql_query($sql,$conn) or die(mysql_error());
78:         $display_block = "<P>You're unsubscribed!</p>";
79:     }
80: }
81: ?>
82: <HTML>
83: <HEAD>
84: <TITLE>Subscribe/Unsubscribe</TITLE>
85: </HEAD>
86: <BODY>
87: <h1>Subscribe/Unsubscribe</h1>
88: <?php echo "$display_block"; ?>
89: </BODY>
90: </HTML>
```

Listing 17.1 may be long, but it's not complicated. In fact, it could be longer, were it not for the user-defined functions at the top of the script. One of the reasons for creating your own functions is that you know you will be reusing a bit of code and don't want to continually retype it. Lines 3–9 set up the first function, doDB(), which is simply the database connection you've been making in your lessons for a while now. Lines 11–16 define a function called emailChecker(), which takes an input and returns an output—like most functions do. We'll look at this one in the context of the script, as we get to it.

Line 19 starts the main logic of the script. Because this script performs several actions, we need to determine which action it is currently attempting. If the value of $_POST[op] is not "ds", we know the user has not submitted the form; therefore, we must show it to the user. Lines 21–34 create the subscribe/unsubscribe form, using $_SERVER[PHP_SELF] as the action (line 22), creating a text field called email for the user's email address, and setting up a set of radio buttons (lines 28–29) to find the desired task. At this point, the script breaks out of the if...else construct, skips down to line 82, and proceeds to print the HTML. The form is displayed as shown in Figure 17.1.

FIGURE 17.1
The subscribe/
unsubscribe form.

If the value of $_POST[op] is indeed "ds", however, we need to do something. We have two possibilities: subscribe and unsubscribe. We determine which action to take by looking at the value of $_POST[action]—the radio button group.

In line 36, if $_POST[op] is "ds" and $_POST[action] is "sub", we know the user is trying to subscribe. To subscribe, he will need an email address, so we check for one in lines 38–41. If no address is present, the user is sent back to the form.

If an address is present, we call the doDB() function in line 43 to connect to the database because we need to perform a query (or two). In line 45, we call the second of our user-defined functions: emailChecker(). This function takes an input ($_POST[email]) and processes it. If we look back to lines 12–15, we see that the function is checking for an id value in the subscribers table that matches the value of the input. The function then returns the resultset, $check_result, for use within the larger script.

Note the definition of global variables at the beginning of both user-defined functions in Listing 17.1. These variables need to be shared with the entire script, and so are declared global.

By the Way

Jump down to line 48 to see how $check_result is used: The number of records in $check_result is counted to determine whether the email address already exists in the table. If the number of rows is less than 1, the address is not in the list, and it can be added. The record is added and the response is stored in lines 50–52, and the failure message (if the address is already in the table) is stored in line 55.

At that point, the script breaks out of the if...else construct, skips down to line 82, and proceeds to print the HTML. You'll test this functionality later.

The last combination of inputs occurs if the value of $_POST[op] is "ds" and $_POST[action] is "unsub". In this case, the user is trying to unsubscribe. To unsubscribe, he will need an email address, so we check for one in lines 59–61. If no address is present, the user is sent back to the form.

If an address is present, we call the doDB() function in line 64 to connect to the database. Then, in line 66, we call emailChecker(), which again will return the resultset, $check_result. The number of records in the resultset is counted in line 69, to determine whether the email address already exists in the table. If the number of rows is less than 1, the address is not in the list, and it cannot be unsubscribed. In this case, the response message is stored in lines 71–72. The user is unsubscribed (the record deleted) and the response is stored in lines 75–77, and the failure message (if the address is already in the table) is stored in line 78. At that point, the script breaks out of the if...else construct, skips down to line 82, and proceeds to print the HTML.

Figures 17.2 through 17.5 show the various results of the script, depending on the actions selected and the status of email addresses in the database.

FIGURE 17.2
Successful subscription.

FIGURE 17.3
Subscription
failure.

FIGURE 17.4
Successful
unsubscribe action.

FIGURE 17.5
Unsuccessful
unsubscribe action.

Next, you'll create the form and script that sends along mail to each of your subscribers.

Developing the Mailing Mechanism

With the subscription mechanism in place, you can create a basic form interface
for a script that will take the contents of your form and send it to every address
in your subscribers table. This is another one of those all-in-one scripts, called
sendmymail.php, and it is shown in Listing 17.2.

LISTING 17.2   Send Mail to Your List of Subscribers

```
1:  <?php
2:  if ($_POST[op] != "send") {
3:     //haven't seen the form, so show it
4:     print "
5:     <HTML>
6:     <HEAD>
7:     <TITLE>Send a Newsletter</TITLE>
8:     </HEAD>
9:     <BODY>
10:    <h1>Send a Newsletter</h1>
11:    <form method=\"post\" action=\"$_SERVER[PHP_SELF]\">
12:    <P><strong>Subject:</strong><br>
13:    <input type=\"text\" name=\"subject\" size=30></p>
14:    <P><strong>Mail Body:</strong><br>
15:    <textarea name=\"message\" cols=50 rows=10 wrap=virtual></textarea>
16:    <input type=\"hidden\" name=\"op\" value=\"send\">
17:    <p><input type=\"submit\" name=\"submit\" value=\"Send It\"></p>
18:    </FORM>
```

LISTING 17.2   Continued

```
19:     </BODY>
20:     </HTML>";
21:
22: } else if ($_POST[op] == "send") {
23:     //want to send form, so check for required fields
24:     if (($_POST[subject] =="") || ($_POST[message] == "")) {
25:         header("Location: sendmymail.php");
26:         exit;
27:     }
28:
29:     //connect to database
30:     $conn = mysql_connect("localhost", "joeuser", "somepass")
31:         or die(mysql_error());
32:     mysql_select_db("testDB",$conn)  or die(mysql_error());
33:
34:     //get emails from subscribers list
35:     $sql = "select email from subscribers";
36:     $result = mysql_query($sql,$conn) or die(mysql_error());
37:
38:     //create a From: mailheader
39:     $headers = "From: Your Mailing List <you@yourdomain.com>";
40:
41:     //loop through results and send mail
42:     while ($row = mysql_fetch_array($result)) {
43:         set_time_limit(0);
44:         $email = $row['email'];
45:         mail("$email", stripslashes($_POST[subject]),
46:             stripslashes($_POST[message]), $headers);
47:         print "newsletter sent to: $email<br>";
48:     }
49: }
50: ?>
```

The main logic of the script starts right there at line 2, where we determine
whether the user has seen the form yet. If the value of $_POST[op] is not "send",
we know the user has not submitted the form; therefore, we must show it to her.
Lines 4–20 create the form for sending the newsletter, which uses
$_SERVER[PHP_SELF] as the action (line 11), creates a text field called subject for
the subject of the mail, and creates a textarea called message for the body of the
mail to be sent. At this point, the script breaks out of the if...else construct and
the HTML is printed. The form is displayed as in Figure 17.6.

If the value of $_POST[op] is indeed "send", however, we have to send the form to
the recipients. Before we send, we must check for the two required items:
$_POST[subject] and $_POST[message]. If either of these items is not present, the
user is redirected to the form again.

FIGURE 17.6
Form for sending
the bulk mail.

If the required items are present, the script moves on to lines 30–32, which connect to the database. The query is issued in line 36, which grabs all the email addresses from the subscribers table. There is no order to these results, although you could throw an order by clause in there if you want to send them out in alphabetical order.

Line 39 creates a From: mail header, which is used inside the upcoming while loop, when mail is sent. This header ensures that the mail looks like it is from a person and not a machine. The while loop, which begins on line 42, extracts the email addresses from the resultset one at a time. On line 43, we use the set_time_limit() function to set the time limit to 0, or "no limit." Doing so allows the script to run for as long as it needs to.

By the Way

> Because all the script in Listing 17.2 does is execute the mail() function numerous times, it does not take into account the queuing factors in actual mailing list software, which are designed to ease the burden on your outgoing mail server. Using set_time_limit() does not ease its burden; it just allows the script to continue to run when it might have timed out before.

In line 45, the mail is sent using the mail() function, inserting the values from the form where appropriate. Line 46 prints a message to the screen for you, to show who should have received the mail. In Figures 17.7 and 17.8, you can see the outcome of the script.

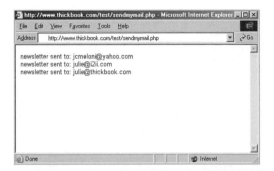

FIGURE 17.7
Mail has been
sent!

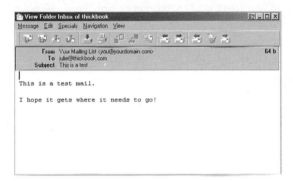

FIGURE 17.8
The mail arrived
safely.

Summary

In this hands-on chapter, you applied your basic PHP and MySQL knowledge
to the creation of a personal mailing list. Included were the database table creation, the subscribe and unsubscribe mechanisms, and the form and script for
sending the mail.

Q&A

Q. *How can I ease the burden on my mail server?*

A. Besides looking into package mailing list software, you can bypass the `mail()` function and talk directly to your SMTP server via a socket connection. Such an example is shown in the PHP Manual for the `fsockopen()` function (`http://www.php.net/manual/fsockopen`), as well as in other developer resource sites.

Q. *Where do bounced messages go?*

A. Bounces go to whatever address you specify in your `From:` or `Reply-to:` mail headers.

Workshop

The workshop is designed to help you anticipate possible questions, review what you've learned, and begin learning how to put your knowledge into practice.

Quiz

1. What function sends mail?

2. What function call causes the script to execute for as long as it needs to run?

Answers

1. This is not a trick question. It's the `mail()` function!

2. `set_time_limit(0)`

CHAPTER 18

Creating an Online Address Book

In this hands-on lesson, your project will be to create a managed, online address book. You will learn the methods for creating the relevant database tables, as well as the forms and scripts for adding, deleting, and viewing database records.

In this chapter, you will learn how to

- ▶ Create relational tables for an online address book
- ▶ Create the forms and scripts for adding and deleting records in the address book
- ▶ Create the forms and scripts for viewing records

Planning and Creating the Database Tables

When you think of an address book, the obvious fields come to mind: name, address, telephone number, email address. However, if you look at your own paper-based address book, you may note that you have several entries for one person. Maybe that person has three telephone numbers, or two email addresses, and so forth. In your online address book, a set of related tables will help alleviate the redundancy and repetition of information.

Table 18.1 shows sample table and field names to use for your online address book. In a minute, you'll create the actual SQL statements, but first you should look at this information and try to see the relationships appear. Ask yourself which of the fields should be primary or unique keys.

TABLE 18.1   Address Book Table and Field Names

Table Name	Field Names
master_name	id, date_added, date_modified, f_name, l_name
address	id, master_id, date_added, date_modified, address, city, state, zipcode, type
telephone	id, master_id, date_added, date_modified, tel_number, type
fax	id, master_id, date_added, date_modified, fax_number, type
email	id, master_id, date_added, date_modified, email, type
personal_notes	id, master_id, date_added, date_modified, note

Notice the use of date-related fields; each table has a date_added and date_modified field in it. The fields will help maintain your data; you may at some point want to issue a query that removes all records that are older than a certain number of months or years, or that removes all records that haven't been updated within a certain period of time.

As you can see in the following SQL statements, the master_name table has two fields besides the ID and date-related fields: f_name and l_name, for first name and last name. The id field is the primary key. No other keys need to be primary or unique, unless you really want to limit your address book to one John Smith, one Mary Jones, and so forth.

> The field lengths for the text fields in the following statements are arbitrary; you can make them as long or as short as you want, within the allowable definition of the field type.

```
mysql> create table master_name (
    -> id int not null primary key auto_increment,
    -> date_added datetime,
    -> date_modified datetime,
    -> f_name varchar (75),
    -> l_name varchar (75)
    -> );
Query OK, 0 rows affected (0.01 sec)
```

The address table has the basic primary key id field and the date_added and date_modified fields. In addition, you should now see where the relationship will be made—through the use of the master_id field. The master_id will be equal to the id field in the master_name table, matching the person whose address this is. The master_id field is not a unique key because it is a perfectly valid assumption that one person may have several address entries. We see this in the type field, which is defined as an enumerated list containing three options: home, work, or other. A person may have one or more of all three types, so no other keys are present in this table besides the primary key id. Assuming this particular address book contains only United States addresses, we round out the table with address, city, state, and zipcode fields.

```
mysql> create table address (
    -> id int not null primary key auto_increment,
    -> master_id int not null,
    -> date_added datetime,
    -> date_modified datetime,
    -> address varchar (255),
    -> city varchar (30),
    -> state char (2),
    -> zipcode varchar (10),
    -> type enum ('home', 'work', 'other')
    -> );
Query OK, 0 rows affected (0.01 sec)
```

The telephone, fax, and email tables are all variations on the same theme:

```
mysql> create table telephone (
    -> id int not null primary key auto_increment,
    -> master_id int not null,
    -> date_added datetime,
    -> date_modified datetime,
    -> tel_number varchar (25),
    -> type enum ('home', 'work', 'other')
    -> );
Query OK, 0 rows affected (0.01 sec)
```

```
mysql> create table fax (
    -> id int not null primary key auto_increment,
    -> master_id int not null,
    -> date_added datetime,
    -> date_modified datetime,
    -> fax_number varchar (25),
    -> type enum ('home', 'work', 'other')
    -> );
Query OK, 0 rows affected (0.00 sec)
```

```
mysql> create table email (
    -> id int not null primary key auto_increment,
    -> master_id int not null,
    -> date_added datetime,
    -> date_modified datetime,
    -> email varchar (150),
    -> type enum ('home', 'work', 'other')
    -> );
Query OK, 0 rows affected (0.00 sec)
```

The personal_notes table also follows the same sort of pattern, except that master_id a unique key and allows only one notes record per person:

```
mysql> create table personal_notes (
    -> id int not null primary key auto_increment,
    -> master_id int not null unique,
    -> date_added datetime,
    -> date_modified datetime,
    -> note text
    -> );
Query OK, 0 rows affected (0.00 sec)
```

Now that your tables are created, you can work through the forms and scripts for managing and viewing your records.

Creating a Menu

Your online address book will contain several actions, so it makes sense to create a menu for your links. Listing 18.1 creates a menu for all the scripts you will create in this section, called mymenu.php.

LISTING 18.1   Address Book Menu

```
 1: <html>
 2: <head>
 3: <title>My Address Book</title>
 4: </head>
 5: <body>
 6: <h1>My Address Book</h1>
 7:
 8: <P><strong>Management</strong>
 9: <ul>
10: <li><a href="addentry.php">Add an Entry</a>
11: <li><a href="delentry.php">Delete an Entry</a>
12: </ul>
13:
14: <P><strong>Viewing</strong>
15: <ul>
16: <li><a href="selentry.php">Select a Record</a>
17: </ul>
18: </body>
19: </html>
```

Figure 18.1 shows the output of Listing 18.1. You'll tackle each of these items in order, starting with "Add an Entry" in the next section.

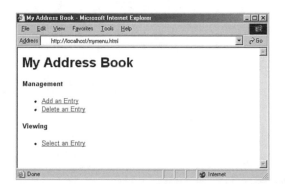

FIGURE 18.1
Address book
menu.

Creating the Record Addition Mechanism

Just because you'll potentially be adding information to six different tables doesn't mean your form or script will be monstrous. In fact, your scripts won't look much different from any of the ones you created in previous lessons, and with practice, you will be able to make these verbose scripts much more stream-lined and efficient.

In Listing 18.2, you can see a basic record addition script, called addentry.php.

LISTING 18.2   Basic Record Addition Script Called addentry.php

```
 1: <?php
 2: if ($_POST[op] != "add") {
 3:    //haven't seen the form, so show it
 4:    $display_block = "<h1>Add an Entry</h1>
 5:    <form method=\"post\" action=\"$_SERVER[PHP_SELF]\">
 6:    <P><strong>First/Last Names:</strong><br>
 7:    <input type=\"text\" name=\"f_name\" size=30 maxlength=75>
 8:    <input type=\"text\" name=\"l_name\" size=30 maxlength=75>
 9:
10:    <P><strong>Address:</strong><br>
11:    <input type=\"text\" name=\"address\" size=30>
12:
13:    <P><strong>City/State/Zip:</strong><br>
14:    <input type=\"text\" name=\"city\" size=30 maxlength=50>
15:    <input type=\"text\" name=\"state\" size=5 maxlength=2>
16:    <input type=\"text\" name=\"zipcode\" size=10 maxlength=10>
17:
18:    <P><strong>Address Type:</strong><br>
19:    <input type=\"radio\" name=\"add_type\" value=\"home\" checked> home
20:    <input type=\"radio\" name=\"add_type\" value=\"work\"> work
21:    <input type=\"radio\" name=\"add_type\" value=\"other\"> other
22:
23:    <P><strong>Telephone Number:</strong><br>
24:    <input type=\"text\" name=\"tel_number\" size=30 maxlength=25>
25:    <input type=\"radio\" name=\"tel_type\" value=\"home\" checked> home
```

LISTING 18.2 Continued

```
26:     <input type=\"radio\" name=\"tel_type\" value=\"work\"> work
27:     <input type=\"radio\" name=\"tel_type\" value=\"other\"> other
28:
29:     <P><strong>Fax Number:</strong><br>
30:     <input type=\"text\" name=\"fax_number\" size=30 maxlength=25>
31:     <input type=\"radio\" name=\"fax_type\" value=\"home\" checked> home
32:     <input type=\"radio\" name=\"fax_type\" value=\"work\"> work
33:     <input type=\"radio\" name=\"fax_type\" value=\"other\"> other
34:
35:     <P><strong>Email Address:</strong><br>
36:     <input type=\"text\" name=\"email\" size=30 maxlength=150>
37:     <input type=\"radio\" name=\"email_type\" value=\"home\" checked> home
38:     <input type=\"radio\" name=\"email_type\" value=\"work\"> work
39:     <input type=\"radio\" name=\"email_type\" value=\"other\"> other
40:
41:     <P><strong>Personal Note:</strong><br>
42:     <textarea name=\"note\" cols=35 rows=5 wrap=virtual></textarea>
43:      <input type=\"hidden\" name=\"op\" value=\"add\">
44:
45:     <p><input type=\"submit\" name=\"submit\" value=\"Add Entry\"></p>
46:     </FORM>";
47:
48: } else if ($_POST[op] == "add") {
49:     //time to add to tables, so check for required fields
50:     if (($_POST[f_name] == "") || ($_POST[l_name] == "")) {
51:         header("Location: addentry.php");
52:         exit;
53:     }
54:
55:     //connect to database
56:     $conn = mysql_connect("localhost", "joeuser", "somepass")
57:         or die(mysql_error());
58:     mysql_select_db("testDB",$conn)  or die(mysql_error());
59:
60:     //add to master_name table
61:     $add_master = "insert into master_name values ('', now(), now(),
62:         '$_POST[f_name]', '$_POST[l_name]')";
63:     mysql_query($add_master) or die(mysql_error());
64:
65:     //get master_id for use with other tables
66:     $master_id = mysql_insert_id();
67:
68:     if (($_POST[address]) || ($_POST[city]) || ($_POST[state]) ||
69:         ($_POST[zipcode])) {
70:         //something relevant, so add to address table
71:         $add_address = "insert into address values ('', $master_id,
72:             now(), now(), '$_POST[address]', '$_POST[city]',
73:              '$_POST[state]', '$_POST[zipcode]', '$_POST[add_type]')";
74:         mysql_query($add_address) or die(mysql_error());
75:     }
76:
77:     if ($_POST[tel_number]) {
78:         //something relevant, so add to telephone table
79:         $add_tel = "insert into telephone values ('', $master_id,
80:          now(), now(), '$_POST[tel_number]',  '$_POST[tel_type]')";
```

LISTING 18.2 Continued

```
81:          mysql_query($add_tel) or die(mysql_error());
82:      }
83:
84:      if ($_POST[fax_number]) {
85:          //something relevant, so add to fax table
86:          $add_fax = "insert into fax values ('', $master_id, now(),
87:           now(), '$_POST[fax_number]', '$_POST[fax_type]')";
88:          mysql_query($add_fax) or die(mysql_error());
89:      }
90:
91:      if ($_POST[email]) {
92:          //something relevant, so add to email table
93:          $add_email = "insert into email values ('', $master_id,
94:              now(), now(), '$_POST[email]', '$_POST[email_type]')";
95:          mysql_query($add_email) or die(mysql_error());
96:      }
97:
98:      if ($_POST[note]) {
99:          //something relevant, so add to notes table
100:         $add_note = "insert into personal_notes values ('', $master_id,
101:             now(), now(), '$_POST[note]')";
102:         mysql_query($add_note) or die(mysql_error());
103:     }
104:
105:     $display_block = "<h1>Entry Added</h1>
106:     <P>Your entry has been added.  Would you like to
107:      <a href=\"addentry.php\">add another</a>?</p>";
108: }
109: ?>
110: <HTML>
111: <HEAD>
112: <TITLE>Add an Entry</TITLE>
113: </HEAD>
114: <BODY>
115: <?php echo $display_block; ?>
116: </BODY>
117: </HTML>
```

This script will perform one of two tasks at any given time: It either shows the record addition form, or it performs all the SQL queries related to adding the record. The logic that determines the task begins at line 2, with a test for the value of $_POST[op]. If the value of $_POST[op] is not "add", the user is not coming from the form and therefore needs to see the form. The HTML for the form is placed in a string called $display_block, from lines 4–55. The script then breaks out of the if...else construct and jumps down to line 110, which outputs the HTML and prints the value of $display_block, in this case the form. This outcome is shown in Figure 18.2.

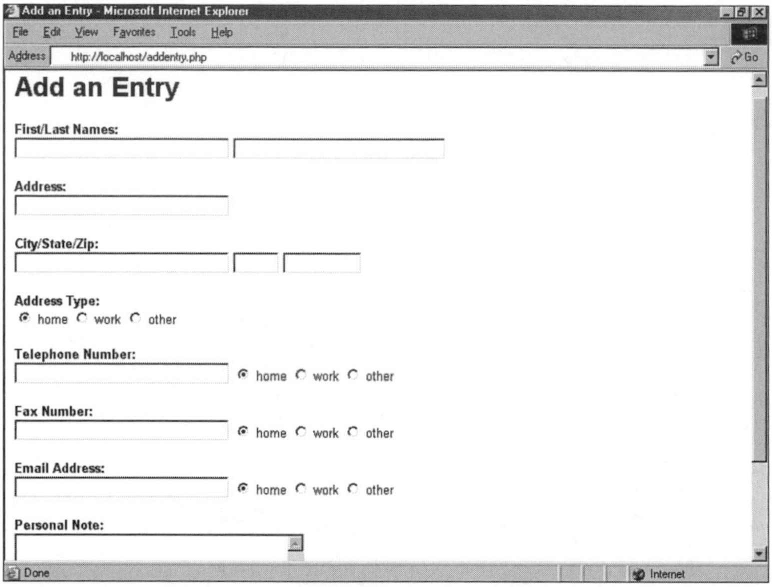

FIGURE 18.2
The record addition
form.

Line 48 begins the second condition if the value of $POST[op] is "add", meaning the user has submitted the form. For the sake of argument, two fields have been designated as required fields: the first name and last name of the person. So, lines 50–53 check for values in $_POST[f_name] and $_POST[l_name] and redirect the user back to the form if either value is missing.

After making it through the check for required fields, we connect to the database in lines 56–59. Next comes the multitude of insertion statements, only one of which is required—the insertion of a record into the master_name table. This occurs on lines 61–63. After the insertion is made, the id of this record is extracted using mysql_insert_id() on line 66. We use this value, now referred to as $master_id, in our remaining SQL queries.

The SQL queries for inserting records into the remaining tables are all conditional. This means that they occur only if some condition is true. In lines 68–69, we see that the condition that must be met is that a value exists for any of the following variables: $_POST[address], $_POST[city], $_POST[state], $_POST[zipcode]. Lines 70–74 create and issue the query if the condition is met.

The same principle holds true for adding to the telephone table (lines 77–82), the fax table (lines 84–89), the email table (lines 91–96), and the personal_notes table (lines 98–103). Once through this set of conditions, the message for the user is placed in the $display_block variable, and the script exits this if...else construct and prints HTML from lines 110–117.

An output of the record addition script is shown in Figure 18.3.

FIGURE 18.3
Adding a record.

Add a few records using this form so that you have some values to play with in the following sections. On your own, try to modify this script in such a way that the values entered in the form are printed to the screen after successful record insertion.

Viewing Records

If you verified your work in the preceding section by issuing queries through the MySQL monitor or other interface, you probably became tired of typing SELECT * FROM... for every table. In this section, you'll create the two-part script that shows you how to select and view records in your database.

Listing 18.3 shows the select-and-view script called selentry.php.

LISTING 18.3 Script Called selentry.php for Selecting and Viewing a Record

```
1: <?php
2: //connect to database
3: $conn = mysql_connect("localhost", "joeuser", "somepass")
4:    or die(mysql_error());
5: mysql_select_db("testDB",$conn)  or die(mysql_error());
6:
7: if ($_POST[op] != "view")  {
8:    //haven't seen the form, so show it
9:    $display_block = "<h1>Select an Entry</h1>";
```

LISTING 18.3   Continued

```
10:
11:      //get parts of records
12:      $get_list = "select id, concat_ws(', ', l_name, f_name) as display_name
13:          from master_name order by l_name, f_name";
14:      $get_list_res = mysql_query($get_list) or die(mysql_error());
15:
16:      if (mysql_num_rows($get_list_res) < 1) {
17:          //no records
18:          $display_block .= "<p><em>Sorry, no records to select!</em></p>";
19:
20:      } else {
21:          //has records, so get results and print in a form
22:          $display_block .= "
23:          <form method=\"post\" action=\"$_SERVER[PHP_SELF]\">
24:          <P><strong>Select a Record to View:</strong><br>
25:          <select name=\"sel_id\">
26:          <option value=\"\">-- Select One --</option>";
27:
28:          while ($recs = mysql_fetch_array($get_list_res)) {
29:              $id = $recs['id'];
30:              $display_name = stripslashes($recs['display_name']);
31:
32:              $display_block .= "<option value=\"$id\">
33:                  $display_name</option>";
34:          }
35:          $display_block .= "
36:          </select>
37:          <input type=\"hidden\" name=\"op\" value=\"view\">
38:          <p><input type=\"submit\" name=\"submit\"
39:              value=\"View Selected Entry\"></p>
40:          </FORM>";
41:      }
42:
43:} else if ($_POST[op] == "view") {
44:
45:      //check for required fields
46:       if ($_POST[sel_id] == "")  {
47:          header("Location: selentry.php");
48:          exit;
49:       }
50:
51:      //get master_info
52:      $get_master = "select concat_ws(' ', f_name, l_name) as display_name
53:          from master_name where id = $_POST[sel_id]";
54:      $get_master_res = mysql_query($get_master);
55:      $display_name = stripslashes(mysql_result($get_master_res,
56:          0,'display_name'));
57:      $display_block = "<h1>Showing Record for $display_name</h1>";
58:      //get all addresses
59:      $get_addresses = "select address, city, state, zipcode, type
60:          from address where master_id = $_POST[sel_id]";
61:      $get_addresses_res = mysql_query($get_addresses);
62:
63:      if (mysql_num_rows($get_addresses_res) > 0) {
64:
```

LISTING 18.3 Continued

```
65:          $display_block .= "<P><strong>Addresses:</strong><br>
66:          <ul>";
67:
68:          while ($add_info = mysql_fetch_array($get_addresses_res)) {
69:              $address = $add_info[address];
70:              $city = $add_info[city];
71:              $state = $add_info[state];
72:              $zipcode = $add_info[zipcode];
73:              $address_type = $add_info[type];
74:
75:              $display_block .= "<li>$address $city $state $zipcode
76:                  ($address_type)";
77:          }
78:
79:          $display_block .= "</ul>";
80:      }
81:
82:      //get all tel
83:      $get_tel = "select tel_number, type from telephone where
84:          master_id = $_POST[sel_id]";
85:      $get_tel_res = mysql_query($get_tel);
86:
87:      if (mysql_num_rows($get_tel_res) > 0) {
88:
89:          $display_block .= "<P><strong>Telephone:</strong><br>
90:          <ul>";
91:
92:          while ($tel_info = mysql_fetch_array($get_tel_res)) {
93:              $tel_number = $tel_info[tel_number];
94:              $tel_type = $tel_info[type];
95:
96:              $display_block .= "<li>$tel_number ($tel_type)";
97:          }
98:
99:          $display_block .= "</ul>";
100:     }
101:
102:     //get all fax
103:     $get_fax = "select fax_number, type from fax where
104:         master_id = $_POST[sel_id]";
105:     $get_fax_res = mysql_query($get_fax);
106:
107:     if (mysql_num_rows($get_fax_res) > 0) {
108:
109:         $display_block .= "<P><strong>Fax:</strong><br>
110:         <ul>";
111:
112:         while ($fax_info = mysql_fetch_array($get_fax_res)) {
113:             $fax_number = $fax_info[fax_number];
114:             $fax_type = $fax_info[type];
115:
116:             $display_block .= "<li>$fax_number ($fax_type)";
117:         }
118:
119:         $display_block .= "</ul>";
```

LISTING 18.3   Continued

```
120:     }
121:
122:     //get all email
123:     $get_email = "select email, type from email where
124:         master_id = $_POST[sel_id]";
125:     $get_email_res = mysql_query($get_email);
126:
127:     if (mysql_num_rows($get_email_res) > 0) {
128:
129:         $display_block .= "<P><strong>Email:</strong><br>
130:         <ul>";
131:
132:         while ($email_info = mysql_fetch_array($get_email_res)) {
133:             $email = $email_info[email];
134:             $email_type = $email_info[type];
135:
136:             $display_block .= "<li>$email ($email_type)";
137:         }
138:
139:         $display_block .= "</ul>";
140:     }
141:
142:     //get personal note
143:     $get_notes = "select note from personal_notes where
144:         master_id = $_POST[sel_id]";
145:     $get_notes_res = mysql_query($get_notes);
146:
147:     if (mysql_num_rows($get_notes_res) == 1) {
148:         $note = nl2br(stripslashes(mysql_result($get_notes_res,0,'note')));
149:
150:         $display_block .= "<P><strong>Personal Notes:</strong><br>$note";
151:     }
152:
153:     $display_block .= "<br><br><P align=center>
154:         <a href=\"$_SERVER[PHP_SELF]\">select another</a></p>";
155: }
156: ?>
157: <HTML>
158: <HEAD>
159: <TITLE>My Records</TITLE>
160: </HEAD>
161: <BODY>
162: <?php echo $display_block; ?>
163: </BODY>
164: </HTML>
```

As with the addentry.php script, the selentry.php script will perform one of two
tasks at any given time: It either shows the selection form, or it performs all the
SQL queries related to viewing the record. No matter which of the two tasks will
be performed, the database still comes into play. Given that, we connect to it in
lines 3–5.

The logic that determines the task begins at line 7, with a test for the value of $_POST[op]. If the value of $_POST[op] is not "view", the user is not coming from the form and therefore needs to see the selection form. A string called $display_block is started in line 9, and this string will be added to throughout this task. We hope that it will ultimately hold a selection form.

In lines 12–14, we select part of the master_name records to build the selection option in the form. For this step, you need only the name and ID of the person whose record you want to select. Line 16 tests for results of the query. If the query has no results, you can't build a form. In this case, the value of $display_block would be filled with an error message and the script would end, printing the resulting HTML to the screen.

However, assume you have a few records in the master_name table. In this case, you have to extract the information from the query results to be able to build the form. This is done in lines 28–33, with form elements written to the $display_block string both above and below it. The script then breaks out of the if...else construct and jumps down to line 110, which outputs the HTML and prints the value of $display_block, in this case the form. This outcome is shown in Figure 18.4.

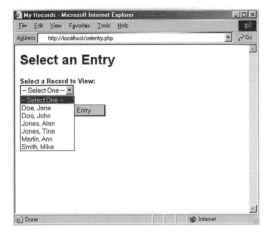

FIGURE 18.4
The record selection form.

Line 43 begins the second condition if the value of $_POST[op] is "view", meaning the user has submitted the form and wants to see a specific record. The required field in this section of the script is $_POST[sel_id], holding the ID from the master_name table of the user selected in the form. If that value does not exist, the user is redirected to the selection form. In lines 52–55, a query obtains the name of the user whose record you want to view. This information is placed in the now-familiar $display_block string, which will continue to be built as the script continues.

Lines 59–80 represent the query against the address table. If the selected individual has no records in the address table, nothing is added to the $display_block string. However, if there are one or more entries, the person is placed in $display_block as unordered list elements, as shown in lines 65–79.

The same principle is followed for records in the telephone (lines 83–100), fax (lines 103–120), and email (lines 123–140) tables. If there are one or more entries, place the results in $display_block. Otherwise, the script moves on. Because there can be only one entry per individual in the personal_notes table, the script checks for the entry beginning in line 143, and moves on if it doesn't exist. If a note exists, it's written in $display_block in lines 147–151.

The final action in this part of the script is to print a link in lines 153–154, in case the user wants to return to the selection screen. After this point, the script exits from the if...else construct and prints the HTML to the screen. Figure 18.5 shows a record from the record selection script, with one entry in each table.

FIGURE 18.5
An individual's record.

Try this script yourself. You should see data only for individuals who have data associated with them. For example, if you have an entry for a friend, and all you have is an email address for that person, you shouldn't see any text relating to address, telephone, fax, or personal notes.

Creating the Record Deletion Mechanism

The record deletion mechanism is virtually identical to the script used to view a record. In fact, you can just take the first 44 lines of Listing 18.3 and paste them into a new file, called `delentry.php`, and make the following changes:

▶ In lines 7, 37, and 43, change `"view"` to `"delete"`

▶ In lines 24 and 39, change `"View"` to `"Delete"`

Starting with a new line 45, the remainder of the code for `delentry.php` is shown in Listing 18.4.

LISTING 18.4 Script Called `delentry.php` for Selecting and Deleting a Record

```
45:    //check for required fields
46:      if ($_POST[sel_id] == "")  {
47:        header("Location: delentry.php");
48:        exit;
49:      }
50:
51:    //issue queries
52:    $del_master = "delete from master_name where id = $_POST[sel_id]";
53:    mysql_query($del_master);
54:
55:    $del_address = "delete from address where id = $_POST[sel_id]";
56:    mysql_query($del_address);
57:
58:    $del_tel = "delete from telephone where id = $_POST[sel_id]";
59:    mysql_query($del_tel);
60:
61:    $del_fax = "delete from fax where id = $_POST[sel_id]";
62:    mysql_query($del_fax);
63:
64:    $del_email = "delete from email where id = $_POST[sel_id]";
65:    mysql_query($del_email);
66:
67:    $del_note = "delete from personal_notes where id = $_POST[sel_id]";
68:    mysql_query($del_master);
69:
70:    $display_block = "<h1>Record(s) Deleted</h1>
71:    <P>Would you like to
72:    <a href=\"$_SERVER[PHP_SELF]\">delete another</a>?</p>";
73: }
74: ?>
75: <HTML>
76: <HEAD>
77: <TITLE>My Records</TITLE>
78: </HEAD>
79: <BODY>
80: <?php echo $display_block; ?>
81: </BODY>
82: </HTML>
```

Picking up with line 45, the script looks for the required field, $_POST[sel_id]. If that value does not exist, the user is redirected to the selection form. In lines 52–68, queries delete all information related to the selected individual, from all tables. Lines 70–72 place a nice message in $display_block, and the script exits and prints the HTML to the screen. An output of the record deletion script is shown in Figure 18.6.

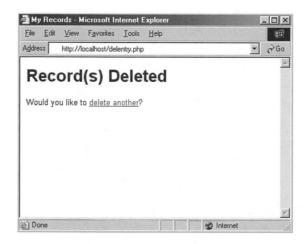

Now go back to the record selection form and note that the individual you deleted is no longer in the selection menu.

Adding Subentries to a Record

At this point, you've learned to add, remove, and view records. What's missing is adding those additional entries to the related tables—entries for home versus work telephone number, for example. All you need to do is make a few changes to existing scripts.

In the selentry.php script in Listing 18.3, change lines 153–154 to read

```
$display_block .= "<P align=center>
<a href=\"addentry.php?master_id=$_POST[sel_id]\">add info</a> ...
<a href=\"$_SERVER[PHP_SELF]\">select another</a></p>";
```

This change simply adds a link to the addentry.php script and also passes it a variable called $master_id.

Now we need to modify the addentry.php script in Listing 18.2 to account for its dual purposes. Here is a summary of the changes to the original script.

Replace the first 10 lines of the original addentry.php script with the following snippet:

```php
<?php
if (($_POST[op] != "add") || ($_GET[master_id] != "")) {
    //haven't seen the form, so show it
    $display_block = "
    <h1>Add an Entry</h1>
    <form method=\"post\" action=\"$_SERVER[PHP_SELF]\">";

    if ($_GET[master_id] != "") {
        //connect to database
        $conn = mysql_connect("localhost", "joeuser", "somepass")
                    or die(mysql_error());
        mysql_select_db("testDB",$conn)  or die(mysql_error());

        //get first, last names for display/tests validity
        $get_names = "select concat_ws(' ', f_name, l_name) as
                    display_name from master_name where id = $_GET[master_id]";
        $get_names_res = mysql_query($get_names) or die(mysql_error());

        if (mysql_num_rows($get_names_res) == 1) {
            $display_name = mysql_result($got_names_res,0,'display_name');
        }
    }

    if ($display_name != "") {
        $display_block .= "<P>Adding information for
                        <strong>$display_name</strong>:</p>";
    } else {
        $display_block .= "
        <P><strong>First/Last Names:</strong><br>
        <input type=\"text\" name=\"f_name\" size=30 maxlength=75>
        <input type=\"text\" name=\"l_name\" size=30 maxlength=75>";
    }
    $display_block .= "<P><strong>Address:</strong><br>
```

This snippet simply moves around the form elements, printing the first and last name fields only if they contain a new record. If they contain an addition to a record, the individual's name is extracted from the database for aesthetic purposes as well as for a validity check of the ID.

Next, find this line:

```
<input type=\"hidden\" name=\"op\" value=\"add\">
```

Beneath it, add the following:

```
<input type=\"hidden\" name=\"master_id\" value=\"$_GET[master_id]\">
```

This modification ensures the known value of master_id is passed along to the
next task.

Identify what were lines 49–67 of the original script, beginning with the comment
time to add to tables and ending with obtaining the value of $master_id.
These lines should be replaced with the following:

```
//time to add to tables, so check for required fields
if (((($_POST[f_name] == "") || ($_POST[1_name] == "")) &&
        ($_POST[master_id] == "")) {
    header("Location: addentry.php");
    exit;
}

//connect to database
$conn = mysql_connect("localhost", "joeuser", "somepass")
        or die(mysql_error());
mysql_select_db("testDB",$conn)  or die(mysql_error());

if ($_POST[master_id] == "") {
    //add to master_name table
    $add_master = "insert into master_name values ('', now(),
                now(), '$_POST[f_name]', '$_POST[1_name]')";
    mysql_query($add_master) or die(mysql_error());
    //get master_id for use with other tables
    $master_id = mysql_insert_id();
} else {
    $master_id = $_POST[master_id];
}
```

These lines modify the check for required fields, allowing the script to continue
without values for first and last names, but only if it has a $_POST[master_id]
value. Then the script connects to the database to perform all the additions we
want it to, but it skips the addition to the master_name table if a value for
$_POST[master_id] exists.

Finally, in the section of the script that handles the insertion into the
personal_notes table, change INSERT into to REPLACE into to handle an update
of the notes field.

The new script should look like Listing 18.5.

LISTING 18.5   New addentry.php Script

```
1: <?php
2: if (($_POST[op] != "add") || ($_GET[master_id] != "")) {
3:     //haven't seen the form, so show it
4:     $display_block = "
5:     <h1>Add an Entry</h1>
6:     <form method=\"post\" action=\"$_SERVER[PHP_SELF]\">";
7:
8:     if ($_GET[master_id] != "") {
```

LISTING 18.5   Continued

```
 9:          //connect to database
10:          $conn = mysql_connect("localhost", "joeuser", "somepass")
11:                     or die(mysql_error());
12:          mysql_select_db("testDB",$conn)  or die(mysql_error());
13:
14:          //get first, last names for display/tests validity
15:          $get_names = "select concat_ws(' ', f_name, l_name) as
16:                  display_name from master_name where id = $_GET[master_id]";
17:          $get_names_res = mysql_query($get_names) or die(mysql_error());
18:
19:          if (mysql_num_rows($get_names_res) == 1) {
20:              $display_name = mysql_result($get_names_res,0,'display_name');
21:          }
22:      }
23:
24:      if ($display_name != "") {
25:          $display_block .= "<P>Adding information for
26:                      <strong>$display_name</strong>:</p>";
27:      } else {
28:          $display_block .= "
29:      <P><strong>First/Last Names:</strong><br>
30:      <input type=\"text\" name=\"f_name\" size=30 maxlength=75>
31:      <input type=\"text\" name=\"l_name\" size=30 maxlength=75>";
32:      }
33:  $display_block .= "<P><strong>Address:</strong><br>
34:      <input type=\"text\" name=\"address\" size=30>
35:
36:      <P><strong>City/State/Zip:</strong><br>
37:      <input type=\"text\" name=\"city\" size=30 maxlength=50>
38:      <input type=\"text\" name=\"state\" size=5 maxlength=2>
39:      <input type=\"text\" name=\"zipcode\" size=10 maxlength=10>
40:
41:      <P><strong>Address Type:</strong><br>
42:      <input type=\"radio\" name=\"add_type\" value=\"home\" checked> home
43:      <input type=\"radio\" name=\"add_type\" value=\"work\"> work
44:      <input type=\"radio\" name=\"add_type\" value=\"other\"> other
45:
46:      <P><strong>Telephone Number:</strong><br>
47:      <input type=\"text\" name=\"tel_number\" size=30 maxlength=25>
48:      <input type=\"radio\" name=\"tel_type\" value=\"home\" checked> home
49:      <input type=\"radio\" name=\"tel_type\" value=\"work\"> work
50:      <input type=\"radio\" name=\"tel_type\" value=\"other\"> other
51:
52:      <P><strong>Fax Number:</strong><br>
53:      <input type=\"text\" name=\"fax_number\" size=30 maxlength=25>
54:      <input type=\"radio\" name=\"fax_type\" value=\"home\" checked> home
55:      <input type=\"radio\" name=\"fax_type\" value=\"work\"> work
56:      <input type=\"radio\" name=\"fax_type\" value=\"other\"> other
57:
58:      <P><strong>Email Address:</strong><br>
59:      <input type=\"text\" name=\"email\" size=30 maxlength=150>
60:      <input type=\"radio\" name=\"email_type\" value=\"home\" checked> home
61:      <input type=\"radio\" name=\"email_type\" value=\"work\"> work
62:      <input type=\"radio\" name=\"email_type\" value=\"other\"> other
63:
64:      <P><strong>Personal Note:</strong><br>
```

LISTING 18.5 Continued

```
65:     <textarea name=\"note\" cols=35 rows=5 wrap=virtual></textarea>
66:     <input type=\"hidden\" name=\"op\" value=\"add\">
67:     <input type=\"hidden\" name=\"master_id\" value=\"$_GET[master_id]\">
68:
69:     <p><input type=\"submit\" name=\"submit\" value=\"Add Entry\"></p>
70:     </FORM>";
71:
72: } else if ($_POST[op] == "add") {
73:     //time to add to tables, so check for required fields
74:     if ((($_POST[f_name] == "") || ($_POST[l_name] == "")) &&
75:     ($_POST[master_id] == "")) {
76:         header("Location: addentry.php");
77:         exit;
78:     }
79:
80:     //connect to database
81: $conn = mysql_connect("localhost", "joeuser", "somepass")
82: or die(mysql_error());
83: mysql_select_db("testDB",$conn)  or die(mysql_error());
84:
85:     if ($_POST[master_id] == "") {
86:         //add to master_name table
87:         $add_master = "insert into master_name values ('', now(),
88:         now(), '$_POST[f_name]', '$_POST[l_name]')";
89:         mysql_query($add_master) or die(mysql_error());
90:         //get master_id for use with other tables
91:         $master_id = mysql_insert_id();
92:     } else {
93:         $master_id = $_POST[master_id];
94:     }
95:
96:     if (($_POST[address]) || ($_POST[city]) || ($_POST[state]) ||
97:         ($_POST[zipcode])) {
98:         //something relevant, so add to address table
99:         $add_address = "insert into address values ('', $master_id,
100:             now(), now(), '$_POST[address]', '$_POST[city]',
101:             '$_POST[state]', '$_POST[zipcode]', '$_POST[add_type]')";
102:         mysql_query($add_address) or die(mysql_error());
103:     }
104:
105:     if ($_POST[tel_number]) {
106:         //something relevant, so add to telephone table
107:         $add_tel = "insert into telephone values ('', $master_id,
108:          now(), now(), '$_POST[tel_number]', '$_POST[tel_type]')";
109:         mysql_query($add_tel) or die(mysql_error());
110:     }
111:
112:     if ($_POST[fax_number]) {
113:         //something relevant, so add to fax table
114:         $add_fax = "insert into fax values ('', $master_id, now(),
115:          now(), '$_POST[fax_number]', '$_POST[fax_type]')";
116:         mysql_query($add_fax) or die(mysql_error());
117:     }
118:
119:     if ($_POST[email]) {
```

LISTING 18.5 Continued

```
120:            //something relevant, so add to email table
121:            $add_email = "insert into email values ('', $master_id,
122:                now(), now(), '$_POST[email]',  '$_POST[email_type]')";
123:            mysql_query($add_email) or die(mysql_error());
124:        }
125:
126:        if ($_POST[note]) {
127:            //something relevant, so add to notes table
128:            $add_note = "replace into personal_notes values ('', $master_id,
129:                now(), now(), '$_POST[note]')";
130:            mysql_query($add_note) or die(mysql_error());
131:        }
132:
133:        $display_block = "<h1>Entry Added</h1>
134:        <P>Your entry has been added.  Would you like to
135:         <a href=\"addentry.php\">add another</a>?</p>";
136:    }
137: ?>
138: <HTML>
139: <HEAD>
140: <TITLE>Add an Entry</TITLE>
141: </HEAD>
142: <BODY>
143: <?php echo $display_block; ?>
144: </BODY>
145: </HTML>
```

You can try out this revised script by selecting a record to view and then following the add info link. You should see a form like Figure 18.7.

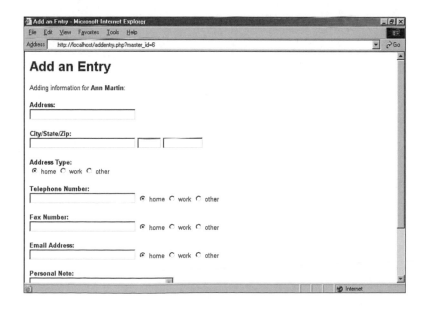

FIGURE 18.7
Adding to a record.

After submitting this form, you can go back through the selection sequence and view the record to verify that your changes have been made.

Summary

In this hands-on chapter, you applied your basic PHP and MySQL knowledge to the creation of a personal address book. You learned how to create the database table and scripts for record addition, removal, and simple viewing. You also learned the process for adding multiple records attached to a single master entry.

Workshop

The workshop is designed to help you anticipate possible questions, review what you've learned, and begin learning how to put your knowledge into practice.

Quiz

1. When passing a variable through the query string, which superglobal does it belong in?

2. How many records in the address, email, telephone, and fax tables can you have for each individual in your master_name table?

Answers

1. The $_GET superglobal.

2. As many as you want—it's relational!

Activities

1. Go through each of the administration scripts and modify the code so that a link to the menu is printed at the bottom of each screen.

2. Use the second version of the addentry.php script to add secondary contact information to records in your database. Figure 18.8 shows how a record will look after secondary contact information is added to it.

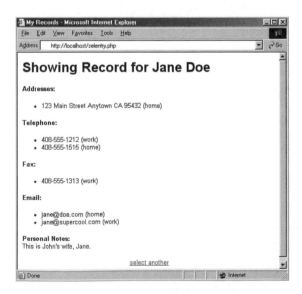

FIGURE 18.8
An individual's record with multiple entries in tables.

CHAPTER 19

Creating a Simple Discussion Forum

In this chapter, you'll learn the design process behind a simple discussion forum. This includes developing the database tables, user input forms, and display of the results. When broken into pieces like this, such a task seems quite simple—and it is!

In this chapter, you will learn

▶ How to create the tables, input forms, and display of a simple discussion forum

Designing the Database Tables

Think of the basic components of a forum: topics and posts. A forum—if properly used by its patrons—should have several topics, and each of those topics will have one or more posts by users. Knowing that, you should realize that the posts are tied to the topics through a key field. This key forms the relationship between the two tables.

Think about the requirements for the topics themselves. You definitely need a field for the title, and subsequently you may want fields to hold the creation time and the identification of the user who created the topic. Similarly, think of the requirements for the posts: You want the text of the post, the time it was created, and the person creating it. Most importantly, you need that key to tie the post to the topic.

The following two table creation statements create these tables, called forum_topics and forum_posts:

```
mysql> create table forum_topics (
    -> topic_id int not null primary key auto_increment,
    -> topic_title varchar (150),
    -> topic_create_time datetime,
    -> topic_owner varchar (150)
    -> );
Query OK, 0 rows affected (0.03 sec)
```

```
mysql> create table forum_posts (
    -> post_id int not null primary key auto_increment,
    -> topic_id int not null,
    -> post_text text,
    -> post_create_time datetime,
    -> post_owner varchar (150)
    -> );
Query OK, 0 rows affected (0.00 sec)
```

By the Way

> In this forum example, we will identify users by their email addresses and not require any sort of login sequence.

You should now have two empty tables, waiting for some input. In the next section, you'll create the input forms for adding a topic and a post.

Creating the Input Forms and Scripts

Before you can add any posts, you must add a topic to the forum. It is common practice in forum creation to add the topic and the first post in that topic at the same time. From a user's point of view, it doesn't make much sense to add a topic and then go back, select the topic, and add a reply. You want the process to be as smooth as possible.

Listing 19.1 shows the form for a new topic creation, which includes a space for the first post in the topic.

LISTING 19.1   Form for Adding a Topic

```
 1: <html>
 2: <head>
 3: <title>Add a Topic</title>
 4: </head>
 5: <body>
 6: <h1>Add a Topic</h1>
 7: <form method=post action="do_addtopic.php">
 8: <p><strong>Your E-Mail Address:</strong><br>
 9: <input type="text" name="topic_owner" size=40 maxlength=150>
10: <p><strong>Topic Title:</strong><br>
11: <input type="text" name="topic_title" size=40 maxlength=150>
12: <P><strong>Post Text:</strong><br>
13: <textarea name="post_text" rows=8 cols=40 wrap=virtual></textarea>
14: <P><input type="submit" name="submit" value="Add Topic"></p>
15: </form>
16: </body>
17: </html>
```

Seems simple enough—the three fields shown in the form, which you can see in Figure 19.1, are all you need to complete both tables; your script and database can fill in the rest. Save Listing 19.1 as something like addtopic.html and put it in your Web server document root so that you can follow along.

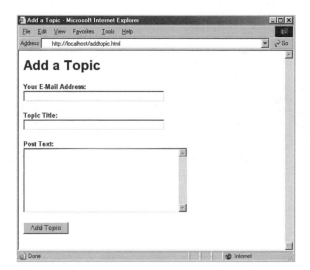

FIGURE 19.1
The topic creation form.

To create the entry in the forum_topics table, you use the topic_title and topic_owner fields from the input form. The topic_id and topic_create_time fields will be filled in automatically. Similarly, in the forum_posts table, you use the post_text and topic_owner fields from the input form, and the post_id, post_create_time, and the topic_id fields will be filled in automatically. Because you need a value for the topic_id field to be able to complete the entry in the forum_posts table, you know that query must happen after the query to insert the record in the forum_topics table.

Listing 19.2 creates the script to add these records to the table.

LISTING 19.2   Script for Adding a Topic

```
 1: <?php
 2: //check for required fields from the form
 3: if ((!$_POST[topic_owner]) || (!$_POST[topic_title])
 4:      || (!$_POST[post_text])) {
 5:    header("Location: addtopic.html");
 6:    exit;
 7: }
 8:
 9: //connect to server and select database
10: $conn = mysql_connect("localhost", "joeuser", "somepass")
```

LISTING 19.2   Continued

```
11:     or die(mysql_error());
12: mysql_select_db("testDB",$conn)  or die(mysql_error());
13:
14: //create and issue the first query
15: $add_topic = "insert into forum_topics values ('', '$_POST[topic_title]',
16:     now(), '$_POST[topic_owner]')";
17: mysql_query($add_topic,$conn) or die(mysql_error());
18:
19: //get the id of the last query
20: $topic_id = mysql_insert_id();
21:
22: //create and issue the second query
23: $add_post = "insert into forum_posts values ('', '$topic_id',
24:     '$_POST[post_text]', now(), '$_POST[topic_owner]')";
25: mysql_query($add_post,$conn) or die(mysql_error());
26:
27: //create nice message for user
28: $msg = "<P>The <strong>$topic_title</strong> topic has been created.</p>";
29: ?>
30: <html>
31: <head>
32: <title>New Topic Added</title>
33: </head>
34: <body>
35: <h1>New Topic Added</h1>
36: <?php echo $msg; ?>
37: </body>
38: </html>
```

Lines 3–7 check for the three required fields we need to complete both tables. If either one of these fields is not present, the user is redirected to the original form.

Lines 10–12 form the database connection, which should be familiar to you by now. Lines 15–17 create and insert the first query, which adds the topic to the forum_topics table. Note that the first field is left blank, so the automatically incrementing number is added by the system. Similarly, the now() function is used to time stamp the record with the current time. The other fields in the record are completed using values from the form.

Line 20 shows the use of a very handy function: mysql_insert_id(). This function retrieves the primary key ID of the last record inserted into the database by this script. In this case, mysql_insert_id() gets the id value from the forum_topics table, which will become the entry for the topic_id field in the forum_posts table.

Lines 23–25 create and insert the second query, again using a mixture of information known and supplied by the system. Line 28 simply creates a message for the user, and the rest of the script rounds out the display.

Save this listing as do_addtopic.php—the name of the action in the previous script—and place it in the document root of your Web server. Complete the form and then submit it, and you should see the New Topic Added message. Figures 19.2 and 19.3 show the sequence of events.

FIGURE 19.2
Adding a topic and first post.

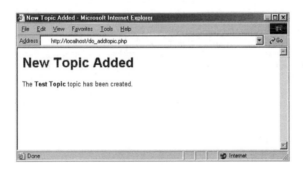

FIGURE 19.3
Successful addition of a topic and first post.

In the next section, you'll put together two more pieces of the puzzle: displaying the topics and posts, and replying to a topic.

Displaying the Topic List

Now that you have a topic and at least one post in your database, you can display this information and let people add new topics or reply to existing ones. In Listing 19.3, we take a step back and create a topic listing page. This page will show the basic information of each topic and provide the user with a link to add a new topic; you already have the form and script for that. This script would actually be an entry page for your forum.

LISTING 19.3   Topic Listing Script

```
 1: <?php
 2: //connect to server and select database
 3: $conn = mysql_connect("localhost", "joeuser", "somepass")
 4:     or die(mysql_error());
 5: mysql_select_db("testDB",$conn)  or die(mysql_error());
 6:
 7: //gather the topics
 8: $get_topics = "select topic_id, topic_title,
 9: date_format(topic_create_time,  '%b %e %Y at %r') as fmt_topic_create_time,
10: topic_owner from forum_topics order by topic_create_time desc";
11: $get_topics_res = mysql_query($get_topics,$conn) or die(mysql_error());
12: if (mysql_num_rows($get_topics_res) < 1) {
13:     //there are no topics, so say so
14:     $display_block = "<P><em>No topics exist.</em></p>";
15: } else {
16:     //create the display string
17:     $display_block = "
18:     <table cellpadding=3 cellspacing=1 border=1>
19:     <tr>
20:     <th>TOPIC TITLE</th>
21:     <th># of POSTS</th>
22:     </tr>";
23:
24:      while ($topic_info = mysql_fetch_array($get_topics_res)) {
25:         $topic_id = $topic_info['topic_id'];
26:         $topic_title = stripslashes($topic_info['topic_title']);
27:         $topic_create_time = $topic_info['fmt_topic_create_time'];
28:         $topic_owner = stripslashes($topic_info['topic_owner']);
29:
30:         //get number of posts
31:         $get_num_posts = "select count(post_id) from forum_posts
32:             where topic_id = $topic_id";
33:         $get_num_posts_res = mysql_query($get_num_posts,$conn)
34:             or die(mysql_error());
35:         $num_posts = mysql_result($get_num_posts_res,0,'count(post_id)');
36:
37:         //add to display
38:         $display_block .= "
39:         <tr>
40:         <td><a href=\"showtopic.php?topic_id=$topic_id\">
41:             <strong>$topic_title</strong></a><br>
42:         Created on $topic_create_time by $topic_owner</td>
43:         <td align=center>$num_posts</td>
44:         </tr>";
45:     }
46:
47:     //close up the table
48:     $display_block .= "</table>";
49: }
```

LISTING 19.3   Continued

```
50: ?>
51: <html>
52: <head>
53: <title>Topics in My Forum</title>
54: </head>
55: <body>
56: <h1>Topics in My Forum</h1>
57: <?php echo $display_block; ?>
58: <P>Would you like to <a href="addtopic.html">add a topic</a>?</p>
59: </body>
60: </html>
```

Although Listing 19.3 looks like a lot of code, it's actually many small, simple concepts you've already encountered. Lines 3–5 make the connection to the database, in preparation for issuing queries. Lines 8–10 show the first of these queries, and this particular one selects all the topic information, in order by descending date. In other words, display the topic that was created last (the newest topic) at the top of the list. In the query, notice the use of the date_format() function to create a much nicer date display than the one stored in the database.

Line 12 checks for the presence of any records returned by the query. If no records are returned, and therefore no topics are in the table, you'll want to tell the user. Line 14 creates this message. At this point, if no topics existed, the script would break out of the if...else construct and be over with; the next action would occur at line 51, which is the start of the static HTML. If the script ended here, the message created in line 14 would be printed in line 57, and you would see something like Figure 19.4.

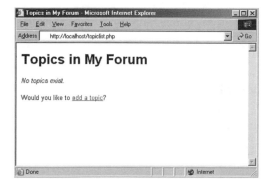

FIGURE 19.4
No topics found.

If, however, you have topics in your forum_topics table, the script continues at line 15. At line 17, a block of text is started, containing the beginnings of an

HTML table. Lines 18–22 set up a table with two columns: one for the title and one for the number of posts. The text block is stopped momentarily, and at line 24 we begin to loop through the results of the original query.

The while loop in line 24 says that while there are elements to be extracted from the result set, extract each row as an array called $topic_info, and use the field names as the array element to assign the value to a new variable. So, the first element we try to extract is the topic_id field, on line 25. We set the value of $topic_id to $topic_info['topic_id'], meaning that we get a local value for $topic_id from an array called $topic_info, containing a slot called topic_id. Continue doing this for the $topic_title, $topic_create_time, and $topic_owner variables in lines 26–28. The stripslashes() function removes any escape characters that were input into the table at the time of record insertion.

In lines 31–35 we issue another query, in the context of the while loop, to get the number of posts for that particular topic. In line 38, we continue the creation of the $display_block string, using the concatenation operator (.=) to make sure this string is tacked on to the end of the string we have created so far. In line 40, we create the HTML table column to display the link to the file that will show the topic (showtopic.php), and also print the topic owner and creation time. The second HTML table column, on line 43, shows the number of posts. On line 45, we break out of the while loop, and in line 48 add the last bit to the $display_block string to close the table. The remaining lines print the HTML for the page, including the value of the $display_block string.

If you save this file as topiclist.php and place it in your Web server document root, and if you have topics in your database tables, you may see something like Figure 19.5.

FIGURE 19.5
Topics are
available.

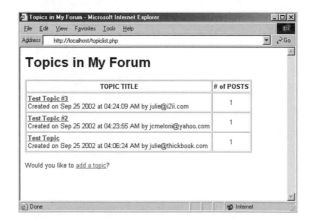

Displaying the Posts in a Topic

As you may have guessed, the next item on the task list is to build that showtopic.php file, to show the topic's postings. Listing 19.4 does just that.

LISTING 19.4 Script to Show Topic Posts

```
 1: <?php
 2: //check for required info from the query string
 3: if (!$_GET[topic_id]) {
 4:     header("Location: topiclist.php");
 5:     exit;
 6: }
 7:
 8: //connect to server and select database
 9: $conn = mysql_connect("localhost", "joeuser", "somepass")
10:     or die(mysql_error());
11: mysql_select_db("testDB",$conn)  or die(mysql_error());
12:
13: //verify the topic exists
14: $verify_topic = "select topic_title from forum_topics where
15:     topic_id = $_GET[topic_id]";
16: $verify_topic_res = mysql_query($verify_topic, $conn)
17:     or die(mysql_error());
18:
19: if (mysql_num_rows($verify_topic_res) < 1) {
20:     //this topic does not exist
21:     $display_block = "<P><em>You have selected an invalid topic.
22:     Please <a href=\"topiclist.php\">try again</a>.</em> </p>",
23: } else {
24:     //get the topic title
25:     $topic_title = stripslashes(mysql_result($verify_topic_res,0,
26:         'topic_title'));
27:
28:     //gather the posts
29:     $get_posts = "select post_id, post_text, date_format(post_create_time,
30:         '%b %e %Y at %r') as fmt_post_create_time, post_owner from
31:         forum_posts where topic_id = $_GET[topic_id]
32:         order by post_create_time asc";
33:
34:     $get_posts_res = mysql_query($get_posts,$conn) or die(mysql_error());
35:
36:     //create the display string
37:     $display_block = "
38:     <P>Showing posts for the <strong>$topic_title</strong> topic:</p>
39:
40:     <table width=100% cellpadding=3 cellspacing=1 border=1>
41:     <tr>
42:     <th>AUTHOR</th>
43:     <th>POST</th>
44:     </tr>";
45:
46:     while ($posts_info = mysql_fetch_array($get_posts_res)) {
47:         $post_id = $posts_info['post_id'];
48:         $post_text = nl2br(stripslashes($posts_info['post_text']));
```

LISTING 19.4 Continued

```
49:        $post_create_time = $posts_info['fmt_post_create_time'];
50:        $post_owner = stripslashes($posts_info['post_owner']);
51:
52:        //add to display
53:        $display_block .= "
54:        <tr>
55:        <td width=35% valign=top>$post_owner<br>[$post_create_time]</td>
56:        <td width=65% valign=top>$post_text<br><br>
57:         <a href=\"replytopost.php?post_id=$post_id\"><strong>REPLY TO
58:         POST</strong></a></td>
59:        </tr>";
60:    }
61:
62:    //close up the table
63:    $display_block .= "</table>";
64: }
65: ?>
66: <html>
67: <head>
68: <title>Posts in Topic</title>
69: </head>
70: <body>
71: <h1>Posts in Topic</h1>
72: <?php echo $display_block; ?>
73: </body>
74: </html>
```

In Listing 19.4, lines 3–6 check for the existence of a value for topic_id in the GET query string. Because we're showing all the posts in a selected topic, we need to know which topic, and this is the manner in which the information is given to us. If a value in $_GET[topic_id] does not exist, the user is redirected to the topic listing page.

If you made it past the check for a topic_id, lines 9–11 make the connection to the database, in preparation for issuing queries. Lines 14–17 show the first of these queries, and this one is used to validate that the topic_id sent in the query string is actually a valid entry, by selecting the associated topic_title for the topic in question. If the validation fails the test in line 19, a message is created in lines 21–22, and the script breaks out of the if...else statement and finishes up by printing HTML. This output looks like Figure 19.6.

If, however, the topic is valid, we extract the value of topic_title in line 25, again using stripslashes() to remove any escape characters. Next, the query is issued in lines 29–32 to gather all the posts associated with that topic, in ascending order by time. In this case, newest posts are at the bottom of the list. At line 37, a block of text is started, containing the beginnings of an HTML table. Lines 40–44 set up a table with two columns: one for the author of the post and one for the post text itself. The text block is stopped momentarily and at line 46 we begin to loop through the results of the original query.

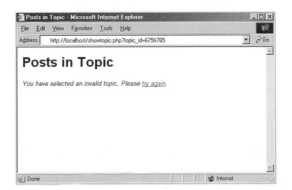

FIGURE 19.6
Invalid topic selected.

The while loop in line 46 says that while there are elements to be extracted from the result set, extract each row as an array called $posts_info, and use the field names as the array element to assign the value to a new variable. So, the first element we try to extract is the post_id field, on line 47. We set the value of $post_id to $posts_info['post_id'], meaning that we get a local value for $post_id from an array called $posts_info, containing a slot called post_id. Continue doing this for the $post_text, $post_create_time, and $post_owner variables in lines 48–50. The stripslashes() function is again used to remove any escape characters, and the nl2br() function is used on the value of $posts_info[post_text], to replace all newline characters with HTML <br> characters.

In line 53, we continue the creation of the $display_block string, using the concatenation operator (.=) to make sure this string is tacked on to the end of the string we have created so far. In line 54, we create the HTML table column to display the author and creation time of the post. The second HTML table row, on line 56, shows the text of the post as well as a link to reply to the post. On line 60, we break out of the while loop and on line 63 add the last bit to the $display_block string to close the table. The remaining lines print the HTML for the page, including the value of the $display_block string.

If you save this file as showtopic.php, place it in your Web server document root, and if you have posts in your database tables, you may see something like Figure 19.7.

A one-post topic is boring, so let's finish up this chapter by creating the script to add a post to a topic.

FIGURE 19.7
Posts in a topic.

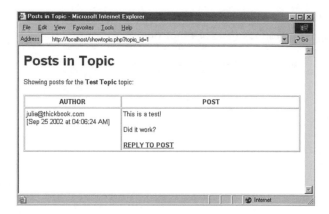

Adding Posts to a Topic

In this final step, you will create replytopost.php, which will look remarkably similar to the form and script used to add a topic. Listing 19.5 shows the code for this all-in-one form and script.

LISTING 19.5   Script to Add Replies to a Topic

```
1: <?php
2: //connect to server and select database; we'll need it soon
3: $conn = mysql_connect("localhost", "joeuser", "somepass")
4:     or die(mysql_error());
5: mysql_select_db("testDB",$conn)  or die(mysql_error());
6:
7: //check to see if we're showing the form or adding the post
8: if ($_POST[op] != "addpost") {
9:    // showing the form; check for required item in query string
10:    if (!$_GET[post_id]) {
11:        header("Location: topiclist.php");
12:        exit;
13:    }
14:
15:      //still have to verify topic and post
16:    $verify = "select ft.topic_id, ft.topic_title from
17:     forum_posts as fp left join forum_topics as ft on
18:     fp.topic_id = ft.topic_id where fp.post_id = $_GET[post_id]";
19:
20:    $verify_res = mysql_query($verify, $conn) or die(mysql_error());
21:    if (mysql_num_rows($verify_res) < 1) {
22:        //this post or topic does not exist
23:        header("Location: topiclist.php");
24:        exit;
25:    } else {
26:        //get the topic id and title
27:        $topic_id = mysql_result($verify_res,0,'topic_id');
28:        $topic_title = stripslashes(mysql_result($verify_res,
```

LISTING 19.5   Continued

```
29:            0,'topic_title'));
30:
31:        echo "
32:        <html>
33:        <head>
34:        <title>Post Your Reply in $topic_title</title>
35:        </head>
36:        <body>
37:        <h1>Post Your Reply in $topic_title</h1>
38:        <form method=post action=\"$_SERVER[PHP_SELF]\">
39:
40:        <p><strong>Your E-Mail Address:</strong><br>
41:        <input type=\"text\" name=\"post_owner\" size=40 maxlength=150>
42:
43:        <P><strong>Post Text:</strong><br>
44:        <textarea name=\"post_text\" rows=8 cols=40 wrap=virtual></textarea>
45:
46:        <input type=\"hidden\" name=\"op\" value=\"addpost\">
47:        <input type=\"hidden\" name=\"topic_id\" value=\"$topic_id\">
48:
49:        <P><input type=\"submit\" name=\"submit\" value=\"Add Post\"></p>
50:
51:        </form>
52:        </body>
53:        </html>";
54:    }
55: } else if ($_POST[op] -- "addpost") {
56:    //check for required items from form
57:    if ((!$_POST[topic_id]) || (!$_POST[post_text]) ||
58:    (!$_POST[post_owner])) {
59:        header("Location: topiclist.php");
60:        exit;
61:    }
62:
63:    //add the post
64:    $add_post = "insert into forum_posts values ('', '$_POST[topic_id]',
65:     '$_POST[post_text]', now(), '$_POST[post_owner]')";
66:    mysql_query($add_post,$conn) or die(mysql_error());
67:
68:    //redirect user to topic
69:    header("Location: showtopic.php?topic_id=$topic_id");
70:    exit;
71: }
72: ?>
```

Lines 3–5 make the database connection at the outset of the script. Although you're performing multiple tasks depending on the status of the form (whether it's being shown or submitted), both conditions require database interaction at some point.

Line 8 checks to see whether the form is being submitted. If the value of $_POST[op] is not "addpost", the form has not yet been submitted. Therefore, it must be shown. Before showing the form, however, you must check for that one required item; lines 10–13 check for the existence of a value for post_id in the GET query string. If a value in $_GET[post_id] does not exist, the user is redirected to the topic listing page.

If you made it past the check for a topic_id, lines 17–20 issue a complicated-looking query that gets the topic_id and topic_title from the forum_topics table, based on the only value that you know: the value of the post_id. This query both validates the existence of the post and gets information you will need later in the script. Lines 21–24 act on the results of this validity test, again redirecting the user back to the topiclist.php page.

If the post is valid, you extract the value of topic_id and topic_title in lines 27–29, again using stripslashes() to remove any escape characters. Next, the entirety of the form for adding a post is printed to the screen, and that's it for this script until the form submission button is clicked. In the form, you see that the action is $_SERVER[PHP_SELF] on line 38, indicating that this script will be recalled into action. Two hidden fields are present, in lines 46 and 47, which hold the information that needs to be passed along to the next iteration of the script.

Moving along to line 55, this block of code is executed when the script is reloaded and the value of $_POST[op] (one of the hidden fields in the form) is "addpost". This block checks for the presence of all required fields from the form (lines 57–61) and then, if they are all present, issues the query to add the post to the database (lines 64–66). After the post is added to the database, the showtopic.php page is reloaded (lines 69–70), showing the user's new post along in the line.

If you save this file as replytopost.php and place it in your Web server document root, try it out and you may see something like Figures 19.8 and 19.9.

FIGURE 19.8
Preparing to add a post.

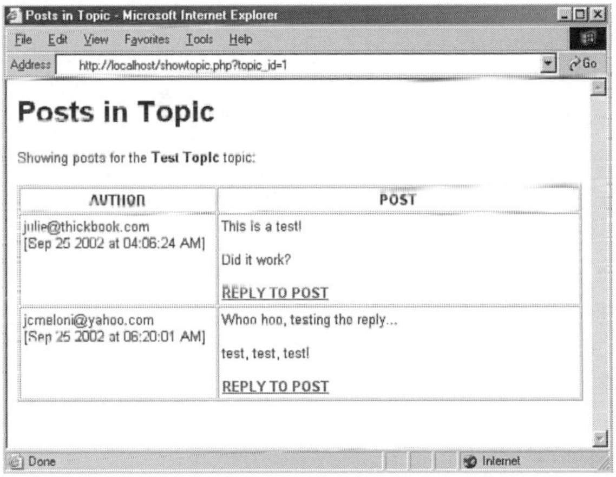

FIGURE 19.9
A post was added to the list.

Summary

To take an idea from inception through to fruition, you should follow a design process. This process essentially says "think before you act." Discuss rules, requirements, and objectives; then create the final version of your normalized tables. In this chapter, you applied this knowledge to the creation of a simple discussion form, using PHP and MySQL to create input forms and display pages for topics and posts.

## CHAPTER 20

Creating an Online Storefront

In this hands-on lesson, the project is creating a generic online storefront. You will learn the methods for creating the relevant database tables, as well as the scripts for displaying the information to the user. The examples used in this chapter represent one of an infinite number of possibilities to complete these tasks, and are meant to provide a foundation of knowledge rather than a definitive method for completing this task.

In this chapter, you will learn how to

- ▶ Create relational tables for an online store
- ▶ Create the scripts to display store categories
- ▶ Create the scripts to display individual items

Planning and Creating the Database Tables

Before you tackle the process of creating database tables for an online store, think about the real-life shopping process. When you walk into a store, items are ordered in some fashion: The hardware and the baby clothes aren't mixed together, the electronics and the laundry detergent aren't side by side, and so on. Applying that knowledge to database normalization, already you can see you will need a table to hold categories and a table to hold items. In this simple store, items will each belong to one category.

Next, think about the items themselves. Depending on the type of store you have, your items may or may not have colors, and may or may not have sizes. But all your items will have a name, a description, and a price. Again, thinking in terms of normalization, you can see you will have one general items table and two additional tables that relate to the general items table.

Table 20.1 shows sample table and field names to use for your online storefront. In a minute, you'll create the actual SQL statements, but first you should look at this information and try to see the relationships appear. Ask yourself which of the fields should be primary or unique keys.

TABLE 20.1   Storefront Table and Field Names

Table Name	Field Names
store_categories	id, cat_title, cat_desc
store_items	id, cat_id, item_title, item_price, item_desc, item_image
store_item_size	item_id, item_size
store_item_color	item_id, item_color

As you can see in the following SQL statements, the store_categories table has two fields besides the id field: cat_title and cat_desc, for title and description. The id field is the primary key, and cat_title is a unique field because there's no reason you would have two identical categories.

```
mysql> create table store_categories (
    -> id int not null primary key auto_increment,
    -> cat_title varchar (50) unique,
    -> cat_desc text
    -> );
Query OK, 0 rows affected (0.03 sec)
```

The store_items table has five fields besides the id field, none of which are unique keys. The lengths specified in the field definitions are arbitrary; you should use whatever best fits your store. The cat_id field relates the item to a particular category in the store_categories table. This field is not unique because you will want more than one item in each category. The item_title, item_price, and item_desc (for description) fields are self-explanatory. The item_image field will hold a filename—in this case, the file is assumed to be local to your server—which you will use to build an HTML <IMG> tag when it's time to display your item information.

```
mysql> create table store_items (
    -> id int  not null primary key auto_increment,
    -> cat_id int not null,
    -> item_title varchar (75),
    -> item_price float (8,2),
    -> item_desc text,
    -> item_image varchar (50)
    -> );
Query OK, 0 rows affected (0.00 sec)
```

Both the `store_item_size` and `store_item_color` tables contain optional information: If you sell books, they won't have sizes or colors, but if you sell shirts, they will. For each of these tables, no keys are involved because you can associate as many colors and sizes with a particular item as you want.

```
mysql> create table store_item_size (
    -> item_id int not null,
    -> item_size varchar (25)
    -> );
Query OK, 0 rows affected (0.00 sec)

mysql> create table store_item_color (
    -> item_id int not null,
    -> item_color varchar (25)
    -> );
Query OK, 0 rows affected (0.00 sec)
```

These are all the tables necessary for a basic storefront—that is, for displaying the items you have for sale. Chapter 21, "Creating a Shopping Cart Mechanism," integrates the user experience into the mix. For now, just concentrate on your inventory.

In Chapter 18, "Creating an Online Address Book," you learned how to use PHP forms and scripts to add or delete records in your tables. If you apply the same principles to this set of tables, you can easily create an administrative front end to your storefront. We won't go through that process in this book, but feel free to do it on your own. At this point, I am confident you know enough about PHP and MySQL to complete the tasks.

For now, simply issue MySQL queries, via the MySQL monitor or other interface, to add information to your tables. Following are some examples, if you want to follow along with sample data.

Inserting Records into the `store_categories` Table

The following queries create three categories in your `store_categories` table: hats, shirts, and books.

```
mysql> insert into store_categories values
    -> ('1', 'Hats', 'Funky hats in all shapes and sizes!');
Query OK, 1 row affected (0.01 sec)

mysql> insert into store_categories values ('2', 'Shirts', 'From t-shirts to
sweatshirts to polo shirts and beyond, we have them all.');
Query OK, 1 row affected (0.00 sec)
```

```
mysql> insert into store_categories values ('3', 'Books', 'Paperback,
hardback, books for school and books for play, you name it, we have it.');
Query OK, 1 row affected (0.00 sec)
```

In the next section, we'll add some items to the categories.

Inserting Records into the `store_items` Table

The following queries add three item records to each category. Feel free to add many more.

```
mysql> insert into store_items values ('1', '1', 'Baseball Hat', '12.00',
'Fancy, low-profile baseball hat.', 'baseballhat.gif');
Query OK, 1 row affected (0.00 sec)

mysql> insert into store_items values ('2', '1', 'Cowboy Hat', '52.00',
'10 gallon variety', 'cowboyhat.gif');
Query OK, 1 row affected (0.01 sec)

mysql> insert into store_items values ('3', '1', 'Top Hat', '102.00',
'Good for costumes.', 'tophat.gif');
Query OK, 1 row affected (0.00 sec)

mysql> insert into store_items values ('4', '2', 'Short-Sleeved T-Shirt',
'12.00', '100% cotton, pre-shrunk.', 'sstshirt.gif');
Query OK, 1 row affected (0.00 sec)

mysql> insert into store_items values ('5', '2', 'Long-Sleeved T-Shirt',
'15.00', 'Just like the short-sleeved shirt, with longer sleeves.',
'lstshirt.gif');
Query OK, 1 row affected (0.00 sec)

mysql> insert into store_items values ('6', '2', 'Sweatshirt', '22.00',
'Heavy and warm.', 'sweatshirt.gif');
Query OK, 1 row affected (0.00 sec)

mysql> insert into store_items values ('7', '3', 'Jane\'s Self-Help Book',
'12.00', 'Jane gives advice.', 'selfhelpbook.gif');
Query OK, 1 row affected (0.00 sec)

mysql> insert into store_items values ('8', '3', 'Generic Academic Book',
'35.00', 'Some required reading for school, will put you to sleep.',
'boringbook.gif');
Query OK, 1 row affected (0.00 sec)

mysql> insert into store_items values ('9', '3', 'Chicago Manual of Style',
'9.99', 'Good for copywriters.', 'chicagostyle.gif');
Query OK, 1 row affected (0.00 sec)
```

Inserting Records into the `store_item_size` Table

The following queries associate sizes with one of the three items in the `shirts` category and a generic "one size fits all" size to each of the hats (assume they're strange hats). On your own, insert the same set of size associations for the remaining items in the `shirts` category.

```
mysql> insert into store_item_size values (1, 'One Size Fits All');
Query OK, 1 row affected (0.00 sec)

mysql> insert into store_item_size values (2, 'One Size Fits All');
Query OK, 1 row affected (0.00 sec)

mysql> insert into store_item_size values (3, 'One Size Fits All');
Query OK, 1 row affected (0.00 sec)

mysql> insert into store_item_size values (4, 'S');
Query OK, 1 row affected (0.00 sec)

mysql> insert into store_item_size values (4, 'M');
Query OK, 1 row affected (0.00 sec)

mysql> insert into store_item_size values (4, 'L');
Query OK, 1 row affected (0.00 sec)

mysql> insert into store_item_size values (4, 'XL');
Query OK, 1 row affected (0.00 sec)
```

Inserting Records into the `store_item_color` Table

The following queries associate colors with one of the three items in the `shirts` category. On your own, insert color records for the remaining shirts and hats.

```
mysql> insert into store_item_color values (1, 'red');
Query OK, 1 row affected (0.00 sec)

mysql> insert into store_item_color values (1, 'black');
Query OK, 1 row affected (0.00 sec)

mysql> insert into store_item_color values (1, 'blue');
Query OK, 1 row affected (0.00 sec)
```

Displaying Categories of Items

Believe it or not, the most difficult task in this project is now complete. Compared to thinking up categories and items, creating the scripts used to display the information is easy! The first script you will make is one that lists categories and items. Obviously, you wouldn't want to list all categories and all items all at once as soon as the user walks in the door, but you do want to give the user the option of immediately picking a category, seeing its items, and then picking another category. In other words, this script will serve two purposes: It will show the categories and then show the items in that category.

Listing 20.1 shows the code for `seestore.php`.

LISTING 20.1 Script to View Categories

```
1: <?php
2: //connect to database
3: $conn = mysql_connect("localhost", "joeuser", "somepass")
4:    or die(mysql_error());
5: mysql_select_db("testDB",$conn)  or die(mysql_error());
6:
7: $display_block = "<h1>My Categories</h1>
8: <P>Select a category to see its items.</p>";
9:
10: //show categories first
11: $get_cats = "select id, cat_title, cat_desc from
12:    store_categories order by cat_title";
13: $get_cats_res = mysql_query($get_cats) or die(mysql_error());
14:
15: if (mysql_num_rows($get_cats_res) < 1) {
16:    $display_block = "<P><em>Sorry, no categories to browse.</em></p>";
17: } else {
18:
19:    while ($cats = mysql_fetch_array($get_cats_res)) {
20:        $cat_id  = $cats[id];
21:        $cat_title = strtoupper(stripslashes($cats[cat_title]));
22:        $cat_desc = stripslashes($cats[cat_desc]);
23:
24:         $display_block .= "<p><strong><a
25:         href=\"$_SERVER[PHP_SELF]?cat_id=$cat_id\">$cat_title</a></strong>
26:         <br>$cat_desc</p>";
27:
28:        if ($_GET[cat_id] == $cat_id) {
29:            //get items
30:            $get_items = "select id, item_title, item_price
31:            from store_items where cat_id = $cat_id
32:             order by item_title";
33:            $get_items_res = mysql_query($get_items) or die(mysql_error());
34:
35:            if (mysql_num_rows($get_items_res) < 1) {
36:                $display_block = "<P><em>Sorry, no items in
37:                 this category.</em></p>";
38:            } else {
39:
40:                $display_block .= "<ul>";
41:
42:                while ($items = mysql_fetch_array($get_items_res)) {
43:                    $item_id  = $items[id];
44:                    $item_title = stripslashes($items[item_title]);
45:                    $item_price = $items[item_price];
46:
47:                    $display_block .= "<li><a
```

LISTING 20.1   Continued

```
48:                          href=\"showitem.php?item_id=$item_id\">$item_title</a>
49:                          </strong> (\$$item_price)";
50:                 }
51:
52:                 $display_block .= "</ul>";
53:             }
54:         }
55:     }
56: }
57: ?>
58: <HTML>
59: <HEAD>
60: <TITLE>My Categories</TITLE>
61: </HEAD>
62: <BODY>
63 :<?php echo $display_block; ?>
64: </BODY>
65: </HTML>
```

Given the length of scripts you saw in Chapter 18, these 65 fully functional lines should be a welcome change. In lines 3–5, the database connection is opened because regardless of which action the script is taking—showing categories or showing items in categories—the database is necessary.

In lines 7–8, the $display_block string is started, with some basic page title information. Lines 11–13 create and issue the query to retrieve the category information. Line 15 checks for categories; if none are in the table, a message is printed to the user and that's all this script does. However, if categories are found, the script moves on to line 19, which begins a while loop to extract the information.

In the while loop, lines 20–22 retrieve the ID, title, and description of the category. String operations are performed to ensure that no slashes are in the text and that the category title is in uppercase for display purposes. Lines 24–26 place the category information, including a self-referential page link, in the $display_block string. If a user clicks the link, she will return to this same script, except with a category ID passed in the query string. The script checks for this value in line 28.

If a $cat_id value has been passed to the script because the user clicked on a category link in hopes of seeing listed items, the script builds and issues another query (lines 30–33) to retrieve the items in the category. Lines 42–53 check for items and then build an item string as part of $display_block. Part of the information in the string is a link to a script called showitem.php, which you'll create in the next section.

After reaching that point, the script has nothing left to do, so it prints the HTML and value of $display_block. Figure 20.1 shows the outcome of the script when accessed directly; only the category information shows.

FIGURE 20.1
Categories in the
store.

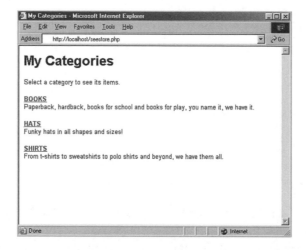

In Figure 20.2, you see what happens when the user clicked on the HATS link: The script gathered all the items associated with the category and printed them on the screen. The user can still jump to another category on this same page, and it will gather the items for that category.

FIGURE 20.2
Items within a cate-
gory in the store.

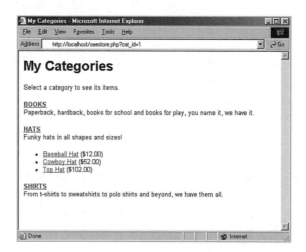

The last piece of the puzzle for this chapter is the creation of the item display page.

Displaying Items

The item display page in this chapter will simply show all the item information. In the next chapter, you'll add a few lines to it to make it function with an "add to cart" button. So for now, just assume this is a paper catalog.

Listing 20.2 shows the code for showitem.php.

LISTING 20.2   Script to View Item Information

```
 1: <?php
 2: //connect to database
 3: $conn = mysql_connect("localhost", "joeuser", "somepass")
 4:     or die(mysql_error());
 5: mysql_select_db("testDB",$conn)  or die(mysql_error());
 6:
 7: $display_block = "<h1>My Store - Item Detail</h1>";
 8:
 9: //validate item
10: $get_item = "select c.cat_title, si.item_title, si.item_price,
11: si.item_desc, si.item_image from store_items as si left join
12: store_categories as c on c.id = si.cat_id where si.id = $_GET[item_id]";
13:
14: $get_item_res - mysql_query($get_item) or dio (myoql_crror());
15:
16: if (mysql_num_rows($get_item_res) < 1) {
17:     //invalid item
18:     $display_block .= "<P><em>Invalid item selection.</em></p>";
19: } else {
20:     //valid item, get info
21:     $cat_title = strtoupper(stripslashes(
22:         mysql_result($get_item_res,0,'cat_title')));
23:     $item_title = stripslashes(mysql_result($get_item_res,0,'item_title'));
24:     $item_price = mysql_result($get_item_res,0,'item_price');
25:     $item_desc = stripslashes(mysql_result($get_item_res,0,'item_desc'));
26:     $item_image = mysql_result($get_item_res,0,'item_image');
27:
28:     //make breadcrumb trail
29:     $display_block .= "<P><strong><em>You are viewing:</em><br>
30:     <a href=\"seestore.php?cat_id=$cat_id\">$cat_title</a>
31:     &gt; $item_title</strong></p>
32:
33:     <table cellpadding=3 cellspacing=3>
34:     <tr>
35:     <td valign=middle align=center><img src=\"$item_image\"></td>
36:     <td valign=middle><P><strong>Description:</strong><br>$item_desc</p>
37:     <P><strong>Price:</strong> \$$item_price</p>";
38:
39:     //get colors
40:     $get_colors = "select item_color from store_item_color where
41:      item_id = $item_id order by item_color";
42:     $get_colors_res = mysql_query($get_colors) or die(mysql_error());
43:
44:     if (mysql_num_rows($get_colors_res) > 0) {
45:
46:         $display_block .= "<P><strong>Available Colors:</strong><br>";
```

LISTING 20.2   Continued

```
47:
48:          while ($colors = mysql_fetch_array($get_colors_res)) {
49:              $item_color = $colors['item_color'];
50:
51:              $display_block .= "$item_color<br>";
52:          }
53:      }
54:
55:      //get sizes
56:      $get_sizes = "select item_size from store_item_size where
57:          item_id = $item_id order by item_size";
58:      $get_sizes_res = mysql_query($get_sizes) or die(mysql_error());
59:
60:      if (mysql_num_rows($get_sizes_res) > 0) {
61:
62:          $display_block .= "<P><strong>Available Sizes:</strong><br>";
63:
64:          while ($sizes = mysql_fetch_array($get_sizes_res)) {
65:              $item_size = $sizes['item_size'];
66:
67:              $display_block .= "$item_size<br>";
68:          }
69:      }
70:
71:      $display_block .= "
72:      </td>
73:      </tr>
74:      </table>";
75:
76: }
77: ?>
78: <HTML>
79: <HEAD>
80: <TITLE>My Store</TITLE>
81: </HEAD>
82: <BODY>
83: <?php echo $display_block; ?>
84: </BODY>
85: </HTML>
```

In lines 3–5, the database connection is opened because information in the database forms all the content of this page. In line 7, the $display_block string is started, with some basic page title information.

Lines 10–14 create and issue the query to retrieve the category and item information. This particular query is a table join. Instead of selecting the item information from one table and then issuing a second query to find the name of the category, this query simply joins the table on the category ID to find the category name.

Line 16 checks for a result; if there is no matching item in the table, a message is printed to the user and that's all this script does. However, if item information is found, the script moves on and gathers the information in lines 21–26.

In lines 29–31, you create what's known as a "breadcrumb trail." This is simply a navigational device used to get back to the top-level item in the architecture. Those are fancy words that mean "print a link so that you can get back to the category."

In lines 33–37, you continue to add to the $display_block, setting up a table for information about the item. You use the values gathered in lines 21–26 to create an image link, print the description, and print the price. What's missing are the colors and sizes, so lines 39–53 select and print any colors associated with this item, and lines 55–69 gather the sizes associated with the item.

Lines 71–74 wrap up the $display_block string, and because the script has nothing left to do, it prints the HTML and value of $display_block. Figure 20.3 shows the outcome of the script when selecting the cowboy hat from the hats category. Of course, your display will differ from mine, but you get the idea.

FIGURE 20.3
The cowboy hat item page.

That's all there is to creating a simple item display. In the next chapter, you'll modify this script so that it can add the item to a shopping cart.

Summary

In this hands-on chapter, you applied your basic PHP and MySQL knowledge to the creation of a storefront display. You learned how to create the database table and scripts for viewing categories, item lists, and single items.

Workshop

The workshop is designed to help you anticipate possible questions, review what you've learned, and begin learning how to put your knowledge into practice.

Quiz

1. Which PHP function was used to uppercase the category title strings?

2. Why don't the `store_item_size` and `store_item_color` tables contain any primary or unique keys?

Answers

1. `strtoupper()`

2. Presumably, you will have items with more than one color and more than one size. Therefore, `item_id` is not a primary or unique key. Also, items may have the same colors or sizes, so the `item_color` and `item_size` fields must not be primary or unique either.

## CHAPTER 21

Creating a Shopping Cart Mechanism

In this hands-on chapter, you will integrate a shopping cart and checkout procedure into the storefront that you created in the previous chapter. You will be shown the methods for creating the relevant database tables as well as the scripts for adding and deleting cart items. Once again, the examples used in this chapter represent one of an infinite number of possibilities to complete these tasks, and are meant as working examples rather than the definitive guide for building an online store.

In this chapter, you will learn

- ▶ How to create relational tables for the shopping cart and checkout portion of an online store
- ▶ How to create the scripts to add and remove cart items
- ▶ Some methods for processing transactions, and how to create your checkout sequence

Planning and Creating the Database Tables

Because the goal of this chapter is to provide the user with a way to select and order items, you can imagine what the tables will be—first and foremost, you need a cart table! In addition to the cart table, you'll need a table to store orders, along with one to store the items purchased as part of each order.

The following SQL statements were used to create the three new tables, starting with the store_shoppertrack table. This is the table used to hold items as users add them to their shopping cart.

> The field lengths used to define these tables were chosen arbitrarily to accommodate several possible inputs. Please feel free to modify the lengths to meet your specific needs.
>
> **By the Way**

```
mysql> create table store_shoppertrack (
    -> id int not null primary key auto_increment,
    -> session_id varchar (32),
    -> sel_item_id int,
    -> sel_item_qty smallint,
    -> sel_item_size varchar(25),
    -> sel_item_color varchar(25),
    -> date_added datetime
    -> );
Query OK, 0 rows affected (0.01 sec)
```

In this table, the only key is the id field for the record. The session_id cannot be unique; otherwise, users could order only one item from your store, which is not a good business practice. The session_id identifies the user. The sel_* fields are the selections by the user: the selected item, the selected quantity of the item, and the selected color and size of the item. Finally, there's a date_added field. Many times, users place items in their cart and never go through the checkout process. This practice leaves straggling items in your tracking table, which you may want to clear out periodically. For example, you might want to delete all cart items more than a week old—this is where the date_added field is helpful.

The next table holds the order information:

```
mysql> create table store_orders (
    -> id int not null primary key auto_increment,
    -> order_date datetime,
    -> order_name varchar (100),
    -> order_address varchar (255),
    -> order_city varchar (50),
    -> order_state char(2),
    -> order_zip varchar(10),
    -> order_tel varchar(25),
    -> order_email varchar(100),
    -> item_total float(6,2),
    -> shipping_total float(6,2),
    -> authorization varchar (50),
    -> status enum('processed', 'pending')
    -> );
Query OK, 0 rows affected (0.00 sec)
```

The only key field in the store_orders table is the id. For the sake of brevity in this lesson, an assumption is made that the billing and shipping addresses of the user are the same, and that this store sells only to United States addresses. It's simple enough to add another block of fields for shipping address information, if you want to do so. Also, this table assumes that you are not storing credit-card information, which you shouldn't do unless you have super-encrypted the information and are positive your firewall is secure. This table is based on the idea of real-time, credit-card processing. You'll learn a few transaction options at the end of this lesson.

The final table is the table to hold the line items in each order, store_orders_items:

```
mysql> create table store_orders_items (
    -> id int not null primary key auto_increment,
    -> order_id int,
    -> sel_item_id int,
    -> sel_item_qty smallint,
    -> sel_item_size varchar(25),
    -> sel_item_color varchar(25),
    -> sel_item_price float(6,2)
    -> );
Query OK, 0 rows affected (0.00 sec)
```

The sel_* fields should look familiar—with the exception of sel_item_price, they are the same fields that appear in the store_shoppertrack table! The primary key is the id field, and the order_id field is used to tie each line item to the appropriate record in store_orders. The sel_item_price field is included here, as opposed to simply relating to the item record because you might have occasion to change the pricing in your item record. If you change the price in the item record, and you relate the sold line items to the current catalog price, your line item prices won't reflect what the user actually paid.

With your tables all squared away, we can move on to adding an item to the user's shopping cart.

Integrating the Cart with Your Storefront

In this section, you'll make modifications to the showitem.php script from Chapter 20, "Creating an Online Storefront." The goal is to transform the item information page into an item information page with a form for selecting colors, sizes, and quantities.

In the original script, insert the following before line 2:

```
session_start();
```

Because the shopping cart elements are attached to the user through a session ID, the session must be started. The next changes don't occur until what was line 37 of the original script, so that's where we start Listing 21.1.

LISTING 21.1   New Lines in `showitem.php`

```
37:          <P><strong>Price:</strong> \$$item_price</p>
38:          <form method=post action=\"addtocart.php\">";
39:     //get colors
40:     $get_colors = "select item_color from store_item_color where
41:          item_id = $item_id order by item_color";
42:     $get_colors_res = mysql_query($get_colors) or die(mysql_error());
43:
44:     if (mysql_num_rows($get_colors_res) > 0) {
45:
46:          $display_block .= "<P><strong>Available Colors:</strong>
47:          <select name=\"sel_item_color\">";
48:
49:          while ($colors = mysql_fetch_array($get_colors_res)) {
50:               $item_color = $colors['item_color'];
51:               $display_block .=
52:                "<option value=\"$item_color\">$item_color</option>";
53:          }
54:
55:          $display_block .= "</select>";
56:     }
57:
58:     //get sizes
59:     $get_sizes = "select item_size from store_item_size where
60:          item_id = $item_id order by item_size";
61:     $get_sizes_res = mysql_query($get_sizes) or die(mysql_error());
62:
63:     if (mysql_num_rows($get_sizes_res) > 0) {
64:
65:          $display_block .= "<P><strong>Available Sizes:</strong>
66:          <select name=\"sel_item_size\">";
67:
68:          while ($sizes = mysql_fetch_array($get_sizes_res)) {
69:               $item_size = $sizes['item_size'];
70:               $display_block .= "
71:                <option value=\"$item_size\">$item_size</option>";
72:          }
73:
74:          $display_block .= "</select>";
75:     }
76:
77:     $display_block .= "
78:     <P><strong>Select Quantity:</strong>
79:     <select name=\"sel_item_qty\">";
80:
81:     for($i=1; $i<11; $i++) {
82:          $display_block .= "<option value=\"$i\">$i</option>";
83:     }
84:
85:     $display_block .= "
86:     </select>
87:     <input type=\"hidden\" name=\"sel_item_id\" value=\"$_GET[item_id]\">
88:     <P><input type=\"submit\" name=\"submit\" value=\"Add to Cart\"></p>
89:     </form>
90:      </td>
91:     </tr>
```

LISTING 21.1 Continued

```
92:    </table>";
93: }
94: ?>
95: <HTML>
96: <HEAD>
97: <TITLE>My Store</TITLE>
98: </HEAD>
99: <BODY>
100: <?php echo $display_block; ?>
101: </BODY>
102: </HTML>
```

The first change is at what was line 37, where the $display_block string is continued to include the beginning <form> element. The action of the form is a script called addtocart.php, which you will create in the next section.

The next change occurs at line 47, where the $display_block string is continued to include the opening tag of a <select> element, named sel_item_color. In lines 51–52, the colors are put into <option> elements for the user to choose from, instead of simply printing on the screen. Line 55 closes the <select> element.

The same types of changes are made for item sizes. Lines 66–67 reflect the continuation of the $display_block string to include the <select> element, named sel_item_size. Lines 70–71 write the colors in <option> elements, and line 74 closes the <select> element.

Lines 77–83 are additions to the script. These lines create a <select> element, called sel_item_qty, for the user to pick how many items to purchase. Line 86 closes this <select> element, and line 87 adds a hidden field for the item_id. Line 88 adds the submit button and line 89 closes the form. The remaining lines are unchanged from the original script.

When viewing the cowboy hat item using the new version of showitem.php, you would see Figure 21.1, reflecting the addition of the form elements.

The next step is to create the addtocart.php script.

FIGURE 21.1
The new cowboy
hat item page.

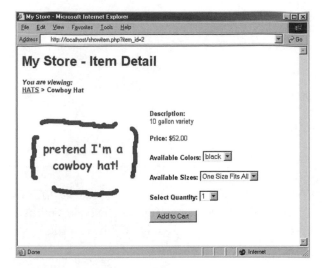

Adding Items to Your Cart

The addtocart.php script will simply write information to the
store_shoppertrack table, and redirect the user to the view of the shopping cart.
We'll create the addtocart.php script in Listing 21.2, and then tackle the
showcart.php script next.

LISTING 21.2   The addtocart.php **Script**

```
 1: <?php
 2: session_start();
 3:
 4: //connect to database
 5: $conn = mysql_connect("localhost", "joeuser", "somepass")
 6: or die(mysql_error());
 7: mysql_select_db("testDB",$conn)  or die(mysql_error());
 8:
 9: if ($_POST[sel_item_id] != "") {
10:    //validate item and get title and price
11:    $get_iteminfo = "select item_title from store_items
12:        where id = $_POST[sel_item_id]";
13:    $get_iteminfo_res = mysql_query($get_iteminfo)
14:        or die(mysql_error());
15:
16:    if (mysql_num_rows($get_iteminfo_res) < 1) {
17:        //invalid id, send away
18:        header("Location: seestore.php");
19:        exit;
20:    } else {
21:        //get info
22:        $item_title =  mysql_result($get_iteminfo_res,0,'item_title');
24:
```

LISTING 21.2 Continued

```
25:        //add info to cart table
26:        $addtocart = "insert into store_shoppertrack values
27:         ('', '$PHPSESSID', '$_POST[sel_item_id]', '$_POST[sel_item_qty]',
28:         '$_POST[sel_item_size]', '$_POST[sel_item_color]', now())";
29:
30:        mysql_query($addtocart);
31:
32:        //redirect to showcart page
33:        header("Location: showcart.php");
34:        exit;
35:
36:    }
37: } else {
38:    //send them somewhere else
39:    header("Location: seestore.php");
40:    exit;
41: }
42: ?>
```

Line 2 continues the user session, which is important because you will need to capture the user's session ID to write to the store_shoppertrack table. Lines 5–7 make the database connection, and line 9 begins the validation of the actions.

In line 9, the script verifies that a value is present in $_POST[sel_item_id], meaning the user came to this script from a form. If there is no value, the script jumps down to line 37 and sends the user away in line 39, and that's it for the script.

However, if there is a value in $_POST[sel_item_id], the next action is to verify that it is a valid value. Lines 11–14 create and issue a SQL query to gather the title of the selected item. Line 16 checks for a result; if there is no result, the user is again redirected away in line 18.

If the selected item is a valid item, the script continues on to line 22 and extracts the value from the result set. The script now has enough information to add the item selection to the store_shoppertrack table, which it does in lines 26–30.

After the query has been issued, the user is redirected to showcart.php, which will contain all cart items. You'll create this in the next section.

Viewing the Cart

Now that you can add items to a cart, you'll want to see them! Listing 21.3 shows the code for showcart.php.

LISTING 21.3   The `showcart.php` Script

```php
1: <?php
2: session_start();
3: //connect to database
4: $conn = mysql_connect("localhost", "joeuser", "somepass")
5:     or die(mysql_error());
6: mysql_select_db("testDB",$conn)  or die(mysql_error());
7:
8: $display_block = "<h1>Your Shopping Cart</h1>";
9:
10: //check for cart items based on user session id
11: $get_cart = "select st.id, si.item_title, si.item_price, st.sel_item_qty,
12: st.sel_item_size, st.sel_item_color from store_shoppertrack as st
13: left join store_items as si on si.id = st.sel_item_id where
14: session_id = '$PHPSESSID'";
15:
16: $get_cart_res = mysql_query($get_cart) or die(mysql_error());
17:
18: if (mysql_num_rows($get_cart_res) < 1) {
19:     //print message
20:     $display_block .= "<P>You have no items in your cart.
21:     Please <a href=\"seestore.php\">continue to shop</a>!</p>";
22:
23: } else {
24:     //get info and build cart display
25:     $display_block .= "
26:     <table celpadding=3 cellspacing=2 border=1 width=98%>
27:     <tr>
28:     <th>Title</th>
29:     <th>Size</th>
30:     <th>Color</th>
31:     <th>Price</th>
32:     <th>Qty</th>
33:     <th>Total Price</th>
34:     <th>Action</th>
35:     </tr>";
36:
37:     while ($cart = mysql_fetch_array($get_cart_res)) {
38:         $id = $cart['id'];
39:         $item_title = stripslashes($cart['item_title']);
40:         $item_price = $cart['item_price'];
41:         $item_qty = $cart['sel_item_qty'];
42:         $item_color = $cart['sel_item_color'];
43:         $item_size = $cart['sel_item_size'];
44:
45:         $total_price = sprintf("%.02f", $item_price * $item_qty);
46:
47:         $display_block .= "<tr>
48:         <td align=center>$item_title <br></td>
49:         <td align=center>$item_size <br></td>
50:         <td align=center>$item_color <br></td>
51:         <td align=center>\$ $item_price <br></td>
52:         <td align=center>$item_qty <br></td>
53:         <td align=center>\$ $total_price</td>
54:         <td align=center><a href=\"removefromcart.php?id=$id\">remove</a></td>
55:         </tr>";
```

LISTING 21.3 Continued

```
56:    }
57:
58:    $display_block .= "</table>";
59: }
60: ?>
61: <HTML>
62: <HEAD>
63: <TITLE>My Store</TITLE>
64: </HEAD>
65: <BODY>
66: <?php echo $display_block; ?>
67: </BODY>
68: </HTML>
```

Line 2 continues the user session, which is important because you need to match the user's session ID with the records in the store_shoppertrack table. Lines 4–6 make the database connection, and line 8 begins the $display_block string, with a heading for the page.

Lines 10–14 represent a joined query, in which the user's saved items are retrieved. The id, sel_item_qty, sel_item_size, and sel_item_color fields are extracted from store_shoppertrack, and the item_title and item_price fields are retrieved from the store_items table, based on the matching information from store_shoppertrack. In other words, instead of printing 2 for the selected item, Cowboy Hat is shown as the title. Line 16 issues the query, and line 18 checks for results.

If there are no results, the user has no items in the store_shoppertrack table, and a message is written to the $display_block string and the script exits and shows the message.

If there are indeed results, the beginning of an HTML table is created in lines 25–35, with columns defined for all the information in the cart (and then some). Line 37 begins the while loop to extract each item from the store_shoppertrack, and this loop continues until line 56, printing the information in the proper table cell.

In line 54, you see a link created for a removal script, which you will create in the next section. Line 58 closes the table, and the script finishes up and prints HTML to the screen in lines 59–68.

Now, go back to an item page and add the item to your cart. After the items are written to the store_shoppertrack table, you should be redirected to the showcart.php page, and your newly selected items should be displayed. Figure 21.2 shows my cart after adding some items.

FIGURE 21.2
Items added
to cart.

The next step is to create the removefromcart.php script.

Removing Items from Your Cart

The removefromcart.php script is quite short because all it does is issue a query and redirect the user to another script. Inevitably, a user will want to weed items out of his cart, and this script enables him to do just that. Listing 21.4 shows the complete script.

LISTING 21.4   The removefromcart.php Script

```
1: <?php
2: session_start();
3: //connect to database
4: $conn = mysql_connect("localhost", "joeuser", "somepass")
5:     or die(mysql_error());
6: mysql_select_db("testDB",$conn)  or die(mysql_error());
7:
8: if ($_GET[id] != "") {
9:     $delete_item = "delete from store_shoppertrack where
10:     id = $_GET[id] and session_id = '$PHPSESSID'";
11:     mysql_query($delete_item) or die(mysql_error());
12:
13:     //redirect to showcart page
14:     header("Location: showcart.php");
15:     exit;
16:
17: } else {
18:     //send them somewhere else
19:     header("Location: seestore.php");
20:     exit;
21: }
22: ?>
```

Line 2 continues the user session because you need to match the user's session ID with the records in the store_shoppertrack table. Lines 4–6 make the database connection, and line 8 checks for a value in $_GET[id]. If a value does not exist in $_GET[id], the user is not clicking the link from her cart and, thus, is sent away in line 19.

If a value exists in $_GET[id], a SQL query (lines 9–10) is issued (line 11) and the user is redirected to the showcart.php script (line 14), where the item should no longer show up. Try it and see!

Payment Methods and the Checkout Sequence

Several commerce methods exist when it comes time to pay for the purchases in the shopping cart. The "right" method for you depends on your business— merchant accounts through banking institutions often require you to have a business license, a reseller's permit, and other pieces of paper proving you're a legitimate business. If you're simply a person who has a few items to sell, you might not want to go through all that paperwork. However, you still have options!

Regardless of the payment method you choose, one thing is certain: If you are passing credit-card information over the Web, you must do so over an SSL connection. Obtaining an SSL certificate and installing it on your system is covered in Chapter 28, "Setting Up a Secure Web Server." You do not have to use this secure connection during the user's entire shopping experience, just from the point at which sensitive information is captured, such as the checkout form.

Creating the Checkout Form

At this point in the book, you should be well versed in creating a simple form. At the beginning of this chapter, the store_orders table was created with fields to be used as a guideline for your form:

- ▶ order_name
- ▶ order_address
- ▶ order_city
- ▶ order_state
- ▶ order_zip

- ▶ order_tel

- ▶ order_email

Additionally, your form will need fields for the credit-card number, expiration date, and the name on the credit card. Another nice feature is to repeat the user's shopping cart contents with an item subtotal, so the customer remembers what he's paying for and approximately how much the order will cost. Also at this point of the checkout sequence, you offer any shipping options you might have. Shipping and sales tax would be calculated in the next step of the process.

From the point of clicking the submit button on the form, the checkout sequence depends on the payment method you are using. The next section goes through the basic steps and offers suggestions on various methods of payment processing.

Performing the Checkout Actions

If you have obtained a merchant account through your bank, you can utilize real-time payment services such as VeriSign's PayFlo Pro. PHP has a built-in set of functions that, when used with the PayFlo libraries from VeriSign, enable you to create a simple script to handle the credit-card transaction. You can learn more about PayFlo Pro at the VeriSign Web site: http://www.verisign.com/products/payflow/pro/index.html. The PHP manual section for PayFlo functions is at http://www.php.net/manual/en/ref.pfpro.php.

VeriSign's product is one of several transaction-processing gateways that exist for use by merchants. Your bank will usually provide a list of merchants it prefers you to use. If you stray from your bank's list of preferred vendors, be sure to research your selected vendor thoroughly, to avoid any delays with deposits and to ensure you're getting the best deal.

After you have selected a transaction processor, your checkout script should follow a path like the following:

1. Total the items, add tax, add shipping. This gives you the total amount to authorize from the credit card.

2. Perform credit-card authorization for the total amount.

3. You will receive either a success or failure response from your card processing routine. If the response is a failure, print a message to the user, and the transaction is over. If the response is a success, continue to step 4.

4. Write the basic order information to a table like `store_orders`, including the authorization code you will receive upon successful authorization. Get the `id` value of this record using `mysql_insert_id()`.

5. For each item in the shopping cart that is tied to this user, insert a record into `store_orders_itemmap`. Each record will reference the `id` (as `order_id`) gathered in the previous step.

6. Delete the shopping cart items for this user.

7. Display the order with authorization code in place of the credit-card information on the screen, so the user can print it and hold it as a receipt. You can also send this information via email to the user.

Each of the steps listed previously—with the exception of the actual payment authorization code—are the same simple steps you have been using throughout this book, and there's no reason to make them more difficult than they need to be!

Summary

In this hands-on lesson, you applied your basic PHP and MySQL knowledge to the integration of a shopping cart into the storefront from the previous chapter. Included were the database table creation, modifications to the item detail page, and new scripts for adding and removing cart items.

Workshop

The workshop is designed to help you anticipate possible questions, review what you've learned, and begin learning how to put your knowledge into practice.

Quiz

1. When removing an item from the cart, why do you suppose that the query validates the session ID of the user against the record?

2. What would be a reason not to store the price in a hidden field when adding to the cart?

Answers

1. Users should be able to remove only their own items.

2. If you stored the price in a hidden field, a rogue user could change that value before posting the form, therefore, writing whatever price he wanted into the `store_shoppertrack` table, as opposed to the actual price.

CHAPTER 22

Creating a Simple Calendar

This chapter will pull together the lessons you've learned so far regarding the PHP language and building small applications. In this chapter, you'll continue your learning in the context of creating a small calendar.

In this chapter, you will learn

- ▶ How to build a simple calendar script
- ▶ How to build a class library to generate date pull-downs in HTML forms

Building a Simple Display Calendar

You'll use the date and time functions you learned in Chapter 8, "Working with Strings, Dates, and Time," to build a calendar that will display the dates for any month between 1980 and 2010. The user will be able to select both month and year with pull-down menus, and the dates for the selected month will be organized according to the days of the week. We will be working with two variables—one for month and one for year—which the user will supply. These pieces of information will be used to build a timestamp based on the first day of the month defined. If the user input is invalid or absent, the default will be the first day of the current month.

Checking User Input

When the user opens the calendar application for the first time, it will be without submitting any information. Therefore, we must ensure that the script can handle the fact that the variables for month and year may not be defined. We could use the isset() function for this, which returns false if the variable passed to it has not been defined. However, let's use checkdate() instead, which not only will see if the variable exists, but will also do something meaningful with it, namely, validate that it is a date. Listing 22.1 shows the fragment of code that checks for month and year variables coming from a form, and builds a timestamp based on them.

LISTING 22.1 Checking User Input for the Calendar Script

```php
 1: <?php
 2: if (!checkdate($_POST['month'], 1, $_POST['year'])) {
 3:     $nowArray = getdate();
 4:     $month = $nowArray['mon'];
 5:     $year = $nowArray['year'];
 6: } else {
 7:     $month = $_POST['month'];
 8:     $year = $_POST['year'];
 9: }
10: $start = mktime (12, 0, 0, $month, 1, $year);
11: $firstDayArray = getdate($start);
12: ?>
```

Listing 22.1 is a fragment of a larger script, so it does not produce any output itself. In the `if` statement on line 2, we use `checkdate()` to test whether the month and year have been provided by a form. If they have not been defined, `checkdate()` returns `false` because the script cannot make a valid date from undefined `month` and `year` arguments. This approach has the added bonus of ensuring that the data submitted by the user constitutes a valid date.

If the date is not valid, we use `getdate()` on line 3 to create an associative array based on the current time. We then set values for `$month` and `$year` ourselves, using the array's `mon` and `year` elements (lines 4 and 5). If the variables have been set from the form, we put the data into `$month` and `$year` variables so as not to touch the values in the original `$_POST` superglobal.

Now that we are sure that we have valid data in `$month` and `$year`, we can use `mktime()` to create a timestamp for the first day of the month (line 10). We will need information about this timestamp later on, so on line 11, we create a variable called `$firstDayArray` that will store an associative array returned by `getdate()` and based on this timestamp.

Building the HTML Form

We need to create an interface by which users can ask to see data for a month and year. For this, we will use SELECT elements. Although we could hard-code these in HTML, we must also ensure that the pull-downs default to the currently chosen month, so we will dynamically create these pull-downs, adding a SELECT attribute to the OPTION element where appropriate. The form is generated in Listing 22.2.

LISTING 22.2 Building the HTML Form for the Calendar Script

```
 1: <?php
 2: if (!checkdate($_POST['month'], 1, $_POST['year'])) {
 3:     $nowArray = getdate();
 4:     $month = $nowArray['mon'];
 5:     $year = $nowArray['year'];
 6: } else {
 7:     $month = $_POST['month'];
 8:     $year = $_POST['year'];
 9: }
10: $start = mktime (12, 0, 0, $month, 1, $year);
11: $firstDayArray = getdate($start);
12: ?>
13: <html>
14: <head>
15: <title><?php echo "Calendar:".$firstDayArray['month']."
16:   ".$firstDayArray['year'] ?></title>
17: <head>
18: <body>
19: <form method="post" action="<?php echo "$_SERVER[PHP_SELF]"; ?>">
20: <select name="month">
21: <?php
22: $months = Array("January", "February", "March", "April", "May",
23: "June", "July", "August", "September", "October", "November", "December");
24: for ($x=1; $x <= count($months); $x++) {
25:     echo"<option value=\"$x\"";
26:     if ($x == $month) {
27:         echo " SELECTED";
28:     }
29:     echo ">",$months[$x 1]."",
30: }
31: ?>
32: </select>
33: <select name="year">
34: <?php
35: for ($x=1980; $x<=2010; $x++) {
36:     echo "<option";
37:     if ($x == $year) {
38:         echo " SELECTED";
39:     }
40:     echo ">$x";
41: }
42: ?>
43: </select>
44: <input type="submit" value="Go!">
45: </form>
46: </body>
47: </html>
```

Having created the $start timestamp and the $firstDayArray date array (lines
2–11), let's write the HTML for the page. Notice that we use $firstDayArray to
add the month and year to the TITLE element on lines 15 and 16.

Line 19 is the beginning of our form. To create the SELECT element for the month pull-down, we drop back into PHP mode on line 21 to write the individual OPTION tags. First, we create an array called $months in lines 22 and 23 that contains the 12 month names. We then loop through this array, creating an OPTION tag for each name (lines 24–30). This would probably be an overcomplicated way of writing a simple SELECT element were it not for the fact that we are testing $x (the counter variable in the for statement) against the $month variable on line 26. If $x and $month are equivalent, we add the string SELECTED to the OPTION tag, ensuring that the correct month will be selected automatically when the page loads. We use a similar technique to write the year pull-down on lines 35–41. Finally, back in HTML mode, we create a submit button on line 44.

We now have a form that can send the month and year parameters to itself, and will default either to the current month and year, or the month and year previously chosen. If you save this listing as listing22.2.php, place it in your Web server document root, and access it with your Web browser, you should see something like Figure 22.1 (your month and year may differ).

FIGURE 22.1
The calendar form.

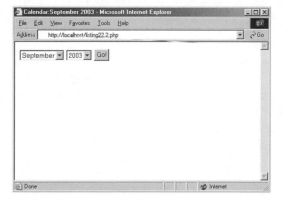

Creating the Calendar Table

We now need to create a table and populate it with dates for the chosen month. We do this in Listing 22.3, which represents the complete calendar script.

LISTING 22.3   The Complete Calendar Script

```
1: <?php
2: define("ADAY", (60*60*24));
3: if (!checkdate($_POST['month'], 1, $_POST['year'])) {
4:     $nowArray = getdate();
5:     $month = $nowArray['mon'];
6:     $year = $nowArray['year'];
7: } else {
```

LISTING 22.3   Continued

```
8:      $month = $_POST['month'];
9:      $year = $_POST['year'];
10:   }
11: $start = mktime (12, 0, 0, $month, 1, $year);
12: $firstDayArray = getdate($start);
13: ?>
14: <html>
15: <head>
16: <title><?php echo "Calendar:".$firstDayArray['month']."
17:   ".$firstDayArray['year'] ?></title>
18: <head>
19: <body>
20: <form method="post" action="<?php echo "$_SERVER[PHP_SELF]"; ?>">
21: <select name="month">
22: <?php
23: $months = Array("January", "February", "March", "April", "May",
24: "June", "July", "August", "September", "October", "November", "December");
25: for ($x=1; $x <= count($months); $x++) {
26:     echo"<option value=\"$x\"";
27:     if ($x == $month) {
28:         echo " SELECTED";
29:     }
30:     echo ">".$months[$x-1]."";
31: }
32: ?>
33: </select>
34: <select name="year">
35: <?php
36: for ($x=1080; $x<=2010; $x++) {
37:     echo "<option";
38:     if ($x == $year) {
39:         echo " SELECTED";
40:     }
41:     echo ">$x";
42: }
43: ?>
44: </select>
45: <input type="submit" value="Go!">
46: </form>
47: <br>
48: <?php
49: $days = Array("Sun", "Mon", "Tue", "Wed", "Thu", "Fri", "Sat");
50: echo "<TABLE BORDER=1 CELLPADDING=5><tr>\n";
51: foreach ($days as $day) {
52:     echo "<TD BGCOLOR=\"#CCCCCC\" ALIGN=CENTER><strong>$day</strong></td>\n";
53: }
54: for ($count=0; $count < (6*7); $count++) {
55:     $dayArray = getdate($start);
56:     if (($count % 7) == 0) {
57:         if ($dayArray['mon'] != $month) {
58:             break;
59:         } else {
60:             echo "</tr><tr>\n";
61:         }
62:     }
```

LISTING 22.3 Continued

```
63:    if ($count < $firstDayArray['wday'] || $dayArray['mon'] != $month) {
64:        echo "<td> </td>\n";
65:    } else {
66:        echo "<td>".$dayArray['mday']."    </td>\n";
67:        $start += ADAY;
68:    }
69: }
70: echo "</tr></table>";
71: ?>
72: </body>
73: </html>
```

Because the table will be indexed by days of the week, we loop through an array of day names in lines 51–53, printing each to its own cell on line 52. All the real magic of the script happens in the final for statement beginning on line 54.

We initialize a variable called $count and ensure that the loop will end after 42 iterations. This is to make sure that we will have enough cells to populate with date information. Within the loop, we transform the $start variable into a date array with getdate(), assigning the result to $dayArray (line 55). Although $start is the first day of the month during the loop's initial execution, we will increment this timestamp by 24 hours for every iteration.

On line 56, we test the $count variable against the number 7 using the modulus operator. The block of code belonging to this if statement will therefore only be run when $count is either zero or a multiple of 7. This is our way of knowing whether we should end the loop altogether or start a new row.

After we have established that we are in the first iteration or at the end of a row, we can go on to perform another test on line 57. If the mon (month number) element of the $dayArray is no longer equivalent to the $month variable, we are finished. Remember that $dayArray contains information about the $start timestamp, which is the current place in the month that we are displaying. When $start goes beyond the current month, $dayArray['mon'] will hold a different figure than the $month number provided by user input. Our modulus test demonstrated that we are at the end of a row, and the fact that we are in a new month means that we can leave the loop altogether. Assuming, however, that we are still in the month that we are displaying, we end the row and start a new one on line 60.

In the next if statement, on line 63, we determine whether to write date information to a cell. Not every month begins on a Sunday, so it's likely that we will start with an empty cell or two. Few months will finish at the end of one of our rows, so it's also likely that we will need to write a few empty cells before we close the table. We have stored information about the first day of the month in $firstDayArray; in particular, we can access the number of the day of the week in $firstDayArray['wday']. If $count is smaller than this number, we know that we haven't yet reached the correct cell for writing. By the same token, if the $month variable is no longer equal to $dayArray['mon'], we know that we have reached the end of the month (but not the end of the row, as we determined in our earlier modulus test). In either case, we write an empty cell to the browser on line 64.

In the final else clause on line 65, we can do the fun stuff. We have already determined that we are within the month that we want to list, and that the current day column matches the day number stored in $firstDayArray['wday']. Now we must use the $dayArray associative array that we established early in the loop to write the day of the month and some blank space into a cell.

Finally, on line 67, we need to increment the $start variable, which contains our date stamp. We simply add the number of seconds in a day to it (we defined this value in line 2), and we're ready to begin the loop again with a new value in $start to be tested.

If you save this listing as listing22.3.php, place it in your Web server document root, and access it with your Web browser, you should see something like Figure 22.2 (your month and year may differ).

FIGURE 22.2
The calendar form and script.

Creating a Calendar Library

Because dates are ubiquitous in Web interfaces, and because working with dates is often comparatively complicated, let's look at creating a class library to automate some of the work that dates can present. Along the way, we will revisit some of the techniques we have already covered.

The simple date_pulldown library created in this instance will consist of three separate select elements: one for day of the month, one for month, and one for year. When a user submits a page, the script checks the form input. If there is a problem with the input, we will refresh the page with the user's input still in place. This is very easy to accomplish with text boxes, but is more of a chore with pull-down menus. Pages that display information pulled from a database present a similar problem. Data can be entered straight into the value attributes of text type input elements. Dates will need to be split into month, day, and year values, and then the correct option elements selected.

The date_pulldown class aims to make date pull-downs sticky (so that they will remember settings from page to page) and easy to set. In order to create our class, we first need to declare it and create a constructor.

By the Way

> A *constructor* is a function that exists within a class, and which is automatically called when a new instance of the class is created.

We can also declare some class properties. The following snippet shows the beginning of the class:

```
 1: class date_pulldown {
 2:     var $name;
 3:     var $timestamp = -1;
 4:     var $months = array("Jan", "Feb", "Mar", "Apr", "May", "Jun",
 5:             "Jul", "Aug", "Sep", "Oct", "Nov", "Dec");
 6:     var $yearstart = -1;
 7:     var $yearend = -1;
 8:
 9:     function date_pulldown($name) {
10:         $this->name = $name;
11:     }
```

We first declare the $name property. This will be used to name the HTML select elements. The $timestamp property will hold a Unix timestamp. The $months array property contains the strings we will display in our month pull-down. The $yearstart and $yearend properties are both set to –1 pending initialization.

They will eventually hold the first and last years of the range that will be presented in the year pull-down.

The constructor is very simple. It accepts a string, which we assign to the $name
property. Now that we have the basis of our class, we need a set of methods by
which the client code can set the date. The snippet continues as follows:

```
12:     function setDate_global( ) {
13:         if (!$this->setDate_array($GLOBALS[$this->name])) {
14:             return $this->setDate_timestamp(time());
15:         }
16:
17:         return true;
18:     }
19:
20:     function setDate_timestamp($time) {
21:         $this->timestamp = $time;
22:         return true;
23:     }
24:
25:     function setDate_array($inputdate) {
26:         if (is_array($inputdate) &&
27:             isset($inputdate['mon']) &&
28:             isset($inputdate['mday']) &&
29:             isset($inputdate['year'])) {
30:
31:             $this->timestamp = mktime(11, 59, 59,
32:                 $inputdate['mon'], $inputdate['mday'], $inputdate['year']);
33:
34:             return true;
35:         }
36:
37:         return false;
38:     }
```

Of these methods, setDate_timestamp() is the simplest. It requires a Unix timestamp, which it assigns to the $timestamp property.

The setDate_array() method expects an associative array with at least three
keys: 'mon', 'mday', and 'year'. These fields will contain data in the same format as in the array returned by getdate(). This means that setDate_array() will
accept a hand-built array such as

```
array('mday'=> 20, 'mon'=>9, 'year' => 2003);
```

or the result of a call to getdate():

```
getdate(1032787181);
```

It is no accident that the pull-downs we will build later will be constructed to produce an array containing 'mon', 'mday', and 'year' fields. The method uses the mktime() function to construct a timestamp, which is then assigned to the $timestamp variable.

The setDate_global() method is called by default. It attempts to find a global variable with the same name as the object's $name property. This is passed to setDate_array(). If this method discovers a global variable of the right structure, it uses that variable to create the $timestamp variable. Otherwise, the current date is used.

The ranges for days and months are fixed, but years are a different matter. We create a few methods to allow the client coder to set her own range of years (although we also provide default behavior):

```
39:     function setYearStart($year) {
40:         $this->yearstart = $year;
41:     }
42:
43:     function setYearEnd($year) {
44:         $this->yearend = $year;
45:     }
46:
47:     function getYearStart() {
48:         if ($this->yearstart < 0) {
49:             $nowarray = getdate(time());
50:             $this->yearstart = $nowarray[year]-5;
51:         }
52:
53:         return $this->yearstart;
54:     }
55:
56:     function getYearEnd() {
57:         if ($this->yearend < 0) {
58:             $nowarray = getdate(time());
59:             $this->yearend = $nowarray[year]+5;
60:         }
61:         return $this->yearend;
62:     }
```

The setYearStart() and setYearEnd() methods are straightforward. A year is directly assigned to the appropriate property. The getYearStart() method tests whether the $yearstart property has been set. If it has not been set, getYearStart() assigns a $yearstart value five years before the current year. The getYearEnd() method performs a similar operation. We're now ready to create the business end of the class:

```
 63:    function output() {
 64:        if ($this->timestamp < 0) {
 65:            $this->setDate_global();
 66:        }
 67:        $datearray = getdate($this->timestamp);
 68:        $out  = $this->day_select($this->name, $datearray);
 69:        $out .= $this->month_select($this->name, $datearray);
 70:        $out .= $this->year_select($this->name, $datearray);
 71:        return $out;
 72:    }
 73:
 74:    function day_select($fieldname, $datearray)  {
 75:        $out = "<select name=\"$fieldname"."[mday]\">\n";
 76:        for ($x=1; $x<=31; $x++) {
 77:            $out .= "<option value=\"$x\"".($datearray['mday']==($x)
 78:                ?" SELECTED":"").">".sprintf("%02d", $x ) ."\n";
 79:        }
 80:        $out .= "</select>\n";
 81:        return $out;
 82:    }
 83:
 84:    function month_select($fieldname, $datearray) {
 85:        $out = "<select name=\"$fieldname"."[mon]\">\n";
 86:        for ($x = 1; $x <= 12; $x++) {
 87:            $out .= "<option value=\"".($x)."\"".($datearray['mon']==($x)
 88:                ?" SELECTED":")."> ".$this->months[$x-1]."\n";
 89:        }
 90:        $out .= "</select>\n";
 91:        return $out;
 92:    }
 93:
 94:    function year_select($fieldname, $datearray) {
 95:        $out = "<select name=\"$fieldname"."[year]\">";
 96:        $start = $this->getYearStart();
 97:        $end = $this->getYearEnd();
 98:        for ($x= $start; $x < $end; $x++) {
 99:            $out .= "<option value=\"$x\"".($datearray['year']==($x)
100:                ?" SELECTED":"").">$x\n";
101:        }
102:        $out .= "</select>\n";
103:        return $out;
104:    }
105: }
```

The output() method orchestrates most of this code. It first checks the $timestamp property. Unless the client coder has called one of the setDate methods, $timestamp will be set to [ms]1 and setDate_global() will be called by default. The timestamp is passed to the getdate() function to construct a date array, and a method is called for each pull-down to be produced.

The day_select() method simply constructs an HTML select element with an option element for each of the 31 possible days in a month. The object's current date is stored in the $datearray argument variable, which is used during the construction of the element to set the selected attribute of the relevant option element. The `sprintf()` function formats the day number, adding a leading zero to days 1–9. The `month_select()` and `year_select()` methods use similar logic to construct the month and year pull-downs.

Why did we break down the output code into four methods, rather than simply creating one block of code? When we build a class, we have two kinds of user in mind: the client coder who will want to instantiate a `date_pulldown` object, and the client coder who will want to subclass the `date_pulldown` class to refine its functionality. For the former, we want to provide a simple and clear interface to the class's functionality. The coder can instantiate an object, set its date, and call the `output()` method. For the latter, we want to make it easy to change discrete elements of the class's functionality. By putting all the output code into one method, we would force a child class that needed to tweak output to reproduce a lot of code that is perfectly usable. By breaking this code into discrete methods, we allow for subclasses that can change limited aspects of functionality without disturbing the whole. If a child class needs to represent the year pull-down as two radio buttons, for example, the coder can simply override the `year_select()` method.

Listing 22.4 contains some code that calls the library class. Before you try to execute this code, take all the class snippets we've covered and put them into a file called `date_pulldown.class.php`, and place this file in the document root of your Web server. You'll be calling it in a moment, so it had better be there!

LISTING 22.4 Using the `date_pulldown` **Class**

```
1:  <html>
2:  <head>
3:  <title>Listing 22.4 Using the date_pulldown Class</title>
4:  </head>
5:  <?php
6:  include("date_pulldown.class.php");
7:  $date1 = new date_pulldown("fromdate");
8:  $date2 = new date_pulldown("todate");
9:  $date2 = new date_pulldown("foundingdate");
10: $date3->setYearStart(1972);
11: if (empty($foundingdate)) {
12:     $date3->setDate_array(array('mday'=>26, 'mon'=>4, 'year'=>1984));
13: }
14: ?>
15: <body>
16: <form>
17: <P><strong>From:</strong><br>
18: <?php echo $date1->output(); ?>
19: <P><strong>To:</strong><br>
20: <?php echo $date2->output(); ?>
```

LISTING 22.4 Continued

```
21: <P><strong>Company Founded:</strong><br>
22: <?php echo $date3->output(); ?>
23: <P><input type="submit" name="submit" value="submit"></p>
24: </form>
25: </body>
26: </html>
```

We include the `date_pulldown.class.php` on line 6, and once we have included the class file, we can use all of its methods. We use the class's default behavior for all the pull-downs apart from `"foundingdate"`. For this object, we override the default year start, setting it to 1972 on line 10. On line 12, we assign this pull-down an arbitrary date that will be displayed until the form is submitted.

This is only the front end of a form, with no action or method; you need to supply your own action or method in order for this to actually do something!

By the Way

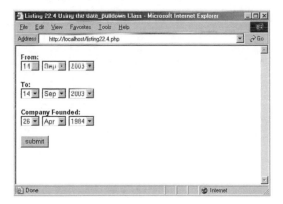

FIGURE 22.3
The pull-downs generated by the date pulldown class.

Summary

In this chapter, you pulled together the PHP date-related functions you learned about earlier in the book to work within a calendar application. You learned how to test the validity of an input date using `checkdate()`. You worked through an example script, which applies some of the tools you have looked at, and built a class library that automates some of the more tedious aspects of working with dates in forms.

Q&A

Q. *Are there any functions for converting between different calendars?*

A. Yes. PHP provides an entire suite of functions that cover alternative calendars. You can read about these in the official PHP manual at `http://www.php.net/manual/en/ref.calendar.php`.

Workshop

The workshop is designed to help you anticipate possible questions, review what you've learned, and begin learning how to put your knowledge into practice.

Quiz

1. What PHP function did we use to check the validity of a date?

2. What PHP function did we use to create a timestamp?

3. What PHP function did we use to create an associative array of date-related information?

Answers

1. `checkdate()`

2. `mktime()`

3. `getdate()`

Activity

Use your fancy new date pull-down class in the context of your own form. Create a back-end script that takes the selected dates and displays their input.

CHAPTER 23

Restricting Access to Your Applications

This chapter explains how to use Apache to restrict access to parts of a Web site based on the identity of the user or on information about the request. On the application side, you can create your own mechanism for user validation and check the validity of your users through cookies.

In this chapter, you will learn

- ▶ How to restrict access based on the user, client IP address, domain name, and browser version
- ▶ How to use the user management tools provided with Apache
- ▶ How to store and retrieve cookie information
- ▶ How to use cookies for authentication

Authentication Overview

Authorization and authentication are common requirements for many Web sites. *Authentication* establishes the identity of parties in a communication. You can authenticate yourself by something you know (a password, a cookie), something you have (an ID card, a key), something you are (your fingerprint, your retina), or a combination of these elements. In the context of the Web, authentication is usually restricted to the use of passwords and certificates.

Authorization deals with protecting access to resources. You can authorize based on several factors, such as the IP address the user is coming from, the user's browser, the content the user is trying to access, or who the user is (which is previously determined via authentication).

Apache includes several modules that provide authentication and access control and that can be used to protect both dynamic and static content. You can either use one of these modules or implement your own access control at the application level and provide customized login screens, single sign-on, and other advanced functionality.

Client Authentication

Users are authenticated for tracking or authorization purposes. The HTTP specification provides two authentication mechanisms: basic and digest. In both cases, the process is the following:

1. A client tries to access restricted content in the Web server.

2. Apache checks whether the client is providing a username and password. If not, Apache returns an HTTP 401 status code, indicating user authentication is required.

3. The client reads the response and prompts the user for the required username and password (usually with a pop-up window).

4. The client retries accessing the Web page, this time transmitting the username and password as part of the HTTP request. The client remembers the username and password and transmits them in later requests to the same site, so the user does not need to retype them for every request.

5. Apache checks the validity of the credentials and grants or denies access based on the user identity and other access rules.

In the basic authentication scheme, the username and password are transmitted in clear text, as part of the HTTP request headers. This poses a security risk because an attacker could easily peek at the conversation between server and browser, learn the username and password, and reuse them freely afterward.

The digest authentication provides increased security because it transmits a digest instead of the clear text password. The digest is based on a combination of several parameters, including the username, password, and request method. The server can calculate the digest on its own and check that the client knows the password, even when the password itself is not transmitted over the network.

By the Way

> A *digest algorithm* is a mathematical operation that takes a text and returns another text, a digest, which uniquely identifies the original one. A good digest algorithm should make sure that, at least for practical purposes, different input texts produce different digests and that the original input text cannot be derived from the digest. MD5 is the name of a commonly used digest algorithm.

Unfortunately, although the specification has been available for quite some time, only very recent browsers support digest authentication. This means that for practical purposes, digest authentication is restricted to scenarios in which you have control over the browser software of your clients, such as in a company intranet.

In any case, for both digest and basic authentication, the requested information itself is transmitted unprotected over the network. A better choice to secure access to your Web site involves using the HTTP over SSL protocol, as described in Chapter 27, "Setting Up a Secure Web Server."

User Management Methods

When the authentication module receives the username and password from the client, it needs to verify that they are valid against an existing repository of users. The usernames and passwords can be stored in a variety of back ends. Apache bundles support for file- and database-based authentication mechanisms. Third-party modules provide support for additional mechanisms such as Lightweight Directory Access Protocol (LDAP) and Network Information Services (NIS).

Apache Authentication Module Functionality

Apache provides the basic framework and directives to perform authentication and access control. The authentication modules provide support for validating passwords against a specific back end. Users can optionally be organized in groups, easing management of access control rules.

Apache provides three built-in directives related to authentication that will be used with any of the authentication modules: AuthName, AuthType, and Require.

AuthName accepts a string argument, the name for the authentication realm. A *realm* is a logical area of the Web server that you are asking the password for. It will be displayed in the browser pop-up window.

AuthType specifies the type of browser authentication: basic or digest.

Require enables you to specify a list of users or groups that will be allowed access. The syntax is Require user followed by one or more usernames, or Require group followed by one or more group names. For example:

```
Require user joe bob
```

or

```
Require group employee contractor
```

If you want to grant access to anyone who provides a valid username and password, you can do so with

```
Require valid-user
```

With the preceding directives, you can control who has access to specific virtual hosts, directories, files, and so on. Although authentication and authorization are separate concepts, in practice they are tied together in Apache. Access is granted based on specific user identity or group membership. Some third-party modules, such as certain LDAP-based modules, allow for clearer separation between authentication and authorization.

The authentication modules included with Apache provide

- **Back-end storage**—Provide text or database files containing the username and group information

- **User management**—Supply tools for creating and managing users and groups in the back-end storage

- **Authoritative information**—Specify whether the results of the module are authoritative

By the Way

> Sometimes users will not be allowed access because their information is not found in the user database provided by the module, or because no authentication rules matched their information. In that case, one of two situations will occur:
>
> - If the module specifies its results as authoritative, a user will be denied access and Apache will return an error.
> - If the module specifies its results as not authoritative, other modules can have a chance of authenticating the user.
>
> This enables you to have a main authorization module that knows about most users, and to be able to have additional modules that can authenticate the rest of the users.

File-Based Authentication

The mod_auth Apache module provides basic authentication via text files containing usernames and passwords, similar to how traditional Unix authentication works with the /etc/passwd and /etc/groups files.

Back-End Storage

You need to specify the file containing the list of usernames and passwords and, optionally, the file containing the list of groups.

The users file is a Unix-style password file, containing names of users and encrypted passwords. The entries look like the following, on Unix, using the crypt algorithm:

```
admin:iFrlxqg0Q6RQ6
```

and on Windows, using the MD5 algorithm:

```
admin:$apr1$Ug3.....$jVTedbQWBKTfXsn5jK6UX/
```

The groups file contains a list of groups and the users who belong to each one of them, separated by spaces, such as in the following entry:

```
web: admin joe Daniel
```

The AuthUserFile and the AuthGroupFile directives take a path argument, pointing to the users file and the groups file. The groups file is optional.

User Management

Apache includes the htpasswd utility on Unix and htpasswd.exe on Windows; they are designed to help you manage user password files. Both versions are functionally identical, but the Windows version uses a different method to encrypt the password. The encryption is transparent to the user and administrator. The first time you add a user, you need to type

```
/usr/local/apache2/bin/htpasswd -c file userid
```

where *file* is the password file that will contain the list of usernames and passwords, and *userid* is the username you want to add. You will be prompted for a password, and the file will be created. For example, on Linux/Unix, the line

```
/usr/local/apache2/bin/htpasswd -c /usr/local/apache2/conf/htusers admin
```

will create the password file /usr/local/apache2/conf/htusers and add the admin user.

Similar functionality exists on Windows, where the command-line operation might look something like the following:

```
htpasswd -c "C:\Program Files\Apache Group\Apache2\conf\htusers" admin
```

The -c command-line option tells htpasswd that it should create the file. When you want to add users to an existing password file, do not use the -c option; otherwise, the file will be overwritten.

It is important that you store the password file outside the document root and thus make it inaccessible via a Web browser. Otherwise, an attacker could download the file and get a list of your usernames and passwords. Although the passwords are encrypted, when you have the file, it is possible to perform a brute-force attack to try to guess them.

Authoritative

The AuthAuthoritative directive takes a value of on or off. By default, it is on, meaning that the module authentication results are authoritative. That is, if the user is not found or does not match any rules, access will be denied.

Using mod_auth

Listing 23.1 shows a sample configuration, restricting access to the private directory in the document root to authenticated users present in the htusers password file. Note that the optional AuthGroupFile directive is not present.

LISTING 23.1   File-Based Authentication Example

```
1: <Directory /usr/local/apache2/htdocs/private>
2: AuthType Basic
3: AuthName "Private Area"
4: AuthUserFile /usr/local/apache2/conf/htusers
5: AuthAuthoritative on
6: Require valid-user
7: </Directory>
```

Database File-Based Access Control

Storing usernames and passwords in plain text files is convenient, but they do not scale well. Apache needs to open and read the files sequentially to look for a particular user. When the number of users grows, this operation becomes very time-consuming. The mod_auth_dbm module enables you to replace the text-based files with indexed database files, which can handle a much greater number of users without performance degradation. mod_auth_dbm is included with Apache but is not enabled by default. Enabling this module occurs when configuring Apache to be built, using the --enable-module=dbm option.

Back-End Storage

The mod_auth_dbm module provides two directives, AuthDBMUserFile and AuthDBMGroupFile, that point to the database files containing the usernames and groups. Unlike plain text files, both directives can point to the same file, which combines both users and groups.

User Management

Apache provides a Perl script (dbmmanage on Unix and dbmmanage.pl on Windows) that allows you to create and manage users and groups stored in a database file.

Under Unix, you might need to edit the first line of the script to point to the location of the Perl interpreter in your system. On Windows, you need to install the additional MD5 password package. If you are using ActiveState Perl, start the Perl package manager and type

```
install Crypt-PasswdMD5
```

To add a user to a database on Unix, type

```
dbmmanage dbfile adduser userid
```

On Windows, type

```
perl dbmmanage.pl dbfile adduser userid
```

You will be prompted for the password, and the user will be added to the existing database file or a new file will be created if one does not exist.

When adding a user, you can optionally specify the groups it belongs to as comma-separated arguments. The following command adds the user daniel to the database file /usr/local/apache2/conf/dbmusers and makes it a member of the groups employee and engineering:

```
dbmmanage /usr/local/apache2/conf/dbmusers adduser daniel employee,engineering
```

If you ever need to delete the user daniel, you can issue the following command:

```
dbmmanage dbfile delete daniel
```

The dbmmanage program supports additional options. You can find complete syntax information in the dbmmanage manual page or by invoking dbmmanage without any arguments.

> Apache 2.0 provides an additional utility, htdbm, that does not depend on Perl and provides all the functionality that dbmmanage does.

By the Way

Using Apache for Access Control

The mod_access module, enabled by default, allows you to restrict access to resources based on parameters of the client request, such as the presence of a specific header or the IP address or hostname of the client.

Implementing Access Rules

You can specify access rules using the `Allow` and `Deny` directives. Each of these directives takes a list of arguments such as IP addresses, environment variables, and domain names.

Allow/Deny Access by IP Addresses

You can deny or grant access to a client based on its IP address:

```
Allow from 10.0.0.1 10.0.0.2 10.0.0.3
```

You can also specify IP address ranges with a partial IP address or a network/mask pair. Additionally, you can specify the first one, two, or three bytes of an IP address. Any IP address containing those will match this rule. For example, the rule

```
Deny from 10.0
```

will match any address starting with 10.0, such as 10.0.1.0 and 10.0.0.1.

You can also utilize the IP address and the netmask; the IP address specifies the network and the mask specifies which bits belong to the network prefix and which ones belong to the nodes. The rule

```
Allow from 10.0.0.0/255.255.255.0
```

will match IP addresses 10.0.0.1, 10.0.0.2, and so on, to 10.0.0.254.

You can also specify the network mask via high-order bits. For example, you could write the previous rule as

```
Allow from 10.0.0.0/24
```

Allow/Deny Access by Domain Name

You can control access based on specific hostnames or partial domain names. For example, `Allow from example.com` will match `www.example.com`, `foo.example.com`, and so on.

Enabling access rules based on domain names forces Apache to do a reverse DNS lookup on the client address, bypassing the settings of the `HostNameLookups` directive. This has performance implications.

Allow/Deny Access Based on Environment Variables

You can specify access rules based on the presence of a certain environment variable by prefixing the name of the variable with env=. You can use this feature to grant or deny access to certain browsers or browser versions, to prevent specific sites from linking to your resources, and so on. For this example to work as intended, the client needs to transmit the User-Agent header.

For example:

```
BrowserMatch MSIE iexplorer
Deny from env=iexplorer
```

Because the client sends the User-Agent header, it could possibly be omitted or manipulated, but most users will not do so and this technique will work in most cases.

Allow/Deny Access to All Clients

The keyword all matches all clients. You can specify Allow from all or Deny from all to grant or deny access to all clients.

Evaluating Access Rules

You can have several Allow and Deny access rules. You can choose the order in which the rules are evaluated by using the Order directive. Rules that are evaluated later have higher precedence. Order accepts one argument, which can be Deny,Allow, Allow,Deny, or Mutual-Failure. Deny,Allow is the default value for the Order directive. Note that there is no space in the value.

Deny,Allow

Deny,Allow specifies that Deny directives are evaluated before Allow directives. With Deny,Allow, the client is granted access by default if there are no Allow or Deny directives or the client does not match any of the rules. If the client matches a Deny rule, it will be denied access unless it also matches an Allow rule, which will take precedence because Allow directives are evaluated last and have greater priority.

Listing 23.2 shows how to configure Apache to allow access to the /private location to clients coming from the internal network or the domain example.com and deny access to everyone else.

LISTING 23.2   Sample `Deny,Allow` **Access Control Configuration**

```
1: <Location /private>
2:   Order Deny,Allow
3:   Deny from all
4:   Allow from 10.0.0.0/255.255.255.0  example.com
5: </Location>
```

Allow,Deny

`Allow,Deny` specifies that `Allow` directives are evaluated before `Deny` directives. With `Allow,Deny`, the client is denied access by default if there are no `Allow` or `Deny` directives or if the client does not match any of the rules. If the client match-es an `Allow` rule, it will be granted access unless it also matches a `Deny` rule, which will take precedence.

Note that the presence of `Order Allow,Deny` without any `Allow` or `Deny` rules causes all requests to the specified resource to be denied because the default behavior is to deny access.

Listing 23.3 allows access to everyone except a specific host.

LISTING 23.3   Sample `Allow,Deny` **Access Control Configuration**

```
1: <Location /some/location/>
2:   Order Allow,Deny
3:   Allow from all
4:   Deny from host.example.com
5: </Location>
```

Mutual-Failure

In the case of `Mutual-Failure`, the host will be granted access only if it matches an `Allow` directive *and* does not match any `Deny` directive.

Combining Apache Access Methods

In previous sections, you learned how to restrict access based on user identity or request information. The `Satisfy` directive enables you to determine whether both types of access restrictions must be satisfied in order to grant access. `Satisfy` accepts one parameter, which can be either `all` or `any`.

`Satisfy all` means that the client will be granted access if it provides a valid username and password *and* passes the access restrictions. `Satisfy any` means the client will be granted access if it provides a valid username and password *or* passes the access restrictions.

Why is this directive useful? For example, you might want to provide free access to your Web site to users coming from an internal, trusted address, but require users coming from the Internet to provide a valid username and password. Listing 23.4 demonstrates just that.

LISTING 23.4   Mixing Authentication and Access Control Rules

```
1: <Location /restricted>
2: Allow from 10.0.0.0/255.255.255.0
3: AuthType Basic
4: AuthName "Intranet"
5: AuthUserFile /usr/local/apache2/conf/htusers
6: AuthAuthoritative on
7: Require valid-user
8: Satisfy any
9: </Location>
```

By the Way

Access control based on connection or request information is not completely secure. Although it provides an appropriate level of protection for most cases, the rules rely on the integrity of your DNS servers and your network infrastructure. If an attacker gains control of your DNS servers, or your routers or firewalls are incorrectly configured, he can easily change authorized domain name records to point to his machine or pretend he is coming from an authorized IP address.

Limiting Access Based on HTTP Methods

In general, you want your access control directives to apply to all types of client requests, and this is the default behavior. In some cases, however, you want to apply authentication and access rules to only certain HTTP methods such as GET and HEAD.

The <Limit> container takes a list of methods and contains the directives that apply to requests containing those methods. The complete list of methods that can be used is GET, POST, PUT, DELETE, CONNECT, OPTIONS, TRACE, PATCH, PROPFIND, PROPPATCH, MKCOL, COPY, MOVE, LOCK, and UNLOCK.

The <LimitExcept> section provides complementary functionality, containing directives that will apply to requests not containing the listed methods.

Listing 23.5 shows an example from the default Apache configuration file. The <Limit> and <LimitExcept> sections allow read-only methods but deny requests to any other methods that can modify the content of the file system, such as PUT. For more information on the myriad options available here, see the Apache documentation at http://httpd.apache.org/docs-2.0/mod/core.html.

LISTING 23.5   Restricting Access Based on Rule

```
 1: <Directory /home/*/public_html>
 2:    AllowOverride FileInfo AuthConfig Limit
 3:    Options MultiViews Indexes SymLinksIfOwnerMatch IncludesNoExec
 4:    <Limit GET POST OPTIONS PROPFIND>
 5:      Order Allow,Deny
 6:      Allow from all
 7:    </Limit>
 8:    <LimitExcept GET POST OPTIONS PROPFIND>
 9:      Order Deny,Allow
10:      Deny from all
11:    </LimitExcept>
12: </Directory>
```

In the next section, you'll learn about restricting access on the application side based on information found in cookies.

Introducing Cookies

On the application side, you can use cookies within your PHP scripts to control access to certain areas of your Web site. A *cookie* is a small amount of data stored by the user's browser in compliance with a request from a server or script. A host can request that up to 20 cookies be stored by a user's browser. Each cookie consists of a name, value, and expiry date, as well as host and path information. An individual cookie is limited to 4KB.

After a cookie is set, only the originating host can read the data, ensuring that the user's privacy is respected. Furthermore, the user can configure her browser to notify her of all cookies set, or even to refuse all cookie requests. For this reason, cookies should be used in moderation and should not be relied on as an essential element of an environment design without first warning the user.

The Anatomy of a Cookie

A PHP script that sets a cookie might send headers that look something like this:

```
HTTP/1.1 200 OK
Date: Tue, 26 Aug 2003 13:39:58 GMT
Server: Apache/2.0.47 (Unix) PHP/4.3.3
X-Powered-By: PHP/4.3.3
```

```
Set-Cookie: vegetable=artichoke; path=/; domain=yourdomain.com
Connection: close
Content-Type: text/html
```

As you can see, this Set-Cookie header contains a name/value pair, path, and domain. The name and value will be URL-encoded. Should it be present, an expires field is an instruction to the browser to "forget" the cookie after the given time and date. The path field defines the position on a Web site below which the cookie should be sent back to the server. The domain field determines the Internet domains to which the cookie should be sent. The domain cannot be different from the domain from which the cookie was sent, but can nonetheless specify a degree of flexibility. In the preceding example, the browser will send the cookie to the server yourdomain.com and the server www.yourdomain.com.

If the browser is configured to store cookies, it will then keep this information until the expiry date. If the user points the browser at any page that matches the path and domain of the cookie, it will resend the cookie to the server. The browser's headers might look something like this:

```
GET / HTTP/1.0
Connection: Keep-Alive
User-Agent: Mozilla/4.0 (compatible; MSIE 6.0; Windows 98)
Host: www.yourdomain.com
Accept: image/gif, image/x-xbitmap, image/jpeg, image/pjpeg, image/png, */*
Accept-Encoding: gzip
Accept-Language: en,pdf
Accept-Charset: iso-8859-1,*,utf-8
Cookie: vegetable=artichoke
```

A PHP script will then have access to the cookie in the environment variable HTTP_COOKIE or as part of the $_COOKIE superglobal:

```
echo "$_SERVER[HTTP_COOKIE]<BR>";   // prints "vegetable=artichoke"
echo getenv("HTTP_COOKIE")."<BR>";   // prints "vegetable=artichoke"
echo $_COOKIE['vegetable']."<BR>";   // prints "artichoke"
```

Setting a Cookie with PHP

You can set a cookie in a PHP script in two ways. You can use the header() function to set the Set-Cookie header. The header() function requires a string that will then be included in the header section of the server response. Because headers are sent automatically for you, header() must be called before any output at all is sent to the browser:

```
header ("Set-Cookie: vegetable=artichoke; expires=Wed, 27-Aug-03 14:39:58 GMT;
path=/; domain=yourdomain.com");
```

Although not difficult, this method of setting a cookie would require you to build a function to construct the header string. Formatting the date as in this example and URL-encoding the name/value pair would not be a particularly arduous task. It would, however, be an exercise in wheel reinvention because PHP provides a function that does just that.

The setcookie() function does what the name suggests—it outputs a Set-Cookie header. For this reason, it should be called before any other content is sent to the browser. The function accepts the cookie name, cookie value, expiry date in Unix epoch format, path, domain, and integer that should be set to 1 if the cookie is only to be sent over a secure connection. All arguments to this function are optional apart from the first (cookie name) parameter.

Listing 23.6 uses setcookie() to set a cookie.

LISTING 23.6   Setting and Printing a Cookie Value

```
1: <?php
2: setcookie("vegetable", "artichoke", time()+3600, "/", "yourdomain.com", 0);
3: ?>
4: <html>
5: <head>
6: <title>Listing 23.6 Setting and printing a cookie value</title>
7: </head>
8: <body>
9: <?php
10: if (isset($_COOKIE[vegetable])) {
11:    echo "<p>Hello again, your chosen vegetable is $_COOKIE[vegetable]</p>";
12: } else {
13:    echo "<p>Hello you. This may be your first visit</p>";
14: }
15: ?>
16: </body>
17: </html>
```

Even though we set the cookie (line 2) when the script is run for the first time, the $_COOKIE[vegetable] variable will not be created at this point. A cookie is read only when the browser sends it to the server. This will not happen until the user revisits a page in your domain. We set the cookie name to "vegetable" on line 2 and the cookie value to "artichoke". We use the time() function to get the current time stamp and add 3600 to it (there are 3,600 seconds in an hour). This total represents our expiry date. We define a path of "/", which means that a cookie should be sent for any page within our server environment. We set the domain argument to "yourdomain.com", which means that a cookie will be sent to any server in that group. Finally, we pass 0 to setcookie(), signaling that cookies can be sent in an insecure environment.

Passing `setcookie()` an empty string (`""`) for string arguments or `0` for integer fields will cause these arguments to be skipped.

By the Way

> With using a dynamically created expiration time in a cookie, as in the preceding example, note the expiration time is created by adding a certain number of seconds to the current system time of the machine running Apache and PHP. If this system clock is not accurate, it is possible that it may send an expiration time in the cookie which has already passed.

Deleting a Cookie

Officially, to delete a cookie, you should call `setcookie()` with the name argument only:

```
setcookie("vegetable");
```

This approach does not always work well, however, and should not be relied on. It is safest to set the cookie with a date you are sure has already expired:

```
setcookie("vegetable", "", time()-60, "/", "yourdomain.com", 0);
```

You should also ensure that you pass `setcookie()` the same path, domain, and secure parameters as you did when originally setting the cookie.

Restricting Access Based on Cookie Values

Now for the fun part—using your cookie skills to restrict access to parts of your Web site! Suppose you created a login form that checked for values against a database. If the user is authorized, you send a cookie that says as much. Then, for all pages you want to restrict only to authorized users, you check for the specific cookie. If the cookie is present, the user can see the page. If the cookie is not present, the user is either sent back to the login form, or a message regarding access restrictions can be printed to the screen.

We'll go through each of these steps in the next few sections.

Creating the Authorized Users Table

When you're integrating user accounts into a Web-based application, it is most common to store the user-specific information in a database table. The information in this table can then be used to authorize the user and grant access to areas of the site that are specifically for these "special" users.

The following table creation command will create a table called auth_users in your MySQL database, with fields for the ID, first name, last name, email address, username, and password:

```
mysql> create table auth_users (
    ->  id int not null primary key auto_increment,
    ->  f_name varchar(50),
    ->  l_name varchar(50),
    -> email varchar(150),
    -> username varchar(25),
    ->  password varchar (75)
    ->);
Query OK, 0 rows affected (0.03 sec)
```

The following INSERT command puts a record in the auth_users table for a user named John Doe, with an email address of john@doe.com, a username of jdoe, and a password of doepass:

```
mysql> insert into auth_users values ('', 'John', 'Doe', 'john@doe.com',
    -> 'jdoe', password('doepass'));
Query OK, 1 row affected (0.00 sec)
```

This INSERT command should be self-explanatory, with the exception of the use of the password() function. When this function is used in the INSERT command, what is stored in the table is in fact not the actual password, but a hash of the password.

When you view the contents of the auth_users table, you will see the hash in the password field, as follows:

```
mysql> select * from auth_users;
+----+--------+--------+--------------+----------+-----------------+
¦ id ¦ f_name ¦ l_name ¦ email        ¦ username ¦ password        ¦
+----+--------+--------+--------------+----------+-----------------+
¦  1 ¦ John   ¦ Doe    ¦ john@doe.com ¦ jdoe     ¦ 2fae5c9d478ec4b1 ¦
+----+--------+--------+--------------+----------+-----------------+
1 row in set (0.01 sec)
```

Although it may look like it is encrypted, a **hash** is in fact not an encrypted bit of information. Instead, it is a "fingerprint" of the original information. Hashes are generally used, like fingerprints, to perform matches. In this case, when you check your user's password, you will be checking that the hash of the input matches the stored hash. Using hashes alleviates the need—and security risk—of storing actual passwords.

Creating the Login Form and Script

After you authorize users in your table, you need to give them a mechanism for proving their authenticity. In this case, a simple two-field form will do, as shown in Listing 23.7.

LISTING 23.7 User Login Form

```
 1: <html>
 2: <head>
 3: <title>Listing 23.7 User Login Form</title>
 4: </head>
 5: <body>
 6: <H1>Login Form</H1>
 7: <FORM METHOD="POST" ACTION="listing23.8.php">
 8: <P><STRONG>Username:</STRONG><BR>
 9: <INPUT TYPE="text" NAME="username"></p>
10: <P><STRONG>Password:</STRONG><BR>
11: <INPUT TYPE="password" NAME="password"></p>
12: <P><INPUT TYPE="SUBMIT" NAME="submit" VALUE="Login"></P>
13: </FORM>
14: </body>
15: </html>
```

Put these lines into a text file called listing23.7.php, and place this file in your Web server document root. In Listing 23.8, you'll create the script itself, which the form expects to be called listing23.8.php.

LISTING 23.8 User Login Script

```
 1: <?php
 2: //check for required fields from the form
 3: if ((!$_POST[username]) || (!$_POST[password])) {
 4:    header("Location: listing23.7.php");
 5:    exit;
 6: }
 7:
 8: //connect to server and select database
 9: $conn = mysql_connect("localhost", "joeuser", "somepass")
10:    or die(mysql_error());
11: mysql_select_db("testDB",$conn)  or die(mysql_error());
12:
13: //create and issue the query
14: $sql = "select f_name, l_name from auth_users where username =
15:    '$_POST[username]' AND password = password('$_POST[password]')";
16: $result = mysql_query($sql,$conn) or die(mysql_error());
17:
18: //get the number of rows in the result set; should be 1 if a match
19: if (mysql_num_rows($result) == 1) {
20:
21: //if authorized, get the values of f_name l_name
22: $f_name = mysql_result($result, 0, 'f_name');
23: $l_name = mysql_result($result, 0, 'l_name');
```

LISTING 23.8   Continued

```
24:
25:  //set authorization cookie
26:  setcookie("auth", "1", 0, "/", "yourdomain.com", 0);
27:
28:  //prepare message for printing, and user menu
29:  $msg = "<P>$f_name $l_name is authorized!</p>";
30:  $msg .= "<P>Authorized Users' Menu:";
31:  $msg .= "<ul><li><a href=\"listing23.9.php\">secret page</a></ul>";
32:
33:  } else {
34:
35:  //redirect back to login form if not authorized
36:  header("Location: listing23.7.php");
37:  exit;
38:  }
39:  ?>
40:  <HTML>
41:  <HEAD>
42:  <TITLE>Listing 23.8 User Login</TITLE>
43:  </HEAD>
44:  <BODY>
45:  <? print "$msg"; ?>
46:  </BODY>
47:  </HTML>
```

Put these lines into a text file called listing23.8.php, and place this file in your Web server document root. In a moment, you'll try it out, but first let's examine what the script is doing.

Line 3 checks for the two required fields from the form. They are the only two fields in the form: username and password. If either one of these fields is not present, the script will redirect the user back to the login form. If the two fields are present, the script moves along to lines 9–11, which connect to the database server and select the database to use, in preparation for issuing the SQL query to check the authenticity of the user. This query, and its execution, is found in lines 14–16. Note that the query checks the hash of the password input from the form against the password stored in the table. These two elements must match each other, and also belong to the username in question, in order to authorize the user.

Line 19 tests the result of the query by counting the number of rows in the result set. The row count should be exactly 1 if the username and password pair represents a valid login. If this is the case, the mysql_result() function is used in lines 22–23 to extract the first and last names of the user. These names are used for aesthetic purposes only. Line 26 sets the authorization cookie. The name of the cookie is auth and the value is 1. If a 0 is put in the time slot, the cookie will last as long as this user's Web browser session is open. When the user closes the browser, the cookie will expire. Lines 29–31 create a message for display, including a link to a file we will create in a moment.

Finally, lines 33–38 handle a failed login attempt. In this case, the user is simply redirected back to the login form.

Go ahead and access the login form, and input the valid values for the John Doe user. When you submit the form, the result should look like Figure 23.1.

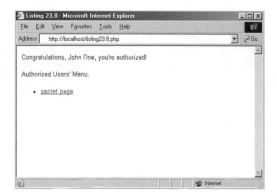

FIGURE 23.1
Successful login result.

Try to log in with an invalid username and password pair, and you should be redirected to the login form. In the next (and final) section, you will create the listing23.9.php script, which will read the authentication cookie you have just set and act accordingly.

Testing for the auth Cookie

The last piece of this puzzle is to use the value of the auth cookie to allow a user to access a private file. In this case, the file in question is shown in Listing 23.9.

LISTING 23.9   Checking for auth Cookie

```
 1: <?php
 2: if ($_COOKIE[auth] == "1") {
 3:   $msg = "<p>You are an authorized user.</p>";
 4: } else {
 5:   //redirect back to login form if not authorized
 6:   header("Location: listing23.7.php");
 7:   exit;
 8: }
 9. ?>
10: <html>
11: <head>
12: <title>Listing 23.9 Accessing a restricted page </title>
```

LISTING 23.9 Continued

```
13: </head>
14: <body>
15: <?php print "$msg"; ?>
16: </body>
17: </html>
```

From the menu shown in Figure 23.1, click the secret page link. Because you are an authorized user, you should see a result like Figure 23.2.

FIGURE 23.2
Accessing the secret page as an authorized user.

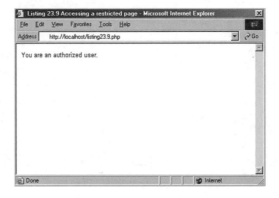

Close your browser and attempt to access listing23.9.php directly. You will find that you cannot, and will be redirected to the login form because the cookie is not set.

Summary

This chapter explained how to use Apache features to restrict access to your Web site based on the identity of the remote user and information from the HTTP request or network connection. It also covered some authentication modules included with Apache and additional tools that you can use to create and manage your user and group databases.

Additionally, you were introduced to using cookies and learned to use the setcookie() function to set cookies on the user's browser. You then learned to use cookie values to allow access to specific parts of your PHP application.

Q&A

Q. *I have a Unix system. Can I use* `/etc/passwd` *as my user database?*

A. Although using `/etc/passwd` might seem convenient, it is advisable that you do not use the existing `/etc/passwd` file for authenticating users of your Web site. Otherwise, an attacker who gains access to a user of your Web site will also gain access to the system. Keep separate databases and encourage users to choose different passwords for their system accounts and Web access. Periodically run password checkers that scan for weak passwords and accounts in which the username is also the password.

Q. *Why am I asked for my password twice in some Web sites?*

A. Your browser keeps track of your password so that you do not have to type it for every request. The stored password is based on the realm (`AuthName` directive) and the hostname of the Web site. Sometimes you can access a Web site via different names, such as `yourdomain.com` and `www.yourdomain.com`. If you are authorized to access a certain restricted area of `yourdomain.com` but are redirected or follow a link to `www.yourdomain.com`, you will be asked again to provide the username and password because your browser thinks it is a completely different Web site.

Q. *Are there any serious security or privacy issues raised by cookies?*

A. A server can access a cookie set only from its own domain. Although a cookie can be stored on the user's hard drive, there is no other access to the user's file system. It is possible, however, to set a cookie in response to a request for an image. So, if many sites include images served from a third-party ad server or counter script, the third party may be able to track a user across multiple domains.

Workshop

The workshop is designed to help you anticipate possible questions, review what you've learned, and begin learning how to put your knowledge into practice.

Quiz

1. What are the advantages of database files over plain text files for storing user authentication information?

2. Can you name some disadvantages of HTTP basic authentication?

3. What function is designed to allow you to set a cookie on a visitor's browser?

Answers

1. Database files are much more scalable because they can be indexed. This means that Apache does not need to read the file sequentially until a match is found for a particular user, but rather can jump to the exact location.

2. One disadvantage is that the information is transmitted in clear text over the network. This means that unless you are using SSL, it is possible for an attacker to read the packets your browser sends to the server and steal your password. Another disadvantage is that HTTP authentication does not provide a means for customizing the login (except the realm name). It is very common for Web sites to implement custom login mechanisms using HTML forms and cookies.

3. The `setcookie()` function allows you to set a cookie (although you could also output a `Set-Cookie` header using the `header()` function).

Activity

Practice using the various types of authentication—both server-based and with PHP—on your development server. Get a feel for the differences between basic HTTP authentication and something you devise on your own.

CHAPTER 24

Logging and Monitoring Web Server Activity

This chapter describes how the logging system in Apache works and how you can customize it—which information to store and where to do it. Additionally, you will learn to use PHP and MySQL to log specific items of interest to you, outside the realm of the Apache log files.

In this chapter, you will learn how to

- ▶ Understand Apache log formats and logging levels
- ▶ Rotate and analyze Apache logs
- ▶ Interpret common errors that might appear in your logs
- ▶ Create scripts that log specific items to database tables
- ▶ Create custom reports based on these logging tables

Standard Apache Access Logging

Using Apache's basic logging features, you can keep track of who visits your Web sites by logging accesses to the servers hosting them. You can log every aspect of the requests and responses, including the IP address of the client, user, and resource accessed. You need to take three steps to create a request log:

1. Define **what** you want to log—your log format.

2. Define **where** you want to log it—your log files, a database, an external program.

3. Define **whether** or not to log—conditional logging rules.

Deciding What to Log

You can log nearly every aspect associated with the request. You can define how your log entries look by creating a log format. A *log format* is a string that contains text mixed with log formatting directives. Log formatting directives start with a % and are followed by a directive name or identifier, usually a letter indicating the piece of information to be logged. When Apache logs a request, it scans the string and substitutes the value for each directive. For example, if the log format is This is the client address %a, the log entry is something like This is the client address 10.0.0.2. That is, the logging directive %a is replaced by the IP address of the client making the request. Table 24.1 provides a comprehensive list of all formatting directives.

TABLE 24.1 Log Formatting Directives

Formatting Options	Explanation
Data from the Client	
%a	Remote IP address, from the client.
%h	Hostname or IP address of the client making the request. Whether the hostname is logged depends on two factors: The IP address of the client must be able to resolve to a hostname using a reverse DNS lookup, and Apache must be configured to do that lookup using the HostNameLookups directive, explained later in this chapter. If these conditions are not met, the IP address of the client will be logged instead.
%l	Remote user, obtained via the identd protocol. This option is not very useful because this protocol is not supported on the majority of the client machines, and the results can't be trusted anyway because the client provides them.
%u	Remote user from the HTTP basic authentication protocol.
Data from the Server	
%A	Local IP address, from the server.
%D	Time it took to serve the request in microseconds.
%{env_variable}e	Value for an environment variable named *env_variable*.
%{time_format}t	Current time. If {time_format} is present, it will be interpreted as an argument to the Unix strftime function. See the logresolve Apache manual page for details.
%T	Time it took to serve the request, in seconds.
%v	Canonical name of the server that answered the request.

TABLE 24.1 Continued

Formatting Options	Explanation
Data from the Server	
%V	Server name according to the `UserCanonicalName` directive.
%X	Status of the connection in the server. A value of x means the connection was aborted before the server could send the data. A + means the connection will be kept alive for further requests from the same client. A - means the connection will be closed.
Data from the Request	
%{cookie_name}C	Value for a cookie named cookie_name.
%H	Request protocol, such as HTTP or HTTPS.
%m	Request method such as GET, POST, PUT, and so on.
%{header_name}i	Value for a header named header_name in the request from the client. This information can be useful, for example, to log the names and versions of your visitors' browsers.
%r	Text of the original HTTP request.
%q	Query parameters, if any, prefixed by a ?.
%U	Requested URL, without query parameters.
%y	Username for the HTTP authentication (basic or digest).
Data from the Response	
%b, %B	Size, in bytes, of the body of the response sent back to the client (excluding headers). The only difference between the options is that if no data was sent, %b will log a - and %B will log 0.
%f	Path of the file served, if any.
%t	Time when the request was served.
%{header_name}o	Value for a header named header_name in the response to the client.
%>s	Final status code. Apache can process several times the same request (internal redirects). This is the status code of the final response.

The Common Log Format (CLF) is a standard log format. Most Web sites can log requests using this format, and the format is understood by many log processing and reporting tools. Its format is the following:

```
"%h %l %u %t \"%r\" %>s %b"
```

That is, it includes the hostname or IP address of the client, remote user via identd, remote user via HTTP authentication, time when the request was served, text of the request, status code, and size in bytes of the content served.

By the Way

> You can read the Common Log Format documentation of the original W3C server at `http://www.w3.org/Daemon/User/Config/Logging.html`.

The following is a sample CLF entry:

```
10.0.0.1 - - [26/Aug/2003:11:27:56 -0800] "GET / HTTP/1.1" 200 1456
```

You are now ready to learn how to define log formats using the LogFormat directive. This directive takes two arguments: The first argument is a logging string, and the second is a nickname that will be associated with that logging string.

For example, the following directive from the default Apache configuration file defines the Common Log Format and assigns it the nickname common:

```
LogFormat "%h %l %u %t \"%r\" %>s %b" common
```

You can also use the LogFormat directive with only one argument, either a log format string or a nickname. This will have the effect of setting the default value for the logging format used by the TransferLog directive, explained in "Logging Accesses to Files" later in this chapter.

The HostNameLookups **Directive**

When a client makes a request, Apache knows only the IP address of the client. Apache must perform what is called a *reverse DNS lookup* to find out the hostname associated with the IP address. This operation can be time-consuming and can introduce a noticeable lag in the request processing. The HostNameLookups directive allows you to control whether to perform the reverse DNS lookup.

HostNameLookups can take one of the following arguments: on, off, or double. The default is off. The double lookup argument means that Apache will find out the hostname from the IP and then will try to find the IP from the hostname. This process is necessary if you are really concerned with security, as described in `http://httpd.apache.org/docs-2.0/dns-caveats.html`. If you are using hostnames as part of your Allow and Deny rules, a double DNS lookup is performed regardless of the HostNameLookups settings.

If HostNameLookups is enabled (on or double), Apache will log the hostname. This does cause extra load on your server, which you should be aware of when making the decision to turn HostNameLookups on or off. If you choose to keep HostNameLookups off, which would be recommended for medium-to-high traffic sites, Apache will log only the associated IP address. There are plenty of tools to resolve the IP addresses in the logs later. Refer to the "Managing Apache Logs" section later in this chapter. Additionally, the result will be passed to CGI scripts via the environment variable REMOTE_HOST.

The IdentityCheck **Directive**

At the beginning of the chapter, we explained how to log the remote username via the identd protocol using the %l log formatting directive. The IdentityCheck directive takes a value of on or off to enable or disable checking for that value and making it available for inclusion in the logs. Because the information is not reliable and takes a long time to check, it is switched off by default and should probably never be enabled. We mentioned %l only because it is part of the Common Log Format. For more information on the identd protocol, see RFC 1413 at http://www.rfc-editor.org/rfc/rfc1413.txt.

Environment Variables

The CustomLog directive accepts an environment variable as a third argument. If the environment variable is present, the entry will be logged; otherwise, it will not. If the environment variable is negated by prefixing an ! to it, the entry will be logged if the variable is *not* present.

The following example shows how to avoid logging images in GIF and JPEG format in your logs:

```
SetEnvIf Request_URI "(\.gif|\.jpg)$" image
CustomLog logs/access_log common env=!image
```

> **By the Way**
>
> The regular expression used for pattern matching in this and other areas of the httpd.conf file follow the same format for regular expressions in PHP and other programming languages.

Status Code

You can specify whether to log specific elements in a log entry. At the beginning of the chapter, you learned that log directives start with a %, followed by a directive identifier. In between, you can insert a list of status codes, separated by commas. If the request status is one of the listed codes, the parameter will be logged; otherwise, a - will be logged.

For example, the directive identifier %400,501{User-agent}i logs the browser name and version for malformed requests (status code 400) and requests with methods not implemented (status code 501). This information can be useful for tracking which clients are causing problems.

You can precede the method list with an ! to log the parameter if the methods are implemented:

```
%!400,501{User-agent}i
```

Logging Accesses to Files

Logging to files is the default way of logging requests in Apache. You can define the name of the file using the TransferLog and CustomLog directives.

The TransferLog directive takes a file argument and uses the latest log format defined by a LogFormat directive with a single argument (the nickname or the format string). If no log format is present, it defaults to the Common Log Format.

The following example shows how to use the LogFormat and TransferLog directives to define a log format that is based on the CLF but that also includes the browser name:

```
LogFormat "%h %l %u %t \"%r\" %>s %b \"%{User-agent}i\""
TransferLog logs/access_log
```

The CustomLog directive enables you to specify the logging format explicitly. It takes at least two arguments: a logging format and a destination file. The logging format can be specified as a nickname or as a logging string directly.

For example, the directives

```
LogFormat "%h %l %u %t \"%r\" %>s %b \"%{User-agent}i\"" myformat
CustomLog logs/access_log myformat
```

and

```
CustomLog logs/access_log "%h %l %u %t \"%r\" %>s %b \"%{User-agent}i\""
```

are equivalent.

The CustomLog format can take an optional environment variable as a third argument, as explained in the "Environment Variables" section earlier in the chapter.

Logging Accesses to a Program

Both `TransferLog` and `CustomLog` directives can accept a program, prefixed by a pipe sign ¦, as an argument. Apache will write the log entries to the standard input of the program. The program will, in turn, process them by logging the entries to a database, transmitting them to another system, and so on.

If the program dies for some reason, the server makes sure that it is restarted. If the server stops, the program is stopped as well.

The `rotatelogs` utility, bundled with Apache and explained later in this chapter, is an example of a logging program.

As a general rule, unless you have a specific requirement for using a particular program, it is easier and more reliable to log to a file on disk and do the processing, merging, analysis of logs, and so on, at a later time, possibly on a different machine.

> Make sure that the program you use for logging requests is secure because it runs as the user Apache was started with. On Unix, this usually means root because the external program will be started before the server changes its user ID to the value of the User directive, typically nobody.

By the Way

Standard Apache Error Logging

Apache can be configured to log error messages and debug information. In addition to errors generated by Apache itself, CGI errors also will be logged.

Each error log entry is prefixed by the time the error occurred and the client IP address or hostname, if available. As with HTTP request logging, you can log error information to a file or program. On Unix systems, you can also log to the `syslog` daemon. Modules for Apache 1.3 allow you to log to the Windows event log and will likely be ported to Apache 2.0 over time.

You can use the `ErrorLog` directive to define where you want your logs to go. This directive takes one argument, which can be a file, a program, or the `syslog` daemon.

Logging Errors to a File

A file argument indicates the path to the error log file. If the path is relative, it is assumed to be relative to the server root. By default, the error log file will be located in the logs directory and will be named error_log on Unix and error.log on Windows. The following is an example:

```
ErrorLog logs/my_error_log
```

Logging Errors to a Program

You can specify the path to a program, prefixed by a pipe ¦. Apache will log errors to the standard input of the program, and the program will further process them. The following is an example:

```
ErrorLog "¦/usr/local/bin/someprogram"
```

The syslog **Daemon Argument**

On a Unix system, if you specify syslog as an argument, you can log error messages to the Unix system log daemon syslogd. By default, log errors are logged to the syslog facility local7. The facility is the part of the system generating the error. You can specify a facility by providing syslog:*facility* as an argument. Examples of syslog facilities are mail, uucp, local0, local1, and so on. For a complete list, look at the documentation for syslog included with your system (try man syslogd or man syslogd.conf at the command line). The following is an example of logging to syslog:

```
ErrorLog syslog:local6
```

The LogLevel **Directive**

The error information provided by Apache has several degrees of importance. You can choose to log only important messages and disregard informational or trivial warning messages. The LogLevel directive takes an error-level argument. Only errors of that level of importance or higher will be logged.

Table 24.2 specifies the valid values for the LogLevel directive, as specified by the Apache documentation. By default, the LogLevel value is warn. That should be enough for most Apache installations. If you are trying to troubleshoot a specific configuration, you can alter the level to debug.

TABLE 24.2 LogLevel **Options as Described in the Apache Documentation**

Setting	Description	Example
emerg	Emergencies—system is unusable	`Child cannot open lock file. Exiting.`
alert	Action must be taken immediately	`getpwuid: couldn't determine user name from uid.`
crit	Critical conditions	`socket: Failed to get a socket, exiting child.`
error	Error conditions	`Premature end of script headers.`
warn	Warning conditions	`Child process 1234 did not exit, sending another SIGHUP.`
notice	Normal but significant conditions	`httpd: caught SIGBUS, attempting to dump core in...`
info	Informational	`Server seems busy, (You may need to increase StartServers, or Min/MaxSpareServers)...`
debug	Debug-level messages	`Opening config file...`

Managing Apache Logs

Apache provides several tools for managing your logs. Other Apache-specific third-party tools are available and are mentioned here. Because Apache can log requests in the Common Log Format, most generic log processing tools can be used with Apache as well.

Resolving Hostnames

Earlier in the chapter, you learned how to use the HostNameLookups directive to enable or disable hostname resolution at the time the request is made. If HostNameLookups is set to off (the default), the log file will contain only IP addresses. Later, you can use the command-line logresolve utility on Unix or logresolve.exe on Windows to process the log file and convert the IP addresses to hostnames.

logresolve reads log entries from standard input and outputs the result to its standard output. To read to and from a file, you can use redirection, on both Unix and Windows:

```
logresolve < access.log > resolved.log
```

Log-resolving tools are efficient because they can cache results and they do not cause any delay when serving requests to clients.

Log Rotation

In Web sites with high traffic, the log files can quickly grow in size. You need to have a mechanism to rotate logs periodically, archiving and compressing older logs at well-defined intervals.

Log files cannot be removed directly while Apache is running because the server is writing directly to them. The solution is to use an intermediate program to log the requests. The program will, in turn, take care of rotating the logs.

Apache provides the `rotatelogs` program on Unix and `rotatelogs.exe` on Windows for this purpose. It accepts three arguments: a filename, a rotate interval in seconds, and an optional offset in minutes against UTC (Coordinated Universal Time).

For example,

```
TransferLog "¦bin/rotatelogs /var/logs/apachelog 86400"
```

will create a new log file and move the current log to the `/var/logs` directory daily. (At the end of the command, 86400 is the number of seconds in one day.)

If the path to the program includes spaces, you might need to escape them by pre-fixing them with a \ (backslash)—for example, `My\ Documents`. This is especially common in the Windows platform.

If the name of the file includes % prefixed options, the name will be treated as input to the `strftime` function that converts the % options to time values. The manual page for `rotatelogs` contains a complete listing of options, but here's an example:

```
TransferLog "¦bin/rotatelogs /var/logs/apachelog%m_%d_%y 86400"
```

This command will add the current month, day, and year to the log filename.

If the name does not include any %-formatted options, the current time in seconds is added to the name of the archived file.

Merging and Splitting Logs

When you have a cluster of Web servers serving similar content, maybe behind a load balancer, you often need to merge the logs from all the servers in a unique log stream before passing it to analysis tools.

Similarly, if a single Apache server instance handles several virtual hosts, sometimes it is useful to split a single log file into different files, one per each virtual host.

Logtools is a collection of log-manipulation tools that can be found at `http://www.coker.com.au/logtools/`.

Apache includes the `split-file` Perl script for splitting logs. You can find it in the `support` subdirectory of the Apache distribution.

Log Analysis

After you collect the logs, you can analyze them and gain information about traffic and visitor behavior.

Many commercial and freely available applications are available for log analysis and reporting. Two of the most popular open source applications are Webalizer (`http://www.mrunix.net/webalizer/`) and awstats (`http://awstats.sourceforge.net/`).

Wusage is a nice, inexpensive commercial alternative and can be found at `http://www.boutell.com/wusage/`.

Monitoring Error Logs

If you run Apache on a Unix system, you can use the `tail` command-line utility to monitor, in real-time, log entries both to your access and error logs. The syntax is

```
tail -f logname
```

where `logname` is the path to the Apache log file. It will print onscreen the last few lines of the log file and will continue to print entries as they are added to the file.

You can find additional programs that enable you to quickly identify problems by scanning your error log files for specific errors, malformed requests, and so on, and reporting on them:

▶ Logscan can be found at `http://www.garandnet.net/security.php`.

▶ ScanErrLog can be found at `http://www.librelogiciel.com/software/`.

Logging Custom Information to a Database

Creating your own logging tables in MySQL, matched up with snippets of PHP code, can help you to capture access-related information for specific pages of your site. Using this information, you can create customized reports. This method can be much less cumbersome than wading through Apache log files, especially when you are just searching for a subset of access information.

Creating the Database Table

The first step in your custom logging method is to create the database table. The following table creation command will create a table called `access_tracker` in your MySQL database, with fields for an ID, page title, user agent, and date of access:

```
mysql> create table access_tracker (
    -> id int not null primary key auto_increment,
    -> page_title varchar(50),
    -> user_agent text,
    -> date_accessed date
    -> );
```

Next, you'll create the code snippet that will write to this table.

Creating the PHP Code Snippet

As you may have gathered already, *code snippet* essentially means *a little bit of code*. In other words, something that doesn't qualify as a long script, but just serves a simple purpose. In this case, the code snippet in Listing 24.1 will write some basic information to the `access_tracker` table.

LISTING 24.1 Code Snippet for Access Tracking

```
1: <?
2: //set up static variables
3: $page_title = "sample page A";
4: $user_agent = getenv("HTTP_USER_AGENT");
5:
6: //connect to server and select database
```

LISTING 24.1   Continued

```
 7: $conn = mysql_connect("localhost", "joeuser", "somepass") or die(mysql_error());
 8: $db = mysql_select_db("testDB", $conn) or die(mysql_error());
 9:
10: //create and issue query
11: $sql = "insert into access_tracker values
12:    ('', '$page_title', '$user_agent',  now())";
13: mysql_query($sql,$conn);
14: ?>
```

What you'll do with this snippet is simple: Place it at the beginning of every page you want to track. For each page, change the value of $page_title in the snippet to represent the actual title of the page.

Now create a sample script called sample1.php, containing the contents of Listing 24.1 and then the content in Listing 24.2.

LISTING 24.2   Sample HTML Page

```
1: <HTML>
2: <HEAD>
3: <TITLE>Sample Page A</TITLE>
4: </HEAD>
5: <BODY>
6: <h1>Sample Page A</h1>
7: <P>Blah blah blah.</p>
8: </BODY>
9: </HTML>
```

Create a few copies of this file, with different filenames and values for $page_title. Then access these different pages with your Web browser to fill up your logging table.

Creating Sample Reports

When you have the data in your access_tracker table, you can create a simple report screen to disseminate this information. The code in Listing 24.3 creates a report that issues queries to count total results as well as the breakdown of browsers in use.

LISTING 24.3   Creating an Access Report

```
1: <?php
2: //connect to server and select database
3: $conn = mysql_connect("localhost", "joeuser", "somepass")
4:    or die(mysql_error());
5: $db = mysql_select_db("testDB", $conn) or die(mysql_error());
6:
```

LISTING 24.3 Continued

```
 7: //issue query and select results for counts
 8: $count_sql = "select count(page_title) from access_tracker ";
 9: $count_res = mysql_query($count_sql, $conn) or die(mysql_error());
10: $all_count = mysql_result($count_res, 0, "count(page_title)");
11:
12: //issue query and select results for user agents
13: $user_agent_sql = "select distinct user_agent, count(user_agent) as count
14:     from access_tracker group by user_agent order by count desc";
15: $user_agent_res = mysql_query($user_agent_sql, $conn)
16:     or die(mysql_error());
17: //start user agent display block
18: $user_agent_block = "<ul>";
19:
20: //loop through user agent results
21: while ($row_ua = mysql_fetch_array($user_agent_res)) {
22:     $user_agent = $row_ua['user_agent'];
23:     $user_agent_count = $row_ua['count'];
24:     $user_agent_block .= "
25:     <li>$user_agent
26:     <ul>
27:     <li><em>accesses per browser: $user_agent_count</em>
28:     </ul>";
29: }
30:
31: //finish up the user agent block
32: $user_agent_block .= "</ul>";
33:
34: //issue query and select results for pages
35: $page_title_sql = "select distinct page_title, count(page_title) as count
36:     from access_tracker group by page_title order by count desc";
37: $page_title_res = mysql_query($page_title_sql, $conn)
38:     or die(mysql_error());
39: //start page title display block
40: $page_title_block = "<ul>";
41:
42: //loop through results
43: while ($row_pt = mysql_fetch_array($page_title_res)) {
44:     $page_title = $row_pt['page_title'];
46:     $page_count = $row_pt['count'];
47:     $page_title_block .= "
48:     <li>$page_title
49:         <ul>
50:         <li><em>accesses per page: $page_count</em>
51:         </ul>";
52: }
53:
54: //finish up the page title block
55: $page_title_block .= "</ul>";
56:
57:?>
58: <HTML>
59: <HEAD>
60: <TITLE>Access Report</TITLE>
61: </HEAD>
62: <BODY>
```

LISTING 24.3 Continued

```
63: <h1>Access Report</h1>
64: <P><strong>Total Accesses Tracked:</strong> <? echo "$all_count"; ?></p>
65: <P><strong>Web Browsers Used:</strong>
66: <?php print "$user_agent_block"; ?>
67: <P><strong>Individual Pages:</strong>
68: <?php print "$page_title_block"; ?>
69: </BODY>
70: </HTML>
```

Lines 3–5 connect to the database so that you can issue the queries against the
access_tracker table. Lines 8–10 issue the query to select the count of all pages,
and lines 13–15 count the user agent accesses. Line 18 starts an unordered list
block for the results of the user agent query, while lines 21–29 loop through the
results and create the list, which is closed in line 32.

Lines 35–37 create and issue the query to count the individual pages. Line 40
starts an unordered list block for the results of this query, and lines 43–52 loop
through the results and create the list of accessed pages, which is closed in
line 55.

Put these lines into a text file called accessreport.php, and place this file in your
Web server document root. When you access this report, you will see something
like Figure 24.1—your page names, counts, and browsers will be different, but you
get the idea.

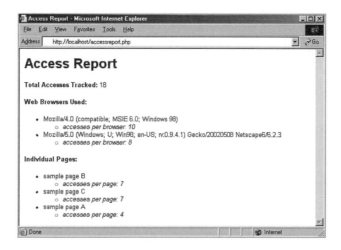

FIGURE 24.1
Custom access
report for tracked
pages.

This sort of tracking is a lot easier than wading through Apache access logs, but I wouldn't recommend completely replacing your access logs with a database-driven system. That's a bit too much database-connection overhead, even if MySQL is particularly nice on your system. Instead, target your page tracking to something particularly important.

Summary

This lesson explained how to log specific information about the requests and errors generated by Apache. You can store the logs in files or databases, or pass them to external programs. You learned about the different utilities available for managing, processing, and analyzing logs, both the ones included with Apache and those available from third parties.

Finally, you saw a simple method for using PHP code snippets and a MySQL database to perform simple access tracking of specific pages. This information was then displayed in a simple access report, built with PHP.

Q&A

Q. *Why wouldn't I want to log images?*

A. In heavily loaded servers, logging can become a bottleneck. If the purpose of logging is to count the number of visitors and analyze their usage of the Web site, you can achieve this result by logging only the HTML pages, not the images contained in them. This reduces the number of hits stored in the logs and the time spent writing them.

Workshop

The workshop is designed to help you anticipate possible questions, review what you've learned, and begin learning how to put your knowledge into practice.

Quiz

1. How would you avoid logging hits from a client accessing your Web site from a particular network?

2. How can you log images to a different file?

Answers

1. In some situations, you may want to ignore requests coming from a particular network, such as your own, so that they do not skew the results. You can do this either by post-processing the logs and removing them or by using the SetEnvIf directive:

```
SetEnvIf Remote_Addr 10\.0\.0\. intranet
CustomLog logs/access_log "%h %l %u %t \"%r\" %>s %b" !intranet
```

2. Earlier in the chapter, you learned how to avoid logging images. Instead of ignoring images altogether, you can easily log them to a separate file, using the same environment variable mechanism:

```
SetEnvIf Request_URI "(\.gif|\.jpeg)$" image
CustomLog logs/access_log common env=!image
CustomLog logs/images_log common env=image
```

CHAPTER 25

Application Localization

The key phrase in *World Wide Web* is *World Wide*. Creating a Web site useful to speakers of different languages is a breeze using PHP and MySQL. The process of preparing your applications for use in multiple locales is called *internationalization*; customizing your code for each locale is called *localization*. In this chapter, you learn some basic tips for performing localization tasks:

▶ How to recognize and prepare for character set differences

▶ How to prepare the structure of your application and produce localized sites

About Internationalization and Localization

First and foremost, neither internationalization nor localization is the same thing as translation. In fact, you can have a fully translated Web site—all in German, all in Japanese, or all in whatever you want—and it will not be considered an internationalized or localized Web site. It will just a translated one. The key aspects to internationalization are as follows:

▶ Externalizing all strings, icons, and graphics

▶ Modifying the display of formatting functions (dates, currency, numbers, and so on)

After you have constructed your application so that your strings are externalized and your formatting functions can change per locale, you can begin the process of localization. Translation is a part of that.

A *locale* is essentially a grouping—in this case, a grouping of the translated strings, graphics, text, and formatting conventions that will be used in the application or Web site to be localized. These groupings are usually referred to by the name of the pervasive language of the application, such as the German locale. Although it might be obvious that the German locale includes text translated into German, it does not mean that the Web site is applicable only to people in Germany—Austrians who speak German would probably utilize a localized German Web site, but it would not be referred to as the Austrian locale.

In the next few sections, you learn about working with different character sets and how to modify your environment to successfully prepare your applications for localization.

About Character Sets

Character sets are usually referred to as *single-byte* or *multibyte* character sets, referring to the number of bytes needed to define a relationship with a character that is used in a language. English, German, and French (among many others) are single-byte languages; only 1 byte is necessary to represent a character such as the letter *a* or the number 9. Single-byte code sets have, at most, 256 characters, including the entire set of ASCII characters, accented characters, and other characters necessary for formatting.

Multibyte code sets have more than 256 characters, including all single-byte characters as a subset. Multibyte languages include traditional and simplified Chinese, Japanese, Korean, Thai, Arabic, Hebrew, and so forth. These languages require more than 1 byte to represent a character. A good example is the word *Tokyo*, the capital of Japan. In English, it is spelled with four different characters, using a total of 5 bytes. However, in Japanese, the word is represented by two syllables, *tou* and *kyou*, each of which uses 2 bytes, for a total of 4 bytes used.

This is a complete simplification of character sets and the technology behind them, but the relevance is this: To properly interpret and display the text of Web pages in their intended language, it is up to you to tell the Web browser which character set to use. This is achieved by sending the appropriate headers before all content.

If you have a set of pages that include Japanese text and you do not send the correct headers regarding language and character set, those pages will render incorrectly in Web browsers whose primary language is not Japanese. In other words, because no character set information is included, the browser assumes that it is to render the text using its own default character set. For example, if your Japanese pages use the Shift_JIS or UTF-8 character set and your browser is set for ISO-8859-1, your browser will try to render the Japanese text using the single-byte ISO-8859-1 character set. It will fail miserably in this unless the headers alert it to use Shift_JIS or UTF-8 and you have the appropriate libraries and language packs installed on your operating system.

The headers in question are the Content-type and Content-language headers, and these can also be set as META tags. Because you have all the tools for a dynamic environment, it's best to both send the appropriate headers before your text and print the correct META tags in your document. The following is an example of the header() function outputting the proper character information for an English site:

```
header("Content-Type: text/html;charset=ISO-8859-1");
header("Content-Language: en");
```

The accompanying META tags would be these:

```
<META HTTP-EQUIV="Content-Type" content="text/html; charset=ISO-8859-1">
<META HTTP-EQUIV="Content-Language" content="en">
```

A German site would use the same character set but a different language code:

```
header("Content-Type: text/html;charset=ISO-8859-1");
header("Content-Language: de");
```

The accompanying META tags would be these:

```
<META HTTP-EQUIV="Content-Type" content="text/html; charset=ISO-8859-1">
<META HTTP-EQUIV="Content-Language" content="de">
```

A Japanese site uses both a different character set and different language code:

```
header("Content-Type: text/html;charset=Shift_JIS");
header("Content-Language: ja");
```

The accompanying META tags would be these:

```
<META HTTP-EQUIV="Content-Type" content="text/html; charset=Shift_JIS">
<META HTTP-EQUIV="Content-Language" content="ja">
```

Environment Modifications

Your environment, as defined in the installation chapters of this book, need not change to handle localized Web sites. Although you can use several language-related settings in Apache, PHP, and MySQL to accommodate localized Web sites, you can also perform all the tasks in this chapter without making any language-related changes to your configuration. Just for your own information, the next few sections point you to the appropriate documentation for internationalization using Apache, PHP, and MySQL.

Configuration Changes to Apache

In Chapter 26, "Apache Performance Tuning and Virtual Hosting," you will learn about the concept of content negotiation using the mod_mime or mod_negotiation modules and the `AddLanguage` and `AddCharset` directives (among others). These directives are used when you manually change the extension of your file and want Apache to interpret the character set to be used based on that extension. However, that is not what we're talking about in this chapter. You want all your localized Web sites to have the same file-naming conventions (such as `index.html` and `company_info.html`) and not have to manually create multiple pages with different language-based extensions to accommodate translated files. Your goal regarding Web site localization is to have a single set of pages filled with the appropriately translated text running from one Web server.

By the Way

> There's nothing wrong with Apache-based content negotiation using multiple files with language-based naming conventions. It's just not the focus of this chapter. You can read more about Apache-based content negotiation at `http://httpd.apache.org/docs-2.0/content-negotiation.html`.

Configuration Changes to PHP

As with Apache, no configuration changes in PHP are required for any tasks in this chapter. However, you can use a host of functions related to the handling of multibyte characters, if you so desire. These functions are found in the PHP manual at `http://www.php.net/mbstring` and must be enabled during the configuration process using this code:

```
--enable-mbstring=LANG
```

Here, `LANG` is a language code, such as `ja` for Japanese, `cn` for simplified Chinese, and so forth. Or, you can use this line to enable all available languages:

```
--enable-mbstring=all
```

When `mbstring` functions are enabled in PHP, you can set several options in the `php.ini` configuration file to properly use these functions. After this is configured, you can use any of the more than 40 `mbstring`-related functions for handling multibtye input in PHP.

The manual entries for these functions are comprehensive and are recommended reading for advanced work with multibyte character sets and dynamic content. You will get by just fine in this chapter without them, although it is recommended that at some point you peruse the manual for your own edification.

Configuration Changes to MySQL

As with Apache and PHP, no explicit changes are needed in MySQL for the localization examples used in this chapter. The default character set used in MySQL is ISO-8859-1, but that does not mean that you are limited only to storing single-byte characters in your database tables. Personally, I have an application that shares MySQL database tables with their normal ISO-8859-1 character set configuration, in which the tables contain English, German, Japanese, and simplified Chinese characters. This usage is partly because grand internationalization and localization features aren't planned for implementation until MySQL 4.1 (see Chapter 31, "Features and Backward Compatibility of MySQL 4.1") and partly because the implementation works fine for my own needs.

For more information on the current language-related elements of MySQL, read the MySQL manual entry at http://www.mysql.com/doc/en/Localisation.html.

Creating a Localized Page Structure

In this section, you look at a functioning example of a localized welcome page that uses PHP to enable a user to select a target language and then receive the appropriate text. The goal of this section is to show an example of externalizing the strings used in this script, which is one of the characteristics of internationalization.

In this script, the user happens upon your English-based Web site but is also presented with an option to browse within the locale of his choice—English, German, or Japanese. Three elements are involved in this process:

- ▶ Creating and using a master file for sending locale-specific header information
- ▶ Creating and using a master file for displaying the information based on the selected locale
- ▶ Using the script itself

Listing 25.1 shows the contents of the master file used for sending locale-specific header information.

LISTING 25.1   Language Definition File

```
 1:  <?php
 2:  if ($_SESSION[lang] == "") {
 3:      $_SESSION[lang] = "en";
 4:      $currLang = "en";
 5:  } else {
 6:      $currLang = $_GET[lang];
 7:      $_SESSION[lang] = $currLang;
 8:  }
 9:  switch($currLang) {
10:      case "en":
11:          define("CHARSET","ISO-8859-1");
12:          define("LANGCODE", "en");
13:      break;
14:
15:      case "de":
16:          define("CHARSET","ISO-8859-1");
17:          define("LANGCODE", "de");
18:      break;
19:
20:      case "ja":
21:          define("CHARSET","UTF-8");
22:          define("LANGCODE", "ja");
23:      break;
24:      default:
25:          define("CHARSET","ISO-8859-1");
26:          define("LANGCODE", "en");
27:      break;
28:  }
29:
30:  header("Content-Type: text/html;charset=".CHARSET);
31:  header("Content-Language: ".LANGCODE);
32:  ?>
```

Save this file as define_lang.php, and place it in the document root of your Web browser. This file defines two constants that will be used in the next script, which is the actual display script. The constants are CHARSET and LANGCODE, corresponding to the character set and language code for each locale. These constants are used in the display script to create the proper META tags regarding character set and language code; although the headers are sent in this script, it's a good idea to ensure that they are part of the page itself, to aid in any necessary input from forms.

Lines 2–8 of Listing 25.1 set up the session value needed to store the user's selected language choice. If no session value exists, the English locale settings are used. If your site were a German site by default, you would change this file to use the German locale by default. This script prepares for the next script, which contains for an input-selection mechanism, by setting the value of $currLang to the result of this input, in line 6.

The switch statement beginning on line 9 contains several case statements designed to assign the appropriate values to the constant variables CHARSET and LANGCODE. Lines 30–31 actually utilize these variables for the first time when dynamically creating and sending the headers for Content-type and Content-language.

Listing 25.2 creates a function that simply stores the externalized strings that will be used in the display script. This example uses two: one to welcome the user to the page (WELCOME_TXT) and one to introduce the language selection process (CHOOSE_TXT).

LISTING 25.2   String Definition File

```
1:  <?php
2:  defineStrings() {
3:    switch($_SESSION[lang]) {
4:        case "en":
5:            define("WELCOME_TXT","Welcome!");
6:            define("CHOOSE_TXT","Choose Language");
7:        break;
8:
9:        case "de":
10:            define("WELCOME_TXT","Willkommen!");
11:            define("CHOOSE_TXT","Sprache auswählen");
12:        break;
13:
14:        case "ja":
15:            define("WELCOME_TXT","[unprintable characters]");
16:            define("CHOOSE_TXT","[unprintable characters]");
17:        break;
18:
19:        default:
20:            define("WELCOME_TXT","Welcome!");
21:            define("CHOOSE_TXT","Choose Language");
22:        break;
23:    }
24: }
25: ?>
```

Use the file lang_strings.php from the CD included with this book to use the actual Japanese characters that cannot be displayed here. Place this file in the document root of your Web browser. This file defines two constants, WELCOME_TXT and CHOOSE_TXT, which are used in the display script. These constants are defined within the context of the function called defineStrings(), although you could just as easily make this file a long switch statement outside the context of the function structure. I've simply put it in a function for the sake of organization and for ease of explanation when it comes time to use the display script.

Finally, it's time to create the display script. Remember, one key element of internationalization is to externalize all strings so that only one master file needs to be used. Listing 25.3 is such an example.

LISTING 25.3   Localized Welcome Script

```
1:  <?
2:  session_start();
3:  include("define_lang.php");
4:  include("lang_strings.php");
5:  defineStrings();
6:  ?>
7:  <HTML>
8:  <HEAD>
9:  <TITLE><? echo WELCOME_TXT; ?></TITLE>
10: <META HTTP-EQUIV="Content-Type" content="text/html; charset=<? echo CHARSET;
?>">
11: <META HTTP-EQUIV="Content-Language" content="<? echo LANGCODE; ?>">
12: <BODY>
13: <h1 align=center><? echo WELCOME_TXT; ?></h1>
14: <p align=center><strong><? echo CHOOSE_TXT; ?></strong><br><br>
15: <a href="<? echo $_SERVER[PHP_SELF]."?lang=en"; ?>"><img src="en_flag.gif"
border=0></a>
16: <a href="<? echo $_SERVER[PHP_SELF]."?lang=de"; ?>"><img src="de_flag.gif"
border=0></a>
17: <a href="<? echo $_SERVER[PHP_SELF]."?lang=ja"; ?>"><img src="ja_flag.gif"
border=0></a>
18: </p>
19: </BODY>
20: </HTML>
```

Save this file as lang_selector.php, and place it in the document root of your Web browser. When visited for the first time, it should look something like Figure 25.1.

FIGURE 25.1
Viewing the language selector for the first time.

Until another language is selected, the default is English; accordingly, the Welcome and Choose Language text appear in English.

Take a look at Listing 25.3—it's a very basic template because all the language-related elements are externalized in the `define_lang.php` or `lang_strings.php` files. All this third file does is display the appropriate results, depending on the selected (or default) locale. Line 5 calls the `defineStrings()` function, which then makes available the appropriate values for the two constant variables. Lines 15–18 display the flags representing the English, German, and Japanese locales, which are clickable. When the user clicks on one of the flags, the locale will change to the new, selected locale, and the strings used will be those appropriate to the new locale. In these links is contained the `lang` variable, which is passed to the script as `$_GET[lang]`. If you look at line 6 of Listing 25.1, you will see how this is used to change the setting regarding the user's preferred locale.

When the user clicks on the German flag, he will see Figure 25.2; when the user clicks on the Japanese flag, he will see Figure 25.3.

FIGURE 25.2
Viewing the German language page.

FIGURE 25.3
Viewing the Japanese language page.

The use of the flag of Great Britain might seem unusual for a book written by an American and with primary distribution in the United States. However, when flags (instead of names of countries) are used as locale selectors, it is more common for the English locale to be represented by the flag of Great Britain rather than the United States of America. As you can imagine, the use of flags for locale selection can get very political. Companies that offer localized versions of their Web sites often have long discussions about how to represent the locale selections—flags, names of countries, names of languages, and so forth. There is no clear-cut answer; the Web sites for Sun Microsystems, Cisco Systems, and IBM use country names, whereas other large corporations use language names, but even Google uses flags. How to display the language selection can definitely be a business decision, but if you have gone through the process of externalizing strings, text, and images and created an internationalized Web site template that is ready to be localized, the format of your locale selection is the least of your concerns.

Summary

In this chapter, you were introduced to the basics of internationalization and localization. You learned the two keys to creating an internationalized site: All strings, text, and graphics are externalized, and so is number, currency, and date formatting. You also learned that neither internationalization nor localization is equivalent to translating text; translation is just one part of localization.

You also learned a little bit about character sets: They can be single-byte or multibyte. You also learned the importance of sending the appropriate language-related headers so that your Web browser can interpret and display your text properly.

Finally, you created a practical example of how to store a locale-related session variable, to determine and send the localized strings to a pre-existing template. This template can be used by all locales because each element was externalized.

Q&A

Q. *How do I go about localizing numbers, dates, and currency using PHP?*

A. Two functions will prove very useful to you in this regard: `number_format()` and `date()`. You have already learned about the `date()` function. To use it in a localized environment, you simply rearrange the month, day, and year elements as appropriate to the locale (MM-DD-YYYY, DD-MM-YYYY, and so forth). The `number_format()` function is used for numbers and currency; it groups the thousandths with a comma, period, or space, as appropriate to the locale. Read the PHP manual entry at `http://www.php.net/number_format` for possible uses.

Workshop

The workshop is designed to help you anticipate possible questions, review what you've learned, and begin learning how to put your knowledge into practice.

Quiz

1. Is English a single-byte or multibyte language? What about Japanese?

2. What two headers related to character encoding are crucial in a localized site?

Answers

1. English is single-byte; Japanese is double-byte.

2. `Content-Type` with the charset indicator, `Content-Language`.

PART VI

Administration and Fine Tuning

CHAPTER 26

Apache Performance Tuning and Virtual Hosting

In this administration-related chapter, consideration will be given to increasing the performance and scalability of your Apache installation. Additionally, you will learn about name-based and IP-based virtual hosting, and DNS and client issues. It explains different mechanisms that can be used to isolate clients from each other and the associated security tradeoffs.

In this chapter, you will learn

- ▶ Which operating system and Apache-related settings can limit the server scalability or degrade performance
- ▶ About several tools for load testing Apache
- ▶ How to fine-tune Apache for optimum performance
- ▶ How to configure Apache to detect and prevent abusive behavior from clients
- ▶ How to configure name-based virtual hosts, IP-based virtual hosts, and the difference between the two
- ▶ About the dependencies virtual hosting has on DNS
- ▶ How to set up scaled-up cookie-cutter virtual hosts

Scalability Issues

This section covers scalability problems and how to prevent them. This is more of a "don't do this" list, explaining limiting factors that can degrade performance or prevent the server from scaling. We will also investigate the proactive tuning of Apache for optimal performance.

Operating System Limits

Several operating system factors can prevent Apache from scaling. These factors are related to process creation, memory limits, and maximum simultaneous number of open files or connections.

> The Unix `ulimit` command enables you to set several of the limits covered in this section on a per-process basis. Please refer to your operating system documentation for details on `ulimit`'s syntax.

Processes

Apache provides settings for preventing the number of server processes and threads from exceeding certain limits. These settings affect scalability because they limit the number of simultaneous connections to the Web server, which in turn affects the number of visitors that you can service simultaneously.

The Apache Multi-Processing Module (MPM) settings are in turn constrained by OS settings limiting the number of processes and threads. How to change those limits varies from operating system to operating system. In Linux 2.0.x and 2.2.x kernels, it requires changing the NR_TASKS defined in /usr/src/linux/include/linux/tasks.h and recompiling the kernel. In the 2.4.x series, the limit can be accessed at runtime from the /proc/sys/kernel/threads-max file. You can read the contents of the file with

```
cat /proc/sys/kernel/threads-max
```

and write to it using

```
echo value > /proc/sys/kernel/threads-max
```

In Linux (unlike most other Unix versions), there is a mapping between threads and processes, and they are similar from the point of view of the OS.

In Solaris, those parameters can be changed in the /etc/system file. Those changes don't require rebuilding the kernel, but might require a reboot to take effect. You can change the total number of processes by changing the max_nprocs entry and the number of processes allowed for a given user with maxuproc.

File Descriptors

Whenever a process opens a file (or a socket), a structure called a *file descriptor* is assigned until the file is closed. The OS limits the number of file descriptors that a given process can open, thus limiting the number of simultaneous connections the Web server can have. How those settings are changed depends on the operating system. On Linux systems, you can read or modify /proc/sys/fs/file-max. On Solaris systems, you must edit the value for rlim_fd_max in the /etc/system file. This change will require a reboot to take effect.

You can find additional information at http://httpd.apache.org/docs/misc/descriptors.html.

Controlling External Processes

Apache provides several directives to control the amount of resources external processes use. This applies to CGI scripts spawned from the server and programs executed via server-side includes, but does apply to PHP scripts which are invoked using the module version, as the module is part of the server process. Support for the following Apache directives (used in httpd.conf) is available only on Unix and varies from system to system:

- ▶ **RLimitCPU**—Accepts two parameters: the soft limit and the hard limit for the amount of CPU time in seconds that a process is allowed. If the max keyword is used, it indicates the maximum setting allowed by the operating system. The hard limit is optional. The soft limit can be changed between restarts, and the hard limit specifies the maximum allowed value for that setting.

- ▶ **RLimitMem**—The syntax is identical to RLimitCPU, but this directive specifies the amount (in bytes) of memory used per process.

- ▶ **RLimitNProc**—The syntax is identical to RLimitCPU, but this directive specifies the number of processes.

These three directives are useful to prevent malicious or poorly written programs from running out of control.

Performance-Related Apache Settings

This section presents you with different Apache settings that affect performance.

File System Access

From a resource standpoint, accessing files on disk is an expensive process, so you should try to minimize the number of disk accesses required for serving a request. Symbolic links, per-directory configuration files, and content negotiation are some of factors that affect the number of disk accesses:

▶ **Symbolic links**—In Unix, a *symbolic link* (or *symlink*) is a special kind of file that points to another file. It is created with the Unix `ln` command and is useful for making a certain file appear in different places.

Two of the parameters that the `Options` directive allows are `FollowSymLinks` and `SymLinksIfOwnerMatch`. By default, Apache won't follow symbolic links because they can be used to bypass security settings. For example, you can create a symbolic link from a public part of the Web site to a restricted file or directory not otherwise accessible via the Web. So, also by default, Apache needs to perform a check to verify that the file isn't a symbolic link. If `SymLinksIfOwnerMatch` is present, it will follow a symbolic link if the same user who created the symbolic link owns the target file.

Because those tests must be performed for every path element and for every path that refers to a filesystem object, they can be expensive. If you control the content creation, you should add an `Options +FollowSymLinks` directive to your configuration and avoid the `SymLinksIfOwnerMatch` argument. In this way, the tests won't take place and performance isn't affected.

▶ **Per-directory configuration files**—As explained in Chapter 2, "Installing and Configuring Apache," it is possible to have per-directory configuration files. These files, normally named `.htaccess`, provide a convenient way of configuring the server and allow for some degree of delegated administration. However, if this feature is enabled, Apache has to look for these files in each directory in the path leading to the file being requested, resulting in expensive filesystem accesses. If you don't have a need for per-directory configuration files, you can disable this feature by adding `AllowOverride none` to your configuration. Doing so will avoid the performance penalty associated with accessing the filesystem looking for `.htaccess` files.

▶ **Content negotiation**—Apache can serve different versions of a file depending on client language or preferences. This can be accomplished with file extensions, but for every request, Apache must access the filesystem repeatedly looking for files with appropriate extensions. If you need to use content negotiation, make sure that you at least use a type-map file, minimizing accesses to disk. Alternatives to Apache-based content negotiation for internationalization purposes can be found in Chapter 25, "Application Localization."

▶ **Scoreboard file**—This is a special file that the main Apache process uses to communicate with its children in certain older operating systems. You can specify its location with `ScoreBoardFile`, but most modern platforms do not require this directive. If this file is required, you might find improved performance if you place it on a RAM disk. A *RAM disk* is a mechanism that allows a portion of the system memory to be accessed as a filesystem. The details on creating a RAM disk vary from system to system.

Network and Status Settings

A number of network-related Apache options can degrade performance:

- ▶ **HostnameLookups**—When HostnameLookups is set to on or double, Apache will perform a DNS lookup to capture the hostname of the client each time the client makes a request. This constant lookup will introduce a delay. The default setting is HostnameLookups off. If you need the hostname in your log files, you can always process the request logs with a log resolver later, and not in real-time.

- ▶ **Accept mechanism**—Apache can use different mechanisms to control how Apache children arbitrate requests. The optimal mechanism depends on the specific platform and number of processors. You can find additional information at http://httpd.apache.org/docs-2.0/misc/perf-tuning.html.

- ▶ **mod_status**—This module collects statistics about the server, connections, and requests, which slows down Apache. For optimal performance, disable this module, or at least make sure that ExtendedStatus is set to off, which is the default.

Load Testing with ApacheBench

You can test the scalability and performance of your site with benchmarking and traffic generation tools. There are many commercial and open-source tools available, each with varying degrees of sophistication. In general, it is very difficult to accurately simulate real-world request traffic because visitors have different navigation patterns, access the Internet using connections with different speeds, stop a download if it is taking too long, press the reload button repeatedly if they get impatient, and so on. As such, some tools record actual network traffic for later replay.

However, for a quick—but accurate—glimpse at basic information regarding your server's capability to handle heavy traffic, the Apache server comes with a simple, but useful, load-testing tool, called ApacheBench, or ab. You can find it in the /bin directory of the Apache distribution.

This tool enables you to request a certain URL a number of times and display a summary of the result. The following command requests the main page of the www.example.com server 1000 times, with 10 simultaneous clients at any given time:

```
# /usr/local/apache2/bin/ab -n 1000 -c 10 http://www.example.com/
```

If you invoke ab without any arguments, you will get a complete listing of command-line options and syntax. Additionally, the trailing slash on the target URL is required, unless a specific page is named.

The result will look similar to the following:

```
This is ApacheBench, Version 2.0.40-dev <$Revision: 1.121.2.1 $> apache-2.0
Copyright (c) 1996 Adam Twiss, Zeus Technology Ltd, http://www.zeustech.net/
Copyright (c) 1998-2002 The Apache Software Foundation, http://www.apache.org/


Benchmarking www.example.com (be patient)
Completed 100 requests
Completed 200 requests
Completed 300 requests
Completed 400 requests
Completed 500 requests
Completed 600 requests
Completed 700 requests
Completed 800 requests
Completed 900 requests
Finished 1000 requests
Server Software:        Apache/2.0.47
Server Hostname:        www.example.com
Server Port:            80

Document Path:          /
Document Length:        8667 bytes

Concurrency Level:      10
Time taken for tests:   64.525026 seconds
Complete requests:      1000
Failed requests:        0
Write errors:           0
Total transferred:      8911000 bytes
HTML transferred:       8667000 bytes
Requests per second:    15.50 [#/sec] (mean)
Time per request:       0.645 - (mean)
Time per request:       0.065 - (mean, across all concurrent requests)
Transfer rate:          134.86 [Kbytes/sec] received

Connection Times (ms)
            min  mean[+/-sd] median    max
Connect:     19    62   59.7 45 727
Processing: 178   572  362.8 478 3151
Waiting:     18   114  176.9 74 1906
Total:      255   634  390.3 536 3301

Percentage of the requests served within a certain time (ms)
  50%    536
  66%    611
  75%    662
  80%    693
  90%    872
  95%   1436
```

```
98%    2162
99%    2461
100%   3301 (longest request)
```

These requests were made over the Internet to a sample server. You should get many more requests per second if you conduct the test against a server in the same machine or over a local network. The output of the tool is self-explanatory. Some of the relevant results are the number of requests per second and the average time it takes to service a request. You can also see how more than 90% of the requests were served in less than one second.

You can play with different settings for the number of requests and with the number of simultaneous clients to find the point at which your server slows down significantly.

Proactive Performance Tuning

Although previous sections explained which settings might prevent Apache from scaling, the following are some techniques for proactively increasing the performance of your server.

Mapping Files to Memory

As explained previously, accesses to disk affect performance significantly. Although most modern operating systems keep a cache of the most frequently accessed files, Apache also enables you to explicitly map a file into memory so that access to disk isn't necessary. The module that performs this mapping is mod_file_cache. You can specify a list of files to memory map by using the MMapFile directive, which applies to the server as a whole. An additional directive in Apache 2.0, CacheFile, takes a list of files, caches the file descriptors at startup, and keeps them around between requests, saving time and resources for frequently requested files.

Distributing the Load

Another way to increase performance is to distribute the load among several servers. This can be done in a variety of ways:

▶ A hardware load balancer directing network and HTTP traffic across several servers, making it look like a single server from the outside.

▶ A software load balancer solution using a reverse proxy with mod_rewrite.

▶ Separate servers providing images, large download files, and other static material. For example, you can place your images in a server called `images.example.com` and link to them from your main server.

Caching

The fastest way to serve content is not to serve it! This can be achieved by using appropriate HTTP headers that instruct clients and proxies of the validity in time of the requested resources. In this way, some resources that appear in multiple pages but don't change frequently, such as logos or navigation buttons, are transmitted only once for a certain period of time.

Additionally, you can use `mod_cache` in Apache 2.0 to cache dynamic content so that it doesn't need to be created for every request. This is potentially a big performance boost because dynamic content usually requires accessing databases, processing templates, and so on, which can take significant resources.

By the Way

> As of this writing, `mod_cache` is still experimental. You can read more about it at `http://httpd.apache.org/docs-2.0/mod/mod_cache.html`.

Reduce Transmitted Data

Another way to reduce the load on the servers is to reduce the amount of data being transferred to the client. This in turn makes your clients' Web site access faster, especially for those over slow links. You can do a number of things to achieve this:

▶ Reduce the number of images.

▶ Reduce the size of your images.

▶ Compress big downloadable files.

▶ Pre-compress static HTML and use content negotiation.

▶ Use `mod_deflate` to compress HTML content. This can be useful if CPU power is available and clients are connecting over slow links. The content will be delivered quicker and the process will be free sooner to answer additional requests.

Network Settings

HTTP 1.1 allows multiple requests to be served over a single connection. HTTP 1.0 enables the same thing with keep-alive extensions. The KeepAliveTimeout directive enables you to specify the maximum time in seconds that the server will wait before closing an inactive connection. Increasing the timeout means that you increase the chance of the connection being reused. On the other hand, it also ties up the connection and Apache process during the waiting time, which can prevent scalability, as discussed earlier in the chapter.

Preventing Abuse

Denial of service (DoS) attacks work by swamping your server with a great number of simultaneous requests, slowing down the server or preventing access altogether to legitimate clients. DoS attacks are difficult to prevent in general, and usually the most effective way to address them is at the network or operating system level. One example is blocking specific addresses from making requests to the server; although you can block those addresses at the Web server level, it is more efficient to block them at the network firewall/router or with the operating system network filters.

Other kinds of abuse include posting extremely big requests or opening a great number of simultaneous connections. You can limit the size of requests and timeouts to minimize the effect of attacks. The default request timeout is 300 seconds, but you can change it with the TimeOut directive. A number of directives enable you to control the size of the request body and headers: LimitRequestBody, LimitRequestFields, LimitRequestFieldSize, LimitRequestLine, and LimitXMLRequestBody.

Robots

Robots, *Web spiders*, and *Web crawlers* are names that describe a category of programs that access pages in your Web site, recursively following your site's links. Web search engines use these programs to scan the Internet for Web servers, download their content, and index it. Normal users use them to download an entire Web site or portion of a Web site for later offline browsing. Normally, these programs are well behaved, but sometimes they can be very aggressive and swamp your Web site with too many simultaneous connections or become caught in cyclic loops.

Well-behaved spiders will request a special file, called robots.txt, that contains instructions about how to access your Web site and which parts of the Web site won't be available to them. The syntax for the file can be found at http://www.robotstxt.org/. By placing a properly formatted robots.txt file in your Web server document root, you can control spider activity. Additionally, you can stop the requests at the router or operating system levels.

Implementing Virtual Hosting

Early Web servers were designed to handle the contents of a single site. The standard way of hosting several Web sites in the same machine was to install and configure different, and separate, Web server instances. As the Internet grew, so did the need for hosting multiple Web sites and a more efficient solution was developed: virtual hosting. Virtual hosting allows a single instance of Apache to serve different Web sites, identified by their domain names. *IP-based* virtual hosting means that each of the domains is assigned a different IP address; *name-based* virtual hosting means that several domains share a single IP address.

Web clients use the domain name server system (DNS) to translate hostnames into IP addresses and vice versa. Several mappings are possible:

▶ **One-to-one**—Means that each hostname is assigned a single, unique IP address. This is the foundation for IP-based virtual hosting.

▶ **One-to-many**—Means that a single hostname is assigned to several IP addresses. This is useful for having several Apache instances serving the same Web site. If each of the servers is installed in a different machine, it is possible to balance the Web traffic among them, improving scalability.

▶ **Many-to-one**—Means that you can assign the same IP address to several hostnames. The client will specify the Web site it is accessing by using the Host: header in the request. This is the foundation for name-based virtual hosting.

When a many-to-one mapping is in place, a DNS server usually can be configured to respond with a different IP address for each DNS query, which helps to distribute the load. This is known as *round robin DNS*. However, if you have the opportunity to utilize a load balancing device instead of relying on a DNS server, doing so will alleviate any problems that may arise when tying your Web server to your DNS server. Utilizing a load balancer will eliminate the possibility that high traffic to your Web server will bring down your DNS server as well.

IP-Based Virtual Hosting

The simplest virtual host configuration is when each host is assigned a unique IP address. Each IP address maps the HTTP requests that Apache handles to separate content trees in their own VirtualHost containers, as shown in the following snippet:

```
Listen 192.168.128.10:80
Listen 192.168.129.10:80

<VirtualHost 192.168.128.10:80>
    DocumentRoot /usr/local/www-docs/host1
</VirtualHost>

<VirtualHost 192.168.129.10:80>
    DocumentRoot /usr/local/www-docs/host2
</VirtualHost>
```

If a DocumentRoot is not specified for a given virtual host, the global setting, specified outside any <VirtualHost> section, will be used. In the previous example, each virtual host has its own DocumentRoot. When a request arrives, Apache uses the destination IP address to direct the request to the appropriate host. For example, if a request comes for IP 192.168.128.10, Apache returns the documents from /usr/local/www-docs/host1.

If the host operating system cannot resolve an IP address used as the VirtualHost container's name and there's no ServerName directive, Apache will complain at server startup time that it can't map the IP addresses to hostnames. This complaint is not a fatal error. Apache will still run, but the error indicates that there might be some work to be done with the DNS configuration so that Web browsers can find your server. A fully qualified domain name (FQDN) can be used instead of an IP address as the VirtualHost container name and the Listen directive binding (if the domain name resolves in DNS to an IP address configured on the machine and Apache can bind to it).

Name-Based Virtual Hosts

As a way to mitigate the consumption of IP addresses for virtual hosts, the HTTP/1.1 protocol version introduced the Host: header, which enables a browser to specify the exact host for which the request is intended. This allows several hostnames to share a single IP address. Most browsers nowadays provide HTTP/1.1 support.

> Although Host: usage was standardized in the HTTP/1.1 specification, some older HTTP/1.0 browsers also provided support for this header.

A typical set of request headers from Microsoft Internet Explorer is shown in Listing 26.1. If the URL were entered with a port number, it would be part of the Host header contents as well.

LISTING 26.1   Request Headers

```
GET / HTTP/1.1
Accept: image/gif, image/x-xbitmap, image/jpeg, image/pjpeg, */*
Accept-Language: en-us
Accept-Encoding: gzip, deflate
User-Agent: Mozilla/4.0 (compatible; MSIE 5.01; Windows NT 5.0)
Host: host1.example.com
Connection: Keep-Alive
```

Apache uses the Host: header for configurations in which multiple hostnames can be shared by a single IP address—the many-to-one scenario outlined earlier this chapter—thus, the description *name-based virtual hosts*.

The NameVirtualHost directive enables you to specify IP address and port combinations on which the server will receive requests for name-based virtual hosts. This is a required directive for name-based virtual hosts. Listing 26.2 has Apache dispatch all connections to 192.168.128.10 based on the Host header contents.

LISTING 26.2   Name-Based Virtual Hosts

```
NameVirtualHost 192.168.128.10
Listen 192.168.128.10:80

<VirtualHost 192.168.128.10>
    ServerName host1.example.com
    DocumentRoot /usr/local/www-docs/host1
</VirtualHost>

<VirtualHost 192.168.128.10>
    ServerName host2.example.com
    DocumentRoot /usr/local/www-docs/host2
</VirtualHost>
```

For every hostname that resolves in DNS to 192.168.128.10, Apache can support another name-based virtual host. If a request comes for that IP address for a hostname that is not included in the configuration file, say host3.example.com, Apache will simply associate the request to the first container in the configuration file; in this case, host1.example.com. The same behavior is applied to requests that are not accompanied by a Host header; whichever container is first in the configuration file is the one that gets the request.

An end user from the example.com domain might have his machine set up with example.com as his default domain. In that case, he might direct his browser to http://host1/ instead of the fully qualified http://host1.example.com/. The Host header would simply have host1 in it instead of host1.example.com. To make sure that the correct virtual host container gets the request, you can use the ServerAlias directive as shown in Listing 26.3.

LISTING 26.3   The ServerAlias Directive

```
NameVirtualHost 192.168.128.10
Listen 192.168.128.10:80

<VirtualHost 192.168.128.10>
    ServerName host1.example.com
    ServerAlias host1
    DocumentRoot /usr/local/www-docs/host1
</VirtualHost>

<VirtualHost 192.168.128.10>
    ServerName host2.example.com
    ServerAlias host2
    DocumentRoot /usr/local/www-docs/host2
</VirtualHost>
```

In fact, you can give ServerAlias a space-separated list of other names that might show up in the Host header so that you don't need a separate VirtualHost container with a bunch of common directives just to handle all the name variants.

HTTP 1.1 forces the use of the Host header. If the protocol version is identified as 1.1 in the HTTP request line, the request *must* be accompanied by a Host header. In the early days of name-based virtual hosts, Host headers were considered a tradeoff: Fewer IP resources were required, but legacy browsers that did not send Host headers were still in use and, therefore, could not access all of the server's virtual hosts. Today, that is not a consideration; there is no statistically significant number of such legacy browsers in use.

Mass Virtual Hosting

In the previous listings, the DocumentRoot directives follow a simple pattern:

```
DocumentRoot /usr/local/www-docs/hostname
```

where *hostname* is the hostname portion of the fully qualified domain name used in the virtual host's ServerName. For just a few virtual hosts, this configuration is fine. But what if there are dozens, hundreds, or even thousands of these virtual hosts? The configuration file can become difficult to maintain. Apache provides a good solution for cookie-cutter virtual hosts with mod_vhost_alias. You can configure Apache to map the virtual host requests to separate content trees with pattern-matching rules in the VirtualDocumentRoot directive. This functionality is especially useful for ISPs that want to provide a virtual host for each one of their users. The following example provides a simple mass virtual host configuration:

```
NameVirtualHost 192.168.128.10
Listen 192.168.128.10:80

VirtualDocumentRoot /usr/local/www-docs/%1
```

The %1 token used in this example's VirtualDocumentRoot directive will be substituted for the first portion of the fully qualified domain name (FQDN). The mod_vhost_alias directives have a language for mapping FQDN components to filesystem locations, including characters within the FQDN.

If we eliminated all the VirtualHost containers and simplified our configuration to the one shown here, the server would serve requests for any subdirectories created in the /usr/local/www-docs directory. If the hostname portion of the FQDN is matched as a subdirectory, Apache will look there for content when it translates the request to a filesystem location.

Although virtual hosts normally inherit directives from the main server context, some of them, such as Alias directives, do not get propagated. For instance, the virtual hosts will not inherit this filesystem mapping:

```
Alias /icons /usr/local/apache2/icons
```

The FollowSymLinks flag for the Options directive is also disabled in this context. However, a variant of the ScriptAlias directive is supported.

The VirtualScriptAlias directive shown in the following snippet treats requests for any resources under /cgi-bin as containing CGI scripts:

```
NameVirtualHost 192.168.128.10
Listen 192.168.128.10:80
VirtualDocumentRoot /usr/local/vhosts/%1/docs
VirtualScriptAlias /usr/local/vhosts/%1/cgi-bin
```

Note that cgi-bin is a special token for that directive; calling the directory just cgi won't work; it must be cgi-bin.

For IP-based virtual hosting needs, there are variants of these directives: VirtualDocumentRootIP and VirtualScriptAliasIP.

Summary

This chapter provided information on Apache and operating system settings that can affect scalability and performance. In most cases, the problems in Web site scalability relate to dynamic content generation and database access. Writing efficient scripts will alleviate issues in those categories. Hardware-related improvements, such as high-quality network cards and drivers, increased memory, and disk arrays can also provide enhanced performance.

With regards to virtual hosting, Apache can be configured to handle virtual hosts in a variety of ways. Whether you need a large number of cookie-cutter virtual hosts, a varied set of different virtual host configurations, or the number of IP addresses you can use is limited, there's a way to configure Apache for your application. Name-based virtual hosting is a common technique for deploying virtual hosts without using up IP addresses. IP-based virtual hosting is another method when you have plenty of IPs available and you want to keep your configuration tidy, with a one-to-one balance of IPs to virtual hosts. Also, if you cannot change your DNS configuration, you have the recourse of using separate port numbers for your virtual hosts.

Q&A

Q. *How can I measure whether my site is fast enough?*

A. Many developers test their sites locally or over an internal network, but if you run a public Web site, chances are good that many of your users will access it over slow links. Try navigating your Web site from a dialup account and make sure that your pages load fast enough, with the rule of thumb being that pages should load in less than three seconds.

Q. *How can I migrate an existing name-based virtual host to its own machine while maintaining continuous service?*

A. If a virtual host is destined to move to a neighboring machine, which by definition cannot have the same IP address, there are some extra measures to take. A common practice is to do something like the following, although many variations on these steps are possible:

1. Set the time-to-live (TTL) of the DNS mapping to a very low number. This increases the frequency of client lookups of the hostname.

2. Configure an IP alias on the old host with the new IP address.

3. Configure the virtual host's content to be served by both name- and IP-address-based virtual hosts.

4. After all the requests for the virtual host at the old IP address diminish (due to DNS caches expiring their old lookups), the server can be migrated.

Q. *Can I mix IP- and name-based virtual hosting?*

A. Yes. If multiple IP addresses are bound, you can allocate their usage a number of different ways. A family of name-based virtual hosts might be associated with each; just use a separate `NameVirtualHost` directive for each IP. One IP might be dedicated as an IP-based virtual host for SSL, for instance, whereas another might be dedicated to a family of name-based virtual hosts.

Quiz

1. Name some Apache settings that might limit scalability or affect Apache performance.

2. Name some operating system settings that might limit scalability.

3. Name some approaches to improve performance.

4. Which VirtualHost container gets a request if the connection uses NameVirtualHost, but no Host header is sent?

5. Is the ServerName directive necessary in a VirtualHost container?

Answers

1. Some of the Apache settings that might affect scalability include FollowSymLinks, SymLinksIfOwnerMatch arguments to the Options directive, enabling per-directory configuration files, hostname lookups, having a scoreboard file, and statistics collection with mod_status.

2. Some operating system settings that might affect scalability include limits for number of processes, open file descriptors, and memory allowed per process.

3. The following are some suggestions for improving performance: load distribution via a hardware load balancer or reverse proxy, data compression, caching, mapping files to memory, and compiling modules statically.

4. Reading the configuration top-to-bottom, the first VirtualHost container is favored. The same behavior occurs if there is a Host header, but no VirtualHost container that matches it.

5. Only when name-based virtual hosts are used. The Host header contents are compared to the contents of the ServerName directive. If a match isn't satisfied, the VirtualHost containers' ServerAlias directive value(s) are checked for matches.

CHAPTER 27

Setting Up a Secure Web Server

This chapter explains how to set up an Apache server capable of secure transactions. In this chapter, you will learn

- ▶ The installation and configuration of the mod_ssl Apache module
- ▶ The SSL/TLS family of protocols and the underlying cryptography concepts
- ▶ What certificates are and how to create and manage them

The Need for Security

As the Internet became mainstream and the number of companies, individuals, and government agencies using it grew, so did the number and type of transactions that needed protection. Those included financial transactions, such as banking operations and electronic commerce, as well as exchange of sensitive information, such as medical records and corporate documents. Three requirements are necessary to carry on secure communications on the Internet: confidentiality, integrity, and authentication.

Confidentiality

Confidentiality is the most obvious requirement for secure communications. If you are transmitting or accessing sensitive information such as your credit-card number or your personal medical history, you certainly don't want a stranger to get hold of it.

Integrity

The information contained in the exchanged messages must be protected from external manipulation. That is, if you place an order online to buy 100 shares of stock, you don't want to allow anyone to intercept the message, change it to an order to buy 1000 shares, or replace the original message. Additionally, you want to prevent an attacker from performing replay attacks, which, instead of modifying the original message, simply resend it several times to achieve a cumulative effect.

Authentication

You need to decide whether to trust the organization or individual you are communicating with. To achieve this, you must authenticate the identity of the other party in the communication.

The science of cryptography studies the algorithms and methods used to securely transmit messages, ensuring the goals of confidentiality, integrity, and authenticity. Cryptanalysis is the science of breaking cryptographic systems.

The SSL Protocol

SSL stands for *Secure Sockets Layer* and TLS stands for *Transport Layer Security*. They are a family of protocols that were originally designed to provide security for HTTP transactions, but that also can be used for a variety of other Internet protocols such as IMAP and NNTP. HTTP running over SSL is referred to as *secure HTTP*.

Netscape released SSL version 2 in 1994 and SSL version 3 in 1995. TLS is an IETF standard designed to standardize SSL as an Internet protocol. It is just a modification of SSL version 3 with a small number of added features and minor cleanups. The TLS acronym is the result of arguments between Microsoft and Netscape over the naming of the protocol because each company proposed its own name. However, the name has not stuck and most people refer to these protocols simply as SSL. Unless otherwise specified, the rest of this chapter refers to SSL/TLS as *SSL*.

You specify that you want to connect to a server using SSL by replacing http with https in the protocol component of a URI. The default port for HTTP over SSL is 443.

The following sections explain how SSL addresses the confidentiality, integrity, and authentication requirements outlined in the previous section. In doing so, it explains, in a simplified manner, the underlying mathematical and cryptographic principles SSL is based on.

Addressing the Need for Confidentiality

The SSL protocol protects data from eavesdropping by encrypting it. Encryption is the process of converting a message, the *plaintext*, into a new encrypted message, the *ciphertext*. Although the plaintext is readable by everyone, the ciphertext is completely unintelligible to an eavesdropper. Decryption is the reverse process, which transforms the ciphertext into the original plaintext.

Usually, encryption and decryption processes involve an additional piece of information: a *key*. If both sender and receiver share the same key, the process is referred to as *symmetric* cryptography. If sender and receiver have different, complementary keys, the process is called *asymmetric* or *public key* cryptography.

Symmetric Cryptography

If the key used to both encrypt and decrypt the message is the same, the process is known as *symmetric cryptography*. DES, Triple-Des, RC4, and RC2 are algorithms used for symmetric key cryptography. Many of these algorithms can have different key sizes, measured in bits. In general, given an algorithm, the greater the number of bits in the key, the more secure the algorithm is and the slower it will run because of the increased computational needs of performing the algorithm.

Symmetric cryptography is relatively fast compared to public key cryptography, which is explained in the next section. Symmetric cryptography has two main drawbacks, however. One is that keys should be changed periodically to avoid providing an eavesdropper with access to large amounts of material encrypted with the same key. The other is the key distribution problem: How to get the keys to each one of the parties in a safe manner? This was one of the original limiting factors, and before the invention of public key cryptography, the problem was solved by periodically having people traveling around with suitcases full of keys.

Public Key Cryptography

Public key cryptography takes a different approach. Instead of both parties sharing the same key, there is a pair of keys: one public and the other private. The public key can be widely distributed, whereas the owner keeps the private key secret. These two keys are complementary—a message encrypted with one of the keys can be decrypted only by the other key.

Anyone wanting to transmit a secure message to you can encrypt the message using your public key, assured that only the owner of the private key—you—can decrypt it. Even if the attacker has access to the public key, he cannot decrypt the communication. In fact, you want the public key to be as widely available as possible. Public key cryptography can also be used to provide message integrity and authentication. RSA is the most popular public key algorithm.

People with public keys will place these keys on public key servers or simply send the keys to others with whom they want to have secure email exchanges. Using the appropriate tools, such as PGP or GnuPG, the sender will encrypt the outgoing message based on the recipient's public key.

The assertion that only the owner of the private key can decrypt it means that with the current knowledge of cryptography and availability of computing power, an attacker will not be able to break the encryption by brute force alone in a reasonable timeframe. If the algorithm or its implementation is flawed, realistic attacks are possible.

> Public key cryptography is similar to giving away many identical padlocks and retaining the key that opens them all. Anybody who wants to send you a message privately can do so by putting it in a safe and locking it with one of those padlocks (public keys) before sending it to you. Only you have the appropriate key (private key) to open that padlock (decrypt the message).

The SSL protocol uses public key cryptography in an initial handshake phase to securely exchange symmetric keys that can then be used to encrypt the communication.

Addressing the Need for Integrity

Performing a special calculation on the contents of the message and storing the result with the message itself can preserve data integrity. When the message arrives at its destination, the recipient can perform the same calculation and compare the results. If the contents of the message changed, the results of the calculation will be different.

Digest algorithms perform just that process, creating message digests. A *message digest* is a method of creating a fixed-length representation of an arbitrary message that uniquely identifies it. You can think of it as the fingerprint of the message. A good message digest algorithm should be irreversible and collision resistant, at least for practical purposes. *Irreversible* means that the original message cannot be obtained from the digest and *collision resistant* means that no two different messages should have the same digest. Examples of digest algorithms are MD5 and SHA.

Message digests alone, however, do not guarantee the integrity of the message because an attacker could change the text *and* the message digest. Message authentication codes, or MACs, are similar to message digests, but incorporate a shared secret key in the process. The result of the algorithm depends both on the message and the key used. Because the attacker has no access to the key, he cannot modify both the message and the digest. HMAC is an example of a message authentication code algorithm.

The SSL protocol uses MAC codes to avoid replay attacks and to assure integrity of the transmitted information.

Addressing the Need for Authentication

SSL uses certificates to authenticate parties in a communication. Public key cryptography can be used to digitally sign messages. In fact, just by encrypting a message with your secret key, the receiver can guarantee it came from you. Other digital signature algorithms involve first calculating a digest of the message, and then signing the digest.

You can tell that the person who created that public and private key pair is the one sending the message. But how can you tie that key to a person or organization that you can trust in the real world? Otherwise, an attacker could impersonate his identity and distribute a different public key, claiming it is the legitimate one. Trust can be achieved by using digital certificates. *Digital certificates* are electronic documents that contain a public key and information about its owner (name, address, and so on). To be useful, the certificate must be signed by a trusted third party (certification authority, or CA) who certifies that the information is correct. There are many different kinds of CAs, as described later in the chapter. Some of them are commercial entities, providing certification services to companies conducting business over the Internet. Companies providing internal certification services create other CAs.

The CA guarantees that the information in the certificate is correct, and that the key belongs to that individual or organization. Certificates have a period of validity and can expire or be revoked. Certificates can be chained so that the certification process can be delegated. For example, a trusted entity can certify companies, which in turn can take care of certifying its own employees.

If this whole process is to be effective and trusted, the certificate authority must require appropriate proof of identity from individuals and organizations before it issues a certificate.

By default, browsers include a collection of root certificates for trusted certificate authorities.

SSL and Certificates

The main standard defining certificates is X.509, adapted for Internet usage. An X.509 certificate contains the following information:

- ▶ **Issuer**—The name of the signer of the certificate
- ▶ **Subject**—The person holding the key being certified
- ▶ **Subject public key**—The public key of the subject
- ▶ **Control information**—Data such as the dates in which the certificate is valid
- ▶ **Signature**—The signature that covers the previous data

You can check a real-life certificate by connecting to a secure server with your browser. If the connection has been successful, a little padlock icon or another visual clue will be added to the status bar of your browser. Depending on your browser, you should be able to click the representative icon in order to view information on the SSL connection and the remote server certificate. Open the `https://www.zend.com/` URL in your browser and analyze the certificate, following the steps outlined in the preceding paragraph. You can see how the issuer of the certificate is Thawte CA. The page downloaded seamlessly because Thawte is a trusted CA that has its own certificates bundled with Internet Explorer and Netscape Navigator.

You can see that both issuer and subject are provided as distinguished names (DN), a structured way of providing a unique identifier for every element on the network. In the case of the Thawte certificate, the DN is C=IL, S=Mehoz Tel Aviv, L=Ramat Gan, O=Zend Technologies, Ltd., CN=`www.zend.com`.

C stands for *country*, S for *state*, L for *locality*, O for *organization*, and CN for *common name*. In the case of a Web site certificate, the common name identifies the fully qualified domain name of the Web site. This is the server name part of the URL; in this case, `www.zend.com`. If this does not match what you typed in the top bar, the browser will issue an error.

SSL Protocol Summary

You have seen how SSL achieves confidentiality via encryption, integrity via message authentication codes, and authentication via certificates and digital signatures.

The process to establish an SSL connection is the following:

1. The user uses his browser to connect to the remote Apache server.

2. The handshake phase begins—the browser and server exchange keys and certificate information.

3. The browser checks the validity of the server certificate, including that it has not expired, that it has been issued by a trusted CA, and so on.

4. Optionally, the server can require the client to present a valid certificate as well.

5. Server and client use each other's public key to securely agree on a symmetric key.

6. The handshake phase concludes and transmission continues using symmetric cryptography.

Obtaining and Installing SSL Tools

SSL support is provided by mod_ssl, an Apache module. This module requires the OpenSSL library—an open-source implementation of the SSL/TLS protocols and a variety of other cryptographic algorithms. OpenSSL is based on the SSLeay library developed by Eric A. Young and Tim J. Hudson.

Due to the restrictions on the distribution of string cryptography and patented intellectual property worldwide, the installation of SSL-related tools varies in its ease from platform to platform. The following sections provide an overview for obtaining and installing SSL-related tools.

OpenSSL

All files and instructions necessary for installing OpenSSL can be found at http://www.openssl.org/. Users of Linux/Unix (and their variants) will find the installation of the OpenSSL software to be similar to installing other system tools. However, the casual Windows user will discover that there are currently no freely distributed pre-compiled binaries. As such, Windows users must compile the OpenSSL tools on their own.

Once you have installed the OpenSSL toolkit, you will have all the necessary elements for creating and manipulating certificates and keys, as well as interfacing with the mod_ssl Apache module.

For Windows Users

Windows users who are familiar with the process of building their own binaries may do so with the OpenSSL source code provided at the OpenSSL Web site. The instructions for compiling OpenSSL on Windows are in the INSTALL.W32 file found in the source distribution. Restating these instructions is beyond the scope of this book; however, you will find they are comprehensive and well-written. The required tools are ActiveState Perl for Windows, and one of the following C compilers:

- ▶ Visual C++
- ▶ Borland C
- ▶ GNU C (Cygwin or MinGW)

Be sure to follow the instructions appropriate to your compiler of choice, as they are quite different for each. You can also find tips from Apache for compiling OpenSSL, at http://httpd.apache.org/docs-2.0/platform/win_compiling.html.

For Linux/Unix Users

If you are running a recent Linux or FreeBSD distribution, OpenSSL might already be installed in your system. Should you need to install OpenSSL, you can download the source from the OpenSSL Web site. Once downloaded, uncompress it and cd into the created directory (replace -version in the following commands with your particular, current version of OpenSSL):

```
# gunzip < openssl-version.tar.gz ¦ tar xvf -
# cd openssl-version
```

Complete installation instructions are found in the INSTALL file, but in short, the config script will help you build the software, which is followed by the make and make install processes.

mod_ssl

In the past, SSL extensions for Apache had to be distributed separately because of export restrictions. Currently, mod_ssl is bundled with Apache 2.0, but only as part of the source distributions. While not an issue for Linux/Unix users, Windows users will find they must build Apache from source in order to build the mod_ssl module; mod_ssl is not distributed in the pre-compiled and distributed binaries. The mod_ssl module depends on the OpenSSL library, so a valid OpenSSL installation is required.

For Windows Users

In order to use mod_ssl, you must build your Apache installation from scratch. In other words, if you followed the installation instructions in Chapter 2, "Installing and Configuring Apache," throw those out and follow the Apache documentation found at http://httpd.apache.org/docs-2.0/platform/win_compiling.html. Again, restating these instructions is beyond the scope of this book, but they will provide you with all the information you need. The core requirements are

- ▶ Installed OpenSSL toolkit
- ▶ Microsoft Visual C++ 5.0 or higher
- ▶ The Windows Platform SDK
- ▶ The awk utility (awk, gawk, or similar)

For Linux/Unix Users

The source distribution used in Chapter 2 should already include the files necessary to use mod_ssl. As such, in order to use mod_ssl, you only need to follow the configure and make/make install process again, with the following addition as part of the configure command:

```
--enable-ssl --with-ssl=/usr/local/ssl/
```

This assumes that you installed OpenSSL in the listed location; if it resides in another directory on your server, simply substitute the location in the preceding command.

If you compiled mod_ssl statically into Apache, you can check whether it is present by issuing the following command, which provides a list of compiled-in modules:

```
# /usr/local/apache2/bin/httpd -l
```

The command assumes that you installed Apache in the /usr/local/apache2 directory.

If mod_ssl was compiled as a dynamic loadable module, the following line must be added or uncommented to the configuration file:

```
LoadModule ssl_module modules/libmodssl.so
```

Managing Certificates

After installing and configuring OpenSSL and mod_ssl, the next step for a work-ing SSL server implementation is to create a server certificate. This section explains in detail how to create and manage certificates and keys by using the openssl command-line tool. For example, if you are using SSL for an e-commerce site, encryption prevents customer data from eavesdroppers, and the certificate enables customers to verify that you are who you claim to be.

> The examples refer to the Unix version of the command-line program openssl. If you are running under Windows, you need to use openssl.exe instead and change the paths of the examples to use backslashes instead of forward slashes. Also, if you installed OpenSSL in a directory unlike the one listed here, simply substitute that directory in the examples.

Creating a Key Pair

You must have a public/private key pair before you can create a certificate request. Assume that the FQDN for the certificate you want to create is www.example.com. (You will need to substitute this name for the FQDN of the machine on which you have installed Apache.) You can create the keys by issuing the fol-lowing command:

```
# /usr/local/ssl/bin/openssl genrsa -des3 -rand file1:file2:file3 \
        -out www.example.com.key 1024
```

The genrsa switch indicates to OpenSSL that you want to generate a key pair.

The des3 switch indicates that the private key should be encrypted and protected by a pass phrase.

The rand switch is used to provide OpenSSL with random data to ensure that the generated keys are unique and unpredictable. Substitute file1, file2, and so on, for the path to several large, relatively random files for this purpose (such as a kernel image, compressed log files, and so on). You can also use /dev/random if it exists on your system. The rand switch is not necessary on Windows because the random data is automatically generated by other means.

The out switch indicates where to store the results.

1024 indicates the number of bits of the generated key.

The result of invoking this command looks like this:

```
625152  semi-random bytes loaded
Generating RSA private key, 1024 bit long modulus
.....++++++
.........................++++++
e is 65537 (0x10001)
Enter PEM pass phrase:
Verifying password - Enter PEM pass phrase:
```

As you can see, you will be asked to provide a pass phrase; choose a secure one. The pass phrase is necessary to protect the private key, and you will be asked for it whenever you want to start the server. You can choose not to protect the key. This is convenient because you will not need to enter the pass phrase during reboots, but it is highly insecure and a compromise of the server means a compromise of the key as well. In any case, you can choose to unprotect the key either by leaving out the -des3 switch in the generation phase or by issuing the following command:

```
# /usr/local/ssl/bin/openssl rsa -in www.example.com.key \
      -out www.example.com.key.unsecure
```

It is a good idea to back up the www.example.com.key file. You can learn about the contents of the key file by issuing the following command:

```
# /usr/local/ssl/bin/openssl rsa -noout -text -in www.example.com.key
```

Creating a Certificate Signing Request

To get a certificate issued by a CA, you must submit what is called a *certificate signing request*. To create a request, issue the following command:

```
# /usr/local/ssl/bin/openssl req -new -key www.example.com.key \
      -out www.example.com.csr
```

You will be prompted for the certificate information:

```
Using configuration from /usr/local/ssl/install/openssl/openssl.cnf
Enter PEM pass phrase:
You are about to be asked to enter information that will be incorporated
into your certificate request.
What you are about to enter is what is called a Distinguished Name or a DN.
There are quite a few fields but you can leave some blank
For some fields there will be a default value,
If you enter '.', the field will be left blank.
-----
Country Name (2 letter code) [AU]:US
State or Province Name (full name) [Some-State]:CA
Locality Name (eg, city) []: San Francisco
Organization Name (eg, company) [Internet Widgits Pty Ltd]:.
```

```
Organizational Unit Name (eg, section) []:.
Common Name (eg, YOUR name) []:www.example.com
Email Address []:administrator@example.com
Please enter the following 'extra' attributes
to be sent with your certificate request
A challenge password []:
An optional company name []:
```

It is important that the `Common Name` field entry matches the address that visitors to your Web site will type in their browsers. This is one of the checks that the browser will perform for the remote server certificate. If the names differ, a warning indicating the mismatch will be issued to the user.

The certificate is now stored in `www.example.com.csr`. You can learn about the contents of the certificate via the following command:

```
# /usr/local/ssl/bin/openssl req -noout -text \
        -in www.example.com.csr
```

You can submit the certificate signing request file to a CA for processing. VeriSign and Thawte are two of those CAs. You can learn more about their particular submission procedures at their Web sites:

- ▶ **VeriSign**—http://www.verisign.com/products/site/index.html

- ▶ **Thawte**—http://www.thawte.com/html/RETAIL/ssl/index.html

Creating a Self-Signed Certificate

You can also create a self-signed certificate. That is, you can be both the issuer and the subject of the certificate. Although this is not very useful for a commercial Web site, it will enable you to test your installation of `mod_ssl`, and to have a secure Web server while you wait for the official certificate from the CA.

```
# /usr/local/ssl/bin/openssl x509 -req -days 30  \
        -in www.example.com.csr -signkey www.example.com.key \
        -out www.example.com.cert
```

You need to copy your certificate `www.example.com.cert` (either the one returned by the CA or your self-signed one) to `/usr/local/ssl/openssl/certs/` and your key to `/usr/local/ssl/openssl/private/`.

Protect your key file by issuing the following command:

```
# chmod 400 www.example.com.key
```

SSL Configuration

The previous sections introduced the (not-so-basic) concepts behind SSL, and you have learned how to generate keys and certificates. Now you can configure Apache to support SSL. The mod_ssl module must either be compiled statically or, if you have compiled as a loadable module, the appropriate LoadModule directive must be present in the file.

Next, you can add the following configuration snippet to your Apache configuration file:

```
Listen 443
<VirtualHost _default_:443>
ServerName www.example.com
SSLEngine on
SSLCertificateFile \
/usr/local/ssl/openssl/certs/www.example.com.cert
SSLCertificateKeyFile \
/usr/loca/ssl/openssl/certs/www.example.com.key
</VirtualHost>
```

This snippet sets up a new virtual host that will listen to port 443 (the default port for HTTPS), and you enable SSL on that virtual host with the SSLEngine directive. The SSLCertificateFile and SSLCertificateKeyfile directives indicate where to find the server's certificate and the file containing the associated key.

Starting the Server

Now you can stop the server if it is running, and start it again. If your key is protected by a pass phrase, you will be prompted for it. After this, Apache will start, and you should be able to connect securely to it via the https://www.example.com/ URL.

If you compiled and installed Apache yourself, in many of the vendor configuration files, you can see that an <ifDefine SSL> block surrounds the SSL directives. That allows for conditional starting of the server in SSL mode. If you start the httpd server binary directly, you can pass it the -DSSL flag at startup. You can also use the apachectl script by issuing the apachectl startssl command. Finally, if you always want to start Apache with SSL support, you can just remove the <ifDefine> section and start Apache in your usual way.

If you are unable to successfully start your server, check the Apache error log for clues about what might have gone wrong. For example, if you cannot bind to the port, make sure that another Apache instance is not running already. You must have administrator privileges to bind to port 443.

Summary

This chapter explained the fundamentals of the SSL protocol and mod_ssl, the Apache module that implements support for SSL. You were given an introduction to installing and configuring OpenSSL and mod_ssl, and how to use the openssl command-line tool for certificate and key generation and management. You can access the mod_ssl reference documentation at http://httpd.apache.org/ docs-2.0/mod/mod_ssl.html for in-depth syntax explanation and additional configuration information. Bear in mind also that SSL is just part of maintaining a secure server, which includes applying security patches, OS configuration, access control, physical security, and so on.

Q&A

Q. *Can I have SSL with name-based virtual hosting?*

A. A question that comes up frequently is how to make name-based virtual hosts work with SSL. The answer is that you currently cannot. Name-based virtual hosts depend on the Host header of the HTTP request, but the certificate verification happens when the SSL connection is being established and no HTTP request can be sent. There is a protocol for upgrading an existing HTTP connection to TLS, but it is mostly unsupported by current browsers (see RFC 2817, at http://www.rfc-editor.org/rfc/rfc2817.txt).

Q. *Can I use SSL with other protocols?*

A. The mod_ssl module implements the SSL protocol as a filter. Other protocols using the same Apache server can easily take advantage of the SSL.

Quiz

1. Name three requirements to carry on secure communications on the Internet.

2. How do you start an SSL-enabled instance of Apache?

Answers

1. Confidentiality, integrity, and authentication.

2. Use the apachectl control script and the command apachectl startssl.

CHAPTER 28

Optimizing and Tuning MySQL

Proper care and feeding of your MySQL server will keep it running happily and without incident. The optimization of your system consists of proper hardware maintenance and software tuning. In this chapter, you will learn

- ▶ Basic hardware and software optimization tips for your MySQL server
- ▶ Key start-up parameters for your MySQL server
- ▶ How to use the OPTIMIZE TABLE command
- ▶ How to use the EXPLAIN command
- ▶ How to use the FLUSH command to clean up tables, caches, and log files
- ▶ How to use SHOW commands to retrieve information about databases, tables, and indexes
- ▶ How to use SHOW commands to find system status information

Building an Optimized Platform

Designing a well-structured, normalized database schema is just half of the optimization puzzle. The other half is building and fine-tuning a server to run this fine database. Think about the four main components of a server: CPU, memory, hard drive, and operating system. Each of these better be up to speed or no amount of design or programming will make your database faster!

- ▶ **CPU**—The faster the CPU, the faster MySQL will be able to process your data. There's no real secret to this, but a 3.0GHz processor is significantly faster than a 1.0GHz processor. With processor speeds now increasing exponentially but with reasonable prices all around, it's not difficult to get a good bang for your buck.

- ▶ **Memory**—Put as much RAM in your machine as you can. You can never have enough, and RAM prices will be at rock bottom for the foreseeable future. Having available RAM can help balance out sluggish CPUs.

▶ **Hard drive**—The proper hard drive will be both large enough and fast enough to accommodate your database server and its traffic. An important measurement of hard-drive speed is its seek time, or the amount of time it takes for the drive to spin around and find a specific piece of information. Seek time is measured in milliseconds, and an average disk-seek time is around 8 or 9 milliseconds. When buying a hard drive, make sure it's big enough to accommodate all the data you'll eventually store in your database and fast enough to find it quickly.

▶ **Operating system**—If you use an operating system that's a resource hog, you have two choices: buy enough resources (that is, RAM) so that it doesn't matter, or use an operating system that doesn't suck away all your resources just so that you can have windows and pretty colors. Also, if you are blessed with a machine that has multiple processors, be sure your operating system can handle this condition and handle it well.

If you put the proper pieces together at the system level, you'll have taken several steps toward overall server optimization.

Using the `benchmark()` Function

You can perform a quick test of your server speed using the `benchmark()` MySQL function to see how long it takes to process a given expression. You can make the expression something simple, such as 10+10, or something more extravagant, such as extracting pieces of dates.

No matter the result of the expression, the result of `benchmark()` will always be 0. The purpose of `benchmark()` is not to retrieve the result of the expression, but to see how long it takes to repeat the expression for a specific number of times. For example, the following command executes the expression 10+10 one million times:

```
mysql> select benchmark(1000000,10+10);
+--------------------------+
| benchmark(1000000,10+10) |
+--------------------------+
|                        0 |
+--------------------------+
1 row in set (0.14 sec)
```

This command executes the date extraction expression, also one million times:

```
mysql> select benchmark(1000000, extract(year from now()));
```

```
+---------------------------------------------+
| benchmark(1000000, extract(year from now())) |
+---------------------------------------------+
|                                           0 |
+---------------------------------------------+
1 row in set (0.20 sec)
```

The important number is the time in seconds, which is the elapsed time for the execution of the function; the first test took 0.14 seconds and the second took 0.20 seconds. You might want to run the same uses of benchmark() multiple times during different parts of day (when your server is under different loads) to get a better idea of how your server is performing.

MySQL Startup Options

MySQL AB provides a wealth of information regarding the tuning of server parameters, much of which the average user will never need to use. So as not to completely overwhelm you with information, this section will contain only a few of the common startup options for a finely tuned MySQL server.

When you start MySQL, a configuration file called my.cnf is loaded. This file contains information ranging from port number to buffer sizes, but can be overruled by command-line startup options. At installation time, my.cnf is placed in the /etc directory, but you can also specify an alternate location for this file during start-up.

In the support-files subdirectory of your MySQL installation directory, you'll find four sample configuration files, each tuned for a specific range of installed memory:

▶ my-small.cnf—For systems with less than 64MB of RAM, where MySQL is used occasionally.

▶ my-medium.cnf—For systems with less than 64MB of RAM, where MySQL is the primary activity on the system, or for systems with up to 128MB of RAM, where MySQL shares the box with other processes. This is the most common configuration, where MySQL is installed on the same box as a Web server and receives a moderate amount of traffic.

▶ my-large.cnf—For a system with 128MB to 512MB of RAM, where MySQL is the primary activity.

▶ my-huge.cnf—For a system with 1GB to 2GB of RAM, where MySQL is the primary activity.

To use any of these as the base configuration file, simply copy the file of your choice to /etc/my.cnf (or wherever my.cnf is on your system) and change any system-specific information, such as port or file locations.

Key Startup Parameters

There are two primary start-up parameters that will affect your system the most: key_buffer_size and table_cache. If you get only two server parameters correctly tuned, make sure they're these two!

The value of key_buffer_size is the size of the buffer used with indexes. The larger the buffer, the faster the SQL command will finish and a result will be returned. Try to find the fine line between finely tuned and over-optimized; you might have a key_buffer_size of 256MB on a system with 512MB of RAM, but any more than 256MB could cause degraded server performance.

A simple way to check the actual performance of the buffer is to examine four additional variables: key_read_requests, key_reads, key_write_requests, and key_writes. You can find the values of these variables by issuing the SHOW STATUS command:

```
mysql> show status;
```

A long list of variables and values will be returned, listed in alphabetical order. Find the rows that look something like this (your values will differ):

```
| Key_read_requests   | 602843  |
| Key_reads           | 151     |
| Key_write_requests  | 1773    |
| Key_writes          | 805     |
```

If you divide the value of key_read by the value of key_reads_requests, the result should be less than 0.01. Also, if you divide the value of key_write by the value of key_writes_requests, the result should be less than 1. Using the previous values, we have results of 0.000250479809834401 and 0.454032712915962, respectively, well within the acceptable parameters. To try to get these numbers even smaller, more tuning could occur by increasing the value of key_buffer_size, but these numbers would be fine to leave as they are.

The other important server parameter is table_cache, which is the number of open tables for all threads. The default is 64, but you might need to adjust this number. Using the SHOW STATUS command, look for a variable called open_tables in the output. If this number is large, the value of table_cache should be increased.

The sample configuration files use various combinations of `key_buffer_size` and `table_cache`, which you can use as a baseline for any modifications you need to make. Whenever you modify your configuration, you'll be restarting your server for changes to take effect, sometimes with no knowledge of the consequences of your changes. In this case, be sure to try your modifications in a development environment before rolling the changes into production.

Optimizing Your Table Structure

An optimized table structure is different from a well-designed table. Table structure optimization has to do with reclaiming unused space after deletions and basically cleaning up the table after structural modifications have been made. The OPTIMIZE TABLE SQL command takes care of this, using the following syntax:

```
OPTIMIZE TABLE table_name[,table_name]
```

For example, if you want to optimize the grocery_inventory table in the testDB database, use

```
mysql> optimize table grocery_inventory;
+-------------------------+----------+----------+----------+
| Table                   | Op       | Msg_type | Msg_text |
+-------------------------+----------+----------+----------+
| testDB.grocery_inventory | optimize | status   | OK       |
+-------------------------+----------+----------+----------+
1 row in set (0.08 sec)
```

The output doesn't explicitly state what was fixed, but the text in the Msg_text column shows that the grocery_inventory table was indeed optimized. If you run the command again, the text will change, showing that it is a useful message:

```
mysql> optimize table grocery_inventory;
+-------------------------+----------+----------+----------------------------+
| Table                   | Op       | Msg_type | Msg_text                   |
+-------------------------+----------+----------+----------------------------+
| testDB.grocery_inventory | optimize | status   | Table is already up to date |
+-------------------------+----------+----------+----------------------------+
1 row in set (0.03 sec)
```

Be aware that the table is locked while it is optimized, so if your table is large, optimize it during scheduled downtime or when little traffic is flowing to your system.

Optimizing Your Queries

Query optimization has a lot to do with the proper use of indexes. The EXPLAIN command will examine a given SELECT statement to see whether it's optimized the best that it can be, using indexes wherever possible. This is especially useful when looking at complex queries involving JOINs. The syntax for EXPLAIN is

```
EXPLAIN SELECT statement
```

The output of the EXPLAIN command is a table of information containing the following columns:

- ▶ table—The name of the table.
- ▶ type—The join type, of which there are several.
- ▶ possible_keys—This column indicates which indexes MySQL could use to find the rows in this table. If the result is NULL, no indexes would help with this query. You should then take a look at your table structure and see whether there are any indexes that you could create that would increase the performance of this query.
- ▶ key—The key actually used in this query, or NULL if no index was used.
- ▶ key_len—The length of the key used, if any.
- ▶ ref—Any columns used with the key to retrieve a result.
- ▶ rows—The number of rows MySQL must examine to execute the query.
- ▶ extra—Additional information regarding how MySQL will execute the query. There are several options, such as Using index (an index was used) and Where (a WHERE clause was used).

The following EXPLAIN command output shows a non-optimized query:

```
mysql> explain select * from grocery_inventory;
+-------------------+------+---------------+------+---------+------+------+------+
| table             | type | possible_keys | key  | key_len | ref  | rows | Extra|
+-------------------+------+---------------+------+---------+------+------+------+
| grocery_inventory | ALL  | NULL          | NULL | NULL    | NULL | 6    |      |
+-------------------+------+---------------+------+---------+------+------+------+
1 row in set (0.00 sec)
```

However, there's not much optimizing you can do with a "select all" query except add a WHERE clause with the primary key. The possible_keys column would then show PRIMARY, and the Extra column would show Where used.

When using EXPLAIN on statements involving JOIN, a quick way to gauge the optimization of the query is to look at the values in the rows column. In the previous example, you have 2 and 1. Multiply these numbers together and you have 2 as your answer. This is the number of rows that MySQL must look at to produce the results of the query. You want to get this number as low as possible, and 2 is as low as it can go!

For a great deal more information on the EXPLAIN command, please visit the MySQL manual at http://www.mysql.com/doc/E/X/EXPLAIN.html.

Using the FLUSH Command

Users with reload privileges for a specific database can use the FLUSH command to clean up the internal caches used by MySQL. Often, only the root-level user has the appropriate permissions to issue administrative commands such as FLUSH.

The FLUSH syntax is

```
FLUSH flush_option
```

The common options for the FLUSH command are

- PRIVILEGES
- TABLES
- HOSTS
- LOGS

You've used the FLUSH PRIVILEGES command before, after adding new users. This command simply reloads the grant tables in your MySQL database, enabling the changes to take effect without stopping and restarting MySQL. When you issue a FLUSH PRIVILEGES command, the Query OK response will assure you that the cleaning process occurred without a hitch.

```
mysql> flush privileges;
Query OK, 0 rows affected (0.10 sec)
```

The FLUSH TABLES command will close all tables currently open or in use and essentially give your MySQL server a millisecond of breathing room before starting back to work. When your caches are empty, MySQL can better utilize available memory. Again, you're looking for the Query OK response:

```
mysql> flush tables;
Query OK, 0 rows affected (0.21 sec)
```

The FLUSH HOSTS command works specifically with the host cache tables. If you are unable to connect to your MySQL server, a common reason is that the maximum number of connections has been reached for a particular host, and it's throwing errors. When MySQL sees numerous errors on connection, it will assume something is amiss and simply block any additional connection attempts to that host. The FLUSH HOSTS command will reset this process and again allow connections to be made:

```
mysql> flush hosts;
Query OK, 0 rows affected (0.00 sec)
```

The FLUSH LOGS command closes and reopens all log files. If your log file is getting to be a burden, and you want to start a new one, this command will create a new, empty log file. Weeding through a year's worth of log entries in one file looking for errors can be a chore, so try to flush your logs at least monthly.

```
mysql> flush logs;
Query OK, 0 rows affected (0.04 sec)
```

Using the SHOW Command

There are several different uses of the SHOW command, which will produce output displaying a great deal of useful information about your MySQL database, users, and tables. Depending on your access level, some of the SHOW commands will not be available to you or will provide only minimal information. The root-level user has the capability to use all the SHOW commands, with the most comprehensive results.

The common uses of SHOW include the following, which you'll soon learn about in more detail:

```
SHOW GRANTS FOR user
SHOW DATABASES [LIKE something]
SHOW [OPEN] TABLES [FROM database_name] [LIKE something]
SHOW CREATE TABLE table_name
SHOW [FULL] COLUMNS FROM table_name [FROM database_name] [LIKE something]
SHOW INDEX FROM table_name [FROM database_name]
SHOW TABLE STATUS [FROM db_name] [LIKE something]
SHOW STATUS [LIKE something]
SHOW VARIABLES [LIKE something]
```

The SHOW GRANTS command will display the privileges for a given user at a given host. This is any easy way to check on the current status of a user, especially if you have a request to modify a user's privileges. With SHOW GRANTS, you can check first to see that the user doesn't already have the requested privileges. For example, see the privileges available to the joeuser user:

```
mysql> show grants for joe@localhost;
+----------------------------------------------------------+
¦ Grants for joeuser@localhost                             ¦
+----------------------------------------------------------+
¦ GRANT USAGE ON *.* TO 'joeuser'@'localhost'
IDENTIFIED BY PASSWORD '34f3a6996d856efd'                  ¦
¦ GRANT ALL PRIVILEGES ON testDB.* TO 'joeuser'@'localhost' ¦
+----------------------------------------------------------+
```

If you're not the root-level user or the joeuser user, you'll get an error. Unless you're the root-level user, you can see only the information relevant to your user. For example, the joeuser user isn't allowed to view information about the root-level user:

```
mysql> show grants for root@localhost;
ERROR 1044: Access denied for user:'joeuser@localhost' to database 'mysql'
```

Be aware of your privilege level throughout the remainder of this chapter. If you are not the root-level user, some of these commands will not be available to you or will display only limited information.

Retrieving Information About Databases and Tables

You've used a few of the basic SHOW commands earlier in this book to view the list of databases and tables on your MySQL server. As a refresher, the SHOW DATABASES command does just that—it lists all the databases on the MySQL server:

```
mysql> show databases;
+-------------------+
¦ Database          ¦
+-------------------+
¦ testDB            ¦
¦ mysql             ¦
+-------------------+
2 rows in set (0.00 sec)
```

After you've selected a database to work with, you can also use SHOW to list the tables in the database. In this example, we're using testDB (your table listing may vary):

```
mysql> show tables;
+--------------------+
| Tables_in_testDB   |
+--------------------+
| grocery_inventory  |
| email              |
| master_name        |
| myTest             |
| testTable          |
+--------------------+
5 rows in set (0.01 sec)
```

If you add OPEN to your SHOW TABLES command, you will get a list of all the tables in the table cache, showing how many times they're cached and in use:

```
mysql> SHOW OPEN TABLES;
+-------------------------+--------------------+
| Open_tables_in_testDB   | Comment            |
+-------------------------+--------------------+
| grocery_inventory       | cached=1, in_use=0 |
| email                   | cached=1, in_use=0 |
| testTable               | cached=1, in_use=0 |
| master_name             | cached=1, in_use=0 |
| myTest                  | cached=1, in_use=0 |
+-------------------------+--------------------+
5 rows in set (0.00 sec)
```

Using this information in conjunction with the FLUSH TABLES command you learned earlier in this chapter will help keep your database running smoothly. If SHOW OPEN TABLES shows that tables are cached numerous times, but aren't currently in use, go ahead and use FLUSH TABLES to free up that memory.

Retrieving Table Structure Information

A very helpful command is SHOW CREATE TABLE, which does what it sounds like—it shows you the SQL statement used to create a specified table:

```
mysql> show create table grocery_inventory;
+-------------------+---------------------------------------------+
| Table             | Create Table                                |
|+------------------+---------------------------------------------+
| grocery_inventory | CREATE TABLE 'grocery_inventory' (
                      'id' int(11) NOT NULL auto_increment,
                      'item_name' varchar(50) NOT NULL default '',
                      'item_desc' text,
                      'item_price' float NOT NULL default '0',
                      'curr_qty' int(11) NOT NULL default '0',
                      PRIMARY KEY  ('id')
                      ) TYPE=MyISAM
+-------------------+---------------------------------------------+
1 row in set (0.00 sec)
```

This is essentially the same information you'd get if you dumped the table schema, but the SHOW CREATE TABLE command can be used quickly if you're just looking for a reminder or a simple reference to a particular table-creation statement.

If you need to know the structure of the table, but don't necessarily need the SQL command to create it, you can use the SHOW COLUMNS command:

```
mysql> show columns from grocery_inventory;
+------------+-------------+------+-----+---------+----------------+
| Field      | Type        | Null | Key | Default | Extra          |
+------------+-------------+------+-----+---------+----------------+
| id         | int(11)     |      | PRI | NULL    | auto_increment |
| item_name  | varchar(50) |      |     |         |                |
| item_desc  | text        | YES  |     | NULL    |                |
| item_price | float       |      |     | 0       |                |
| curr_qty   | int(11)     |      |     | 0       |                |
+------------+-------------+------+-----+---------+----------------+
5 rows in set (0.00 sec)
```

> The SHOW COLUMNS and DESCRIBE commands are aliases for one another and, therefore, do the same thing.

By the Way

The SHOW INDEX command will display information about all the indexes present in a particular table. The syntax is

```
SHOW INDEX FROM table_name [FROM database_name]
```

This command produces a table full of information, ranging from the column name to cardinality of the index. The columns returned from this command are described in Table 28.1.

TABLE 28.1 Columns in the SHOW INDEX Result

Column Name	Description
Table	The name of the table.
Non_unique	1 or 0.
	1 = index can contain duplicates.
	0 = index can't contain duplicates.
Key_name	The name of the index.
Seq_in_index	The column sequence number for the
	Index; starts at 1.
Column_name	The name of the column.

TABLE 28.1   Continued

Column Name	Description
Collation	The sort order of the column, either A (ascending) or NULL (not sorted).
Cardinality	Number of unique values in the index.
Sub_part	On a partially indexed column, this shows the number of indexed characters, or NULL if the entire key is indexed.
Packed	The size of numeric columns.
Comment	Any additional comments.

Another command that produces a wide table full of results is the SHOW TABLE STATUS command. The syntax of this command is

```
SHOW TABLE STATUS [FROM database_name] LIKE 'something'
```

This command produces a table full of information, ranging from the size and number of rows to the next value to be used in an auto_increment field. The columns returned from this command are described in Table 28.2.

TABLE 28.2   Columns in the SHOW TABLE STATUS Result

Column Name	Description
Name	The name of the table.
Type	The table type: MyISAM, BDB, InnoDB, or Gemini.
Row_format	The row storage format: fixed, dynamic, or compressed.
Rows	The number of rows.
Avg_row_length	The average row length.
Data_length	The length of the data file.
Max_data_length	The maximum length of the data file.
Index_length	The length of the index file.
Data_free	The number of bytes allocated but not used.
Auto_increment	The next value to be used in an auto_increment field.
Create_time	The date and time when the table was created (in datetime format).
Update_time	The date and time of when the data file was last updated (in datetime format).

TABLE 28.2 Continued

Column Name	Description
Check_time	The date and time of when the table was last checked (in datetime format).
Create_options	Any extra options used in the CREATE TABLE statement.
Comment	Any comments added when the table was created. Additionally, InnoDB tables will use this column to report the free space in the tablespace.

Retrieving System Status

The SHOW STATUS and SHOW VARIABLES commands will quickly provide important information about your database server. The syntax for these commands is simply SHOW STATUS or SHOW VARIABLES—nothing fancy.

There are no less than 54 status variables as the output of SHOW STATUS, but the most useful are

- ▶ Aborted_connects—The number of failed attempts to connect to the MySQL server. Anytime you see an aborted connection, you should investigate the problem. It could be related to a bad username and password in a script, or your number of simultaneous connections could be set too low.

- ▶ Connections—The aggregate number of connection attempts to the MySQL server during the current period of uptime.

- ▶ Max_used_connections—The maximum number of connections that have been in use simultaneously during the current period of uptime.

- ▶ Slow_queries—The number of queries that have taken more than long_query_time, which defaults to 10 seconds. If you have more than one, it's time to investigate your SQL syntax!

- ▶ Uptime—Total number of seconds the server has been up during the current period of uptime.

You can find a comprehensive list of SHOW STATUS variables and an explanation of their values in the MySQL manual, located at http://www.mysql.com/doc/S/H/SHOW_STATUS.html.

The SHOW VARIABLES command produces even more results than SHOW STATUS—approximately 82! The variables reported from SHOW VARIABLES control the general operation of MySQL and include the following useful tidbits:

- ▶ connect_timeout—Shows the number of seconds the MySQL server will wait during a connection attempt before it gives up.

- ▶ have_innodb—Will show YES if MySQL supports InnoDB tables.

- ▶ have_bdb—Will show YES if MySQL supports Berkeley DB tables.

- ▶ max_connections—The allowable number of simultaneous connections to MySQL before a connection is refused.

- ▶ port—The port on which MySQL is running.

- ▶ table_type—The default table type for MySQL, usually MyISAM.

- ▶ version—The MySQL version number.

You can find a comprehensive list of the variables returned by the SHOW VARIABLES results and an explanation of their values in the MySQL manual at http://www.mysql.com/doc/S/H/SHOW_VARIABLES.html. After you know the values you have, you can change them in your MySQL configuration file or startup command.

Summary

Running an optimized MySQL server starts with the hardware and operating system in use. Your system's CPU should be sufficiently fast, and you should have enough RAM in use to pick up the slack when your CPU struggles. This is especially true if MySQL shares resources with other processes, such as a Web server. Additionally, the hard drive in use is important because a small hard drive will limit the amount of information you can store in your database. The seek time of your hard drive is important—a slow seek time will cause the overall performance of the server to be slower. Your operating system should not overwhelm your machine and should share resources with MySQL rather than using all the resources itself.

Some key startup parameters for MySQL are the values of key_buffer_size and table_cache, among others. Baseline values can be found in sample MySQL configuration files, or you can modify the values of these variables and watch the server performance to see whether you hit on the right result for your environment.

Beyond hardware and software optimization is the optimization of tables, as well as SELECT queries. Table optimization, using the OPTIMIZE command, enables you to reclaim unused space. You can see how well (or not) optimized your queries are by using the EXPLAIN command. The resulting output will show if and when indexes are used, and whether you can use any indexes to speed up the given query.

Paying attention to your MySQL server will ensure that it continues to run smoothly. Basic administration commands, such as FLUSH and SHOW, will help you to recognize and quickly fix potential problems. All these commands are designed to give MySQL a millisecond of rest time and breathing room if it's under a heavy load. Numerous SHOW commands will display structural information about databases, tables, and indexes, as well as how the system is performing.

Q&A

Q. *Can MySQL take advantage of multiple CPUs in a single server?*

A. Absolutely. If your operating system supports multiple CPUs, MySQL will take advantage of them. However, the performance and tuning of MySQL using multiple processors varies, depending on the operating system. For more information, please see the MySQL manual section for your specific operating system: `http://www.mysql.com/doc/0/p/Operating_System_Specific_Notes.html`

Q. *What permission level must I have to use the* `OPTIMIZE` *command?*

A. Any user with `INSERT` privileges for a table can perform `OPTIMIZE` commands. If a user has only `SELECT` permissions, the `OPTIMIZE` command will not execute.

Workshop

The workshop is designed to help you anticipate possible questions, review what you've learned, and begin learning how to put your knowledge into practice.

Quiz

1. Which MySQL function will enable you to run an expression many times over to find the speed of the iterations?

2. Which SQL command will clean up the structure of your tables?

3. Which `FLUSH` command resets the MySQL log files?

4. To quickly determine if MySQL has support for InnoDB tables, would you use `SHOW STATUS` or `SHOW VARIABLES`?

5. Write a SQL statement that will enable you to see the SQL statement used to create a table called `myTable`.

Answers

1. The `benchmark()` function

2. `OPTIMIZE`

3. `FLUSH LOGS`

4. `SHOW VARIABLES`

5. `SHOW CREATE TABLE myTable`

Activities

1. If you have root-level access to your server, change the values of `key_buffer_size` and `table_cache`, and run `benchmark()` functions after each change to see how the execution times differ.

2. Use `OPTIMIZE` on all the tables you have created in your database to clean up any structural issues.

3. Use the `SHOW STATUS` command to retrieve information about your MySQL server, and then issue `FLUSH` commands to clean up the server. After each command, use `SHOW STATUS` again to see which commands affect which results in the `SHOW STATUS` results display.

CHAPTER 29

Software Upgrades

Throughout this book, you've been reminded to seek out information regarding new versions of PHP, Apache, and MySQL, and to be mindful of possible necessary updates. Also, you've been shown how to add functionality to PHP at build time, but only in the context of installing the software. In this short chapter, you'll learn how to update your already-installed software over the normal course of time, without wrecking havoc on your system, including

- ▶ How to keep up-to-date with new software releases
- ▶ How to upgrade MySQL
- ▶ How to upgrade Apache
- ▶ How to upgrade PHP

Staying in the Loop

You should already have bookmarked the Web sites for Apache, PHP, and MySQL. It doesn't matter if you've been using these technologies for one day or six years—there will always be a need to refer back to the sites. The primary reason for visiting the Web sites is to obtain updates for your installed software. Of course, you could always subscribe to an announcements-only mailing list:

- ▶ For MySQL announcements, go to http://lists.mysql.com/ and subscribe to the MySQL Announcements list.
- ▶ For Apache announcements, go to http://www.apache.org/foundation/ mailinglists.html and subscribe to the Apache News and Announcements list.
- ▶ For PHP announcements, go to http://www.php.net/mailing-lists.php and subscribe to the Announcements list.

When to Upgrade

As indicated in the installation chapters, minor version changes occur whenever the developers find it necessary to do so—not on any particular schedule. But just because a minor version change has occurred, that doesn't necessarily mean you should run right out and upgrade your software. Sometimes, however, it does indeed mean this.

The primary instance in which you should immediately upgrade your software is when a security fix is announced. Usually, security issues are not discovered until they are exploited—sometimes in a testing environment but sometimes by a rogue user who just wants to cause trouble for the world. Once a security issue is verified, you can bet that it becomes the top priority for developers to fix, and very quickly you will see an announcement of an upgrade. When that occurs, you should follow suit and upgrade immediately—even if you don't use the particular element that is the cause of the security issue. A hole is a hole—why leave it uncovered?

Here is an example of the Apache changelog, documenting a change that occurred between version 2.0.46 and 2.0.47, that would be an indicator of a need to upgrade:

```
SECURITY [CAN-2003-0254]: Fixed a bug in ftp proxy causing denial of service when
target host is IPv6 but proxy server can't create IPv6 socket. Fixed by the
reporter.
```

A good rule of thumb would be that if the word *security* appears anywhere in the changelog, you should upgrade.

However, if the release is simply a maintenance release, meaning that it contains bugfixes and general enhancements that occur through normal development, you probably don't need to drop everything and upgrade your software. Here are some examples of maintenance items, from the Apache and PHP changelogs:

```
Add support for "streamy" PROPFIND responses. (from Apache changelog)
Fixed bug 21958 (workaround for unusual realpath() on AIX & Tru64). (from PHP
changelog)
```

If nothing in the list of changes is relevant to you, your work, or your environment, you could probably put off the upgrade until scheduled downtime or a rainy day. For example, if all the bugs fixed in a maintenance release of PHP have to do with an AIX or Tru64 platform and you run Linux on Intel architecture, you can put the task aside.

Even if you don't immediately upgrade your software, it's a good idea to stay at least within one or two minor versions of the current production version of the software. Anything past that and it becomes more likely that new features would be added or bugs fixed which are indeed relevant to your work or your environment.

Upgrading MySQL

Whether you use Linux/Unix or Windows, upgrading minor versions of MySQL is quite simple—do the install the new version as if the other version does not exist.

> Before upgrading to a new minor version of MySQL, you should back up your existing databases.

By the Way

MySQL AB has made it quite easy to upgrade within the same base version; 4.0 is a base version, 4.1 will be a base version, and so on. This means that upgrading any minor version in the 4.0.x family is as simple as installing the new software on top of the old software. With the Windows installer, this is all invisible to you, but is exactly what occurs. Linux/Unix users who install from the binary distribution will simply be re-linking the "mysql" symbolic direectory to the new, unpacked distribution, as part of the installation process.

If you run into problems during the upgrade process, there are troubleshooting tips at http://www.mysql.com/doc/en/Upgrade.html. However, upgrading minor versions of MySQL has always been a painless experience for me, on multiple platforms.

Upgrading Apache

Like MySQL, upgrading or rebuilding Apache follows the same process as installing the software in the first place. Windows users have the benefit of an installer application, which will automatically detect the previous version, remove it and install the new one.

For Linux/Unix users, the process also follows the same path as the original installation. When you unpack your new distribution, it will create a directory named with the new version number. For example, if your previous version was 2.0.46 and you are upgrading to 2.0.47, your directories will be named httpd-2.0.46 and httpd-2.0.47, respectively.

The actual installation directory for Apache is determined by you, when you run the `configure` script; for example,

```
# ./configure --prefix=/usr/local/apache2
```

After running the `configure` script in order to build the new version of Apache, just go through the `make` and `make install` process as you did when installing Apache in the first place.

Now, should you want to install your new version of Apache directly over your old version, you can—even with the old `httpd` binary still running. Just be sure to back up your configuration files, in case something goes awry. However, if you are more comfortable installing your new version in a different directory, that's fine too—you'll just have to move all your Web-related files (that is, everything in the document root) to the new directory, and make all appropriate edits to your fresh, new `httpd.conf` file. Whichever method you choose is up to you; one method just requires more file movement and reconfiguration than the other.

After upgrading Apache on Linux/Unix, you should also re-build your PHP module. Windows users do not have a module to re-build, but should ensure the appropriate PHP-related changes are still present in the `httpd.conf` file, related to loading the module residing in the PHP directory tree.

Modifying Apache Without Upgrading

Suppose you need to add or remove functionality from Apache but you are not upgrading to a new minor version. An example would be to add a new module or to upgrade the version of OpenSSL used on your system.

In this case, Linux/Unix users should go to the existing source directory (such as `httpd-2.0.47`) and type `make clean` at the prompt. This will, essentially, reset the makefiles so that you can re-build Apache without relying on previous, cached values. After the `make clean` command, run the `configure` script with your new parameters, and go through the `make` and `make install` process again. You would not need to rebuild the PHP module in this situation.

Upgrading PHP

Given that Linux/Unix users can add so much functionality to PHP, just through various build options, it is likely that you will upgrade or modify PHP more often than Apache or MySQL. Regardless of whether you are upgrading to a new minor version or simply adding new functionality (or removing some you no longer need), the process for modifying or upgrading is exactly the same as installing it in the first place: `configure`, `make`, `make install`. The `make install` step will place the PHP module in the appropriate place in the Apache directory tree. Once your new module is in place, restart Apache—the new version of PHP should be in use.

Windows users have a different set of tasks to perform; adding new functionality to an existing module requires only that the module be activated through changes to `php.ini` and the server restarted. Upgrading to a new minor version requires you to download a new distribution file. The contents of this file are then extracted into a directory named for the version it represents. You must then follow the steps required for installation, regarding the placement of `php.ini` and `php4ts.dll` files, as each version produces a different file. Finally, change any PHP-related pathnames in the Apache `httpd.conf` file, and restart the server—the new version of PHP should be in use.

Summary

This short chapter provided some guidelines for keeping your installations of MySQL, Apache, and PHP current. You learned where to look for updates, and how to weigh the importance of upgrading to a new version. Finally, you learned the step-by-step processes for upgrading or modifying MySQL, Apache, and PHP.

Workshop

The workshop is designed to help you anticipate possible questions, review what you've learned, and begin learning how to put your knowledge into practice.

Quiz

1. What is considered the primary reason for upgrading to a new minor version of any software?

2. What command will clean up previous `makefiles` and cached settings?

Answers

1. Security issues which have been found and fixed by the developers.

2. `make clean`

PART VII

Looking Toward the Future

## CHAPTER 30

Features and Backward Compatibility of PHP 5.0

All PHP-related elements in this book are based on the version 4 family, which has been in production for several years. During that time, the PHP Group and the developers at Zend Technologies have also been working on the next generation of PHP, version 5. Given how full-featured PHP has become since its inception, it's difficult to imagine what the next generation could possibly contain.

In this short chapter, you'll learn about the new features in PHP 5, including

- ▶ An overview of the new object model
- ▶ An overview of other new features
- ▶ When to consider upgrading to PHP 5

What's Wrong With PHP 4?

The "shortcomings" of the version 4 family of PHP depend on whom you talk to. Personally, I don't have any problems with the way PHP 4 works because

- ▶ It's fast
- ▶ It's flexible enough to do what I want it to do while still being fast

Alright, so those aren't very professional-sounding reasons, but they represent the bottom line: If a technology meets your needs, how can it be bad? The answer is, it's not—at least not for me. But if you come to PHP from other programming languages, especially highly structured, specifically object-oriented languages, the crossover to a flexible, procedural language that just happens to handle object-oriented programming can be frustrating. Of course, the ease of use and somewhat hidden robustness is one of the reasons new programmers are drawn to PHP in the first place—the learning curve isn't steep, *and* it gets the job done.

However, this also presents a marketing and positioning problem for PHP within the enterprise. Some Powers That Be may not think PHP is suitable for enterprise-level application development, because it is not a time-tested, structured, object-oriented programming language such as C or even Java. There may not be the time or opportunity for a developer to convince her managers otherwise by showing examples of PHP and C or Java performing the same tasks—if you even can, with the same level of structure, security, reusability, and exception-handling. From these and other problems came the development path for PHP 5, the main purpose of which is to improve the object model, instill a sense of programming discipline, and specifically design a version of PHP that meets the needs of object-oriented developers and allows them to interface with Java, .NET, and other enterprise-level application frameworks.

But where does that leave Joe and Jane Developer, who use don't want anything to do with objects, classes, .NET, or XML—who just want a simple, fast, flexible language they can use to create basic, dynamic Web sites? These developers are not left out in the cold. While PHP 5 contains an enhanced internal scripting engine and a vastly improves OO framework, the PHP Group and Zend Technologies recognizes and appreciates the roots of PHP and the core group of users who have made it so pervasive. As with PHP 4, PHP 5 does not force you to use the elements of the language you don't wish to use. If your applications are written at the basic, procedural level introduced in this book, and that works fine for you, you don't have to change a thing. If you have elements of OO programming, you should read the overview of object-related enhancements in the next section and see how they may impact your applications.

The New Object Model

Because this book did not introduce you to programming in PHP from an object-oriented point of view, this section will not go into detail and show examples of the object model changes in PHP 5. For that, I highly recommend Harry Fuecks' article "PHP5: Coming Soon to a Webserver Near You", at `http://www.sitepoint.com/article/1192/`. This article contains an outstanding dissection of the object-related changes in PHP 5, and how to implement them.

The following bullet points provide an overview of the changes. If you are a Java developer, you will begin to notice strong similarities.

▶ Private and protected variables and methods—Private variables and methods are only accessible from inside the class in which they are declared, while protected variables and methods are available to subclasses as well.

This is a completely new feature in PHP 5 and thus presents no backward-compatibility issues other than you should go back and tighten up the security around your variables and methods.

▶ Introduction of the _constructor() method—In Chapter 7, you learned that constructors are named for the class itself. In the new model, the _constructor() method is used, so that if you happen to change the name of the class, you don't need to change the name of the constructor as well. This is a completely new feature in PHP, but the PHP 4 way of doing things will still work just fine.

▶ Introduction of the _destructor() method—Ensures an object is properly closed and "cleaned up" when it has run its course. This is a completely new feature in PHP, although in both PHP 4 and PHP 5, the built-in garbage collection routines will handle the removal of the object from memory when it is no longer active. The _destructor() method simply allows you to implicitly call for such action.

▶ Abstract classes—Allow a group of subclasses to share a parent class while not directly using the parent class. For example, such a class would only be used to extend other classes, and would not be directly called. This is a completely new feature in PHP 5 and thus presents no backward-compatibility issues other than you might now want to go create a bunch of abstract classes where you previously could not.

▶ Object overloading—The ability to call methods that are not explicitly declared within the class calling them. This is a completely new feature in PHP 5 and thus presents no backward-compatibility issues.

▶ static, final, and constant keywords—are used to further define variables and methods within your classes. The static keyword allows variables and methods to be accessed without instantiating the class that contains them. The final keyword prevents variable or method in a class from being overridden by a subclass. The const keyword declares constants within a class, and only within the class. This is a completely new feature in PHP 5, although workarounds were present in PHP 4 for some of the same functionality. There are no backward-compatibility issues other than you may want to revisit your code and specifically use these keywords where possible.

▶ Autoloading—Allows you to include a class, through the use of the _autoload() function, only when it is instantiated. This is a completely new feature in PHP 5 and thus presents no backward-compatibility issues.

▶ Error handling—Implements a Java-like mechanism to handle errors, whereas error handling in PHP 4 is basically dependent on whatever the developer decides to code into place. Error handling in PHP 5 uses a try...catch control structure, like if...else for exceptions; the goal of which is to separate application data from errors. This is a completely new feature in PHP 5 and thus presents no backward-compatibility issues. However, if you have coded your own error handling into place, it is well worth converting to the try...catch structure.

As you can see, the object model has grown exponentially, and the changes are definitely for the better. While there's nothing wrong with the foundation information regarding objects that you learned about in Chapter 7, "Working with Arrays and Objects," that basic model is like driving a Le Car while PHP 5's object model is like driving a luxurious sedan (BMW, Mercedes, whatever you choose, as long as it's expensive).

Additional New Features

A few other major features will be part of PHP 5, but luckily nothing that renders moot the information you've learned so far in this book! The next few sections provide a glimpse at these features.

SQLite

PHP 5 will contain an embedded database engine, called *SQLite*. This is not at all meant to replace a robust database like MySQL, PostgreSQL, or Oracle. Instead, this simple, speedy little database can store database in both files and memory and thus would be good for something like storing session data and application configuration information—simple INSERTs and SELECTs. While there is not much information currently available regarding the inner workings of this database engine, based on the initial indications of speed it is definitely something to keep an eye on, for uses like those indicated earlier.

XML Support

PHP 4 uses several different third-party libraries to control XML parsing and rendering: Expat, libxml, and Sablotron. Expat is currently relied upon more heavily by developers and is pretty stable, but developers use the other two as well. The point is, PHP 4 has no single stable and reliable XML rendering and parsing mechanism.

With PHP 5, the development group has settled upon one XML library, Gnome's libxml, as the foundation for the DOM extension. This library has been determined to be very fast and full-featured, and thus a good foundation on which to rebuild the XML functionality in PHP.

So, When Should I Upgrade to PHP 5?

If you have a development area, you can download a beta version of PHP 5 and install it. As with all beta releases, there will be bugs as well as items not yet implemented, and even items that are currently implemented that may end up being scrapped before the final release. If you are intrigued by the new featured listed in this chapter, I encourage you to follow the betas as they evolve, installing and testing with each one. You will then be ready to immediately switch to PHP 5 in a production environment, when the PHP Developers Group indicates the first nonbeta is ready for action.

Backward Compatibility

The changelog and PHP manual always indicates when a new implementation will cause problems in previous versions, so at least read the changelog thoroughly if not the manual entries for your favorite functions. However, the vast majority of PHP 5 focuses on additional functionality rather than completely replacing existing elements, you may find that none of your scripts *require* a rewrite. Requiring a rewrite and rewriting scripts for the sake of utilizing new functionality are completely different—you may want to rewrite to take advantage of new object-oriented functionality, but you may not have to. If your code is primarily procedural (as with the scripts in this book), there's a better than 95% chance that no rewrites will be necessary.

Summary

This chapter provided a quick look at the new functionality in PHP 5. You were given a brief rundown of the additions and enhancements to the object model, as well as other grand new items such as vastly improved XML support and the availability of a built-in database called SQLite.

Q&A

Q. *Where can I read more about PHP 5?*

A. Zend Technologies, the creators of the Zend Engine which powers PHP, has a section devoted to "The Future of PHP." This section includes presentations, tutorials, articles and a forum for the exchange of ideas. The URL is `http://www.zend.com/zend/future.php`. For news regarding PHP 5 releases, keep an eye on the PHP Web site at `http://www.php.net/`.

## CHAPTER 31

Features and Backward Compatibility of MySQL 4.1

In this book, you've learned about the core elements of MySQL—how to create and add tables, add records to those tables, how to join the tables and retrieve data, some of the built-in functions available and so forth. You have probably come to your own conclusion that MySQL is a robust database system, and extremely fast at performing tasks. This statement is true. However, the developers at MySQL AB aren't stopping and resting on their laurels—MySQL 4.1 is the next planned major release, and it will include several enhancements which will make it an even better system.

In this short chapter, you'll learn about the new features planned for MySQL 4.1, including

- ▶ The introduction of subqueries and how to use them
- ▶ An overview of internationalization enhancements
- ▶ Information on more minor additions
- ▶ Information on the subsequent major release, MySQL 5.0

Using Subqueries

Arguably the greatest of all the enhancements to MySQL in version 4.1 is the availability to use subqueries. Using subqueries allows you to execute a query to obtain a result set, and then use these results as a condition to another query—all within the same statement. In other words, you have two statements in your single query, the second valid only with the results of the first.

Think of times when you may have run into a situation in your programming when you wanted to get results from multiple tables, but did not want to join the tables due to their complexity or perhaps they weren't fully relational. Your solution may have been to execute the first query and then loop through the results and perform another query. There's nothing wrong with performing the task in that manner and, with compact code, it probably wasn't especially time consuming. However, using a subquery in that same situation would open a whole new world of efficiency.

Subquery Example for Time Tracking

Suppose you have a system in place that allows employees to enter hours spent on particular tasks, on certain dates, for a given company. The table creation and data insertion statements that follow are rudimentary examples of what you might find in such a system.

In the tasks table, the names of tasks and their assigned hours rates are stored:

```
CREATE TABLE tasks (
    task_id tinyint PRIMARY KEY NOT NULL auto_increment,
    task_name varchar(50) NOT NULL default '',
    task_fee float(4,2) NOT NULL default '0.00'
);
INSERT INTO tasks VALUES ('1', 'Programming', '150.00');
INSERT INTO tasks VALUES ('2', 'Database Design', '200.00');
INSERT INTO tasks VALUES ('3', 'Project Management', '150.00');
INSERT INTO tasks VALUES ('4', 'Data Entry', '75.00');
INSERT INTO tasks VALUES ('5', 'Graphic Design', '150.00');
```

In the employees table, the names of employees are stored:

```
CREATE TABLE employees (
    e_id tinyint PRIMARY KEY NOT NULL auto_increment,
    e_fname varchar(50) NOT NULL default '',
    e_lname varchar(50) NOT NULL default ''
);
INSERT INTO employees VALUES ('1', 'John', 'Doe');
INSERT INTO employees VALUES ('2', 'Jane', 'Doe');
INSERT INTO employees VALUES ('3', 'Michael', 'Smith');
INSERT INTO employees VALUES ('4', 'Ralph', 'Jones');
```

In the clients table, the names of clients are stored:

```
CREATE TABLE clients (
    c_id tinyint PRIMARY KEY NOT NULL auto_increment,
    c_name varchar(255) NOT NULL default ''
);
INSERT INTO clients VALUES ('1', 'ABC Company');
INSERT INTO clients VALUES ('2', 'XYZ Company');
INSERT INTO clients VALUES ('3', 'Acme Telesystems');
INSERT INTO clients VALUES ('4', 'GoNutz Inc.');
```

Finally, in the billable_hours table, you have the individual entries. Note that all entries in the billable_hours table use the appropriate ID fields of the employee, client, and tasks tables in order to relate back to the master record for each.

```
CREATE TABLE billable_hours (
    bh_id int PRIMARY KEY NOT NULL auto_increment,
    work_date date,
    e_id tinyint,
    c_id tinyint,
    task_id tinyint,
    billable_time float(4,2) NOT NULL default '0.00'
);
INSERT INTO billable_hours VALUES ('', '2003-08-25', '1', '3', '2', '1.75');
INSERT INTO billable_hours VALUES ('', '2003-08-25', '1', '3', '1', '3.50');
INSERT INTO billable_hours VALUES ('', '2003-08-25', '2', '1', '3', '4.25');
INSERT INTO billable_hours VALUES ('', '2003-08-26', '2', '1', '4', '7.25');
INSERT INTO billable_hours VALUES ('', '2003-08-26', '2', '2', '1', '3.50');
INSERT INTO billable_hours VALUES ('', '2003-08-26', '3', '3', '1', '4.00');
INSERT INTO billable_hours VALUES ('', '2003-09-01', '3', '4', '2', '6.75');
INSERT INTO billable_hours VALUES ('', '2003-09-01', '3', '4', '2', '4.25');
INSERT INTO billable_hours VALUES ('', '2003-09-01', '4', '3', '3', '5.00');
INSERT INTO billable_hours VALUES ('', '2003-09-05', '4', '1', '3', '4.50');
```

Say you wanted to see a list of distinct tasks performed by any employee, for Acme Telesystems—and you weren't using subqueries. First, you'd have to get the ID for Acme Telesystems, and then issue a second query to get the list of tasks:

```
mysql> select c_id from clients where c_name = 'Acme Telesystems';
+------+
| c_id |
+------+
| 3    |
+------+
1 row in set (0.16 sec)


mysql> select distinct t.task_name as theTasks
    -> from billable_hours as bh
    -> left join tasks as t on t.task_id = bh.task_id
    -> where bh.c_id = 3;
+--------------------+
| theTasks           |
+--------------------+
| Database Design    |
| Programming        |
| Project Management |
+--------------------+
3 rows in set (0.22 sec)
```

Using subqueries, those two statements can become one:

```
mysql> select distinct t.task_name as theTasks
    -> from billable_hours as bh
    -> left join tasks as t on t.task_id = bh.task_id
    -> where bh.c_id = (select c_id from clients where c_name = 'Acme
Telesystems');
```

```
+--------------------+
¦ theTasks           ¦
+--------------------+
¦ Database Design    ¦
¦ Programming        ¦
¦ Project Management ¦
+--------------------+
3 rows in set (0.22 sec)
```

Using subqueries in this case has eliminated the first query, and 0.16 seconds from the whole process (plus the time it took to type the first query!).

In general, a subquery is usually a SELECT statement, and this statement must not return more than one column of results. Because you're trying to match one result from the second query to one condition in the first query, you can see where a multi-column SELECT statement in the second query would cause a mismatch error.

You can nest as many subqueries as you want, as long as the basic rules of queries are followed; that is, they must be valid queries and well-structured. Take the following example, which looks for work done by Michael Smith for GoNutz Inc.:

```
mysql> select t.task_name as theTask,
    -> bh.billable_time * t.task_fee as theTotal
    -> from billable_hours as bh
    -> left join tasks as t on t.task_id = bh.task_id
    -> where
    -> (
    -> (bh.c_id = (select c_id from clients where c_name = 'GoNutz Inc.'))
    -> and
    -> (bh.e_id = (select e_id from employees where (e_fname = 'Michael' and
e_lname = 'Smith')))
    -> );
```

```
+-----------------+----------+
¦ theTasks        ¦theTotal  ¦
+-----------------+----------+
¦ Database Design ¦1350.00   ¦
¦ Database Design ¦850.00    ¦
+-----------------+----------+
2 rows in set (0.22 sec)
```

In the next sections, you will learn about some additional enhancements found MySQL 4.1, but it is likely that none will have the same affect on your programming style as the ability to use subqueries in your applications!

Internationalization Enhancements

An out-of-the box installation of MySQL already includes a great deal of support for both single and multi-byte languages, but a few enhancements in version 4.1 will enhance your experience even more.

Primarily, in MySQL 4.1, you will be able to define character sets on a per-column, per-table, and per-database basis. This enhancement will allow for greater consistency and flexibility when developing internationalized application and multilingual web sites. Additionally, MySQL 4.1 will offer Unicode (UTF8) support.

For more information on enhancements related to character sets, please see the MySQL manual at `http://www.mysql.com/doc/en/Charset.html`.

Additional New Functionality

In this section, you'll see more highlights of new functionality that will be introduced in MySQL 4.1. This list is not the full list of changes; for that, you can read the actual changelog entries at `http://www.mysql.com/doc/en/News-4.1.x.html`.

- ▶ Speed enhancements. As if MySQL weren't fast enough, the developers are always finding ways to make it even faster.

- ▶ Table creation using `LIKE`. You can use `CREATE TABLE tablename LIKE othertablename` to create a new table with the exact structure (but no data) as an existing table.

- ▶ Usability enhancements, primarily a help system within the MySQL command-line interface. Typing `UCASE` will provide help for the `UCASE()` MySQL function, for example.

- ▶ `DATE/DATETIME` usage will be changing slightly, in that you will no longer be able to enter data in the format of `YYYYMMDD HHMMSS` instead of `YYYY-MM-DD HH:MM:SS`; all the separators must be used.

- ▶ `TIMESTAMP` will be returned as a string in the `YYYY-MM-DD HH:MM:SS` format, instead of in microseconds.

- ▶ You will be able to specify a length for `BLOB` and `TEXT` fields, and by doing so, MySQL will autmatically change it to its appropriate type.

- ▶ Per-column comments can now be added, and `SHOW FULL COLUMNS FROM tablename` will display these comments.

▶ Spatial extensions will be available to allow the generation, storage, and analysis of geographic features. You can read all about this topic at http://www.mysql.com/doc/en/Spatial_extensions_in_MySQL.html.

With the exception of the date-related changes mentioned earlier, none of these listed enhancements to MySQL are incompatible with previous versions. In the changelog for minor and major releases, MySQL AB will always publish a warning statement, in bold lettering, to indicate when an incompatibility is caused by a new feature.

Looking Further Ahead to MySQL 5.0

As if the changes happening for MySQL 4.1 weren't enough, the developers are already hard at work planning and prototyping features for including in MySQL 5.0. This list of included features will grow dramatically as developers actually get closer to an alpha release, but in general you can look forward to the following in MySQL 5.0:

▶ Stored procedures, based on SQL-99. The developers are also endeavoring to use external languages and implement compatibility with languages such as PL/SQL and T-SQL.

▶ New functionality, such as elementary cursor support.

▶ Additional strides toward standards compliance.

▶ Ongoing speed enhancements.

▶ Continued internationalization and usability enhancements.

As subqueries are to MySQL 4.1, stored procedures are The Big Thing for MySQL 5.0.

Summary

This chapter provided a quick look at what's on tap for MySQL 4.1 and even into MySQL 5.0, although MySQL 4.1 is much nearer on the horizon. You were shown a rudimentary example of using subqueries, and were given a brief rundown of internationalization enhancements and other changes. Again, to keep an eye on the ongoing development of MySQL 4.1, visit http://www.mysql.com/doc/en/News-4.1.x.html.

Q&A

Q. *Can I use MySQL 4.1 now?*

A. While officially an alpha release at the time of this writing, MySQL 4.1 is available for download at `http://www.mysql.com/downloads/mysql-4.1.html`. The installation might be slightly different, in which case be sure to read the accompanying instructions. For example, Windows users will not have a wizard interface for installation, but the installation simply consists of unzipping files into a specified directory.

If you do download and install MySQL 4.1, remember that it is for development use only—you should never use alpha software in a production environment!

Workshop

The workshop is designed to help you anticipate possible questions, review what you've learned, and begin learning how to put your knowledge into practice.

Quiz

1. What is a subquery?

2. True or false: You can have only one level of subqueries.

3. True or false: Installing alpha software in a production environment at my company makes me cooler than my friends.

Answers

1. A query that uses the result set of one query within a conditional statement of another.

2. False. You can have as many as you want, as long as they are well-formed.

3. False. It will make you less employed than your friends.

PART VIII

Appendix

APPENDIX A

Installing MySQL, Apache, and PHP from the CD-ROM

Chapters 1 to 3 deal with obtaining and installing PHP, MySQL, and Apache from their respective locations on the Internet so you can make sure your versions are up to date.

If you want to get started quickly, this appendix will step you through installation from the supplied CD-ROM for both Linux/Unix and Windows systems.

Linux/Unix Installation

Whenever you compile applications from a source archive, the build process is dependent upon your system having the correct development tools and libraries in place.

The instructions below were written with Red Hat Linux specifically in mind, but the steps are the same for a default installation of all other Linux or commercial Unix distributions.

Should you encounter unexpected error messages during compilation, contact your systems administrator or refer to the documentation for your particular operating system.

Begin as the super user (either log in as root or su from a regular system user) and mount the CD-ROM under /mnt on your filesystem.

```
# mount /dev/cdrom /mnt -t iso9660
```

Installing MySQL

Before installing MySQL we need to create a user on the system that will run the MySQL server.

```
# /usr/sbin/groupadd mysql
# /usr/sbin/useradd -g mysql mysql
```

We will put all the source code to be built in the /usr/local/src directory, so let's extract the MySQL archive from the CD-ROM.

```
# cd /usr/local/src
# gunzip < /mnt/MySQL/Linux/tarballs/source/mysql-4.0.15.tar.gz ¦ tar xf -
```

This creates a directory called mysql-4.0.15 containing the source code. Change to the new directory and configure MySQL with the following commands.

```
# cd mysql-4.0.15
# ./configure --prefix=/usr/local/mysql
```

The --prefix compile-time option specifies that the MySQL server and client programs will reside under /usr/local/mysql, which is the same location that is used for a binary install. The default location for a source install is actually /usr/local, so you should change this here to match the location that MySQL would have been installed to in Chapter 2.

Once the configure script has run, we can begin compilation by issuing the make command.

```
# make
```

Issue the make install command to have the newly installed MySQL server, client programs, and libraries copied to their correct places on your system:

```
# make install
```

The next step is to create the default set of tables using the mysql_install_db script. From the source directory, issue the command

```
# scripts/mysql_install_db
```

Next we need to set the permissions on the MySQL data directory so the mysql user we created earlier can run the server and read and write the data files.

```
# chown -R mysql /usr/local/mysql/var
```

Finally, we can start the MySQL server using the mysqld_safe command, and you should see a message like that below.

```
# /usr/local/mysql/bin/mysqld_safe &
[1] 9678
Starting mysqld daemon with databases from /usr/local/mysql/var
```

The command above can be added to your system startup script to ensure the MySQL server is always started following a reboot. For instance, on Red Hat Linux add the command to /etc/rc.d/rc.local.

If you want to test that MySQL is running, use the `mysqladmin status` command to get a short status message from a running server.

```
# /usr/local/mysql/bin/mysqladmin status
Uptime: 8826  Threads: 1  Questions: 10  Slow queries: 0  Opens: 8
Flush tables: 1  Open tables: 2  Queries per second avg: 0.000
```

Installing Apache

Extract the Apache source code from the CD-ROM to /usr/local/src and change to that directory.

```
# cd /usr/local/src
# gunzip < /mnt/Apache/Linux/source/httpd-2.0.47.tar.gz | tar xf -
# cd httpd-2.0.47
```

We want to install Apache under /usr/local/apache2 and configure the Web server to allow Dynamic Shared Objects (DSO), so that we don't need to rebuild Apache to add in PHP support. The `configure` command therefore looks like this:

```
# ./configure --prefix=/usr/local/apache2 --enable-module=so
```

Other compile-time options can be specified above, but for the purposes of this book the example given will be sufficient.

Compile and install Apache, and then start the Web server with the `apachectl` command.

```
# make
# make install
# /usr/local/apache2/bin/apachectl start
```

To test that the Web server is running, open a Web browser and enter the name or IP address of your server as the location. If you are installing Apache on a Linux workstation, you can use `localhost` or `127.0.0.1` to access your server. The default page for a new installation (shown in Figure A.1) tells you that everything has worked.

Installing PHP

Extract the PHP source code from the CD-ROM to /usr/local/src and change to that directory.

```
# cd /usr/local/src
# gunzip < /mnt/PHP/Linux/source/php-4.3.3.tar.gz | tar xf -
# cd php-4.3.3
```

FIGURE A.1
The default Apache
page.

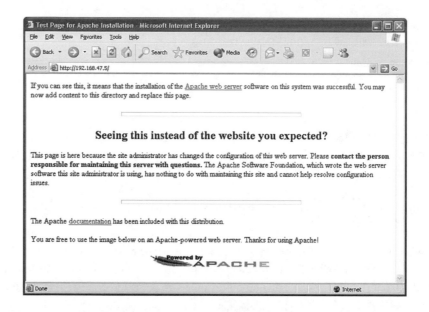

We need PHP to include MySQL support and to link into Apache using DSO using the apxs utility. We'll also use the prefix /usr/local/php for the essential PHP files.

```
# ./configure  --prefix=/usr/local/php \
               --with-mysql=/usr/local/mysql \
               --with-apxs2=/usr/local/apache2/bin/apxs
```

Then use the make and make install commands to compile and install PHP.

```
# make
# make install
```

The apxs utility does most of the hard work here. Once PHP is built, it's copied to the correct place and the Apache configuration modified in order to load the module at start time.

We need to make one more change to the Apache configuration file to instruct the Web server to process any .php file as a PHP script. We'll also activate PHP for files ending .phtml and .html. Edit /usr/local/apache2/conf/httpd.conf and add the following line:

```
AddType application/x-httpd-php .php .phtml .html
```

Restart Apache with the apachectl command to make sure the changes to the configuration file are acted upon.

```
/usr/local/apache/bin/apachectl restart
```

To test that PHP is now a part of your Web server, create a simple script as
/usr/local/apache2/htdocs/index.php that looks like this:

```
<?php
phpinfo();
?>
```

In your Web browser, visit index.php on your new server and you should see a
page giving lots of information on the PHP configuration (Figure A.2).

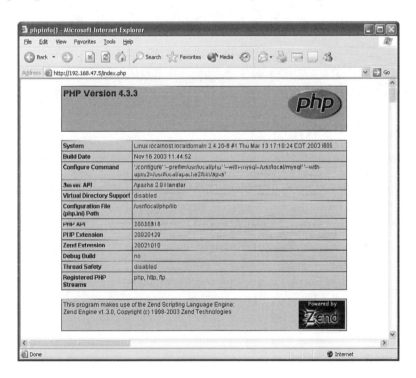

FIGURE A.2
The phpinfo() page.

Windows Installation

The setup files included on the CD-ROM are suitable for Windows 95, 98, NT,
2000, XP, or 2003. Earlier versions of Windows are not supported.

Insert the CD-ROM into your PC and it should autoplay. If the menu screen
shown in Figure A.3 does not appear, double-click the drive icon for your CD-
ROM under My Computer.

FIGURE A.3
The CD-ROM instal-
lation menu.

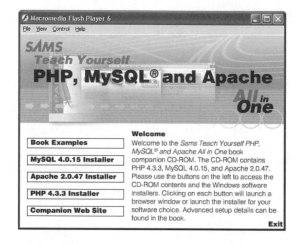

FIGURE A.3
The CD-ROM instal-
lation menu.

Installing MySQL

Click the button in the menu to begin installation of MySQL 4.0.15. At the screen shown in Figure A.4 click Next to continue.

FIGURE A.4
Beginning a MySQL installation.

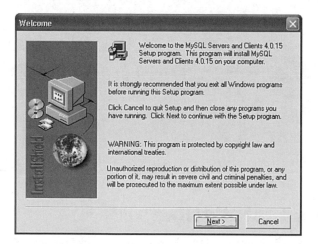

Click Next again after you have seen the release notes and the next screen allows you to choose the destination location for the MySQL files. If you change from the default of C:\mysql be aware that the path used in subsequent steps will also need to be changed.

The next step is to choose the setup type—typical, compact, or custom—as shown in Figure A.5. A typical installation will do the job here, so leave the default item selected and click Next to begin the installation.

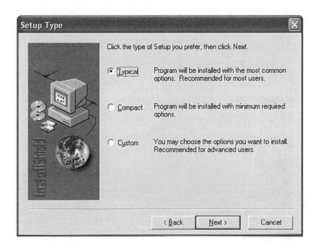

FIGURE A.5
MySQL installation
type selection.

Once the installation program has finished, open up the file explorer to
C:\mysql\bin (if you changed the installation location above, this will be relative
to the folder you selected) and run winmysqladmin.exe. The first time this program is run you will be asked to enter a username and password.

Having done this, the traffic light icon in your system tray indicates the status of
the MySQL server—it should be green. Click the traffic light and select Show Me
to bring up WinMySQLadmin, which shows the connection information for your
server as seen in Figure A.6.

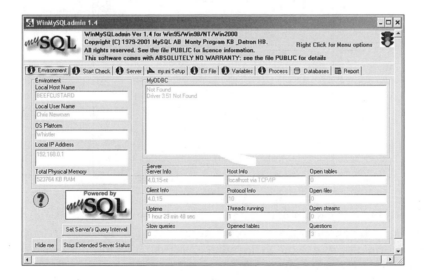

FIGURE A.6
WinMySQLadmin
shows the status
of your MySQL
server.

Installing Apache

Click the button in the menu to begin installation of Apache 2.0.47. At the screen shown in Figure A.7 click Next to continue.

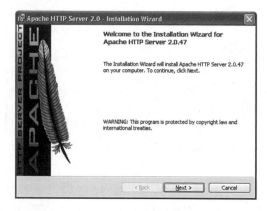

You must accept the license terms on the next screen to continue with the installation, after which you will be shown some release notes. Click Next once you have read these and you will be asked to enter your server information, as seen in Figure A.8.

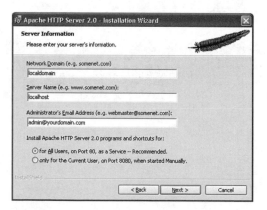

Enter your server's domain and hostname and your email address. If you are installing on a personal workstation, use localhost and localdomain for your server information. Leave the radio button selected on the recommended option to install Apache on port 80.

The next screen asks you to choose a setup type, either typical or custom. The typical setup is just fine, so leave the radio button selected on that option and click next to continue.

Then you are given the opportunity to select the destination folder for the Apache files. By default this is C:\Program Files\Apache Group and this location shouldn't cause you any problems. If you wish to change it, hit the Change button before pressing Next.

Finally Apache is ready to install. Pressing Install will start copying and setting up files onto your system.

Once installation is complete, the Apache server and monitor program will start up and you will see a new icon in your system tray. Double-click this icon to bring up the Service Monitor, which will look like Figure A.9.

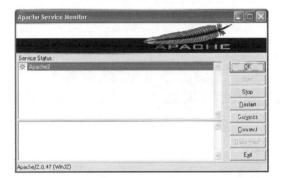

FIGURE A.9
The Apache Service Monitor.

The green light next to Apache2 shows that the service is running and you can verify this by opening up a Web browser and visiting http://localhost/. The default Apache page will be displayed, as shown in Figure A.10.

You can stop or restart the Web server from the Apache Service Monitor using the buttons on the right hand side. Make sure Apache is not running before continuing to install PHP.

Installing PHP

Click the option on the CD-ROM menu to install PHP 4.3.3 and a self-extracting zip archive will open, as shown in Figure A.11.

FIGURE A.10
The default Apache page on a Windows system.

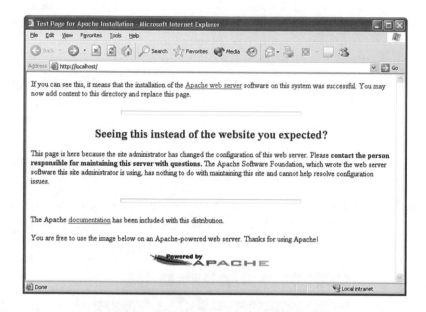

FIGURE A.11
Beginning installation of PHP.

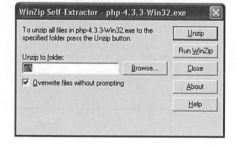

The default location to extract to is C:\ and a new folder called php-4.3.3-Win32 will be created, so you do not need to change the location. Click Extract and the files will be extracted to your system. Close this window when it has finished.

The installation process for PHP still requires manual intervention to add the PHP module to Apache. Using the file explorer, open up the Apache configuration directory—if you used the default location it will be C:\Program Files\Apache Group\Apache2\conf—and edit httpd.conf.

Look for a section that contains a number of LoadModule directives, some of which will be prefixed with a # sign. The last few lines of this section will look like this.

```
LoadModule userdir_module modules/mod_userdir.so
#LoadModule usertrack_module modules/mod_usertrack.so
#LoadModule vhost_alias_module modules/mod_vhost_alias.so
#LoadModule ssl_module modules/mod_ssl.so
```

Add the following line to the `LoadModule` section to tell Apache to load the PHP module on startup.

```
LoadModule php4_module c:/php-4.3.3-Win32/sapi/php4apache2.dll
```

Next search for the `AddType` section with directives that look like this

```
AddType application/x-tar .tgz
AddType image/x-icon .ico
```

Add the following line to tell Apache to process any file ending with `.php` as a PHP script, as well as `.phtml` and `.html` files. You can add more file extensions to this line separated by spaces if you wish.

```
AddType application/x-httpd-php .php .phtml .html
```

We also need to copy `php.ini` and a DLL file to a system location. Under `C:\php-4.3.3-Win32` you will find `php.ini-dist` and `php4ts.dll`. Move `php.ini-dist` to your Windows directory—usually `C:\WINDOWS` or `C:\WINNT`—and rename it as php.ini, and move php4ts.dll to where your DLLs are stored—usually `C:\WINDOWS\SYSTEM` or `C:\WINNT\SYSTEM32`.

To make sure these changes take effect, restart Apache from the Apache Service Monitor. The light next to the Apache2 service should change from red to green indicating that Apache has started.

If you encounter problems starting Apache, check the system events log from Control Panel then Administrative Tools to find the error message.

Now we're ready to check that PHP is working. In the `htdocs` directory in your Apache installation, create a file called `index.php` containing the following lines.

```
<?php
phpinfo();
?>
```

In your Web browser, visit `http://localhost/index.php` and make sure the PHP information page appears, as in Figure A.12.

FIGURE A.12
The phpinfo() page
on a Windows sys-
tem.

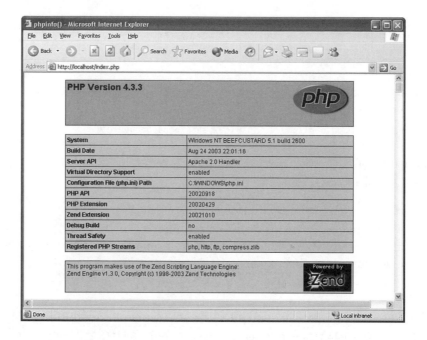

FIGURE A.12
The phpinfo() page on a Windows system.

Troubleshooting

The steps above have been tested with the versions of the software supplied on the CD-ROM that accompanies this book. If you experience installation problems, first of all check that you have followed the steps above exactly. If you continue to have difficulties, the following Web sites may be able to provide assistance:

http://www.mysql.com/doc/P/r/Problems.html

http://httpd.apache.org/docs-2.0/faq/support.html

http://www.php.net/manual/en/faq.build.php

Index

Symbols

A

C

F

G-H

N-O

V

virtual hosting

   DocumentRoot, 491

   IP-based, 491

   name-based, 491-493

VirtualHost containers, 491

W-X-Y-Z

w (write) mode, 223

warn, LogLevel directive option, 457

Web crawlers, 489

Web page structure, application localization, 471-476

Web servers

   Apache, installing (Windows), 32

   troubleshooting, 46

Web sites

   Apache, 29

   awstats, 459

   hosting. See virtual hosting

   Logscan, 460

   MySQL, 8

   MySQL Manual, 551

   performance tools, 485

   PHP, 52, 55, 58

   PHP Manual, 321, 331

   ScanErrLog, 460

   Thawte, 510

   VeriSign, 510

   Webalizer, 459

Web spiders, abuse, preventing, 489

Webalizer, log analysis, 459

WEEKDAY() function, 303

well-known ports, 310, 312

WHERE clause, 283-284, 305, 336

while statements, 84, 100-101

whitespace, 57

width, field width specification, 157-158

wildcards

   %, 22

   *, 22

WINCH, signals, sending, 43

Windows

   Apache

      controlling (commands), 43

      starting, 45

   errors, logging, 455

   installing Apache, 34

   installing Apache on, 32-35

   installing MySQL on, 9-11

   installing PHP on, 55

   integrating PHP with Apache on, 55-56

   OpenSSL library, installing, 506

   rotatelogs.exe programs, logs (rotating), 458

winmysqladmin.exe application, 14

wizards (MySQL installation), 10-11

wordwrap() function, 170-171

wrapping text, 170-171

write (w) mode, 223

writing to files, 228-229

WS-FTP for Windows, 60

X type specifier, 155

X.509, digital certificates, 504

xor operator, 85

>= (greater than or equal to) operator, 84

<= (less than or equal to) operator, 84

< (less than) operator, 84